Modern Turkey

This exciting new textbook provides a broad and comprehensive overview of contemporary Turkey. Placing the country and its people within the context of a rapidly globalizing world, the book covers a diverse range of themes such as politics, economics, international relations, the Turkic world, religion and recent historical background.

Tracing the evolution of Turkey's domestic political and economic systems, and its foreign policy, from the inception of the republic to the present day, the themes covered include:

- the impact of globalization on Turkey's society, politics, economy and foreign policy;
- the role of the EU and the Turkish diaspora in the evolution of Turkish policies;
- the main features and prominent role of Kemalism;
- Turkish foreign policy, and the new challenges and opportunities brought by the end of the cold war;
- the position of Turkey as a 'bridge' between East and West, and the particular and unique dilemmas confronting a Muslim but economically developed, democratized state allied to the West;
- Kurdish identity;
- the Fethullah Gulen movement and the Armenian 'genocide'.

Situating the country as a 'model' for the wider Muslim world, this sophisticated analysis of one of the largest and most important states in the Middle East will be an invaluable resource for scholars and officials interested in Turkish politics and US foreign and security policies, and for students of the Balkan, Middle Eastern, Caucasus and Central Asian regions.

Bill Park is a Senior Lecturer in the Department of Defence Studies, King's College, London University. He has written on Turkey's EU accession prospects, Turkey and ESDP, policies towards Northern Iraq, Turkey–US relations, the Fethullah Gulen movement and the Ergenekon affair.

Modern Turkey

People, state and foreign policy
in a globalized world

Bill Park

Routledge
Taylor & Francis Group

LONDON AND NEW YORK

First published 2012
by Routledge
2 Park Square, Milton Park, Abingdon, Oxon OX14 4RN

Simultaneously published in the USA and Canada
by Routledge
711 Third Ave, New York, NY 10017

Routledge is an imprint of the Taylor & Francis Group, an informa business

British Library Cataloguing in Publication Data
A catalogue record for this book is available from the British Library

Library of Congress Cataloging in Publication Data
Park, Bill.
Modern Turkey: People, state and foreign policy in a globalized world / Bill
Park.
p. cm.
Includes bibliographical references and index.
1. Turkey – Foreign relations. I. Title.
JZ1649.P37 2011
327.561 – dc22   2011004698

ISBN 978-0-415-44370-8 (hbk)
ISBN 978-0-415-44371-5 (pbk)
ISBN 978-0-203-80671-5 (ebk)

Typeset in Times New Roman
by Taylor & Francis Books

Printed and bound in Great Britain by
TJ International Ltd, Padstow, Cornwall

Contents

Acknowledgements

This book is the result of many hours, days, weeks, months and even years spent in my study, more than was originally envisaged in my contract with Routledge. My gratitude is therefore due to Joe Whiting and Suzanne Richardson for their patience and understanding.

The people of Turkey must also receive some credit. By this I mean not only those with whom I am acquainted, and who have shared their thoughts with me in so many different fora while this book has been in preparation, but the millions of Turks in all walks of life who have inspired my fascination with their country. The relentless drama of Turkish political and social life has absorbed me and compelled me to write this book, but the speed and unexpectedness of developments have simultaneously made the task difficult. Turks can guarantee that there are few dull moments in the life of their country, or in the study of it.

Gareth Winrow deserves praise for his apparent readiness, over a period of a couple of years, to listen to my moans and groans during the writing of this book. No doubt the wide range of Oxford pubs that we have sampled together during that time has made the experience more palatable to him.

Above all, though, my gratitude is due to my wife Joanna, whose life with me may sometimes seemed to have been on hold as I spent hour after hour, day after day in my study; and to my daughter Josephine who, although of mathematical rather than political inclination, has nevertheless been more patient than one has the right to expect from a teenager on those occasions when I have chosen to share my thoughts and preoccupations with her. This book, and so much else, is dedicated to both of them.

Acronyms and abbreviations

Many acronyms and abbreviations are introduced in the text of this book. In each instance the full title is given. Below are those that have been used subsequently.

AAA	Armenian Assembly of America
AKP	*Adalet ve Kalkinma Partisi* (Justice and Development Party, sometimes referred to as the JDP)
ANAP	*Anavatan Partisi* (Motherland Party)
AoC	Alliance of Civilizations
AP	*Adalet Partisi* (Justice Party)
ARF	Armenian Revolutionary Federation
BOTAS	*Boru Hatlari ile Petrol Tasima* (Petroleum Pipeline Corporation)
BTC	Baku–Tbilisi–Ceyhan pipeline
CHP	*Cumhuriyet Halk Partisi* (Republican People's Party)
CUP	Committee of Union and Progress
DEP	*Demokratik Emek Partisi* (Democratic Labour Party)
Diyanet	Directorate of Religious Affairs
DP	*Democrat Partisi* (Democratic Party)
DTP	*Demokratik Toplum Partisi* (Democratic Society Party)
EC	European Commission
ECtHR	European Court of Human Rights
EEC	European Economic Community
EU	European Union
FDI	foreign direct investment
GDP	gross domestic product
GNP	gross national product
IMF	International Monetary Fund
ITF	Iraqi Turkmen Front
KDP	Kurdish Democratic Party
KRG	Kurdish Regional Government
LNG	liquefied natural gas
MGK	*Milli Guvenlik Kurulu* (National Security Council)

MHP	*Milliyetci Hareket Partisi* (National Action Party)
MUSIAD	*Mustakil Sanayici ve Isadamlari Dernegi* (Independent Industrialists' and Businessmen's Association)
NATO	North Atlantic Treaty Organization
NGO	nongovernmental organization
OECD	Organization for Economic Cooperation and Development
OIC	Organization of The Islamic Conference
PKK	*Partiya Karkeren Kurdistan* (Kurdish Workers Party)
PLO	Palestine Liberation Organization
PUK	Patriotic Union of Kurdistan
RP	*Refah Partisi* (Welfare Party)
SOCAR	State Oil Company of Azerbaijan
TGNA	Turkish Grand National Assembly
TIKA	*Turk Isbirligi ve Kalkinma Idaresi Baskanligi* (Turkish International Cooperation and Development Agency)
TPAO	*Turkiye Petrolleri Anonim Ortakligi* (Turkish Petroleum Corporation)
TSK	*Turk Silhali Kuvvetleri* (Turkish General Staff)
TUSIAD	*Turk Sanayici ve Isadamlari Dernigi* (Turkish Industry and Business Association)
WMD	weapons of mass destruction

1 Introduction

Globalization, Turks and Turkey

Globalization 'unpackaged': some observations

Over the past couple of decades, enormous attention has been devoted to the phenomenon, or the array of phenomena, known as 'globalization'. Globalization refers to a powerful set of forces and processes that are said to be having a transformative impact on the international system and the states that make it up. So pervasive has the concept become that whole bookshelves in some major academic bookshops are devoted specifically to globalization as a sphere of study seemingly distinct from the field of international relations. One reason for this preoccupation is the perceived recentness of the phenomenon. As one analyst has expressed it, 'globalization did not figure continuously, comprehensively, intensely and with rapidly increasing frequency in the lives of a large proportion of humanity until around the 1960s' (Scholte 2001: 17). However, the same author goes on to assert that 'fully fledged globalization [...] is a fairly new phenomenon', which leaves open the possibility that the modern, intense, comprehensive and speeded-up variant of the phenomenon may have been preceded by more unevenly distributed, slower-paced, perhaps sometimes less penetrating forms – that, in other words, a less-than 'fully fledged globalization' might have older antecedents. We shall return to this thought later in this chapter.

There are many definitions of globalization on offer. Many overlap, others contest. This volume embraces the contested and eclectic nature of globalization, rather than seeking to correct it, and as such might prove a source of frustration to any reader with a stake in one or other particular variant of the phenomenon. One of the better definitions, or at least one particularly suited to the approach and objectives of this volume, states that 'globalization refers to the multiplicity of linkages and interconnections between the states and societies which make the modern world system. It describes the process by which events, decisions and activities in one part of the world can come to have significant consequences for individuals and communities in quite distinct parts of the globe' (McGrew 1992: 23). One key word here is 'multiplicity'. Globalization is made up of a range of phenomena, and can be approached from a range of analytical angles. It includes the perceived deepening and widening of economic interdependence; the greater ease, speed, availability and frequency of communications both electronically and via transportation; the growth of transnational movements, based on ideas and organizations, which might expand the scope for more fluid and transferable loyalties and identities; the globalization of risks, such as environmental degradation and disaster, resource depletion, the proliferation of weapons of mass destruction (WMD) and global epidemics; and so on. The overwhelming sense is of the immediacy of things, of the collapse of time and space (Baylis and Smith 2001: 9).

Economists focus on globalized phenomena such as foreign trade patterns, investment flows across national borders and labour mobility. There is sometimes a hint in this discourse that globalization is desirable as well as inevitable, and that it is closely associated with an ideological predilection for deregulation and free markets. This in turn can lead to globalization being equated to westernization or even Americanization. Political economists sometimes foresee in these and other developments a 'borderless world' in which states and state-based societies are progressively receding in significance and capacity, and are being replaced by a global sphere made up of a 'web of transborder networks' (Scholte 2001: 15). In this world, individual states are unable to exercise much control over the environment or the global financial system, but rather are at the mercy of global environmental and financial developments. Sociologists and cultural theorists identify how such processes and flows might lead to cultural homogenization. Thus, baseball caps, McDonald's burgers, the English language, Hollywood and 'Bollywood' cinema (itself a real or imagined example of cultural emulation), Japanese *anime* (animation) and, more seriously perhaps, women's issues, human rights concerns, environmental awareness and the like, might increasingly be found in all corners of the world. These trends are encouraged or enabled by the internet, cell phones and satellite transmission, and migration and air travel. Robert O. Keohane and Joseph S. Nye famously defined transnational relations as 'contacts, coalitions and interactions across state boundaries that are not controlled by the central foreign policy organs of government' (Keohane and Nye 1973: xi). This definition incorporates relatively informal, unorganized or loosely structured activities and linkages that are not controlled by the state, such as those between criminal gangs, individuals, ideologically sympathetic groups and diasporas. These networks, flows and interactions represent a kind of 'transnationalism from below' (Smith and Guarnizo 1998). States cannot prevent the flow of ideas and loyalties, or the emergence of supraterritorial bonds – between, for example, Muslims, or women, or environmental or human rights campaigners, or the militaries of the North Atlantic Treaty Organization (NATO).

On the other hand, the transnational origins of values, loyalties and norms can be hard to pin down. For example, to what extent might the women's movement in a society such as Turkey's primarily constitute an expression of global interactions and influences rather than a response to the predicaments faced by women domestically, inside Turkey? How do we balance the form that Turkish nationalism takes as a value inculcated in the country's schools, media and institutions, and the same nationalism as a reaction to external pressures on, and challenges to, Turkish identity, values or stakes? Where is the dividing line between those manifestations of Islam in Turkey that are essentially 'national' and exceptional, and those that reflect Turkish society as part and parcel of the global Muslim *umma* (community)? No definitive answer can be given to such questions, beyond the most plausible 'a bit of both'. Above all, how do we determine whether, and to what extent, developments in Turkey are a consequence of, or manifestation of, globalization? Judgements and assumptions must unavoidably guide the assessment of 'how much' of each, but we must also bear in mind that globalization will have influenced the author of this study as well as its subjects. Although this author's assessments are littered throughout this study, and some may indeed be contested, most of them are cautious.

To regulate the flows of people, planes, investment and technology, the political scientist notes the proliferation of, and increasing resort to, regional and global intergovernmental organizations set up in order to address economic and financial, transport, cultural, ideological and many other spheres of activity. Beginning perhaps with the establishment of the International Telegraph Union in 1865, the list now includes bodies as diverse as the International Organization for Migration (IOM), Interpol, the International Seabed Authority (ISA) and the International Atomic Energy Agency (IAEA). There is also a hint at global governance in the role of the United Nations (UN) and its various agencies, such as the World Health Organization (WHO) and the United Nations Development Programme (UNDP). The World Bank and the International Monetary Fund (IMF) are two of the world's most significant 'global governance' organizations – and, pertinent to this volume, have played a major part in both rescuing and, more recently, transforming the Turkish economy in the post-1945 world. Some of this intergovernmental development is on a regional or sub-global rather than global basis. Perhaps the most important regional intergovernmental organization is the European Union (EU), which Turkey aspires to join. The various regional development banks around the world can also be included here. Examples of regional or sub-global bodies of which Turkey is a member include NATO, the Black Sea Economic Cooperation (BSEC) and the transregional Organization of The Islamic Conference (OIC).

Political scientists also attach significance to the explosion of transnational nongovernmental organizations covering a range of functional, ideological, environmental, regulatory, humanitarian and campaigning objectives. They include the Red Cross and the Red Crescent (of which Turkey is a member), Amnesty International, Greenpeace, the International Federation of Football Associations (FIFA) and many others. Some see in the activities and growth of such organizations an emergent global or transnational civil society (Anheier *et al.* 2001). Multinational corporations, companies that operate at a global rather than regional level, such as Toyota or the world's major banks and energy companies, are also examples of transnational nongovernmental organizations. The Arcelik and Beko white goods companies, both owned by the Koc Group, are examples of Turkish-owned companies that manufacture and market on a transnational basis.

Another key word in our definition of globalization is 'process' – or, rather, processes, for they are indeed multiple. These processes might 'interact in specific and contingent ways', they 'are unevenly developed over time and space' and 'are complex and often resisted' (Hay and Marsh 2000: 3). According to what is sometimes dubbed 'second wave theory', globalization and the transnational interactions that make it up are restless, and can be simultaneously challenging, reinforcing, transformative, transcending and creative. Globalization possesses an 'inherent fluidity, indeterminacy and open endedness' leading to 'hybridization' or a 'global melange' rather than to any particular end state, let alone one necessarily compatible with a neoliberal or westernized order (Pieterse 1995: 99–100). It incorporates James N. Rosenau's (1969, 1990) imagery of linkages, 'turbulence' and 'cascades'. Globalization 'is a process that generates contradictory spaces, characterized by contestation, internal differentiation, continuous border crossings' (Sassen 2000: 76). Globalization understood in this way might be more about the journey than it is about arrival. It is not exclusively or necessarily driven by westernization, and might not lead inexorably to homogenization. In the context of our study of the Turkish state, society and foreign policy, this train of thought can lead us to consider the possibility of a range of alternative futures, as a variety of forces, institutions, ideas, identities and events clash and contest in a non-hierarchical way. Turkey's politics, economy, society and values can appear as a battleground, a contested space. Even where trends can be detected and linearity identified, there are nevertheless oscillations, challenges, obstacles and oppositional forces that threaten to overturn, derail or modify what we think we can see. In so far as this volume arrives at findings, that globalization has created turbulence and unpredictability in Turkey will be one of them.

Turks, Turkey and 'globalization' in history

It is then a major purpose of this volume to try to trace and analyse the impact of modern forms of globalizing phenomena on the Turkish state and society, and on their relationships with other states and other societies. However, this volume also embraces the idea that globalization processes are not entirely new phenomena. The evolution of the international system and of the analysis of it reveal numerous developments that can be regarded as precursors or foundation stones to globalization as it is understood today (Baylis and Smith 2001: 7–8). To offer just a few illustrations, the emergence of the 'Silk Route', sprawling overland from China to the Mediterranean via central Asia and the Middle East, can be traced back almost 3000 years, and served as a vehicle for the transmission of languages, belief systems, technologies, textiles, ceramics and people (Beckwith 2009). The world's major religions – Buddhism, Christianity and Islam in particular – have for centuries spread well beyond their historical points of origin via trade, prose-lytizing and conquest. So, too, have some major religious institutions, such as the Roman Catholic Church. The industrialization and 'modernization' of late-nineteenth-century Europe, and the global distribution via imperialism of some of its fruits, such as railway networks and ideas of governance, offer a further illustration. Indeed, imperialism throughout the ages, dating back to Roman times and before, has been a major means for the transmission of people, languages, ideas and technologies. Karl Marx foresaw the globaliza-tion of capitalism, encapsulated by his assertion that developed societies 'simply hold up to the less advanced the mirror of their own future' (Jellissen and Gottheil 2009). W.W. Rostow's idea, developed in the 1950s, that wherever economic growth took off it would essentially follow the same five stages, in effect equated western-style economic growth and development with modernity, and anticipated a near universalization of the process (Rostow 1960). The Hague Conventions of 1899 and 1907, which addressed the laws of war and war crimes, might be regarded as early examples of both interna-tional law and the globalization of norms. Many other examples of centuries-old globalization processes could be offered.

In the Turkish case, ethnic Turkic origins, Islam and the Ottoman past constitute regional and global phenomena that link modern Turkey to the past, but that also form profound elements of its present character and context. To take ethnicity first, if there can be a field of study called 'world history', focusing on the links, contacts, interactions, interminglings, move-ments, influences, integration and conflicts between the peoples of the globe over the centuries of human existence, then 'Turks' are and have long been very much a part of it (Findley 2005). 'Turks', seen as a 'Turkic' people, are not indigenous to Anatolia. The Turkic peoples have contributed considerably to the human movement around the globe that has been going on for cen-turies and has not yet ceased. The population of modern Turkey is heavily descended from the partly Hellenized and other inhabitants of Anatolia who converted to the Islam of the relatively small number of 'Turks' who success-fully conquered and then settled the region (Vali 1971: 1–2; Kinross 1977: 26). It has been said that 'the contemporary Turkish republic arguably has a history going back to […] the Anatolian heritage, extending back long before the Turks arrived there […] and the Turkic or Turko Mongol heri-tage, going back to the earliest Turks and their precursors in inner Asia' (Findley 2005: 5).

People with the ethnonym 'Turk' have their (unrecorded and imperfectly understood) origins in central eastern Mongolia and southern Siberia, to the north-east of China. Today the Turkic Uyghur of modern China and the inhabitants of inner Mongolia loosely inhabit this place of origin, whereas the Turks of Anatolia represent the westernmost edge of a thousand-year-long westward drift of Turkic peoples, depositing the Kazakhs, Uzbeks, Turkmen,

Kyrgyz, Azeri and other Turkic peoples of the modern world along the way (Findley 2005: 3–55; Golden 2005). With the emergence of Turkic states from the ruins of the Soviet Union in the early 1990s into a world of global communications, interlocking economies and, above all, a global energy market, these residues of older forms of globalization collided with its most recent manifestations. The Turks of Anatolia were reminded that they formed part of a wider Turkic world, shared with a people enjoying similar – if distant – ethnic, linguistic, historical and cultural roots. 'The next century will be a Turkish century', declared a celebratory Turkish president, Turgut Ozal, in 1992, as Ankara briefly imagined it could quickly weld the Turkic states and peoples into some kind of united bloc.

Nor can modern Turkey be understood without an appreciation of the impact and presence of Islam in the country. Yet Islam, too, is a transnational or global phenomenon. It is the world's second largest and perhaps its fastest-growing religion, and is distributed over large parts of the globe, notably in the Middle East, Asia and Africa, but with offshoots in Europe, Russia, China and even the Caribbean. Yet its origins date back 1400 years. A little before the moment 'Turks' began to appear in Anatolia, around 1000 years ago, they had converted to Islam – or, rather, had added a strong dose of Islam to their pagan, shamanistic belief systems (Jenkins 2008b: 19–30). Turkish Islam has retained degrees of uniqueness that can in part be explained by the nomadic origins and pre-Anatolian experiences of Turkic peoples, but this can be said of many other 'Islams' too. Modern Turkey is part of the modern Islamic world. Many Turks are devout, and share their faith with Arabs, Iranians, Pakistanis, Malays, Sudanese – and indeed Uyghur. Each year, tens of thousands of Turks join their fellow Muslims in the pilgrimage – the *haj* – to Mecca. Turkey is a member of the OIC, which, with fifty-seven member states, is the second largest international organization in the world after the UN. Its membership is made up of the world's Muslim majority states, and a Turkish national is its current secretary general. In today's globalized world, Islam is not a mere historical residue, but constitutes a major part of that landscape. For others, especially in the wake of 9/11, Islam is a challenge or obstacle to globalization and modernity, at least in some of their guises.

On the Turkish domestic scene, Islam appears to have raised its profile politically and socially in recent years, coinciding quite precisely with the country's striking recent strides towards modernity – the growth of a civil society, the establishment of a diaspora of 'transnational' or 'outer' Turks, a media and communications explosion, enhanced democratization, greater integration into the global economy, and so on. The present AK Party (*Adalet ve Kalkinma Partisi* – AKP) government in Ankara, a result of two substantial electoral successes in 2002 and 2007, has its roots in earlier Turkish political movements and parties similarly inspired by Islam. As we shall see, Islam in part informs the way the AKP governs Turkey and the way it relates to the outside world through its foreign policy. Islam also influences the way in which others approach Turkey – as, for example, with some Christian Democratic opposition to Turkey's EU membership. In short, and along with 'Turkic' identity, Islam fuses Turkey's experience of, and contribution to, earlier forms of globalization with the social, cultural, political and diplomatic choices and dilemmas that confront it in the modern globalized world.

Another respect in which modern Turkey's political, economic and social life is coloured by earlier forms of globalization derives from the fact that it is the primary successor to the Ottoman empire. Ankara's relationship with Greece and other states of the Balkans and Black Sea regions, the particular interest Turkey has taken in the Turkic and Muslim peoples of the former Ottoman provinces in the Balkans in the wake of communism's collapse there, and even shared cultural artefacts such as cuisine, all hark back to this earlier time. Many of modern Turkey's people trace their family and even ethnic roots back to non-Anatolian regions of the Ottoman empire. This was disproportionately so for the Turkish republic's founders. Ataturk himself was born and raised in the now Greek city of Salonika. In recent years, Turkey has also begun to emphasize its past Ottoman links with the Arab world. The foreign policy headache for today's Turkey that the Armenian diaspora is able to generate has its roots in the last years of the Ottoman empire. Yet the playing out in the international political system of the Armenian 'genocide' issue is a manifestation of more recent globalization. As we shall explore (see Chapter 10), the organization, behaviour and impact of the Armenian diaspora has itself been enabled by modern manifestations of globalization – increased and improved methods of communication, the universalization of norms, transnationalism and policy linkages.

Neither current Turkish foreign policy nor its domestic arrangements and tensions can be understood without an appreciation of the impact of the Ottoman experience on the republic's founders. The ideology of Kemalism is at root based on the notion that Ottoman decline and its ultimate collapse derived from the empire's backwardness relative to the economic, technological, military and intellectual dynamism of the European powers. Ataturk's conclusion was that Turkey could regain its place as an advanced and essentially European state and society only by emulating those that had defeated it. This would require that Islam be confined to the private sphere and excluded from the country's political life, that western legal and administrative forms be imported into Turkey, that positivist modes of thought be emulated, and even that western dress codes, cultural forms and the Latin alphabet be adopted by Turkey's largely devout, conservative and illiterate citizens. In the foreign policy arena, it encouraged Turkey's founders to keep the 'backward' Arab world at arm's length.

The Turkish republic offered one of the earliest and most explicit examples of the universalization and hegemonial impact of western norms and practices. Can economic, social and political modernity be attained without an emulation of those western societies that defined what modernity consisted of? Turkey today can be seen as a test case for this question. The novels of Orhan Pamuk, winner in 2006 of the first Nobel Prize to be awarded to a Turkish citizen, are permeated by the tensions created by this attempt by a Muslim, eastern people to internalize western values, practices and patterns of thought. Turkey's post-1945 attachment to western institutions, and its bid to join the EU – Turkey's western and European destiny, in other words – are both a reflection and a source of modern Turkey's globalization, but they are simultaneously rooted in its earlier experiences as an imperial, transnational power. Turkey's European identity can be traced back to the impact and legacy of the European domains of the Ottoman empire.

Foreign policy in a globalized world

As Keohane and Nye observe above, a great deal of what makes up the foreign policy environment of states is 'not controlled by the central foreign policy organs of government'. Put another way, 'globalization's hallmark is acknowledgement of the independent role of both transnational entities [...] and intergovernmental organizations' (Buzan and Weaver 2003: 7). This does not refer simply to the complexities and interdependencies of the 'external' international environment through which states must steer their way. Globalization 'also refers to a "domestic" process of change within states' and to 'the profound transformations in the nature of the state, and in state–society relations, that have developed in recent decades' (Clark 2001: 645). This serves to blur the boundary between what is domestic or internal and what is foreign or external, with the internal and the external interpenetrating each other. Human rights, terrorism, Islam, the economy, crime and identity are all examples of issues that transcend national borders, not least for Turkey, and that are internal and external simultaneously and in an interlocking way. They are also areas where the state and its foreign policy apparatus have to jostle for control, impact and influence with other actors – transnational organizations and movements, intergovernmental bodies, corporations, individuals, diasporas and communities, and so on. The external relations of 'Turkey' cannot simply be understood as the policies pursued by a unitary Turkish state machinery, notwithstanding the preferences of many of the holders of state offices in Ankara. Furthermore, there are 'outside-in' pressures on the state and society that contribute to both their shape and their behaviour. In their conduct of foreign policy, states are obliged to contend with 'mixed actorness'. All of this surely creates severe constraints on a state's capacity to act autonomously, and shapes both its action and what it acts upon.

However, it need not empty the state as a site of 'agency' in foreign policy (Hill 2003: 16–17). Although 'the changing politics of both state and international relations have drawn foreign policy makers in many states to reconfigure their approaches' (Hill 2003: 302), they need not be stymied. States can choose from a broad range of foreign policy styles and contents – to be passive or assertive, to be neutral or aligned, to be isolationist or participatory, to be cooperative or confrontational. States can enhance their domestic capacity, or at least appear to, by piggy-backing on the improved economic welfare and social liberation that is sometimes associated with globalization, or by engaging in multilateral regional and global consultation and governance. They can ride, and domestically benefit from, nationalist backlashes against any excessive external pressures or global homogenization. Fred Halliday has noted the paradox that 'nationalism, the doctrine that proclaims the separateness of peoples, has spread because of, and in reaction against, the international and globalizing trends of the past two hundred years' (Halliday 2001: 442). Of course, nationalism can fragment multinational states, as some argue the Kurds threaten to do in the Turkish case, as much as it can cement national identities. In any case, nationalism itself can be understood as a feature of globalization. One might argue that the Turks 'learned' their nationalism from the Ottoman empire's Christian subject peoples, who in turn 'learned' it from elsewhere in Europe. In some circumstances, the adoption of 'hard power' by states, the resort to coercion or military force, might strengthen the bonds between state and society. States can also gain credence at home by advancing 'transborder as well as national causes' (Scholte 2001: 23) such as Islam, ethnic relatives, human rights, environmental regulation and the like – in other words, by relying more on the 'soft' power instruments of diplomacy, norms and culture. These might be seen as 'inside-out' forms of relationship between a state and its external environment.

In other words, the 'deterritorialization' of so many issues in a globalized world can strengthen as well as weaken the state, or simply coexist with it. Much depends on the nature of the state, the policy choices it makes, and the nature of the society over which it presides. These circumstances might determine not only the degree of 'wriggle room' afforded a state in the international system, but also the nature and content of its bid for greater autonomy. In other words, there are likely to be costs as well as benefits associated with its policy choices, but it can choose which costs it is most prepared to bear. In a postmodern, post-positivist intellectual era, we also cannot help but be aware that such choices might in large measure be determined by the 'socially constructed reality' adopted by a state and its society. Identities and perceptions might be more important determinants of policies and approaches than any elusive or contingent 'reality'. How a people interpret and understand their history, the nature of their self-identity, and the extent to which they perceive the external environment as primarily threatening or benign, will surely influence the way a state and society interact with others. As we shall see, this might be particularly significant in the Turkish case, where the domestic political system and the state's foreign policy priorities have been shaped to a considerable degree by a 'constructed' legacy of the republic's founder, Kemal Ataturk, which led the governing elite of a Muslim and overwhelmingly rural society to stress its western and European, rather than its Middle Eastern and Muslim, credentials. This legacy, and its current significance, will be explored in the early chapters of this volume.

On a related point, much too might hinge on the political nature of the state and on its relationship with the society it represents and governs. To what extent might a state serve as a means of self-expression for a society? To what extent is it open and accommodating to bottom-up pressures and demands from society? Is the foreign policy machinery of the state more or less centralized and controlled, perhaps in the hands of one or just a few individuals? Or is the machinery of state bureaucratized, implying dispersed, sectorized or even incoherent policy outputs? Are some elements of the state – the military, the bureaucracy, domestic lobbies – better able than others to ensure that their agendas, perspectives and interests are heeded in the making of foreign policy? In our consideration of Turkey's external relationships in a globalized world, these domestic considerations, and the interactions between them and the outside world, will constitute a constant theme.

What this volume seeks to do, and what it does not seek to do

Globalization might be said to touch almost everything in the modern world, but in ways that cannot always, or even often, be measured. However, this volume does not try to cover every conceivable way in which modern Turkey – its politics, society and foreign policy – have been affected by globalization. That would be too vast a task, and impossible to achieve. Thus this volume somewhat modestly seeks to identify just a few of the ways in which the ever-increasing interaction of Turkish people and their state with the 'outside' world have had, or are having, a transformative effect. The chapters on Turkey's aspiration to develop as an energy hub, on the appearance of a Turkish emigrant diaspora, on the Armenian 'genocide' issue and on the Gulen movement serve as case studies. There could have been others. Thus this volume does not afford phenomena such as environmentalism, feminism and people- and drug-smuggling anything like the attention they deserve. In any case, we cannot always measure the impact of globalization, or agree on how to define what it is. Much of it is 'in our heads', and is expressed by thought and behaviour patterns the genesis of which cannot be monocausally traced back to some or other impact of globalization. This is to focus on a 'moving target', as Turkey hurtles, stumbles, muddles and seeks to steer its way towards an unpredictable future. This is a study of an ongoing process, or of processes, of change. It is a snapshot in time. It will not attempt prediction but, if there are overall observations to be made in these pages about modern Turkey, it is that globalization has helped to transform Turkish society and to render its domestic politics and foreign policy more contested and more turbulent. It is to be hoped that these pages offer insights into how and why this is the case.

2 The Kemalist legacy

Cult, ideology and political practice

It could be argued that Turkey's evolution over the past few decades has been the story of a tussle between on the one hand the controlling and autarkic inclinations of the republican system established in 1923, and on the other the encroachment of forces unleashed by the pressures of globalization and transnationalism. Thus, in order to assess the impact of globalization on the politics, society and external relations of modern Turkey, we need first to appreciate the republic's starting point. In fact, it has been claimed that 'in the course of the last one hundred and fifty years a clear continuity in social, political and ideological terms can be discerned' in Turkey (Jung and Piccoli 2001: 5). There were indeed numerous continuities between the late Ottoman era and the early decades of the republic, and traces of these early form-ative influences continue to leave their mark on today's Turkey. The distance between state and people, the top-down and elitist approach to governance and reform, the key roles played by the military and the bureaucracy in the preservation of the system and their almost complete identification with it, the commitment to a version of modernity that involved emulation of European practice and a secularization of the state's legal basis, and even the inclination to blur the distinction between foreign enemies and internal opposition – these were features of Turkish political life before 1923 and have been in evidence ever since.

On the other hand, it is an exaggeration to regard the Kemalist revolution as no more than a 'myth' (Jung and Piccoli 2001: 5). The changes wrought were considerable. Yet, in seeking to impose from above 'a cultural revolution without a social revolution, something historically very rare', the post-1923 regime arguably accentuated still further the legacy of elitism and statism carried over from the Ottoman past (Anderson 2008: 8). Certainly, 'the structure of society, the rules of property, the pattern of class relations remained unaltered' by the formation of the republic (Anderson 2008: 5). However, the Kemalist regime quickly evolved into a strong, corporatist and ideological state, which sought to intrude into the lives of its citizens in ways and to an extent that had no Ottoman-era parallels. The new Turkey that emerged arguably mirrored the authoritarian, even totalitarian, states to be found elsewhere in Europe and beyond more than it did Ottomanism.

Indeed, the Turkey that existed in the 1930s has been not inaccurately described as 'an authoritarian statist polity with strong corporatist aspects akin to national socialism' (Poulton 1997: 112). Furthermore, the new regime aspired to engineer not so much a new economic and social order as a new type of individual, one who would be nationalistically Turkish, secular, literate and altogether 'modern'. Turkey's citizens were arguably the world's first Islamic population to be subjected to a determined modernization project (Yavuz and Esposito 2003: xviii), but they were not invariably the receptive guinea pigs of the endeavour. In any case, the tension between continuities and change will be noted throughout this volume.

How, though, are we to characterize the Kemalist system and the body of ideas that underpinned it? The Kemalist system has taken the name of its founder, Mustapha Kemal 'Ataturk' – 'father of the Turks', the surname he gave himself alongside his insistence that all Turks adopt surnames. Yet 'although Kemalism has been transformed into a strict ideology since his death, Ataturk himself was no ideologue' (Rouleau 2006: 104). However, it is also not enough to regard Ataturk as a mere pragmatist (Kinross 1995; Mango 1999). He did make speeches that might be seen as laying the republic's ideological foundations, most notably the address he delivered over six days in October 1927, known as '*Nutuk*' (Alaranta 2008). Based in large measure on the content of this speech, Kemalism went on to evolve as a kind of 'political religion' with its 'dogmas, myths, ethics, and liturgy' (Mateescu 2006: 229). Many of his ideas, such as his sponsorship of an entirely fanciful version of the history of the Turkish people, were quite odd and extraordinarily doctrinaire. Yet there was also an element of impulsiveness at play in the way at which he arrived at some of his policies. Many of the reforms that have since been enshrined as central tenets of Kemalism were discussed and decided by him with no more than a handful of close associates. Events triggered instant reactions from him that have had enduring and far-reaching ramifications, or could prompt the articulation of ideas of which he may hitherto have given little indication.

Ataturk could tolerate neither dissent against the regime's autocratic tendencies nor any questioning of his own authority. He was a personal as well as a political autocrat, and a great deal of his personality has permeated the system that has taken his name. As an ideology, Kemalism has reified the man in the form of a personality cult that placed him above personal or political criticism of any kind, built a mausoleum in his honour, proliferated millions of statues and portraits of him and bestowed on him the titles of the Eternal Leader, the Great Reformer and *Gazi* (a warrior, or one who struggles). It has also reified his ideas, which are constantly rehearsed, cited, chanted and taught, and, like the man, are for many Turks above criticism. One observer, confronted with a national campaign to promote Ataturk's greatness on the *Time* magazine website, not unreasonably likened Turkey's personality cult to that found in North Korea surrounding Kim Il-sung and Kim Jong-il (Morris 2005: 32). It is a moot point whether this cult should be laid primarily at his door, or at the door of those who have since governed in his name. Many 'Kemalist' principles only truly saw the light of day in the wake of his demise. In so far as the policies he introduced represent expressions of a philosophy or ideology, this typically only really took shape and concrete form after the event, and sometimes only subsequent to his death. Indeed, Kemalism can be seen as 'a mere set of political practices' (Mateescu 2006: 231) that emerged adaptively and that have since evolved adaptively, in which the imprint of Ataturk himself is relatively light. Even so, the Kemalist phenomenon is a curious feature for a country that has been so desperate to join the advanced West, and can be seen as sometimes functioning as a barrier to the penetration of ideas from the world beyond the country's borders.

In any case, when Ataturk died in 1938, Kemalism and Turkey were 'neither democratic nor liberal but authoritarian, elitist, and ideological' (Yavuz and Esposito 2003: xx1). Over time, the ideological foundation of the Turkish state hardened into a particular interpretation of the Kemalist legacy – most notably, that secularism equates to state control over and regulation of religious practice and symbolism, and that national unity prohibits accommodation to Kurdish distinctiveness. Adherence to these ideological rigidities remains deeply rooted in large swathes of Turkish civil society as well as in its military hierarchy and state bureaucracy, and the state's attachment to them has served to curtail the growth of a more spontaneous bottom-up democracy – 'for the people, despite the people', as the 1920s Republican People's Party (*Cumhuriyet Halk Partisi* – CHP) slogan expressed it. Indeed, the relationship of the CHP, Turkey's oldest political party, to the Kemalist state and the assumptions upon which the party are built are particularly interesting. The CHP can trace its origins back to Ataturk himself. It was the dominant party during the more or less exclusively one-party period up until 1950, and from its foundation up to this day it has been ardently Kemalist and central to Turkey's political, social and economic evolution. Yet it has never emerged victorious in its own right in a free election.

The other institution most usually associated with the Kemalist order is the Turkish General Staff (*Turk Silhali Kuvvetleri* – TSK) (Jenkins 2001). Under Kemal Ataturk and up until 1960, the military's influence was informal and largely explained by the easy relationship between its civilian rulers, most of whom were former military officers who had been obliged to resign their commissions before they could take up political office, and a military leadership equally committed to the Kemalist revolution. Since 1960, the military's political role has been more overt, although it has varied in degree and form. This more explicit political engagement has coincided with the advent in Turkey of multiparty democracy, beginning with the elections of 1950. The military sees itself as nonpartisan, as representing something akin to a national general will, and as the guardian of the official ideology of Kemalism. The significance of this self-appointed 'guardianship' role should not be underestimated, and it underpinned and helped legitimize the emergence in the 1990s in particular of a 'national security regime' (Cizre 2003) as well as the coups of 1960, 1971 and 1980, the so-called 'postmodern coup' of 1997 and countless lower-profile and continuous interventions in the country's politics. A representative statement of the military's thinking, especially since the 1960s, came in the form of a written statement, issued by the TSK in the wake of comments by the then prime minister, Mesut Yilmaz, in March 1998, critical of the military's leading role in Turkey's struggle with Islamists. The statement declared that 'no matter what position or task is represented, no one, for the sake of his personal interest or aspiration, can display an attitude or make any suggestions or comment that will discourage, confuse, weaken or overshadow the determination of the Turkish armed forces to struggle against separatist or fundamentalist activities that target the country's security' (Kramer 2000: 31). In more recent times, the constitutional court has emerged more strongly as a pre-eminent guardian of the system and of what is presumed to be Ataturk's legacy.

What follows in this chapter is an articulation of that set of political practices, or of ideas, that give Kemalism its unique flavour and that have found themselves in increasing confrontation and conflict with the challenge from forces, both inside and outside Turkey, that are crashing against its defences or eroding its foundations.

Etatism

The new Turkish republic that was established in 1923 was a backward society. Anatolia had always been economically less developed and industrialized than the European regions of the Ottoman empire (Hershlag 1968; Hale 1981; Lewis 2002; Zurcher 2004; Altug *et al.* 2008).[1] Technological levels were low, and such industry as existed was largely foreign owned, as was much of the limited rail and merchant-shipping network. Communications in Anatolia were primitive with few surfaced roads. Turks were mainly poor and illiterate farmers – the national literacy rate stood at around ten per cent in 1927 (Lewis 2002: 310) – living in small and frequently isolated communities, suffering from high infant mortality and low life expectancy. In 1923 there was little that resembled a Turkish middle class. Feudal landlordism was not uncommon, especially in the eastern and Kurdish-populated regions of the country. The socially more elevated Turks had additionally provided the military officers and state bureaucrats of the Ottoman regime. The new republican elite were overwhelmingly from this latter class. They had little understanding of commerce or practical appreciation of economic matters. Indeed they were rather disdainful of it, not least because they associated such activities with the empire's disloyal non-Muslim groups and with the 'capitulations' – rights and privileges afforded to external powers, such as economic concessions – and outside influence that they had fought to throw off. Indeed, largely as a result of the influence of the 'Young Turks', the last years of the empire coincided with a shift of the hitherto open Ottoman economic system towards a 'national economy' that would minimize the role of foreign capital and non-Muslim minorities (Grigoriadis and Kamaras 2008: 54).

Turkey in 1923 was also a broken society. The large-scale destruction of roads, bridges, houses, factories and farms during the decades of conflict that preceded the establishment of the republic made matters worse still. Russians, Greeks, Armenians, British, French and Italians had all made their appearance as enemies to be fought. Such infrastructure as there had been – and in Anatolia there had not been much – was devastated. Trade in 1923 was only a third of its prewar levels (Zurcher 2004: 165). In addition, the brutal sequence of external invasion, occupation, civil conflict, internal migration, famine, lawlessness and disease had significantly transformed the ethnic, cultural and social make-up of Anatolia. In the decade leading up to the founding of the republic, it is reckoned that the population of Anatolia had fallen by almost one-third. Sixty per cent of the Muslim population of Van had died, as had forty per cent of the Muslims of Bitlis and thirty per cent of those of Erzerum. On the other hand, they had been partly replaced by an estimated half a million Muslim immigrants fleeing the ethnic cleansing, pogroms and conflicts of the Balkans, the Caucasus, and Crimea and southern Russia (Poulton 1997: 89). It has been claimed that on the eve of the First World War as many as a quarter of the Muslim population of Anatolia were refugees or the children of refugees from the Balkan, Black Sea or Caucasus regions (Zurcher 2004: 117). One recent study of Turks of Albanian origin in the Samsun region found that they are descended both from Albanians forcibly removed from their Balkan homes in 1878, and from Kosovo Albanians fleeing the massacres of 1912–13 (Genis and Maynard 2009). A still greater number of modern-day Turks are descended from Caucasians (or Circassians, as they are sometimes called) (Kaya 2005; Celikpala 2006). Many of today's Turks have in effect become so over the past century or so.

There is relatively little awareness and few studies of the plight and experiences of these Muslim settlers in Anatolia. This is in considerable contrast with the still sensitive issue of the fate of those whose places – frequently, literally the homes and land – they took, the millions of Greeks and Armenians who had been killed or deported in the years preceding the republic's founding. Even in the small towns and villages of Anatolia, the merchant and artisan class – the blacksmiths, carpenters, tailors as well as shopkeepers and traders – had been mainly Greek, Armenian or Jewish. Now, any that remained were mostly concentrated in Istanbul. Anatolia suffered a massive skill shortage as a consequence. So great was the impact on Anatolian society and its economic prospects that it has been written that 'the biggest break in Turkish social history came not with Ataturk's reforms, but earlier with the departure of the Christians, on whose skills the country had long depended' (Mango 1999: 467). Turkey in 1923 had what we would understand today as the profile of an underdeveloped or 'third world' society and economy, added to which it was – again in today's parlance – a post-conflict zone which had been traumatized by large-scale ethnic cleansing, lawlessness, war and social dislocation. Indeed, it is worth considering that Turkey was then one of the few 'economically underdeveloped' but sovereign states. In 1923, most similarly preindustrial societies were still colonies. Turkey can be considered as a forerunner for the flood of newly decolonized and independent states that joined the international system after 1945, not least as a consequence of its attempt at modernity.

Furthermore, the state was financially broke and additionally obliged by the terms of the Lausanne Treaty to pay off Ottoman debts. Such revenue as it was able to raise came largely from a tax on agricultural produce. The Treaty also forbade the new Turkish government the right to impose tariffs on imports. These impositions contributed to the emergence of a severe balance of payments deficit and a large national debt. Although the new regime focused considerable energy on ensuring its grip on power, it also managed to end the capitulations; nationalize foreign-owned defence, tobacco and transportation companies; establish a mixed private–public-owned bank to assist industry and commerce; create a state monopoly covering tobacco, alcohol, sugar, matches and explosives; extend the country's sparse rail network and subsidize some essential needs such as transportation. Economic growth was quite rapid during the first decade or so of the republic's life, a fact that can largely be explained by the low start base and the need to restore what had been destroyed. By 1930 the gross national product (GNP) was back to roughly its prewar level (Zurcher 2004: 165). The country's large agricultural sector also happily ensured that the country could feed itself.

The 1929 global economic crash forced Ankara to pay more systematic attention to economic policy. This led to an articulation of what had been the largely implicit, unstated underpinnings of economic policy to date. The direction of economic policy became more evident with the 1931 adoption by the ruling CHP of the six 'fundamental and unchanging principles' that were to guide the republic, which today appear as six arrows on the CHP's crest and which were later to appear (and still feature to this day) in the Turkish constitution. These six principles are 'republican, nationalist, populist, etatist, secularist and revolutionary'. Of these, only etatism had not already made an appearance in the Kemalist lexicon (Lewis 2002: 286). It referred to the leading role the state should take in initiating and developing economic projects. For some republicans, the economic measures to which the principle gave rise were seen as essentially short-term and pragmatic, designed to help Turkey overcome the impact of the global recession and to kick-start the country's economic modernization. The state was required to step in to offset the (presumed temporary) unavailability of private capital. For this segment of the country's leadership, economic autarky was a short-term and unavoidable necessity.

For others, such as prime minister and later president Ismet Inonu, it represented a more enduring and principled approach to economic policy. It could reflect residual anti-free-market and anti-western feelings that derived from Turkey's exploited past and that have been a persisting undercurrent in some republican circles ever since. This mindset was to be mirrored decades later by some of the newly independent states of the post-Second World War era. In the 1920s and 1930s, it also mirrored something of the spirit of the age. Turkey was born into an era in which even liberal and democratic societies witnessed unprecedented levels of state involvement in the economy, such as US president Roosevelt's 'New Deal'. Fascism, communism and the various other types of authoritarian project then current in Europe and beyond offered an explicit rejection of the western capitalist model, and an ideologically driven economic protectionism and state direction of economic activity. According to this thinking, the unavailability of private capital, and especially foreign capital, was less the point than was its undesirability. In today's Turkey, many politicians, lawyers and state officials continue to regard privatization and foreign ownership of parts of the economy as contrary to republican ideals and to Turkey's national interests.

As part of its policy of economic etatism, and taking inspiration as well as loans and technical assistance from the Soviet Union, Turkey adopted its first five-year plan in 1933. This created two large state banks or holding companies to finance the government's economic ventures. Beneath these umbrellas, state economic enterprises were established in the mining, heavy industry and chemicals sectors. Textiles, paper, ceramics and glass factories were established to develop the consumer sector of the national economy, but also as part of a drive towards import substitution. Sugar and paper and pulp enterprises were also established with import substitution in mind. This close business–government relationship in Turkey offered little scope or encouragement to foreign investment from the capitalist world. There were successes. Industry's share of GNP rose from a little over ten per cent in 1927 to around sixteen per cent in 1938. Although steep barriers to trade were erected, thereby ensuring minimum interaction between the Turkish economy and the outside world, trade levels nevertheless crept upwards during the 1930s, much of it based on bilateral government-to-government arrangements and around half of it with Nazi Germany and its statist allies (Zurcher 2004: 199). As just one illustration of Turkey's affinity with Europe's more authoritarian regimes, in 1936 Ankara adopted a labour law prohibiting unions and strikes that was a direct copy of fascist Italy's, despite the minuscule size of Turkey's proletariat (Zurcher 2004: 200). Turkey's vast agricultural sector, accounting for between a half and two-thirds of Turkey's GNP in 1927, was largely left to its own devices and remained unproductive and unmodernized, although sufficient for the country's domestic needs.

Although Turkey remained neutral during the Second World War, the additional deprivations and difficulties imposed by the conflict undermined Turkey's second five-year plan, launched in 1939, and deepened still further the state's involvement in the economy. Raw material prices and military expenditure rose, as did inflation and government debt levels. With Inonu installed as president, trade and production were subjected to still greater bureaucratic rules and control. Prices were fixed and raw materials requisitioned.

The economy shrank, many goods were in short supply and black markets proliferated. The mainly Greek, Armenian and Jewish business class was confronted with racially inspired and crippling tax burdens and even with forced labour (Lewis 2002: 297–302). Overall, although circumstances had conspired to narrow the economic options available to its leadership, the first three decades of the Turkish republic's existence offered little evidence that its natural inclination was to adopt either the economic approach or the political practices of the more liberal western powers. Turkey's economy at the end of the Second World War was decidedly state-dominated, autarkic and only minimally integrated into wider global economic and financial networks.

From Ottomans to Turks

In so many respects, the republic's leaders were the direct descendants of the late Ottoman years. They had been part of the 'Young Turk' movement – more formally known as the Committee of Union and Progress (CUP) – during the last years of the empire. This movement had been composed of Ottoman soldiers, bureaucrats and intellectuals committed to a version of modernity that would feature constitutionalism, economic reform and independence from external powers. Eighty-five per cent of Ottoman civil servants and ninety-three per cent of its staff officers retained their positions in the new republic (Poulton 1997: 88). Although some were attached to ideas of freedom that had taken hold in Europe more generally, the Ottoman reformism with which they had been associated 'laid the foundations for the specific way of Turkish modernization: a top down modernization centred around a military–bureaucratic elite' (Jung and Piccoli 2001: 30). Guided by its leader Kemal Ataturk, this elite set itself the task of dragging a socially and economically backward Turkey towards what it believed to be a European-style modernity (Jung and Piccoli 2001: 11–108). Although suspicious of Europe, they – or, rather, Ataturk – interpreted the downfall of the Ottoman empire as testimony both to its relative social, cultural and intellectual backwardness and to Europe's relative dynamism. Their task, as laid down and initiated by Ataturk, was both to embrace what was seen as Europe's positivism and rationalism and to discard Anatolian superstition and conservatism, in order to secure Turkey's membership of the advanced, civilized and essentially European world.

Some of the consequent reforms had an absurdist quality to them – the banning of the fez, for example, and the adoption of western headgear in its place. Some were progressive, such as the 1934 extension of the vote to women, ninety per cent of whom were illiterate at the time. During the 1920s, Turks lost the sultanate but acquired surnames, the Latin alphabet in place of the Arabic, and a reformed and written Turkish language replete with more purely Turkish and often newly invented words to replace the Arabic and Persian words of which it had been purged (Lewis 1999). This innovation was accompanied by a mass literacy campaign. One effect of these acts of social engineering was to cut modern Turks off from their Ottoman past. Ottoman Turkish was unintelligible to most Turks anyway, but a consequence has been that later generations of more literate Turks have been unable to read Ottoman inscriptions on historic monuments or to read Ottoman documents. Since the 1920s, this has aided the republic's leaders in their objective of obliterating Turkey's Ottoman legacy wherever they could.

More problematic for its subsequent evolution, however, was the republic's approach to Turkish national identity. Turkish nationalism emerged as a serious political force only during the latter decades of the Ottoman era. The modernizing 'Young Turks', themselves disproportionately non-Anatolian in origin, had initially entertained hopes for a reformed Ottoman entity. However, with the progressive loss of its Christian domains and subjects, the empire's population had become increasingly Islamic – eighty-five per cent by 1912, including its Arab and Kurdish populations. With the loss of pre-dominantly Muslim Albania in 1912, and the stirrings of Arab nationalism, it increasingly appeared as if only its Anatolian rump would remain. This pre-saged a shift of identity from Ottomanism – but to what? Europeans had long designated the Muslim people of Anatolia as 'Turks' but the Ottoman elite rarely did, other than pejoratively. Nor had the Ottomans been inclined towards adopting the epithet 'Turkish' for their imperial domains, in which half the population was non-Muslim and half the Muslim population was non-Turkish (Vali 1971: 4). Now, a kind of cultural Turkish nationalism emerged (Poulton 1997: 92–101; Lewis 2002: 323–61). This often extended beyond the Turks of Anatolia to the wider Turkic world of central Asia and elsewhere, and there was even a flurry of interest, shared by some CUP leaders, in replacing the multinational Ottoman empire with a pan-Turanian (pan-Turkic) one extending to the borders of China. More broadly, the growth of Turkish nationalism can be seen as both a reaction to, and an emulation of, the European and Ottoman Christian nationalisms that preceded it.

However, what was a Turk? How should a Turk be distinguished from an Ottoman subject, or from a Greek or an Armenian? The empire had been composed of *millets* – partly self-governing religious communities. Non-Muslims had been tolerated, but treated differently – not allowed to serve in the Ottoman army, for example, and required to pay higher rates of tax. Even those members of religious minorities who spoke Turkish were defined according to their religion. Furthermore, the nationalist movements of the empire were also based chiefly on religious identity. Thus Greeks defined themselves as such by their adherence to Greek Christian Orthodoxy rather than by whether their spoken language was Greek or Turkish. In these struggles, it became clear that the Sunni Muslims of Anatolia had retained their loyalty to the Ottoman state. It also became clear that they shared with CUP members a growing resentment of the demands of the Christian minorities and the sponsorship these groups received from the country's external rivals. Anatolia's Muslim poor also resented the better material well being their Christian neighbours so frequently, but not invariably, enjoyed. Thus it transpired that the Muslim Turks and Kurds of Anatolia were left as the only remaining 'loyalists'. These, along with the Muslim refugees from surrounding Christian territories who were happy to regard themselves as, or to become, 'Turks', were to constitute the citizens of the new republic. Although there is something in the assertion that 'Muslimness was a *sine qua non* for becoming a Turk' (Yavuz and Esposito 2003: xx) in that it distinguished them from the Christian minorities, it clearly did not apply to the Ottoman empire's former Arab subjects. Furthermore, the new republic's relations with its Kurdish Muslim citizens were also to take a fraught turn.

The roots of Turkey's Kurdish problem

Initially, it appeared that the loyal Turkish and Kurdish communities would equally emerge as the core citizens of the Turkish republic. In his speeches both before and after he became president of the republic, Ataturk referred – 'whether in sincerity or deceit' (McDowall 1996: 187) – to Turks and Kurds as distinctive groups united by Islam. Thus, in a 1920 address to the Turkish Grand National Assembly (TGNA), Ataturk referred to the assembly membership as 'composed of not only Turks, not only Circassians, not only Kurds, not only Laz [...] they belong to a mass composed of elements of Islam [...] there are Turks as well as Kurds. We do not differentiate them' (Koker 2010: 54–55). What united them was the loyalty both had shown to the Ottoman cause, and their Muslim faith. Indeed, Kurds had willingly fought on the Ottoman and nationalist sides during the previous years of conflict. However, although fragmented by tribe, language, religion and geography, it was simultaneously evident that some kind of separate Kurdish identity existed even then.

The emerging and distinctively Turkish nationalism of the republican elite was doomed to conflict in some form with this elemental Kurdish identity (McDowall 1996: 184–213). A 'nation' had to be built in order to better secure the Anatolian geographical space that remained in the wake of the empire's break-up. The unease of Turkey's new rulers was intensified by international sympathy for Kurdish self-determination, and by the British inclination to offer the Kurds of what is now northern Iraq a degree of autonomy. In any case, the new regime's centralizing measures were themselves sufficient to prompt a reaction from the notoriously independent Kurdish tribes and sheiks. Ataturk's March 1924 abolition of the caliphate – the term used to depict the commander or protector of the world's Sunni Islam community, and which had been held by Ottoman rulers for 400 years – appeared to galvanize their enmity. The so-called Sheik Said revolt of 1925, named after the Kurdish religious and tribal chief who nominally led it, aimed both at Kurdish self-rule and the restoration of the caliphate. Ankara's crackdown was severe, enduring, and above all decisive in the shaping of the Kemalist republic, such that the revolt 'became a symbol of state inflexibility not yet abandoned' (McDowall 1996: 198). Although urban, non-tribal and Alevi Kurds did not participate significantly in the revolt, there were nevertheless widespread deportations of Kurds to western Turkey, Kurdish villages were destroyed, hundreds executed, livestock killed and martial law declared throughout the Kurdish-inhabited areas of south-eastern Turkey. Some tribes sought refuge in Syria, Iraq, Iran and Azerbaijan. Yet Kurdish revolts continued throughout the 1920s and 1930s, prompting ever more severe repression of Kurds and, increasingly, of any form of dissent. In 1927, the British ambassador to Turkey likened the treatment of the Kurds to that of the Armenians a decade or so earlier (McDowall 1996: 199), and Kurdish exiles began to establish links with their Armenian counterparts (McDowall 1996: 203), links that continue to resurface to this day.

In the wake of the Sheik Said revolt, the process of 'Turkification' intensified. Armenians and Greeks had been removed from Anatolia essentially as a consequence of their presumed disloyalty. This presumption now applied to Kurds too. However, there were additional facets to the republican elite's increasing propensity to denigrate the Kurds and Kurdishness. The relative economic backwardness of the Kurdish regions – made worse by the expulsion of the Armenian population – their relative religiosity, and the tribal and feudal relationships that survived amongst the Kurds, all now appeared as obstacles to the modernizing and secularizing aspirations of the Kemalists. This could take on a racist hue, as reflected in the remark by Tawfiq Rustu, Turkey's foreign minister from 1925 until 1938, that 'their cultural level is so low, their mentality so backward, that they cannot be simply in the general Turkish body politic [...] they will die out, economically unfitted for the struggle for life in competition with the more advanced and cultured Turks' (McDowall 1996: 200). A recent observer described the 'blend of revulsion and pity [...] that forms the attitude of Turk towards Kurd' even today (de Bellaigue 2009: 254).

Within a few years of the establishment of the republic, Ankara progressively embarked on a policy that simultaneously sought to 'Turkify' the Kurds, deny the very existence of Kurds as anything other than corrupted Turks, brutally suppress them and economically and socially neglect the predominantly Kurdish-inhabited regions of the country. As the Kemalists sought to tighten their hold over the country, the new republic took on an increasingly ethnically Turkish quality. Turkish place names began to replace Kurdish ones – a policy given renewed impetus by the 1960 coup leaders – and Turkish emerged as the only permitted language in the country's courts, bureaucracy and educational establishments, thereby effectively excluding Kurdish speakers from both government posts and educational opportunity. The term 'Kurdistan' disappeared from official usage. The prohibition on Kurdish was lifted in 1950, only to be reimposed by the 1980 coup leaders. Traces of these approaches towards Turkey's Kurdish minority have been evident throughout almost the entire life of the republic.

In 1934, a law divided Turkey into three zones: ethnically and culturally 'pure' Turkish areas; regions earmarked for the deportation of non-Turkish

speakers (that is, Kurdish speakers); and entirely non-Turkish-speaking localities, which were to be evacuated (McDowall 1996: 207; Jongerden 2001).
Although it proved impossible to fully implement these provisions, the law
nevertheless offered an indication both of the state of mind of Turkey's governing elite and of the pressures Turkey's Kurdish population were now
subjected to. It seems that the 1960 coup leaders similarly considered trans-
migrating Kurds from Turkey's south-east with Turks from the Black Sea
region.[2] Forced evacuations and the razing of Kurdish villages again occurred
from the late 1980s, as the battle against the Kurdish Workers Party (*Partiya
Karkeren Kurdistan* – PKK) intensified. The most significant military
campaign to date against rebellious Kurds took place in the late 1930s in the
province of Dersim, renamed Tunceli and home to a mostly Zaza-speaking
population of the Alevi faith. This involved the bulk of the Turkish army and
included aerial bombardment of Kurdish villages, in which Sabiha Gokcen,
Ataturk's adopted daughter and Turkey's first female pilot, participated. An
unknown number of Kurds lost their lives – the most frequently quoted figure
is 13,000 – and again there were mass deportations, widespread acts of brutality and the destruction of homes and villages. The military permanently
garrisoned and in effect occupied the Dersim region, as it did much of the
country's south-east. It has been claimed that the atmosphere in the region is
little changed to this day (de Bellaigue 2009). Foreigners were not allowed to
travel east of the Euphrates until 1965 (McDowall 1996: 210). Official
archives relating to the events in Dersim/Tunceli province remain closed,
but the deputy leader of the CHP, former senior diplomat Onur Oymen,
reignited the issue in November 2009 with remarks that appeared to justify
the repressive measures taken in 1937–38 (Seibert 2009). Condemnations followed, notably from the Alevi community, but so did declarations of support.
That so senior a political figure should even see fit to utter such remarks
illustrates just how unreconstructed are some elements of Turkey's Kemalist
and nationalist establishment.

   The continuities between the context of Turkish suppression of Kurdishness
in the 1920s and 1930s and the context of Ankara's more recent denials of
Kurdish rights are striking. Ankara's 1929 warning to Iran not to support the
Kurdish rebels prompted Iranian security cooperation with Turkey that
has echoes today. The relative acquiescence of the international community
has similarly been mirrored in recent decades, as has the impact of the campaign against Kurdish particularism on Turkey's wider democratization and
the role of the military in Turkey's domestic political development. When, in
1999, the Turkish ban on the renowned Kurdish film *Yol*, made in 1982, was
lifted, the appearance of the word 'Kurdistan' in the film remained exorcised.
The suppression of Kurdishness is inseparable from the early development
of Kemalism and of the Turkish republic. With the massacre and expulsion of
Anatolia's Armenians by its CUP predecessors, it profoundly altered the
country's social, political and even economic trajectory. Both campaigns
continue to bedevil Turkey's tranquillity.

Racially and culturally based social engineering projects have long enjoyed global currency, not only in Hitler's Germany but elsewhere in central and eastern Europe, and also in Australasia, North America and southern Africa. The colonial practice of deploying certain ethnic groups to perform specific tasks – which for example deposited large numbers of Asians from the Indian subcontinent in east Africa and the Caribbean, or French *pieds noirs* in Algeria, and above all dispersed African slaves to the western hemisphere – might all be seen as manifestations of earlier ages when distinctions of 'race' and 'culture' formed the basis for policies of exclusion, deportation or extermination. 'Nation-building' projects throughout the post-1945 newly decolonized world have also frequently led to policies and practices aimed at the forcible eradication of racial, ethnic and cultural differences and to widespread intercommunal tensions and conflict. Critics of Turkey sometimes overlook the sadly widespread prevalence of such events. On the other hand, few countries have sought to deny or excuse their past and present 'misdemeanours' with quite the energy that Turkey has. As we shall see later in this volume (see Chapter 10), there is still a pronounced Turkish inclination to downplay the massacres of Armenians, and Turkey has similarly had difficulty moving on from the brutally repressive approach towards its Kurdish citizens that first saw the light of day in the early years of the republic's life. A more globalized world has vastly complicated Turkey's endeavours to disguise aspects of its past, and indeed of its present.

Turkish nationalism

A major explanatory factor behind Turkey's resistance to the adoption of a more contrite approach to the Armenian fate, or a more inclusive embrace of its Kurdish citizens, is the intensity of Turkish nationalism (Guney 2006–07; Uslu 2008a). This phenomenon has its roots in the early years of the republic, and its depth and ubiquity are perhaps the most enduring and universal legacy of Kemalism. Nationalist sentiment can also serve as a barrier to Turkey's absorption of external influences, and sometimes generates a negative reaction to them. Guided by Kemal's tutelage and inspiration, the early republic's construction of foundations on which to base Turkish nationalism – the explicit and deliberate development of an 'imagined community', in the language of Benedict Anderson (1991) – frequently took racist, xenophobic and absurd forms that derived in some degree from the racial theories current in Europe in the 1920s and 1930s. Thus the Turkish history thesis, propagated by one of Ataturk's adopted daughters, Afet Inan, insisted that the Turks of central Asia constituted the world's first civilized people, who, through their nomadism, had provided the root of all other world civilizations. It further claimed that Turks had migrated to Anatolia centuries before the appearance of Greek and other cultures associated with the region, and constituted its prehistoric inhabitants. Thus the Hittites and Sumerians were deemed Turkic peoples. The thesis also incorporated the idea that Islam had been adopted pragmatically by the Turks, had never been fully internalized by them, and in any case accounted for only a relatively brief period in the long history of the Turkish people. Islam could thus be regarded as a superficial and transient phenomenon for Turks. Such ideas made it possible to insist that Kurds were simply 'mountain Turks' whose geographical and cultural isolation had led them to stray from their native Turkish language and culture. These notions were afforded added currency in the wake of the 1960 coup. Associated with the history thesis was the Sun language theory, which asserted that Turks were the originators of language itself and that all other languages were thus derived from or linked to it (Cagaptay 2002; Arkman 2006). These ideas were taught in high schools and universities, were explained as the products of scientific and rational thought and have left their mark to this day.[3] In less extreme forms, some of the basic underpinnings of these ideas can still be found in Turkish textbooks and histories and in official and semi-official documents.

The Turkish state and leading institutions, such as the TSK, the CHP and the education system, have propagated nationalist sentiment from the republic's very inception, and its presence in Turkish society is ubiquitous. Its impact has been reinforced by the prohibitions that have been, and still are, placed on the development and airing of alternative national and social discourses in Turkey. Article 301 of the Turkish penal code, moderately reformed in 2008, makes it illegal to 'insult' Turkishness or to denigrate the government or institutions of the state, including the military. The writers Orhan Pamuk and Elif Shafak, and the Armenian spokesman Hrant Dink – who was assassinated by a Turkish nationalist in January 2007 – are just some of the many individuals who have fallen foul of the Article. Questioning Turkish policy towards the Armenian genocide or the Kurdish problem is viewed with particular severity. Indeed, querying whether a political opponent or outspoken citizen has Kurdish, Armenian or Jewish blood is a not infrequent occurrence in Turkey. CHP deputies have questioned whether president Abdullah Gul and foreign minister Davutoglu are of Armenian descent, and a best-selling book written by an arch Kemalist has wondered whether prime minister Erdogan and other leading AKP figures are 'crypto Jews' (Akyol 2010). Immediately prior to General Yasir Buyukanit's 2006 appointment as chief of the TSK, the Islamic end of Turkey's political spectrum seem to have been behind a whispering campaign to the effect that he was a converted Jew.

School textbooks, university courses, official publications, military training, films, the media and even officially sanctioned mosque sermons are all replete with intensely nationalistic material. The ubiquity of the Turkish flag is striking. At the start of each day, school children are obliged to recite the words, first uttered by Ataturk and appearing everywhere on plaques throughout the country, 'How happy are those who can call themselves a Turk'. Turkey contains numerous nationalist movements, including the National Action Party (*Milliyetci Hareket Partisi* – MHP) and the so-called

'Grey Wolves'. Retired military officers are particularly active in the country's various nationalist pressure groups. The TSK, through the pronouncements of its senior officers, the content of its website and the materials it makes available to schools and universities, not least those relating to the denial of genocide against the Armenians, is a major instrument of nationalist propaganda. Turkish nationalism is not infrequently defensive, xenophobic, racist and illiberal. Today, Turkish nationalist sentiment extends beyond Turkey's Kemalist core and permeates the entire society, and its themes 'are a common denominator of political parties of all different shades' (Guney 2006–07: 20). In recent years, it has been incited still further by a host of developments, including European coolness towards Turkey's EU accession, the diplomatic and political falling out with Washington, the Kurdish issue, international pressure relating to the Armenian issue, and internal democratization. It is at root a creation of the 1920s and 1930s, however, and of a state elite confronted with the challenge of creating an identity for the assortment of people inhabiting the Anatolian rump territory they had inherited. It is a product of a very successful nation-building exercise, and a means to encourage the Anatolian masses to switch their allegiances to the new republic. It is one of Kemalism's most enduring legacies, and a contributory factor in Turkey's difficulties in adapting to the realities of a globalized and transnationalized world.

Secularism

It was the abolition of the caliphate in 1924 that sparked the Sheik Said revolt, but the secularism introduced by the Turkish republic's founders sought to penetrate and indeed transform Turkish society more broadly. Islam, and the Sufi brotherhoods that constituted a defining characteristic of Turkish society and its relationship to religion, offered an alternative and competing source of authority and inspiration as well as, in Mustafa Kemal's eyes, a source of superstition and an obstacle to Turkish society's advancement. As he said in 1925, 'I flatly refuse to believe that today, in the luminous presence of science, knowledge, and civilization in all its aspects, there exist, in the civilized community of Turkey, men so primitive as to seek their material and moral well being from one or another sheik [...] the republic of Turkey cannot be the land of the sheiks, dervishes, disciples, and lay brothers' (Lewis 2002: 410–11). The Ottoman regime had long based much of its legal system on secular and legal principles derived from European practice, but the new regime went further. Secular law was now applied to social matters such as marriage, divorce and the rights of women. The brotherhoods were banned, their assets impounded, their ceremonies prohibited and their leaders persecuted. Formal religious education disappeared altogether from Turkey. Prayers were to be in Turkish, not Arabic. In 1924, a Directorate of Religious Affairs (known as *Diyanet*) was established, which in time took on the responsibility of training and appointing imams and approving their sermons.

Thus the regime did not seek to ban Islam, but to control it as a social and political force and to confine it to the private and spiritual sphere (Yavuz 2003a; Jenkins 2008b; Rabasa and Larrabee 2008). Imams became state employees and religious organization an arm of the state. Faith continued to play a part in the lives of many Turks, of course, including those of some high-ranking members of the Kemalist elite. Indeed, it seems probable that the major impact of the state's campaign to minimize Islam's autonomy and the role it could play in the country's political and public life was to alienate great swathes of society from the state and its governing elite, and to elevate religion as a vehicle for opposition to it. It has been argued that 'the rural and pious masses of Anatolia remained largely unaffected by the cultural reengineering' of Kemalism (Taspinar 2007: 118), that Turkey is still a 'torn' society and remains an essentially Islamic and 'eastern' country, notwithstanding the elite's bid to affiliate it with western ideas of modernity (Huntington 1993, 1996). From the Turkish republic's first multiparty elections in 1950, democratization in Turkey has tended to underline the 'centre–periphery' encapsulation of Turkish politics and society (Mardin 1973), according to which Turkey's increased pluralism has enabled Turkey's conservative, provincial and devout hinterland, including the Kurdish south-east, to challenge its Kemalist, secular, 'westernizing' and urban centre.

The present AKP government, which won forty-seven per cent of the electoral vote in 2007, represents these 'peripheral' communities, as indeed to varying degrees did Adnan Menderes's Democratic Party (DP), which emerged victorious from Turkey's first multiparty elections in 1950 and won three elections in succession; the Justice Party (*Adalet Partisi* – AP), which descended from the DP (banned by the 1960 military coup leaders, who also hanged Menderes) and which was electorally popular during the 1960s and 1970s; and Turgut Ozal's Motherland Party (*Anavatan Partisi* – ANAP), which came to power in the 1983 election held in the wake of the 1980 military coup. These parties shared an overlapping lineage in terms of personalities, ideologies, constituencies and historical formation. Necmettin Erbakan's Welfare Party (*Refah Partisi* – RP), which led Turkey's coalition government that was ousted from power by the 1997 'soft coup', was the AKP's less compromising forerunner. Although the challenge to the secular order posed by the AKP and its RP predecessor has been a quite explicit one, the DP, AP and ANAP parties all flirted with a similar constituency and also nibbled at the edges of the secular and Kemalist order. Turkey's devout Anatolian population has generally rewarded these parties with its votes.

Yet each of these parties was banned on the orders of Kemalist military coup leaders determined to uphold the secular character of the republican state. In fact, the present prime minister, Recep Tayyip Erdogan, spent four months in prison for 'inciting religious hatred', and could only take his place as prime minister in March 2003 after constitutional amendments were made after the November 2002 election that permitted him to re-enter the political process. In 2008, the constitutional court voted against banning the ruling AKP by the narrowest of margins, but did vote to overrule a parliamentary attempt to lift the headscarf ban on women attending universities. In other words, secularism has remained as a central tenet of Kemalism, and the constitution continues to assert that the republic is secular and must remain so. Islam remains a securitized issue for the arch Kemalists of the Turkish state elite. The religiously observant are still likely to find themselves purged from the Turkish officer corps. Religious instruction is still monitored and controlled, even if less effectively than hitherto, and individuals displaying religious symbols – such as the headscarf for women or beards for men – remain excluded from public sector employment.

In light of the tempering of Kemalism's harder secularist edge, largely as a result of the political preferences of Turkey's population, what does it mean to assert that Turkey is a secular republic? And what does it mean to argue, as many have done, that it has become more Islamic? The DP lifted the ban on the Arabic call to prayer (which was later reinstated), reopened mosques and built new ones. Currently, there can be few if any countries that have a higher rate of new mosque construction than Turkey. Ozal, in particular, tolerated the activities of the supposedly proscribed brotherhoods, and over the years Islam again resurfaced as a more visible feature of Turkish life, 'in which moderate Islam was again seen by large sections of the mainstream political forces as a component of national identity' (Poulton 1997: 175). Indeed, it has been argued that the brotherhoods, and most especially the *Naksibendi* order, are more influential in modern Turkey than was the case in the Ottoman era, when the religious elite were part of the ruling elite (Mardin 2005). Furthermore, it is claimed that they have endowed Turkey with a populist, nationalistic and increasingly modernizing variant of Islam that has been inclined towards statism – inherited from the Ottoman era as well as absorbed from Kemalism – and disinclined to mount overt religiously inspired challenges to the Kemalist order.

More remarkable still was the adoption by the 1980 coup leaders of the so-called 'Turkish–Islamic synthesis' as a semi-official state ideology in an attempt to turn the country's youth away from political extremes, especially those of the left, and towards a more conservative and patriotic value system. The military regime's hope was that Islam could be used as a servant of the state. Although as a set of ideas it can be traced back to the early twentieth century, or late Ottoman period, the Turkish–Islamic synthesis was reformulated during the 1970s by a group of conservative intellectuals. Its basic assertion is that 'Turkishness and Islam are two essential components of the national culture' (Sen 2010: 61). In practical terms, it meant that in the early 1980s, compulsory religious instruction was reintroduced into elementary and middle schools, that the *Diyanet* was expanded in size and resources, that its Koran classes increased in number, that the country's mosque-building programme expanded, and that the *Imam Hatip* schools, whose function was to train preachers, increased their intake of students. Put another way, the

Kemalist state's involvement in, and funding of, religious education now grew substantially, although there was an attempt to turn the clock back after the 'soft coup' of 1997. In particular, '*Imam Hatip* schools have played a crucial role in terms of the dissemination and legitimization of the main ideas and ideals of Turkish Islamism' (Sen 2010: 66). Over time, the effect of these reforms has been to raise Islam's profile significantly in Turkish social, public and, eventually, political life. Turkish Islam is no longer underground, in so far as it ever was. An increasing number of Turkish politicians, journalists, businessmen and academics, as well as more modestly employed individuals, owe their education to religious schools. Non-state Islamic groups, such as the brotherhoods, have also been free to grow, not least as a consequence of the liberalizing reforms of the 1980s. They, too, share the religious, patriotic and conservative values of the synthesis, but have simultaneously been able to create spheres of philosophical and institutional autonomy from the state. Indeed, a kind of parallel society, with its own networks and elites, has emerged in Turkey in recent decades (Sen 2010: 68).

It has been argued that 'the history of modern Turkey is not that of a conflict between republicanism and sultanism, nor is it a history of strife framed by Islam and secularism. It is a complex, many tiered encounter between "traditional" forces and modernity that have interpenetrated and been transformed over time due to their propinquity' (Mardin 2005: 160). The sponsorship of Islam by Turkey's secular state, and the adoption of Turkish nationalism, statism and a commitment to modernity by both state and non-state Islamic institutions, and the inclination even of the religious bodies to separate religion from politics, all serve to endow both Turkish Islam and Turkish secularism with a high degree of uniqueness (Kuru 2008, 2009). However, the state has ultimately proved itself unable to control the Islamic beast that it inherited from the Ottoman era and that it enabled to grow in its attempt to instil political and social discipline in the country, and that has blossomed still further as a consequence of the country's democratization. Kemalism's desire to banish Islam as far as it could from Turkey's public and political life has failed, and its tendency to securitize Islam and to see it as a threat to the core values of the republic appear not to be shared by the bulk of Turks. Indeed, it seems more plausible to argue not that there has been a two-way interpenetration but that, whilst Turkey's Muslims have frequently embraced modernity and an essentially secular approach to politics, there has thus far been less willingness on the part of at least the further reaches of the Kemalist spectrum to tolerate or accommodate displays of Islamic adherence. At any rate, this issue is at the heart of Turkey's current evolution, and of its relationship with the rest of the world.

3   Kemalism and state security

Becoming Turkey

How was the new, and newly Turkish, state to find its place in the world? Territorially, by 1920 Turkish nationalists had accepted that western Thrace and the Arab lands could remain outside the new republic, and instead based their demands on the National Pact agreed upon that year by an Ottoman but elected and nationalist-dominated parliament meeting in Istanbul (Vali 1971: 14–21; Hale 2000: 44–59; Lewis 2002: 239–62; Zurcher 2004: 133–63). In effect, this declared the intention to base the new Turkish state on the 'Ottoman Muslim' – Turkish and Kurdish – people, thereby rejecting any desire to retain wider Ottoman territorial possessions. It also signalled the defeat of those Turkish nationalists who aspired to base the new state on pan-Turkic (or pan-Turanian) principles. This would have necessitated exploiting the difficulties of the new Soviet regime in a bid to incorporate central Asia and Azerbaijan. However, in 1920, Turkish nationalists were confronted both with the fact that Greek forces, inspired by their Greater Greece or *megali* idea and encouraged by the British in particular, were in occupation of the whole of Thrace and much of western Anatolia; and by the Treaty of Sèvres, drawn up by British and French diplomats and signed by the Sultan's government, also in 1920 but after the adoption of the National Pact earlier in the year. The Treaty of Sèvres aimed to award Thrace and western Anatolia to Greece, envisaged the establishment of Kurdish and Armenian states in eastern Anatolia, offered zones of economic influence to France and Italy, restored the hated 'capitulations' that awarded privileges to foreigners in Turkey and to their economic interests, placed the country under external financial control and planned to put the straits – the Bosphorus and the Dardanelles – under international supervision. In addition, French and Italian troops had joined the British in occupying the straits and had landed on parts of Anatolia's southern coastline. The Sultan's administration, now a mere puppet of the allies, remained the recognized government until November 1922.

It was Kemal Ataturk who took the credit for leading the fight – the Turkish War of Independence – against the Greeks. Turkish forces attained victory in late 1922, but not before widespread atrocities were committed by both sides against the civilian inhabitants of the region. The French and Italians had neither the unity nor the will to take on Turkey's emerging nationalist forces, and soon signalled their readiness to enter into negotiations with them. The British, too, proved unwilling to back their political support for the Greeks with military force. In Anatolia's north-east, Turkey had attacked the independent Armenian state in 1920 and in effect annexed much of its territory. The Soviets simultaneously took over what remained of Armenia, which led to the Turkish–Soviet Treaty of Kars establishing the Turkish–Armenian border at its present location, which ceded Kars, Ardahan and Igdir to Turkey, but incorporated Muslim Adjara and the port city of Batumi (in Georgia) into the Soviet Union. With victory assured, the nationalists under Ataturk's leadership abolished the sultanate. They were now the *de facto* government of a new Turkish republic.

International recognition soon followed with the Treaty of Lausanne, signed in July 1923. This embraced some but not all of the terms of the National Pact of 1920. Turkey would be fully sovereign, with provincial and Anatolian Ankara rather than cosmopolitan and geographically vulnerable Istanbul as its capital. Neither a Kurdish nor an Armenian state would be carved out of Anatolia. Eastern Thrace would be Turkish, but most of the Aegean islands – some of which were to be permanently demilitarized – went to Greece. In light of the bloodletting that had taken place between ethnic Turks and Greeks, it was also agreed that a population exchange should take place between the two countries, involving the transfer of over 1 million Christians from Turkish territory and half a million Muslims from Greece – although this was in large measure a rubber-stamping of the population flows that had already occurred. A small Greek minority remained in Istanbul, and a Muslim minority stayed put in western Thrace, where it outnumbered the local Greeks by more than three to one, although some of the Muslims were Bulgarian- rather than Turkish-speaking (Pomaks) (Vali: 1971: 224). Thousands of these Muslims have since emigrated to Turkey, and the number remaining is a source of dispute between Turkey and Greece, as is their treatment at the hands of the Greek authorities. The Greek population of Istanbul, at more than 100,000 (fourteen per cent of the city's total) at the time of independence (Vali 1971: 222) also drifted to Greece in the ensuing years and was depleted still further in the mid-1950s in the wake of anti-Greek riots ostensibly provoked by the interethnic conflict in British-ruled Cyprus. Today there are only around 4000 Greek inhabitants of Istanbul, although tens of thousands more have retained their Turkish citizenship though residing in Greece. The status of Turkey's Greeks, and especially of Istanbul's Greek Patriarch, is similarly a source of tension today between the two neighbouring states. Both Greece and Turkey have been criticized for their approach to interethnic relations within their national boundaries (Council of Europe 2009).

Three territorial issues remained after the signing of the Lausanne Treaty: the Dodecanese islands and Rhodes; the province of Hatay/Alexandretta, bordering Syria; and the largely Kurdish-populated Mosul province of what is now Iraq. The Lausanne Treaty gave the mostly Greek-inhabited Dodecanese islands to Italy. Although Turkey had retained a claim to them based on their Ottoman past, the Turkish minorities that still resided there and their proximity to the Turkish coastline, Ankara did not see fit to oppose the 1947 transfer of the islands to Greece. Turkey needed allied support against the Soviet threat, and was not in an especially strong diplomatic position given its wartime neutrality. Furthermore, its relations with Greece were good at this time. That the islands were to be demilitarized also sweetened the pill.

With regard to Alexandretta, to Turkey's south-east, the population of which was over one-third Turkish with the rest divided between Sunni, Shia and Christian Arabs and Armenians, it had been agreed at Lausanne that it should be attached to French-ruled Syria, so long as it remained administratively distinct and the rights of Turks were protected. With the approach of Syrian independence, Ankara's opposition to Arab rule of the province mounted. An inconclusive election in Alexandretta was ignored by the French who, keen to retain friendship with Turkey as the prospect of war in Europe loomed, instead allowed Turkish troops jointly to police the province. Another election was held, this time producing a Turkish majority, which enabled Paris to cede the province, called Hatay by the Turks, to Ankara. This was contrary to the undertaking that had been made by France to the League of Nations that it would not cede Syrian territory to any foreign power. Consequently, the League of Nations refused to recognize the transfer. More importantly, this arrangement angered the newly independent state of Syria that emerged in 1946, and undermined relations between Ankara and Damascus for decades to come (Hale 2000: 66–67).

The most immediately problematic territorial issue left unresolved by the Lausanne Treaty, and with major implications for Turkey today, concerned the former Ottoman province of Mosul in British-administered Iraq. Although in 1915 Sherif Hussein, whose son was in due course to become the new Iraqi state's first King, laid claim only to the Ottoman Arab provinces of Baghdad and Basra, over which the British acquired a mandate at the end of World War I, the British had now attached Mosul province to their Baghdad and Basra protectorates (Catherwood 2004). This rendered the lower-lying Arab provinces more defensible and economically more viable. Furthermore, oil had recently been discovered around Kirkuk, thus strengthening the British desire to incorporate Mosul province into a new Iraqi state over which it could exercise control. Ankara, on the other hand, was determined that the new Turkish state should be made up of the non-Arab loyal Muslim inhabitants of the Ottoman empire, namely the Turks and the Kurds, and that Mosul province should become part of Turkey. Furthermore, Kurds – most of whom were in any case to be incorporated into Turkey – had generally fought alongside Turks in establishing the new Turkish state. The province was around three-quarters Kurdish, although Mosul city was mainly Arab and there was also a Turcoman population. Ankara even proposed that a plebiscite be held to establish the wishes of Mosul's population, which the British refused. Instead, the issue was left to a League of Nations International Commission of Inquiry to investigate, which Ankara believed was bound to favour the British perspective, not least because Turkey was not yet a League member. It did, and Mosul was awarded to Iraq in a 1925 judgement. Turkey protested but, unwilling to go to war with the British, had little choice but to back down, in return for a ten per cent share of the province's oil royalties for a twenty-five-year period. In June 1926, Turkey and Britain signed a bilateral treaty recognizing the outcome. Iraq became independent in 1932 but, as we shall see (in Chapter 6), the fate of the Kurdish region of Iraq has again become a Turkish concern in recent years.

Laying the foundations of Turkish foreign policy

Celebrated as Ataturk's victories still are in Turkey, symbolized by the achievement of the country's sovereignty, borders and diplomatic recognition at Lausanne, the predominant sentiment left behind by this period has come to be known as the 'Sèvres complex'. It reflects a reading of history, but is also a national psychosis. Anyone familiar with modern-day Turkey will be aware of the frequency with which Turkish officials, journalists and politicians make reference to it or exhibit its main features (Guida 2008). Turkey's officer corps have been especially attached to its precepts. An entirely representative expression of the syndrome was offered in 2000, when the head of the Military Academy informed its new intake that 'you will see that Turkey has the most internal and external enemies of any country in the world. You will learn about the dirty aspirations of those who hide behind values such as democracy and human rights and who want to take revenge on the republic of Ataturk' (Jenkins 2001: 90). It is a form of paranoia, a conspiracy theory that has been described as 'a virtual siege mentality' (Jenkins 2001: 16), and has frequently and typically informed Ankara's approach to foreign policy issues as diverse as Turkey's relations with the EU, the Cyprus issue and the Armenian 'genocide' question. Ankara's approach to the outside world is conditioned by this sense that Turkey's territorial integrity is insecure and contested and that the country 'is under continual internal and external threat' (Jenkins 2001: 16). A survey conducted in 2006 found that seventy-two per cent of Turks believe that some countries still seek to divide Turkey (Guida 2008: 38). The Sèvres complex is perhaps at its most intense with respect to the country's Kurdish issue, and prime minister Bulent Ecevit's 1994 declaration that 'the fundamental goal of the United States was to create an autonomous region in southeastern Turkey' (Olsen 1996: 102) offers just one illustration of this commonplace Turkish assumption and mindset. In Turkey, 'Sèvres' is shorthand for the widely held Turkish suspicion that external powers, and especially Turkey's 'allies' in the West, are bent on the further dismemberment and weakening of their country.

Although it was indeed aimed at leaving Turkey 'helpless and mutilated, a shadow state' (Lewis 2002: 247) – not least by applying the principle of self-determination to the Kurds and Armenians – it is testimony to the power of Turkey's nationalist narrative that the Sèvres Treaty, which has been described as 'a historically specific' and 'ill thought out and poorly executed' plan that 'failed so lamely' (Robins 2003: 104), has left such a profound legacy. It is a mindset that has frequently encouraged Ankara's policy makers since the birth of the republic to keep the world at arm's length. During the interwar period, it underpinned Ankara's inclination towards distant, if correct, relationships with the western powers, with whom its diplomatic engagement was probably less than that with Moscow. In economic terms, Turkey's autarkic approach was softened only by a cautious readiness to accept aid from the Soviet Union and by barter deals with Europe's other corporatist polities. Indeed, the determination to maintain peaceful relations with Moscow may have been a factor in Ataturk's policy of eschewing any pan-Turkic aspirations (Carley 1996: 6). It may also have ensured that Moscow kept the lid on the Armenian issue. Ataturk's domestic aspiration to westernize Turkish society thus, and perhaps paradoxically, offered 'no reason for constructing an alliance with the western powers' (Hale 2000: 71). Indeed, Turkey remained neutral during the Second World War. One of Ankara's few diplomatic forays during this period was to join Iran, Iraq and Afghanistan in the Saadabad Pact in 1937. This aimed at ensuring mutual non-interference and respect for existing borders, but was also designed to signal to external powers not to aggress against the signatories (Hale 2000: 62). It suggested, too, a strong strain of anti-imperialism in early republican and Kemalist attitudes. Notwithstanding the fact that Turkey had never been directly and explicitly colonized, Turkish foreign policy in the early years of independence bears some resemblance to that pursued by later batches of newly independent states.

Relations with Greece constituted a more immediate priority, and a rapprochement was achieved with Athens in 1930, which lasted until the 1950s. This cleared the way for the signing of a rather unsuccessful Balkan Pact in 1934 to include Romania and Yugoslavia. The detente between Turkey and Greece resolved some outstanding issues between the two states, such as the terms of the population exchange and disputed property claims, and was accompanied by mutual rhetoric that sought to downplay the raw emotions that were a legacy of their bloody separation. There was also a shared suspicion of Italian ambitions in the region. However, this atmosphere could not survive the impact on Greek Cypriots of the trend towards global decolonization during the 1950s and the consequent disruption of the island's inter-communal relationships (Borowiez 2000; Hannay 2005; Mallinson 2005; Dodd 2010), nor could it survive the impact of changes in the world's law of the sea regime during the 1970s, 1980s and 1990s on territorial demarcation in the Aegean (Wilson 1979). Tension over these two issues revealed that the raw emotions between the two peoples had not at all dissipated.

For the most part, the Arab Middle East remained dominated by the British and French during the interwar period. Thus, in so far as Turkey thought at all about this part of its neighbourhood, relations with it were conducted largely via London and Paris. Ankara was in any case generally uninterested in cultivating the Arab world. The shared Ottoman and Islamic past had been superseded by Turkey's construction of its own ethnic Turkish identity. Turkey's attitudes were also coloured by the notion that, in siding with the British against the Ottoman empire during the First World War, the Arabs had proved themselves treacherous (Jung 2005). It has been argued that 'it was events during the relatively short period of Young Turk rule that irretrievably damaged relations between the Turks and the Arabs' (Carley 1996: 9). The fact and the manner of the acquisition by Turkey of Alexandretta/Hatay province arguably demonstrated a rather low Turkish regard for Arab sensitivities and certainly did not endear republican Turkey to Arab public opinion. Ataturk's commitment to secularism, and his view of Islam – and the Arab world – as backward and superstitious, gave additional impetus to Turkey's tendency to turn its back on its Arab neighbours. A senior Turkish commentator once wrote that Turks 'have always considered the middle east to be a kind of quicksand that they would prefer to avoid. Turkish policy has thus been to observe events in the middle east rather than be involved in them' (Birand 1996: 171). This observation applies to the Cold War era as much as it does to the interwar period.

In short, for all the new republic's professed westernization project, Turkish foreign policy in the republic's first few decades can be best characterized as neutralist, anti-imperialist and isolationist. Unsurprisingly, its leaders were preoccupied with domestic political, economic and social development, and needed a respite from what had been so exhausting a period of internal and external conflict. Although it derived in such large measure from the officer-dominated Young Turk movement, the new regime did not possess the resources, the need or the inclination to devote much attention to the modernization of its armed forces, at least until the outbreak of war seemed increasingly likely. In any case, the establishment of the Soviet Union in 1917 and its tightening grip on the Caucasus and central Asia, and the overbearing presence of Britain and France in the former Ottoman possessions in the Middle East and north Africa, afforded little opportunity to conduct a more active foreign policy in extensive swathes of its neighbourhood. Furthermore, Turkey was of relatively little interest to the outside world. It was initially regarded as a defeated power, and as such was excluded from the League of Nations until 1932. Western powers paid little diplomatic attention to it, a state of affairs with which Ankara was mostly quite content.

One exception to this overall picture was the signing of the Montreux Convention in 1936, which offered an early illustration of the importance that geopolitical circumstances could have in Turkey's external relations, an importance that was to become more evident during the Cold War and even more compelling in its wake. The Convention conferred control of the straits to Turkey, which for Turks represented a victory over the Sèvres proposal that the straits be internationally controlled. Although the Convention has survived the test of time, Moscow's dissatisfaction with its terms prompted its 1946 demand that either the littoral states of the Black Sea, or Moscow and Ankara exclusively, should jointly exercise control over the straits (Vali 1971: 181–97). The Convention permits Black Sea powers, such as the Soviet Union (and, today, Russia), to send warships of any size and type, including surfaced submarines, through the straits unimpeded, except in times of war, when Turkey has the right to prevent such passage. The Convention also granted Turkey the right to fortify the straits, and to gather intelligence on passing warships. These clauses proved very useful during the Cold War. Non-Black Sea states, however, could only send ships not exceeding 30,000 tons northwards into the Black Sea in peacetime, they could not stay in the Black Sea for more than twenty-one days, and had to give advance notification of intended passage to the Turkish authorities. The USA, albeit not a signatory to the Convention, has routinely exercised these rights. Moscow's 1946 demands unsurprisingly sought to prevent non-Black Sea warship passage through the straits. Although technological and other developments have led to the occasional raised eyebrow concerning the Convention and Turkey's application of its terms, its provisions have remained generally unchallenged since 1946.

The end of the Cold War and Turkey's emergence as an energy transit route have thrown a different kind of spotlight on the Convention, and subjected it to new strains. The outbreak of armed conflict between the former Soviet states of Russia and Georgia in 2008, and the accession to NATO of two more Black Sea littoral states, Romania and Bulgaria, signify the shifts that have occurred in the region's geostrategic circumstances. The Convention also permits the free passage of merchant shipping through the straits, a right that Ankara now feels uneasy about in light of the massive growth of Black Sea shipping, especially involving the passage of Russian oil tankers, and Istanbul's equally substantial population explosion. Neither present levels of shipping, especially of inflammable oil products, nor Istanbul's growth – its population is approaching 12 million, and with its surrounding conurbation it at least doubles this figure – as part of the global trend towards urbanization, could have been anticipated in 1936. As we shall see, this has produced a different slant on Turkey's appreciation of the Convention.

The emergence of the Cold War: out of the cold?

It is commonly assumed, by Turks and non-Turks alike, that Turkey's post-1945 incorporation into western political structures formed part and parcel of its wider embrace of western values. Yet it can also be argued that 'Turkey was forced into the western camp in the cold war because it was directly threatened by the Soviet Union rather than through an a priori commitment to liberal democracy' (Hale 2000: 110). Soviet pressure to convert the sole

Turkish control of the straits granted to it by the Montreux Convention and demands for a border revision in the north-east of the country were added to concern over Soviet support for the communist side in the ongoing Greek civil war. Moscow's abrupt termination of the 1925 Treaty of Friendship with Turkey, and its generally aggressive and expansionist behaviour elsewhere, not least in neighbouring Iran, impressed upon Ankara the risks this new era posed. Turkey, which had remained neutral during World War II, now began to fear the consequences of its diplomatic isolation.

The Truman Doctrine of 1947 entitled Turkey to US military aid, and Ankara appreciated that a US guarantee to Turkey represented the real prize. However, Britain rather than the USA was the main external actor in the region, thus it was primarily London that Ankara sought to cultivate. In any case, the USA was still struggling with the issue of how far it was willing to commit itself to security pacts in western Europe, let alone beyond. Turkey's approach was thus to lobby for incorporation into any western security pact that emerged (Gonlubol 1975; Athanassopoulou 1998; Hale 2000: 110–19; Kubicek 2008). This offered the best means to ensure indirect US protection. However, some in the USA agreed with the British preference that Turkey should play a role in regional arrangements covering the eastern Mediterranean and Middle East rather than in any western European pact. Neither Washington nor London saw Turkey as integral to Europe or to the Atlantic region – a sentiment shared by many in continental Europe (Kubicek 2008: 25–27) – although both recognized the geostrategic significance of the country. This attitude towards Turkey has persisted, and underpins the reluctance in some quarters to accept Turkey as an EU member. As Giscard d'Estaing, former French president and then head of the EU's constitutional convention, put it in an interview with *Le Monde* in 2002, Turkey is not in Europe, it is not a European country, and it has a 'different culture, a different approach, a different way of life'.[1] Two of the most seasoned American students of Turkey–US relations have observed that 'few Americans are familiar with Turkey, and even well informed Americans tend to share a perception of Turkey as culturally and politically exotic', as 'middle eastern rather than European' (Larrabee and Lesser 2003: 179). Turkey's western diplomatic alignment has had to contend with perceptions such as these since the Cold War's onset.

However, with the perceived hardening of the Soviet menace and the emergence of the Cold War, the outbreak of the Korean War in 1950, the Turkish contribution of 5000 troops to the US-led military effort there and the drive for rearmament in the West, Turkish membership of NATO soon emerged as a strategically attractive option. Turkey's geography could offer a base both for defence and offence against the Soviet Union, and its forces could make a vital contribution to the overall military balance. Turkey's position astride the straits offered control over entry to and egress from the Black Sea, and could bottle up the Soviet Black Sea fleet. Furthermore, the 'loss' of Turkey would represent a serious blow to western security, in the eastern Mediterranean and in the Middle East. In short, Turkey's importance to the West was now considerable and derived from its geo-strategic location. Thus, in 1952, Turkey along with Greece acceded to NATO.

Turkey as an Atlantic ally

With its NATO accession, Turkey was now deluged with US military and economic aid and with American praise. Turkey was progressively tied to the USA through the signing of numerous bilateral and secret agreements rather than through multilateral arrangements under the NATO umbrella. US air and missile bases, communication facilities, military storage sites and naval facilities proliferated (Gonlubol 1975: 33–45). American U2 spy planes took off from bases in Turkey, US nuclear-armed bombers were stationed at Incirlik air base near Adana and dual-control battlefield nuclear weapons – whereby Turkish armed forces controlled the delivery system but US forces controlled the warhead – were introduced into Turkey. They are still there. In the late 1950s, the two states agreed to the deployment of Jupiter medium-range nuclear missiles on Turkish territory. The behaviour of US military personnel in Turkey was governed by US rather than Turkish law, a source of a series of incidents that during the 1960s contributed to the appearance of anti-American sentiment in the country. The US military presence in Turkey functioned with minimum input from the Turkish authorities, as was demon-strated by the 1960 shooting down by the Soviet Union of an American U2 spy plane based in Turkey, and by the 1963 US withdrawal of the Jupiter missiles as a result of understandings arrived at with Moscow during the Cuban missile crisis, but without consultation with Ankara. Turkey could have easily found its territory drawn into a conflict of which it had little prior warning or capacity to control. Turkey had become a forward operating base for US forces, and the country's geographical location was almost all that mattered from Washington's perspective. Again, in the words of a leading US observer, 'Turkey and Turkish–US relations have been prisoners of a narrow concept of geopolitics' (Lesser 2006: 83).

During these Cold War years, in 1948, Turkey also joined the Organization for European Economic Cooperation (OEEC), which had been established to distribute US Marshall Aid. Turkey was also a founding signatory in 1960 of its successor, the Organization for Economic Cooperation and Development (OECD) and the Council of Europe in 1949 (notwithstanding some reserva-tions from Nordic countries in particular), and became an associate member of the European Economic Community (EEC) in 1963. The West's readiness to bring Turkey into the fold of its burgeoning institutional structures served to encourage Ankara in its commitment to pursue a Western path in its domestic development, too. In Cold War Europe, the very idea of the 'West' and even of 'Europe' rather loosely came to mean NATO members, US allies, and other free-market states, in contrast to the excluded communist 'East'. In this way, an imperfectly democratic, economically semi-developed and

Muslim Turkey came to find itself in the 'West'. This was a remarkable transformation in Turkey's global situation, and unsurprisingly it was enthusiastically welcomed by Turkey's elite circle of policy makers. It was also welcomed by the Turkish military, which was lionized by the USA and was by far the major domestic beneficiary of US assistance.

Few relationships could have had more expectation placed on them, and more exaggerated rhetoric expended on them, than this Turkish–US relationship in its first decade or so (Kubicek 2008: 27). Europeans were generally more wary. Turkey's successful lobbying to be allowed into the Council of Europe paradoxically served to draw attention to its human rights failings (Hale 2000: 116–17). By agreeing to expose its domestic political practices to European scrutiny in return for its diplomatic inclusion, Turkey laid itself open to a process that is still in evidence today, by which Turkey's domestic political failings emerge as a problem in its relations with the west, whose 'interference' in Turkey's domestic affairs in turn irritates Turks. Military interaction between Turkey and its European NATO allies, certainly in these early years, was slight, and European attitudes to Turkey were less exclusively focused than American ones on the country's geostrategic value (Buzan and Diez 1999: 45–47). For Ankara, too, 'political relations with the western European nations were important to Turkey mainly because they were partners of the US' (Hale 2000: 174). Turkey's NATO relationship thus largely took the form of a bilateral relationship with the US, and its interaction with the West more broadly in fields other than the strategic remained undeveloped and uncomfortable.

Ankara also did little to improve its relationships with its mainly Arab Middle Eastern neighbourhood during this period. Turkey was one of the earliest states to recognize Israel in 1949. It massed forces on Syria's border in 1957 in response to a feared communist coup there. It allowed the USA to use the Incirlik base to reinforce Lebanon during the 1958 crisis. Above all, Turkey was instrumental in forming the Baghdad Pact in 1955, a 'northern tier' alliance consisting of Turkey, Iraq, Iran, Pakistan and the UK (Hale 2000: 125–30). Ankara's role represented fulfilment of its promise to engage actively in Middle Eastern security arrangements as bait for its NATO admission. Widely regarded by much of the Arab world as a vehicle to perpetuate western intrusion into the region, particularly in the wake of the Suez crisis in 1956, it has been claimed that the Baghdad Pact 'precipitated the Arab countries' alignment with the Soviet Union, it stimulated the rise of radical ideologies, and cast Turkey in the image of a docile tool of western powers' (Karpat 1975: 116). In any case, with Iraq's withdrawal in 1959 in the wake of the 1958 coup against the pro-western regime there, the Pact was transformed into the now entirely non-Arab Central Treaty Organization (CENTO). It survived, ineffectually, until the Shah's overthrow in 1979.

Broadly, Ankara's reaction to the failure of the Baghdad Pact, helped by a change of government in Turkey, was to 'disengage from intra middle eastern disputes, while seeking correct rather than cordial relations with all states in the region', based on a prevailing Turkish view of the Arab world as 'complex, unstable, impenetrable and unintelligible' (Robins 2003: 99–100). Furthermore, Ankara failed to respond to Moscow's 1953 post-Stalin withdrawal of its territorial demands on Turkey, or to the opportunities offered by Krushchev's diplomacy of 'peaceful coexistence'. As an indication of the exclusiveness of its western alignment, Ankara strongly criticized the idea of 'neutrality' as an appropriate Cold War stance at the Afro-Asian Bandung Conference in 1955, which was a precursor to the nonaligned movement. As a consequence of these rigidities, Ankara's diplomatic position was, by the early 1960s, a somewhat lonely one. The Cold War had brought Turkey from a position of neutrality into an unequal alliance with Washington, but it had won few other friends, and in some quarters was regarded with considerable suspicion. Western Europeans – then as now – sometimes failed to reciprocate the Turkish elite's attachment to a European 'destiny', and both Europe and the Middle East tended to regard Turkey as peripheral, external, as at or beyond the boundaries of their respective regions. Ankara had failed to engage with, and had even stood in opposition to, some of the broader political trends then current in global politics, such as third-world radicalism and nonalignment. It had traded on its geostrategic location on the southern flank of the Soviet Union and its proximity to the Middle East, and its military prowess had been enhanced as a result, but it was also now strategically exposed and dependent. Indeed, and especially from a European security perspective, it has been convincingly argued that Turkey's main function was to insulate regional 'security complexes' from each other by virtue of its limited interactions with each of the regions that surrounded it (Buzan and Diez 1999; Diez 2005). For Europe, Turkey constituted a welcome physical barrier to the volatile Middle East region, rather than a bridge to it. In any case, former imperial countries such as the UK and France engaged far more with the Middle East than did Turkey.

The trials and tribulations of the US relationship

Before long, Ankara would become aware of the extent of Turkey's exposure and dependence, and the fact that its strategic location meant that its alliance with the USA was primarily a function of US objectives and interests, 'a by product of other more prominent concerns' (Larrabee and Lesser 2003: 165), and did not necessarily imply respect for Turkey's. There had been tension as early as the mid-1950s over US objections to the manner in which its economic aid packages to Turkey had been distributed by the government for domestic political advantage, but the 1963 withdrawal of Jupiter missiles was one of the first foreign policy differences to set alarm bells ringing in Ankara. Turkey had steadfastly supported Washington during the Cuban missile crisis, notwithstanding the fact that the presence of Jupiter missiles rendered it highly likely that Turkish soil would constitute a high-priority Soviet target in the event of a nuclear exchange. Although Ankara had little choice but to acquiesce in the withdrawal of the missiles, given Washington's failure to consult properly with Ankara, it was unsurprising that questions were asked in Turkey about the one-sidedness of its transatlantic alliance.

Such questioning became still more insistent in the wake of the crisis over Cyprus that erupted in 1963. The island had attained independence from the UK in 1960 (after a prolonged struggle by Greek Cypriot) forces on the basis of a complicated power-sharing arrangement designed to protect the interests of the Turkish Cypriot minority on the island. The UK, Greece and Turkey were designated as guarantor powers to the agreement. When the Greek side elected to abrogate the agreement in 1963, intercommunal strife broke out. Both Greece and Turkey felt impelled to involve themselves in the island's affairs on behalf of their respective ethnic communities. Turkey, in particular, seriously considered intervening militarily, which as a guarantor power it believed it was entitled to do. Fearing that a Turkish landing was imminent, US president Lyndon Johnson wrote a letter to Ankara which made two main points. One was that 'the United States cannot agree to the use of any United States supplied military equipment for a Turkish intervention in Cyprus under present circumstances'. Then, drawing attention to the NATO expectation that member states do not wage war on each other, Johnson went on to add that 'I hope you will understand that your NATO allies have not had a chance to consider whether they have an obligation to protect Turkey against the Soviet Union if Turkey takes a step which results in Soviet intervention without the full consent and understanding of its NATO allies' (Vali 1971: 129–46; Bilge 1975; Gonlubol 1975: 17–18; Harris 1975: 59–66; Hale 2000: 148–54).

This was devastating to Turkey, whose loyalty to and trust in the USA had seemed so boundless. As one US official put it more recently, in the wake of the 'Johnson letter' the Ankara–Washington relationship 'never really recovered the initial closeness' (Arnett 2006: 36). Turks had been given a lesson that has since been repeatedly reinforced – that where US and Turkish interests and perspectives in Turkey's neighbourhood do not coincide, Washington could be expected to relegate Ankara's concerns. As Robert Komer, later to become US ambassador to Turkey, expressed it in 1963, 'We never really decided in our own minds whether to treat Turkey primarily as a NATO partner [...] or as an underdeveloped country' (Kuniholm 1996: 59). Given the scale of US economic aid to Turkey at this time, this is perhaps not surprising. The asymmetry in power was perhaps too great for it to be otherwise. However, proud Turks of all persuasions were now more questioning of the utility of the transatlantic alliance, and in particular of the possible mismatch between Turkish regional interests and those of the USA as a global power. The Turkish left, in particular, began to exhibit an anti-Americanism that has since become a familiar feature of Turkish politics across the political spectrum.

One result of this questioning was the 1969 Defence Cooperation Agreement, which reduced and to some degree codified the US military presence in Turkey. The Agreement affirmed Turkish sovereignty over, and the NATO rather than bilateral character of, the various installations in Turkey. Turkey had already refused the USA permission to use bases in Turkey for refuelling or for resupply of Israel during the 1967 Arab–Israeli war, and in 1973 Ankara prevented direct US combat and logistical support to Israel via Turkey. Indeed, for all the value Washington has attached to Turkey's geo-political situation, Ankara has repeatedly restricted US access to Incirlik and other facilities whenever Middle Eastern crises have broken out (Bolme 2007). The crisis following Turkey's 1974 invasion of Cyprus worsened Turkish–US relations still further. Ankara retaliated to a US congressional embargo on military equipment transfers to Turkey by suspending US operations at military installations in Turkey. Ankara also refused to assist in the failed US hostage rescue attempt in Iran in 1980. Tensions over the amount and quality of US economic and military aid to Turkey, Turkey's human rights record, threatened congressional support for Armenian genocide claims, and even concerns over Turkey's domestic opium production, much of which ended up as narcotics sold illegally on the streets of US cities (Robins 2007a), continued to bedevil Turkish–US relations throughout the remainder of the Cold War. In July 2010, former US ambassador to Ankara Ross Wilson warned the first-ever US House of Representatives Foreign Affairs Committee hearing into Turkish foreign policy that, when contemplating Turkish–US relations, 'there have always been ups and downs in US–Turkish relations. Those who think they remember the halcyon days of yore should read their history' (Wilson 2010).

On the periphery

Another impact of the 'Johnson letter' incident was, as one Turkish commentator put it, to swing Turkish foreign policy 'from one sidedness to many sidedness' (Vali 1971: 133). Turkey had found itself diplomatically isolated during the Cyprus crisis, and this too reinforced the sense in Ankara that too many eggs had been put in the US diplomatic basket. It is arguable that the logic of this assertion was not fully followed up until the 2002 election of the AKP government, and that in any case it took the end of the Cold War to render it feasible, but there was certainly a greater multidimensionality to Turkish foreign policy from the mid-1960s onwards (Altunisik 2009), as well as a distinct anti-American strain. Of course, Soviet behaviour, such as the invasions of Czechoslovakia in 1968 and Afghanistan in 1979 and its naval build-up in the eastern Mediterranean, could generally be relied upon to maintain the geostrategic cement of Turkish–US relations for the remainder of the Cold War, such that Ankara's distancing from the West had its limits. However, from the mid-1960s onwards, Turkish–Soviet relations thawed markedly, in a belated acknowledgement by Ankara of the wider 'peaceful coexistence' that had already been embraced by East and West. This notably took the form of Soviet economic assistance, which by the late 1970s had transformed Turkey into perhaps the biggest recipient of Soviet aid (Hale 2000: 151). This was accompanied by a relaxation of relationships with other communist states of Europe.

In the wake of the oil price hikes associated with the 1973 Arab–Israeli war, Turkey's trade with its oil-rich Arab neighbours increased substantially and its general tone towards the region softened. Ankara recognized the Palestine Liberation Organization (PLO) in 1976 and permitted it to open an Ankara office in 1979. In fact there had always been widespread sympathy in Turkey for the Palestinian plight and support for Israeli withdrawal to its prewar borders. However, this did not extend to a readiness to rupture relations with Israel nor to a wider engagement with Middle Eastern politics. Ankara's relations with its Arab neighbours remained mostly bilateral and largely economic in content. Turkey participated in, but did not become a full member of, the OIC, and continued to be wary of Arab radicalism, especially Syria's, of the complexity of intra-Arab relationships and of the region's Islamism.

Nor did Europe offer an alternative focus for Turkish diplomacy at this time. In most important respects, Turkey's NATO relationship remained essentially a bilateral one with Washington. Although Turkey and the EEC signed the Ankara Agreement in 1963, which released funds for economic restructuring in Turkey, laid out a road map towards a customs union and held out the hope of eventual Turkish membership, Turkey's economy was nowhere near ready to warrant serious consideration for membership at this time. Turkey's continuing economic difficulties, the military coups of 1971 and 1980, the 1974 invasion of Cyprus and continuing human rights concerns, combined to ensure that politically Turkey continued to be held at arm's length by most European states. Furthermore, Greek accession to the European Community (EC) in 1981 provided Athens with ample opportunity to obstruct progress in Turkish–EC relations.

All in all, Turkey remained remarkably isolated and friendless throughout much of the Cold War. Except for a brief flirtation under the stewardship of Bulent Ecevit in the 1970s, it had held itself aloof from the broader global trends of nonalignment that had absorbed much of the rest of the developing world. Its relations with Europe and the Middle East were undeveloped, notwithstanding the Ottoman past it shared with the latter, while the 'iron curtain' combined with Ankara's own disinclination and limitations to curtail contact with the Balkans, central Asia or the Caucasus region. The Cold War had served as a vehicle to bring Turkey out of its interwar isolation, but this fell far short of a fuller engagement with global or even regional developments. Turkey's much vaunted geopolitical significance remained 'both its blessing and its curse' (Robins 1996: 183). For both internal and external political and economic reasons, Turkey remained peripheral to, or even excluded from, each of the regions it abutted, and geographical circumstance could not overcome this fact. Washington lionized Turkey but also used it, and even in this relationship 'the cultural and economic dimension remains undeveloped' to this day, as it did throughout the Cold War (Lesser 2006: 93).

'Kemalist' geopolitics

Even as Turkey's Kemalist elites were becoming more questioning of the US alliance, they remained attached to the view that Turkey's geopolitical and geostrategic circumstances drove the country's foreign and security policy choices. After all, it was Turkey's location that had attracted external interest, helped bring Turkey closer to the western world and encouraged the USA to assist in building up its military prowess. Militaries everywhere are convinced of the vital contribution they make to national security, and are inclined to emphasize and even exaggerate the seriousness of external threats to it. In Turkey, the military emerged as a very powerful and influential factor in the determination of the country's security agenda and foreign policy (Ozcan 2001). Weak governments and an undeveloped civil society offered little resistance to the military's capacity to determine the security agenda, which in any case was shared by much of the civilian Kemalist elite and reinforced by the ubiquitous nationalist propaganda in the country's educational establishments and media. Indeed, Turkey's high school curriculum has since 1926 featured a compulsory course in 'National Security', designed and taught by the military (Bilgin 2007: 745–46). Turkey adopted a 'hard' approach to national security, putting great emphasis on national sovereignty and territorial integrity, on the prevalence of external threats and on the desirability of high levels of military preparedness. It could be seen as a 'national security state' or 'garrison state', adopting a 'realist' or Hobbesian view of the international political system, prioritizing security above democracy or economic advantage and institutionalizing the mindset that goes with it (Ripsman and Paul 2010: 10–12). Thus the Turkish military has enjoyed enormous areas of institutional autonomy, its funding and behaviour have generally been above criticism and beyond scrutiny, and it has been able to intimidate or persuade the country's political elites through its domination of Turkey's MGK (*Milli Guvenlik Kurulu* – National Security Council), its track record of interference in the country's political processes, its resource advantage over its civilian counterparts and the culture of deference to it (Turan 1997; Karaosmanoglu 2000; Narli 2000; Jenkins 2001; Demirel 2005; Akkoyunlu 2007; Michaud-Emin 2007).

Encouraged by Washington, Turkish security policy throughout the Cold War acquired an essentialist and geopolitically deterministic flavour in which 'Turkey's geographical location has been utilized to point to its unique security needs and interests' (Bilgin 2005: 185, 2007). It has been noted that a 'geopolitical culture emerges from a state's encounter with the world. It is conditioned by a series of factors: a state's geographical situation, historical formation and bureaucratic organization, discourses of national identity and traditions of theorizing its relationship to the wider world, and the networks of power that operate within the state' (O'Tuathail 2006: 7). In Turkey's case, its geopolitical culture and its tough zero-sum approach to its neighbourhood have helped create the world that Turkey has encountered and have tended to serve as a self-fulfilling prophecy. Thus Turkey emerged from the Cold War with 'strained relations with virtually all its neighbours' (Mufti 1998: 40). In the words of former president and general staff chief Kenan Evren, uttered in 1989, Turkey was 'bound to be strong since she has very few friends' (Aral 1997: 87). In his preface to Turkey's 2000 Defence White Paper, defence minister Sabahattin Cakmakoglu noted that 'Turkey is located in the centre of a region full of instabilities and uncertainties, such as the middle east, Caucasus and the Balkans, where the balances are in a process of change', and this required the country to pay due attention to its military strength (Bilgin 2005: 186). According to this mode of thought, Turkey is a 'pivotal' (Chase *et al.* 1999) or 'central' state (Bilgin 2007: 748–49), possessing a unique geography and located in one of the world's most conflict-prone regions (Drorian 2005). The driving factor is less the nature of the political regime than 'geography, history, national identity, threat perceptions and alliance relations' (Kazan 2005: 598), seen as objective or 'scientific' rather than constructed factors.

Turkey's purportedly exceptional geopolitical circumstances served to reinforce the Kemalist elite's resistance to democratic consolidation and led it to argue for Turkey's exceptionalism, not least in the context of the country's quest to join the EU. As then prime minister Bulent Ecevit once expressed it, 'Turkey's special geographical conditions require a special type of democracy', and a member of the military hierarchy is quoted as saying that Turkey's geopolitical situation 'does not allow for more democracy' (Bilgin 2005: 186, 2007: 750–51). The shift that took place in the 1990s towards identifying the twin domestic phenomena of Kurdish separatism and Islamism as national security threats that required the military's intervention in Turkey's domestic politics deepened the challenge posed by the security state to the process of democratization. It was this trend that prompted deputy prime minister Mesut Yilmaz's 2001 attack on the 'national security syndrome', which he claimed was too broad in its reach and largely determined beyond the public gaze, and for which he was pilloried by the country's security establishment (Cizre 2003; Bilgin 2005: 187–94). Yet it can be argued that the Kemalist insistence on secularism had an international security as well as a domestic security dimension from the outset (Bilgin 2008). Religion was seen as constituting a barrier to the West's embrace of Turkey as well as to the country's domestic social and political development, and as a factor that could enable and encourage external interference in Turkey's domestic affairs. Similar observations apply to Turkey's domestic Kurdish issue. In fact, Ankara's capacity to contain the Kurdish issue has weakened progressively with the passage of time and the twists and turns of events, as has its ability to resist intellectual challenges to its national security state concept. It also became clear that, in the post-Cold War era at least, far from determining the nature of the Turkish response, Turkey's security challenges have lent themselves to alternative analyses and responses. Yet, as we shall see (in Chapter 7), even Turkey's 'new' foreign policy approach of recent years has drawn heavily on geopolitical modes of thought (Bilgin 2007: 749).

4 Turkey's Europeanization

A journey without an arrival?

A bad beginning

Notwithstanding its commitment to westernization, the Kemalist republic made no serious steps towards political democratization during the first decades of its existence. Turkey did not hold its first free multiparty election until 1950, and only then in part because the country's elite had now come to appreciate that this was what it now meant to be 'western' in the post-1945 world. There was little pressure from below. As we have seen (in Chapter 2), for the republic's leadership the aspiration to 'join' the West derived from a range of impulses, many of which were rooted in the circumstances of the Ottoman collapse and those of the 1920s and 1930s. They included security considerations, an attachment to the idea of economic and technological progress, a sense of 'Europeanness' rooted in the Ottoman empire's diplomatic involvement with, and imperial presence in, Europe, and a degree of disdain for the country's Islamic roots and Islamic neighbours.

Thus the republic's chosen path to modernity did not include a strong attachment to human rights or to democratization, values that since 1945 have become progressively more associated with the idea of 'Europeanization', but which in the 1920s and 1930s were patchy (Risse *et al.* 2001). Indeed, the postwar emergence of these normative values as both a European and global political issue largely passed Turkey by. Even the advent of multiparty democracy did not produce, and has not produced to this day, a full consolidation of democracy in Turkey (Ozbudun 2000). Indeed, the advent of electoral politics could be said to have hindered Turkey's progress, as it has produced challenges to the secular, unitary and authoritarian nature of Turkish state and society, which have in turn provoked the military in particular to intensify its interference in Turkish politics. Turkey's political, bureaucratic and military elite have for so long sought the country's inclusion into the western family in general, and accession to the EU in particular, yet Turkey's alignment with European political norms remains patchy and incomplete (Grigoriadis 2009). In the meantime, it has been swiftly overtaken in the quest for 'Europeanization' by a raft of other European states whose starting point was over forty years of communist rule.

The veteran analyst of Turkey–EU relations Heinz Kramer has observed that, 'from its very beginning, EU–Turkey relations have not been perceived as an integral part of the European integration process by most EU member states. Turkey has always been regarded as an "outsider" to Europe' (Kramer 2006: 24). Notwithstanding the doubts that have long been felt by many in Europe concerning Turkey's European credentials, the Ankara Agreement of 1963 gave Turkey associate member status of the (then) EEC (Kramer 1996; Muftuler-Bac 1999; Onis 2001; Avci 2003). Many Turks have subsequently regarded eventual full membership of the EU as a 'right deriving' from this agreement. In 1987, President Ozal decided to launch a badly timed bid for accession. Although Brussels politely declined, subsequent negotiations did lead to the signing of a customs union with the EU in 1995, the only such agreement ever signed between the EU and another state. Turkey's human rights record, its economic backwardness, political instability and problems with Greece – which acceded to the EU in 1981 – were just some of the more substantive reasons behind the pervasive European coolness towards the prospect of Turkish membership. Turkey's unconsolidated democracy loomed particularly large in European minds as an obstacle to Turkey's accession. If 'Europeanization is [...] understood as a diffusion of European norms and ideas, defined by the European liberal paradigm' (Grigoriadis 2008: 23), then Turkey was deemed by the EU to be insufficiently Europeanized. The values and political practices associated with the Kemalist order constituted barriers to effective norm and ideational transfer to Turkey from the liberal, democratic and civic Europe that had now been consolidated.

Thus at its summit meeting in Luxembourg in 1997, the EU decided against extending formal accession status to Turkey, although it did extend such status to eleven other candidates, ten of which were former communist states. Worse still from Ankara's perspective, the eleventh was (Greek) Cyprus. The EU also decided that actual accession negotiations could begin with Poland, the Czech Republic, Hungary, Estonia, Slovenia – and Cyprus, and that preparations for the other accession candidates would be speeded up. In the event, ten states joined in 2004 – the above-named six, plus Latvia, Lithuania, Slovakia and Malta. They were followed by Bulgaria and Romania in 2007. None of these states had enjoyed a customs union with the EU, which led some in Ankara to conclude that it constituted a waiting room rather than a pre-accession agreement. Condemning the EU's 1997 decision as 'unjust and discriminatory', Ankara suspended political dialogue with Brussels for a time. However, the EU did confirm Turkey's candidate status, and tasked the EC to produce annual progress reports on Turkey, which suggested that Turkey was indeed a candidate 'by implication'.[1] Helped by a change of government in Germany, and notwithstanding the serious objections of Greece and Cyprus, the EU decided in December 1999 to offer Turkey accession status (Park 2000). A decision on whether to commence accession negotiations was delayed until December 2004.

The EU accession process and the AKP: norm transfer in Turkey?

In 1993, the EU adopted the Copenhagen criteria for aspirant members, not least because it was felt that if an enlarged EU was to function satisfactorily, it should also deepen the commonalities between its member states. In the political sphere, the criteria insisted on the 'stability of institutions guaranteeing democracy, the rule of law, human rights and respect for and protection of minorities'. They also required 'the existence of a functioning market economy as well as the capacity to cope with competitive pressure and market forces within the Union' and 'the ability to take on the obligations of membership including adherence to the aims of political, economic & monetary union'.[2] These represented a serious raising of the bar for Turkey, such that the internal political costs of complying with the EU now appeared excessive to many in Ankara's political class, at least until hopes were raised by the 1999 Helsinki decision to accept Turkey as an accession candidate. The reforms associated with the Ozal era during the 1980s and early 1990s focused predominantly on the economic sphere, although they did enable an explosion of media outlets in Turkey, and there was also more space in which Islam and Kurdish identity could express themselves. However, human rights abuses were still widespread, and freedom of speech and association were subjected to severe restrictions. According to PEN International and Human Rights Watch, during the 1990s Turkey had the world's worst record for holding writers and journalists under legal detention. Thus Turkey remained very much out of step with EU norms, politically even more than economically.

However, the Helsinki decision was greeted bullishly in Turkey. It encouraged Turks to believe that eventual EU membership was an achievable goal after all (Kubicek 2005: 365; Vardan 2009: 50–51). Prime minister Ecevit captured this mood of optimism, asserting before he left Helsinki that 'some members of the EU may think it will take many years for Turkey to become a full member. But I am convinced that given the dynamism of the Turkish people and their attachment to democracy, we will achieve this objective in a far shorter period'.[3] The hope was that, as one Turkish analyst expressed it, 'the possibility of full membership provides the much needed discipline or the external anchor required to legitimize the reform process' (Onis 1999: 120). More cautiously, and perhaps more realistically, foreign minister Ismail Cem hinted at a Turkish exceptionalism when he noted that 'Turkey is not just any candidate. Turkey has a different identity and a very different historical experience to the others'.[4] To many European observers it was evident that, 'in practice, it would require generations before Turkey's civic and political culture could take the same form as that found in the EU's core' (Buzan and Diez 1999: 50).

Encouraged by the real prospect of accession signalled by the Helsinki decision, Ankara published a 1000-page National Programme in early 2001, laying out the steps it intended to take in order to align Turkey with EU *acquis* (Park 2001; Rumford 2002). Although the programme met with serious opposition in Turkey, Ankara did at last embark energetically on a reform programme designed to align Turkish legal, political, administrative and economic practices with those of the EU. Reform activity intensified still further after the AKP's election victory in November 2002, although it slowed again once the actual EU accession negotiations began in October 2005 (Ozbudun 2007; Onis 2008b). A series of harmonization packages was passed in parliament (packages of amendments to existing laws, the penal code and the constitution, designed to bring Turkey into line with EU accession requirements, in some instances involving the introduction of laws implementing earlier constitutional amendments). Between them these legal packages extended, on paper at least, freedom of expression, of religion, of the press, of association and of assembly. The right to a free trial was enhanced, and the death penalty abolished. The commitment to equality of the sexes was tightened up. The grounds for the prohibition and closure of political parties were restricted. The MGK, which had traditionally been dominated by the military and constituted the chief formal mechanism through which the TSK's influence on domestic political affairs was exercised, became a predominantly civilian body chaired by a civilian. Governments were no longer obliged to give priority to the MGK's recommendations, and its meetings were to be held less frequently. Greater civilian oversight of military expenditure was introduced. State security courts, on which military judges sat and which had been established in 1982 to deal with cases involving a somewhat widely defined understanding of state security, were abolished. Restrictions on the use of languages other than Turkish (such as Kurdish) in education and broadcasting were softened.

Politics and civil society

Under the AKP in particular, Turkey has appeared to become a more open society in other ways, too, although the country's secularists and Kemalists might dispute this. The government has sought to establish dialogue with the Alevi and Roma communities which, in the past, have more typically simply been ignored where not discriminated against (Ademi 2010; Subasi 2010).[5] It has also sought to desecuritize the Kurdish issue in Turkey with its so-called 'Kurdish opening' aimed, at least rhetorically, at addressing the problem via dialogue and greater democratization (Candar 2009a; Cizre 2009; Aytac 2010). For all its undoubted flaws and biases, the 'Ergenekon' investigation into the extralegal activities of the so-called 'deep state' – the unexplained murders, mysterious accidents, disappearances, violent incidents, alleged coup plans and the like that have long punctuated Turkish political life and that are widely thought to have involved state officials – at last held out some prospect both that the details might come to light, and that the immunity for so long enjoyed by agents of the state and their criminal associates might be curtailed (Park 2008b; Jenkins 2009; Kavakci 2009; Kaya 2009; Unver 2009).

Turkish society has undergoing transformation below the level of the central state and government too. It is not without reason that 'Turkish civil society has traditionally been portrayed as weak, passive, and controlled', although at times this might have been exaggerated (Kubicek 2005: 366). After all, there was no shortage of civil society groups representing the far right, the far left, organized labour and Islamist and Kurdish factions, contributing to the mayhem that preceded the 1980 coup, but these were mostly of an oppositional nature. Indeed, around 20,000 nongovernmental organizations (NGOs), constituting around half the total, were closed down by the military in the wake of the 1980 coup (Simsek 2004: 48). As recently as 2009, the chair of one of the most prominent Turkish civil society groups, the Independent Industrialists' and Businessmen's Association (*Mustakil Sanayici ve Isadamlari Dernegi* – MUSIAD), a conservative association generally regarded as loosely supportive of the governing AKP, could write of the 'non-democratic, semi authoritarian constitutional and legal characteristics of the Turkish polity, the non-institutionalized party system, a weak and non-democratic civil society' (Vardan 2009: 50). Yet by 2004 there were estimated to be in excess of 100,000 civil society groups in Turkey (Kubicek 2005: 368), and their explosive growth continues. The sub-state organization of Turkish society that is now so abundantly evident dates back to Ozal's liberalizing reforms of the 1980s. Today, it includes business associations, women's groups, environmental lobbies, human rights activists, think tanks and Islamist, Alevi and Kurdish groups (CIVICUS Civil Society Index Report for Turkey, undated). University conferences investigating the Armenian 'genocide' issue have been held against a backdrop of ever-greater readiness to openly discuss and acknowledge the events of 1915. There have been mass demonstrations protesting against the January 2007 murder in Istanbul of Armenian activist Hrant Dink and decrying the lack of progress in the investigation.

Turkish society today is altogether less passive, less deferential, far noisier, better organized, more pluralistic and more diverse than it was just a few decades ago, and the EU accession process has in many ways served as both a means and an end of this transformation. Many of these groups function as transmitters of EU values and dynamics to Turkish society, or as lobbyists to the EU, or both. Indeed, a variety of EU sources has helped fund the growth of Turkish NGOs (Seyrek 2004). Some of the EU's support for civil society can be traced back to the 2004 decision to open accession negotiations with Turkey, when the European Commission called for a strengthened political and cultural dialogue between EU and Turkish citizens (Hulsse 2006: 320–22). The EU's pressure for administrative reform in Turkey has similarly galvanized the traditionally weak and dependent system of local government in Turkey. More city councils have emerged, and more open budgetary, planning and accountability systems have been introduced. It has been claimed that here, too, 'the major impact of Europeanization at the local level has been the increased awareness of the opportunities for asserting more political and economic power' and to intensify 'local demands for more financial and political autonomy from the centre' (Celenk 2009: 55).

However, this expanded civil society often serves to mirror and even enlarge the wider cleavages and polarities in Turkish society. Business associations are organized primarily around their relationship to the secular state or, alternatively, are based on various political representations of Islam. There are Islamic and secular women's movements, Islamic and secular human rights movements, lobbies for the rights of homosexuals and organized groups opposing them from an Islamic perspective, Kurdish rights groups and Turkish nationalist movements to counter them. Turkish nationalist and Kemalist groups have energetically and virulently opposed those calling for recognition of the Armenian 'genocide' and for investigation of the state's involvement or negligence in the death of Hrant Dink. In other words, the emergence of civil society in Turkey should not be interpreted as a kind of mirror imaging of what can typically be found in Europe. Rather, 'the diversity of Turkish NGOs illustrates how different interpretations of human rights can be constructed according to cultural, national, or religious prerequisites' (Duncker 2006/07: 52).

Furthermore, Turkey's secular movements do not necessarily share the tolerance and inclusivity that their western counterparts usually strive towards, while Turkey's Islamic NGOs quite often do not share what might be regarded as archetypal western values on such matters as family law and relations, gender equality, freedom of religion and expression, and the cultural rights of minorities. Indeed, their values correspond in large measure to those expressed by African, Asian and Islamic countries in documents such as the African Banjul Charter of 1981,[6] the Islamic Cairo Declaration of 1990,[7] and the Asian Bangkok Declaration of Human Rights of 1993,[8] and at gatherings such as the World Conference on Human Rights, held in Vienna in 1993. This serves as a reminder both that 'global' values are not necessarily either universal or western in origin, and that some elements in Turkish society, particularly those on the Islamic or nationalist ends of the spectrum, might hold values closer to those of their developing-world counterparts than those prevalent in EU societies. In this sense, the Turkish experience suggests that 'democratization' does not in any simple and straightforward way equate to 'westernization'.

Turkey and the international norms regime

Respect for the rights of minorities has emerged as a key platform in Europe's postwar evolution. In 1995 the Council of Europe, which has long emphasized the importance of minority rights and of which Turkey has been a member since 1949, opened the Framework Convention for the Protection of National Minorities for signature.[9] It declares that the protection of the rights and freedoms of national minorities, individually and collectively, is an integral element in the protection of human rights. It prohibits discrimination against minorities and calls for their equality before the law. The convention encourages signatories to promote the economic, social, political and cultural life of minorities, and to preserve the essential elements of minority identities such as religion, language, traditions and cultural heritage. Minorities should be granted freedom of association and of political and religious expression. They should be free to adopt personal and place names in their minority language, be educated in it, have access to media and converse freely with others of the same ethnic, linguistic, religious or cultural minority across state boundaries. The convention came into force in 1998 with the acquisition of twelve ratifications. To date, Turkey is one of just four Council of Europe states that have neither signed nor ratified the convention. In November 2010, Turkey assumed the six-month chairmanship of the Committee of Ministers of the Council of Europe.

As we have noted, in recent years the EU has similarly elevated its emphasis on the 'common values' upon which it is based. These are stressed in the Charter of the Fundamental Rights of the Union,[10] proclaimed at Nice in December 2000 and given legal status by the passage of the Lisbon Treaty,[11] which came into force on 1 December 2009. The charter's preamble declares that 'the Union is founded on the values of respect for human dignity, freedom, democracy, equality, the rule of law, and respect for human rights, including the rights of persons belonging to minorities'. Turkey would be expected to embrace these provisions on accession. At the time of writing, Turkey has yet to ratify all European Court of Human Rights (ECtHR) protocols. It is also the only Council of Europe member not to have signed the Rome Statute of the International Criminal Court (ICC), which the EU has been so central to establishing and to which all EU members have acceded (Cakmak 2005). On the other hand, it should be noted that a group of Turkish NGOs, organized as the Turkish National Coalition for the ICC, are affiliated to the international coalition of ICC supporters,[12] and also that in 2004 AKP prime minister Erdogan promised Turkish accession to the ICC.[13]

It has been argued that 'generally speaking, Turkey has opted to resist being a party to international arrangements on human rights' and 'has been sometimes indifferent, sometimes ambivalent and sometimes suspicious toward international human rights regimes' (Narli 2000: 115). In fact, with the incentive provided by the 1999 Helsinki decision, Turkey did make great progress in signing and ratifying international human rights instruments.[14] Even so, there is still some tardiness in Turkey's readiness to embrace global (or western) human and minority rights norms and conventions. Thus Article 27 of the International Covenant on Civil and Political Rights, a UN treaty which came into force in 1976, declares that 'in those States in which ethnic, religious or linguistic minorities exist, persons belonging to such minorities shall not be denied the right, in community with the other members of their group, to enjoy their own culture, to profess and practise their own religion, or to use their own language'.[15] Turkey ratified the treaty in 2006, one of the most recent of the 113 parties to the treaty to have done so.

However, it also has the longest list of reservations and qualifications of all parties to the treaty, one of which declares that Ankara will interpret the treaty 'in accordance with the related provisions and rules of the Constitution of the Republic of Turkey and the Treaty of Lausanne of 24 July 1923 and its Appendixes'.[16] The UN General Assembly Declaration on the Rights of Persons belonging to National or Ethnic, Religious and Linguistic Minorities, issued in December 1992,[17] also refers to the obligation of states to protect the existence of minorities within their borders, to promote their identities, to enable education in minority languages, to permit transborder contact with other members of the same minority, and to associate freely. Interventions by the international community in places such as former Yugoslavia and East Timor further suggest that there has been a shift in favour of minority rights even if at the expense of national sovereignties.

Article 3 of Turkey's constitution declares unambiguously that 'the Turkish state, with its territory and nation, is an indivisible entity. Its language is Turkish'.[18] In a document replete with references to the indivisibility of the 'nation' and of its territory, the constitution goes on to assert that 'everyone bound to the Turkish state through the bond of citizenship is a Turk' (Article 66). It also warns that no privilege should be granted and no sovereignty exercised by any individual, group or class. This insistence on territorial and national indivisibility and the unitary character of the Turkish state has been something of a *leitmotif* of Turkish officials and politicians over the years, and has typically taken on an inflexible, uncompromising and ideologically rigid flavour. The Treaty of Lausanne by which the Turkish republic was established refers only to non-Muslim minorities (Jews, Greeks and Armenians), to whom it grants language, religious and cultural rights.[19] In practice, however, even their activities are very tightly curtailed. Their schools receive no state funding, Turkish Muslims are appointed by the state to act as their school principals, and the state's Minorities Committee maintains tight control over their activities. For example, a summer camp for minority schoolchildren could not go ahead because it was deemed a threat to national security. Furthermore, only Turkish nationals can serve as clergy for the recognized minorities, which poses a particular difficulty for the country's Greek community. Non-Muslim minorities not recognized by the Lausanne Treaty, such as the Syrian Orthodox community, are not allowed to operate schools at all (Yildiz 2007; US Department of State 2009). Combined with the constitution, the Lausanne Treaty left little scope for the protection of the rights of Muslim minorities such as the Kurds, or even for the recognition of their minority status.[20]

The state of play in 2009: the European Commission's progress report on Turkey

The annual progress reports on Turkey produced by the EC, although noting that progress has been made year on year, continue to find deficiencies in

Turkey's democratization. Each report is replete with calls for fuller implementation of legal changes made, demands that legal arrangements be clarified and the identification of omissions in the reform programme. Indeed, Turkey's failure to properly implement the legal and constitutional changes it makes is a recurring theme. To take the *Turkey 2009 Progress Report* (European Commission 2009) – released ten years after the 1999 Helsinki decision – for purposes of illustration and for insight into Turkey's democratic deficiencies, overall the report found that there had been little progress 'on effective implementation of political and constitutional reforms' during the previous year. Noting that the pro-Kurdish Democratic Society Party (*Demokratik Toplum Partisi* – DTP) faced closure by the constitutional court for engaging in activities against the unity and integrity of the country, the report concludes that 'Turkey still needs to bring its legislation on political parties in line with European standards'. Indeed, subsequent to the publication of the report, the DTP was closed by order of the court. In 2008, even the ruling AKP narrowly avoided closure by the constitutional court for its allegedly anti-secularist activities.

The Commission's 2009 report also noted that, in the run-up to local elections held in March 2009, Turkey's Supreme Electoral Board made controversial last-minute decisions concerning matters such as the documentation required to be eligible to vote and the banning of headscarves for ballot box observers. It also noted that 'no progress has been made on devolution of powers to local governments'. With respect to the required administrative reform, the report opined that 'further developing a professional, independent, accountable, transparent and merit based civil service remain priorities', and that there were concerns over the politicization of the country's administrative machinery. The report also expressed its concerns 'about the independence, impartiality and efficiency of the judiciary', about the pressure put on the legal process, about failures in the investigations of some high-profile crimes such as the assassination of the Armenian journalist Hrant Dink and about 'violations of procedural rights of the accused' with respect to the Ergenekon case. Furthermore, it found that corruption was both pervasive and largely unaddressed, and that governance overall was insufficiently transparent (European Commission 2009: 7–12).

As regards civilian oversight of the military, Brussels had welcomed the June 2009 passage of legislation that, for the first time in Turkey, empowered civilian courts to try military personnel in peacetime, and that removed the remaining powers of military courts to try civilians in peacetime, 'thus aligning Turkey with EU practices'. In January 2010, however, and subsequent to the publication of the report, the constitutional court again threw the law into confusion by overturning the right of civilian courts to try military personnel. The report asserted that the scope of Turkey's military courts too 'needs to comply with EU practice'. More seriously, the report observed that, notwithstanding the reform of the MGK, 'the armed forces have continued to exercise undue political influence via formal and informal mechanisms.

Senior members of the armed forces have expressed on a large number of occasions their views on domestic and foreign policy issues going beyond their remit, including on Cyprus, ethnicity, the southeast, secularism, political parties and other nonmilitary matters'. Furthermore, 'no change has been made to the Turkish Armed Forces Internal Service Law or to the Law on the National Security Council. These define the roles and duties of the Turkish military and grant the military wide room for manoeuvre by providing a broad definition of national security'. It also remained the case that 'no progress has been made on strengthening legislative oversight of the military budget and expenditure. Likewise, the Defence Industry Support Fund, from which most procurement projects are financed, had survived as an extra budgetary fund excluded from parliamentary scrutiny. Parliament has no mandate to develop security and defence policies' (European Commission 2009: 10). The revelations and allegations of the ongoing Ergenekon investigation had also not cast Turkey in an especially good light.

Turkey hardly fared better in the Commission's 2009 progress report with respect to human and minority rights. Although the report declared that 'there is an increasingly open and free debate in Turkish society, including on issues traditionally perceived as sensitive', it also noted that Turkey had yet to ratify all protocols of the European Convention of Human Rights (ECHR). During the year covered by the report, Turkey had been judged by the ECtHR to be in violation of the ECHR almost 400 times. Indeed, Turkey is second only to Russia in the number of human rights cases open before the court. The report also found that in Turkey 'implementation of ECtHR judgments requiring legislative measures is delayed, sometimes for several years'. The ratification of the Optional Protocol to the UN Convention against Torture had also been much delayed. Efforts to implement and apply safeguards against torture and ill-treatment were found wanting in the report, and the effectiveness of proceedings against law enforcement agents was similarly doubted. Although a 2008 amendment to Article 301 of the Turkish Criminal Code – which renders insult to Turkey, Turkish ethnicity or Turkish government institutions a criminal offence – had reduced resort to it, a raft of other existing laws put 'journalists, writers, publishers, politicians, academics and others at risk of investigation, prosecution, conviction and imprisonment and could therefore result in self censorship'. The military, politicians and the judiciary had all been found to put undue pressure on media outlets during the period covered by the report (European Commission 2009: 14–18). The report offers information on constraints on the freedom of association and assembly, on the restrictions of various kinds imposed on non-Muslim and Alevi religious groups and on women and other minorities. It thus concludes that 'full respect for and protection of language, culture and fundamental rights, in accordance with European standards have yet to be fully achieved' (European Commission 2009: 28).

With respect to cultural rights, of significance to the issue of Turkey's Kurdish minority, 'restrictions remain, particularly on use of languages other than Turkish in private TV and radio broadcasting, political life, education and contacts with public services. The legal framework on the use of languages other than Turkish is open to restrictive interpretations, and implementation is inconsistent'. The reforms had introduced scope for education and broadcasting in the Kurdish language. However, there remained no provision of Kurdish language education in the state sector and limitations on access of Kurdish speakers to social services. The use of Kurdish in political life remained illegal, and a number of DTP MPs, mayors and members were prosecuted as a result of it. However, even the use of Kurdish in nonpolitical contexts could result in legal and official harassment. More widely, although the report welcomed the initiation by the government of a 'wide ranging public debate – covering cultural, political and economic matters – on the Kurdish issue', it also noted that with respect to the Kurdish south-east of the country, 'the use made of the anti-terror legislation, which provides a wide definition of terrorism, has resulted in undue restrictions on the exercise of fundamental freedoms, such as freedom of expression and freedom of association, in the region. In several instances, the law has been used to punish non-violent opinions, in particular on the Kurdish issue' (European Commission 2009: 29–31).

The language used by human rights organizations such as Human Rights Watch[21] and Amnesty International[22] to describe affairs in Turkey is, if anything, harsher than that deployed by the EC. Turkey's membership of the Council of Europe has similarly led to persistent and critical scrutiny of its human rights failings, and the 2009 report on Turkey by that body's commissioner for human rights similarly finds much to criticize.[23] In 2010, Turkey was placed 106th in the world, and bottom in western Europe, on a press freedom index compiled by Freedom House. The apparently politically motivated tax fine imposed on the Dogan media group, the blocking of *YouTube* and other internet sites for 'insulting' Ataturk and an increase in prosecutions of journalists for offences against Article 301 were amongst the reasons given for the low ranking.[24] *Reporters Sans Frontieres* placed Turkey 122nd out of 175 states in 2010, a fall of twenty places compared with the previous year.[25] The US State Department's 2008 report on human rights in Turkey offers little reprieve from this general picture (US Department of State 2008). Clearly, after decades of ambition and years of reform, Turkey still has some way to go before it meets European or wider western norms.

Polarization or nationalist reaction?

If it is true that the 'domestic politics of nation states have become increasingly transnationalized', then this is 'especially true for Turkey, since all features of its domestic politics are under the constant scrutiny of the European Union' (Duncker 2006/07: 52). Furthermore, and notwithstanding the continued deficiencies noted above, it has been the AKP government, representing Turkey's seemingly less westernized, more traditional, conservative and devout masses, and the upwardly mobile elites that have been drawn from them, which has taken Turkey's reformism, internationalism and democratization further than any of its Kemalist predecessors – at least this was true for its first few years in office. In contrast, the main domestic bulwark of Kemalism, the CHP, has increasingly presented itself as a force for 'resistance to globalization, the EU, and the social mobilization of conservative members of society' (Taspinar 2007; Kosebalaban 2009: 92; Karaveli 2010). As Turkey's relationship with the EU has developed, so its Kemalists have been increasingly troubled by the impact of the accession process on what they regard as the country's sovereignty and exceptionalism, and particularly hurt by the sense of rejection that the process has so widely engendered in Turkey. They also fear that the reform obligations emanating from the EU accession process lend support to Islamist demands and to Kurdish identity politics, and are sceptical that the cause of either Turkey's democratization or its stability is furthered as a consequence (Gokalp and Unsar 2008).

The so-called 'e-memorandum' that appeared on the TSK website in April 2007, which declared that 'the Turkish Armed Forces maintain their sound determination to carry out their duties stemming from laws to protect the unchangeable characteristics of the Republic of Turkey', offered just one example of the increasingly evident tension between the EU's requirements of Turkey and the Kemalist mindset. The TSK was concerned that the secular character of the republic was threatened by the proposed elevation to the presidency of the AKP's Abdullah Gul. The memorandum was followed by huge secularist demonstrations against Gul, organized by an NGO staffed chiefly by retired military officers, the Association of Kemalist Thought. Following a legal challenge mounted by the CHP to Gul's presidential candidacy, Erdogan called a general election which was won handsomely by the AKP with almost forty-seven per cent of the vote. Gul was subsequently elected as president of the republic (Balkir 2007). Similarly, the constitutional court's 2008 consideration of a ban on the ruling AKP offered an illustration of how Turkey's constitutional exigencies can undermine the country's democratic credentials. The frequently defensive, self-justificatory and unapologetic tone of the CHP's and TSK's reaction to the Ergenekon revelations, and the CHP's unconstructive approach to both the 'Kurdish opening' and the AKP's early 2010 proposals for constitutional reform, provide further evidence. Indeed, a number of commentators have detected that the EU issue has itself emerged as a source of an intensified cleavage in Turkish society (Onis 2007; Patterson 2008; Kosebalaban 2009; Kubicek 2009), in which the Kemalist heartland is increasingly discomforted by the reforms introduced to align Turkey with EU norms. Turkey thus appears as a polarized or 'torn' society. The twin processes of democratization and globalization on the one hand, and the impact of the EU accession process on the other, have amplified the fault lines between the Kemalist elite, which sought to modernize Turkey by excluding its peripheral population and by maintaining centralized state power, and that very Turkish periphery, which with the support of liberals has utilized the EU process and the forces of globalization in order to mount its challenge to the existing order (Karaveli 2010).

The accession process also appears to have generated a nationalist backlash in Turkey, centred on, but by no means confined to, Kemalism's supporters (Guney 2006–07; Uslu 2008a). Nationalism is perhaps the deepest and most strongly felt political sentiment in Turkey, and is arguably Kemalism's most enduring and widely internalized legacy to Turkish society and political culture. Its burgeoning and extraordinarily high profile is associated with a growing disillusion with, and even opposition to, the EU specifically and the West more generally, and serves to strengthen resistance to change in its more 'Europeanized' forms. Washington's Iraq adventure provided most of the impetus behind the intense anti-Americanism that has also swept across Turkish society. The EU's December 2006 suspension of negotiations on eight of the thirty-five chapters that constitute the accession process, and its refusal to close any of the remaining chapters until a resolution of the Cyprus issue is found, provides an additional element in the Turkish population's frustration with the EU. Indeed, the perceived unfairness and pro-Greek bias of Europe's approach to the Cyprus problem is in itself an issue for Turks. The frequent observations that emanate chiefly from Europe's Christian Democratic circles to the effect that Turkey's Muslim character in effect debars it from acquiring a properly European identity or EU membership has also, understandably, led to a growing Turkish disillusion with the EU project. The EU accession process has enabled many Turks to better appreciate the extent and depth of European unease concerning Turkey's European credentials, with arguably predictable consequences.

Is Turkey on the road to Europeanization?

It seems manifest that liberalism, the rule of law, tolerance and institutional autonomy enjoy somewhat shallow and fragile roots in Turkey, while authoritarianism, nepotism and nationalism remain deeply entrenched and ubiquitous characteristics of Turkey's political psyche. Furthermore, it would appear that external pressures on Turkey have encouraged some of these more negative traits more than they have helped augment the more positive ones. Many countries have far poorer human rights records than Turkey's. What is remarkable in the Turkish case, however, is that Ankara has proclaimed its European destiny since the inception of the republic, and since 1963 has regarded itself as a candidate country for membership of Europe's main political institutions. Of course there has been progress in Turkey, and it might well be true that 'Turkey–EU relations historically move in terms of cycles. At the end of each cycle Turkey moves closer to and becomes more integrated with the EU' (Onis 2008b: 35) – in other words, that Turkey's Europeanization is still an ongoing process, but one that will take time. We might also agree with the need to distinguish 'between internalization

of democratic norms as opposed to changes in instrumental, utilitarian cal-
culation', and that perhaps the former will yet follow the latter (Ertugal 2005:
64–65; Kubicek 2005: 364).

However, as yet it is far from clear that commitment to democratic reform
is especially well supported in Turkey, by elites or the public, or that its
norms have been deeply internalized. Thus 'the process of EU accession or
Europeanization [...] so far has not initiated a process of value change for
the major political elites' (Celenk 2009: 57). This is so even though 'the EU is
a central – even towering – figure in the Turkish reform progress' (Kubicek
2005: 373). In the absence of external pressure, especially from Brussels,
Turkey sometimes appears almost as prone to regress as progress, or at any
rate to stand still. The internal drive to Europeanize appears weak, and
it remains unclear that even the intense external pressure the country has
come under will prove strong enough to enable the hurdles to democratization
to be overcome. The domestic polarization that the EU accession process
seems to have inflamed has not helped. In short, it is hard to avoid the conclusion that, at best, 'Turkish policy makers have been meticulous and careful
to meet the demands from the EU, but not to do more than those demands
require' (Cakmak 2005: 120). Even that proposition does not hold for the
years preceding 1999.

What is the root problem?

Why have Turkey's democratization and adaptation to wider European norms
been so difficult and so incomplete? A simple answer is that the very ruling
class that has been so loud in its proclamation of that destiny had also founded, defended and benefited from a system of governance that has obstructed
its fulfilment. The Kemalist top-down, bureaucratic approach to modernity,
underpinned by a pervasive nationalism, statism, authoritarianism and a
culture of insecurity and insularity, has paradoxically served to block progress
towards the liberal internationalism now so associated with the West. Nor
does the paradox end there. Turkey's experiment with multiparty democracy
has meant that Turkey's religious classes and provinces, its Kurds and its
excluded classes in general have become increasingly visible in the country's
political, social and economic life. In the 1957 and 1977 elections, the Kemalist CHP received just over forty per cent of the vote, but these represent
their highest electoral achievements since the republic's establishment. In the
1950, 1954 and 1957 elections, they were beaten by the DP led by Adnan
Menderes, which in 1954 received almost fifty-eight per cent of the popular
vote. During the 1960s, in the wake of the coup that ousted the DP government, the CHP was forced into coalition governments with the DP's success-
or, the Justice Party (*Adalet Partisi* – AP) of Suleyman Demirel. He was
ousted by the 1971 coup, but the 1970s, too, witnessed successive coalition
governments. After the 1980 coup, the CHP was banned, along with all
other existing political parties. In any case, Turgut Ozal, whose electoral

constituency was not dissimilar to that of the DP in the 1950s and the AKP today, and who was tolerated rather than favoured by the 1980 coup leaders, emerged as the dominant political figure of the decade. The CHP has never fully recovered from the 1980 temporary ban. In 1995 it attained only ten per cent of the vote, and in 1999 it sank to a still lower level of electoral unpopularity. In the 2007 general election, the CHP won just over twenty per cent of the vote, less than half the forty-seven per cent received by the victorious AKP. In other words, the party most associated with the Kemalist order has been unable to form a government without coalition partners, if at all, and it has been repeatedly outvoted by political parties deriving their support from the peripheral population of Turkey's Anatolian hinterland.

Thus Turkey's political evolution has progressively pushed the Kemalist political elite onto the defensive, notwithstanding the repeated bans and curtailments of Islamist and Kurdish parties. Instead, it and the class it represents have been obliged to rely on their unelected sympathizers firmly ensconced in the courts, the state bureaucracy, the media and, above all, the military. The restrictive provisions of the 1982 constitution, drawn up under the tutelage of the 1980 coup leaders, rigorously enforced by Turkey's secular and nationalistic legal profession, have also been instrumental in keeping the system's challengers at bay. The relative electoral weakness of Kemalism's political class has also been a major factor encouraging the military to emerge as the primary, or at least the ultimate, defenders of the Kemalist legacy. This in turn has served to disrupt any consolidation of democracy that might otherwise have evolved.

The role of the military

The emergence of multiparty electoral politics in Turkey coincided with, or resulted in, the more explicit engagement of the country's military establishment in its domestic politics. Electoral politics in Turkey have been interspersed with military coups, in 1960, 1971 and 1980. In 1997, a so-called 'postmodern' or 'soft' coup was mounted against the Islamist-led coalition government, forced out of power by a TSK-inspired campaign of intimidation, threat and crisis. However, only the 1980 coup took the form of a direct military takeover of the country by the military high command, and even in that instance a technocratic government of civilians was appointed to run the day-to-day business of government and to help draft a new constitution and new laws. The 1960 coup by junior officers, which has been described by one Turkish observer as 'an attempt to restore the Kemalist hegemony' (Kosebalaban 2009: 86), and by another as 'a reaction of the state elite to the increased power of the political elite and thus the periphery' (Celenk 2009: 49), produced what many have regarded as Turkey's most liberal constitution, although as with the 1980 coup it also led to a severe crackdown on political activism, including the 1961 execution of prime minister Adnan Menderes.

In short, the military's engagement with domestic politics in Turkey has not followed an entirely consistent pattern, but it has always led to the re-establishment of civilian rule as well as that of the Kemalist order, as far as possible. Civil–military relations during the 1960s took the form of a 'silent partnership' (Narli 2000: 112–13) until rising political and social disorder led to the events of 1971. The 1971 coup by memorandum, described by one Turkish scholar as a 'reequilibration of democracy' (Ozbudun 2000: 24), led to the resignation of the existing government and the installation of a multiparty technocratic government appointed and presided over by the military against a background of martial law. However, there was no suspension of the constitution (although some more restrictive amendments were introduced), no ban on political parties and no dissolution of the TGNA. Interestingly, however, many of the military's subsequently familiar 'reserved domains', designed largely to preserve its own autonomy and independence from civilian intrusion – such as restrictions on external auditing, control over its own personnel policies, and the expansion of the powers of martial law courts – can be dated to the events of 1971 (Ozbudun 2000: 111–12).

The uneasy political–military coexistence of the 1970s paralleled a return to a period of still more violent disorder, in which the loss of 5000 or so lives in largely left–right gang warfare was accompanied by a breakdown in relations between the main political figures and a consequent governmental paralysis, until the TSK stepped in again in 1980. After a period of repression, the country was again returned to a system of multiparty elections, and the TSK reluctantly accepted the 1983 victory of the Motherland Party (ANAP), led by Turgut Ozal, in its electoral competition with two military-sponsored rivals. Between, and since, these more dramatic moments, the TSK's influence has been brought to bear both formally via institutional and constitutional arrangements, and informally through its public pronouncements and its access to opinion formers, policy officials and the like.

It is not without value to note the 'tutelary powers' (Ozbudun 2000: 105–10) the TSK has awarded itself when seeking to explain Turkey's unique civil–military relationships. Key to this, in legislative terms, is the Turkish Armed Forces Internal Service Law of 1961, itself apparently identical to a 1935 law (Jenkins 2007: 343), which endows the armed forces with the responsibility 'for defending both the Turkish fatherland and the Turkish republic as defined by the Constitution'. This responsibility was also enshrined in the 1982 Constitution drawn up in the wake of the 1980 coup, and in the 1983 National Security Council Law, and is generally taken to refer to protection both of the republic's secular inheritance and against internal and external threats to the country's territorial integrity. Indeed, the EC's *Turkey 2007 Progress Report* bemoaned the fact that these regulations granted the military 'a wide margin of manoeuvre by providing a broad definition of national security' (European Commission 2007: 9).

In short, the Turkish military is a highly politicized institution, whose self-appointed role is to ensure Turkey's continued progress towards its European destiny and to defend the unitary and secular Kemalist state. Clearly there is some tension between these goals, as there is between the TSK's politically high profile and its EU aspirations. There is a historical and cultural context to the military's self-identification, as it stems from the Kemalist top-down and state-centric revolution in which the task of 'democracy' is to identify rational solutions to problems rather than to serve as a mechanism for reconciling conflicting interests. In this positivist formulation, political parties can be disdainfully regarded as divisive, anti-communitarian and excessively motivated by self-interest rather than the public good (Karaosmanoglu 1993). The military has liked to present itself as nonpartisan, as representing something akin to a national general will and as the guardian of the official ideology of Kemalism. Furthermore, this self-image has been deepened by the intensely propagandistic inculcation of patriotism and Kemalist values by the military's educational and socialization system (Jenkins 2001: 21–33). It was perhaps only a little hyperbolic for products of this system to have asserted that, at the upper reaches of the military hierarchy, this has produced 'a singular, self replicating class of generals, towering over an institution with a single mindset' (Aydinli *et al.* 2006: 82). However, neither this mindset, nor the forms and legacies of the Turkish military's involvement in the country's domestic politics, nor Turkey's record of political instability since the introduction of multiparty elections, has notably advanced the cause of Turkey's 'Europeanization'.

Political culture

Yet, just as 'it would be misleading to look at Turkish democratization from a binary perspective, juxtaposing an authoritarian military against democratically inclined civilian politicians' (Akkoyunlu 2007: 36), so it would also be inaccurate to portray Turkey's less democratic features as exclusive to one or other end of the political and social spectrum. Even putting military intervention to one side, democratization in Turkey has not proceeded smoothly. Politicians have generally been associated with corruption and nepotism, politics has been personalized and has lacked a spirit of bipartisanship and a culture of compromise, and political parties have generally enjoyed only the shallowest of roots in Turkish society. Governments have typically been formed from weak and fractious coalitions between power brokers and their supporters, perhaps most particularly during the 1990s. Furthermore, Turkish society has experienced bouts of extreme disorder since the advent of multiparty democracy, as in the 1960s and 1970s, which the political elite seemed unable or even unwilling to combat. The weakness of Turkey's political institutions has left a vacuum, providing – in the language of Samuel Finer – both the 'opportunity' and the 'motive' for military intervention in the country's politics to add to the 'mood' of an already patriotic and politicized military (Finer 2002). Put another way, the enduring weakness of Turkish democracy has functioned as a 'trigger' for the military's political interventions (Guney and Karatekelioglu 2005: 442–43).

Although elements of the leftist intelligentsia became more questioning of the military's role after the 1971 coup, and were joined in their doubts by the right of centre in the wake of the post-1980-coup crackdown on the politically active across the entire spectrum, such sentiments have not been as widespread as would have been expected from a more fully democratized political culture (Demirel 2005: 259–60). The more usual popular response in Turkey towards the military's role in the restoration of order has been acquiescence or even positive approval. Turkey's 'army-nation' has been inclined to regard the military as a legitimate political actor, as more trustworthy and responsible than civilian politicians, and as a necessary bulwark against disorder. This widely held sentiment has reduced the readiness of the population at large to defend democracy (Demirel 2005: 254–55). In this context, the popular inclination to rely on the military to sort out Turkey's political mess may have made a contribution of its own to the faltering progress of Turkish democratization. For swathes of Turkish society, 'democracy' remains something endowed from above. This widespread national indulgence towards a politically active military has meant that, for the TSK, there has been little in the way of a major 'inhibiting factor' (again from Finer) which has functioned to dissuade the military from entering the political fray. Perhaps only far leftists, pro-Kurds and Islamists have exhibited a sustained discomfort with the Turkish military's domestic political role (Narli 2000: 116). It is too early to judge whether the Ergenekon investigation in Turkey will more profoundly undermine the TSK's political legitimacy across Turkish society.

Thus both the political classes and the populace at large have played their part in Turkey's thwarted democratization. Particularly in the context of the increased fragmentation of party politics in Turkey in the wake of Ozal's death in 1993, coupled with a strengthening of the military's leverage over Turkey's politics and an intensification of its concern with the twin domestic threats of Islamism and Kurdish separatism, political parties of most persuasions exhibited a readiness to cultivate the military for their own ends. True Path Party (*Dogru Yol Partisi* – DYP) leader Tansu Ciller not only gave the military a free hand in its struggle with the PKK, both at home and in northern Iraq, but also sought its assistance in her struggle against her Welfare Party (RP) rival. Support for the 1997 coup extended beyond the CHP, and most parties openly sympathized with the TSK's virulent attack on then prime minister Mesut Yilmaz's criticism of the TSK's political role (Demirel 2003: 14–17). Overall, few observers would dissent from the assessment that the approach Turkish politicians have adopted towards civil–military relations has typically been short-term, selective and unprincipled, suggesting that the democratic idea of civilian supremacy over the military has not been as internalized by civilians as one might normally expect in a functioning political democracy.

European doubts: insurmountable conditionality?

Turkey's path towards EU accession is conditional. However, in Turkey's case the conditionality is not confined to the country's capacity and willingness to adapt to the EU's *acquis*. A solution to the division of Cyprus must also be found before Turkey can be admitted. This remains so even though, in separate referenda held in 2004 on the Annan Plan to end the division, the Greek Cypriot electorate rejected and the Turkish Cypriot side accepted the proposals. Greek Cypriot accession to the EU was not made conditional on a settlement, and (Greek) Cyprus was allowed to accede one week after its electorate voted 'no' to the settlement proposals. The self-styled Turkish Republic of Northern Cyprus (TRNC) has since remained diplomatically and economically embargoed, and the failure to arrive at an agreement serves as an obstacle to Turkey's EU accession. Thus the incentives for the Greek Cypriot side to compromise are now minimal, and it is hard to see what Ankara or the TRNC can offer short of an almost complete capitulation to Nicosia's requirements, which are in essence for a more centralized system of governance on the island than the Turkish Cypriots can countenance. In short, at the time of writing and short of a miraculous turn of events, no solution to the island's division appears forthcoming (Hannay 2005; Mallinson 2005; Ulusoy 2009; Dodd 2010).

Even more problematic, however, is the essentialist opposition to Turkish EU membership that can be found in Europe. This is derived from Turkey's Islamic character, and is a sentiment most frequently and strongly held amongst Europe's Christian Democrats. Although these objections are often accompanied by references to Turkey's poor unconsolidated democracy, human rights record and relative economic backwardness, at root there is a feeling that the Turkish state and its society are simply not European. This has led to the idea that Turkey might be offered a 'privileged partnership' rather than full membership, an alternative currently most strongly advocated amongst politicians, public opinion and governments in France, Germany and Austria. Although one might wonder whether such attitudes would have much traction were Turkish political culture and economic performance to resemble more closely those found in core Europe, this attitude nevertheless amounts to an insurmountable obstacle to Turkey's EU accession in the absence of a change of governments or minds in Europe. Furthermore, in so far as Europe's 'Turkophobia' can be linked to phenomena such as immigration or Islamic terrorism, and even if it is more deeply rooted in identification of the Turks as Europe's 'other', this source of opposition to Turkey's EU accession demonstrates that in Europe, too, the impact of globalization processes can be to generate negative reactions and barriers to further transnational exchange. In short, both in Turkey and in Europe it is far from self-evident that transnational and global forces have been sufficient to overcome either the realities or the perception of Turkey's non-European character.

5　From autarky to globalization
Turkey's economic transition

Turkish contradictions

According to the IMF, 'economic "globalization" is a historical process, the result of human innovation and technological progress. It refers to the increasing integration of economies around the world, particularly through the movement of goods, services, and capital across borders'. It notes that 'the term "globalization" began to be used more commonly in the 1980s, reflecting technological advances that made it easier and quicker to complete international transactions – both trade and financial flows'. It observes too that 'a common denominator which appears to link nearly all high growth countries together is their participation in, and integration with, the global economy'. However, it also warns that 'integrating with the global economy is, as economists like to say, a *necessary*, but not *sufficient*, condition for economic growth. For globalization to be able to work, a country cannot be saddled with problems endemic to many developing countries, from a corrupt political class, to poor infrastructure, and macroeconomic instability' (IMF 2008).

For all its oft-quoted commitment to westernization, Turkey missed out on the first few decades of economic globalization, understood as a process set in train in the early postwar years. Partly, but not entirely, this was due precisely to the corruption, poor infrastructure and macroeconomic instability identified by the IMF as an obstacle to progress. The circumstances of the Turkish republic's birth and the values of most of its founders produced a closed, self-sufficient, government-directed and autarkic economic system (Hershlag 1968; Hale 1981; Lewis 2002; Zurcher 2004). Although Turkey joined most of the key institutions of the newly globalizing world of the post-Second World War era, it did not begin to seriously rethink its macroeconomic management until the 1980s. It was not unusual in this. For example, India and some central and south American economies mirrored Turkey in their initial reluctance or inability to embrace economic globalization. Other countries, many of them Islamic, continue to this day to hold themselves aloof as far as they are able from integration into the global economy.

Two factors bring an element of uniqueness to the Turkish case, however. One is that Turkey's ruling elite entertained an explicit vision, one that had few parallels elsewhere in the developing world, that Turkey should join, be embraced by and become an integral part of the 'West'. Yet Turkey's state authorities combined this aspiration with an incompatible adherence to national control over the economy and an approach to macroeconomic management that was generally unhelpful to the professed longer-term objective. The second factor that gives a particular flavour to the Turkish case is that its political landscape continues to host an element of reluctance to embrace, or ability to fully appreciate, the changes necessary to integrate more fully with the global economy. Many in Turkey's elite, paradoxically more notably those who claim to take their inspiration from Kemalism, appear still to have only incompletely internalized the requirements and desirability of globalization or economic westernization. There is a sense that, if there had been an absence of external pressure, Turkey might not have come as far as it has and could even revert back towards earlier practices. Given that few developing economies have been subjected to the kind of external pressure that the EU, the IMF, the World Bank, other global financial institutions, and of course the USA have put on Turkey, this is a substantive point. Turkey's EU accession bid, and Washington's attachment to Turkey's strategic location, have exposed it to pressures that a different regional context might not have attracted. However, even if one rejects the degree of uniqueness claimed for Turkey here, a consideration of the Turkish relationship with the forces of economic globalization offers an interesting case study of the issues that developing world economies face in the modern era.

The advent of democracy and the beginnings of economic westernization: a false dawn?

As we have seen, Turkey's economy at the end of the Second World War was largely self-sufficient, protectionist and barely engaged in external trade. With its 1950 election, Turkey at last adopted a multiparty political system. Furthermore, in each of the 1950, 1954 and 1957 elections, the DP emerged victorious. Its support base was the small farmers, small traders and new businessmen who felt both excluded from, and stifled by, the state's economic policies, and religious elements from the market towns and villages of Anatolia. The DP's electoral victories over the CHP reflected the degree of alienation from the regime felt by many provincial and rural Turks. Small farmers had seen little improvement in their lives, but had come to resent the intrusions of the ideologues and tax collectors of the government. One illustration of the gap between the favoured Kemalist urban heartlands and the forgotten provinces is that by 1953, only 0.025 per cent of Turkey's 40,000 villages had been linked up to the electric grid. Although national production of electricity had grown tenfold since 1923, eighty per cent of the supply went to Istanbul, Ankara and Izmir (Zurcher 2004: 206).

The advent of multiparty democracy in Turkey can be seen as an element in its post-1945 Cold War-era 'westernization'. The post-1945 world also witnessed a growth in international economic institutions and management. In large measure, the objective of these interlocking institutions was to prevent a resort to the kind of trade protectionism which had contributed to the 1930s depression. It was a world created and led by a democratic free-market USA that had emerged from the war triumphant and powerful. Put another way, the advent of what today is commonly understood as economic globalization can reasonably be traced back to these early postwar years. Partly in order to ingratiate itself with, and win the protection of, the USA, Turkey ensured it was formally part of this process of global economic management from the very beginning. It joined the IMF in 1947, the first year of that institution's existence. In 1948, it was one of eighteen founder members of the OEEC, established to distribute and manage US Marshall Aid to Europe's war-torn economies. Indeed, even before the 1950 election, Ankara had embarked on some limited economic liberalization and had devalued the lira in order to endear itself to these two organizations. Turkey was also a founding signatory to the establishment of the OEEC's successor organization, the OECD, in 1960. In 1951, Turkey as a developing country acceded to the General Agreement on Tariffs and Trade (GATT), which had come into force on 1 January 1948. It joined the World Bank in 1947 and the International Finance Corporation in 1956. Turkey also became an associate member of the EEC with the signing of the 1963 Ankara Agreement.

The new DP government was in a rush to modernize, but it only dimly appreciated how this might be achieved and sustained. Its largely rural and provincial political constituency created a political imperative to support prices for agricultural products and for other basic essentials. The DP was also sympathetic to those commercial interests that had supported it and to the free-market principles both they and Ankara's US benefactors favoured. However, in the DP's approach to governance there was more than a hint of the patronage politics and clientelism – the targeted allocation of public money to ensure or maintain political support – that would in time become a core feature of Turkish economic management and political practice, perhaps particularly so during Turkey's more democratic interludes. Furthermore, private investment, both foreign and domestic, remained scarce and tax revenue deficient. Any dreams of privatization that were entertained were killed off by a combination of the absence of funds for private investment and domestic political considerations. This lack of alternative sources of revenue obliged the government to raise funds for its programmes in other ways, such as printing money or exploiting the country's strategic location in order to borrow from abroad. In this the USA willingly obliged.

Thus government direction and ownership of much of Turkey's economic infrastructure remained intact, and bureaucratic controls were left in place, as were import barriers and import substitution policies. The importation of machinery did ensure that the country's bid for modernization led directly to quite impressive economic growth rates, although high population growth ensured that the per capita improvement was less marked. This, too, has ever since remained a feature of Turkish economic development. However, the consequence of all this was inflation and a massive national debt, combined with a balance of trade deficit as the country continued to import oil products, raw materials and machinery that its own underindustrialized economy was incapable of producing. Turkey's remained a mainly agricultural, low-productivity, low-technology economy only thinly integrated into the wider global economy. On the world stage, Turkey was a trading minnow, and foreign direct investment (FDI) into Turkey – which, along with trade, constituted one of the core indicators of the new economic globalization – was similarly pitiful when measured against the record of other developing economies, especially those in the Far East.

By 1958 Ankara had become one of the very first clients of an IMF standby agreement, obliging it to take the advice of the IMF and World Bank and cut government spending, reduce domestic subsidies and devalue the currency in return for a new loan package. Turkey had taken the first step towards becoming what was later described as an 'economic protectorate' (Hanke 2001) of the IMF, now having entered into nineteen 'arrangements' with the organization since becoming a member. It had also embarked on a now familiar boom-and-bust economic cycle that would intensify dramatically when, from the 1980s onwards, the country's economic managers experimented more boldly with economic liberalization and global integration. However, in the aftermath of the 1960 military ousting of the DP from office, Turkey reverted to its familiar embrace of government-led economic planning. During the 1960s and 1970s, five-year plans were reintroduced, import substitution and trade barriers were again enthusiastically embraced, and the large state-owned or -directed oligopolies were encouraged to expand their activities, enabled in large measure by imported technology and raw materials. Around forty per cent of industrial production in Turkey was generated by these cosseted state-owned enterprises, which were inefficient, overmanned and guided largely by political considerations.

The national indebtedness, inflationary pressures, inefficiencies and balance of payments deficits that Ankara's macroeconomic management inevitably spawned rendered the Turkish economy uniquely vulnerable to global economic downturns. The crunch – or one of many such crunches – came in the 1970s. The globally traded price of energy, which Turkey was now importing in increasing quantities, rocketed in price, thus worsening Turkey's balance of payments problems and stoking its inflationary pressures. The recession triggered in the West by higher energy prices had a negative impact on both Turkey's exports and the remittances from its workers abroad, on which it had increasingly come to rely to bridge its payments gap. As the crisis worsened, Ankara resorted to the short-sighted measures that until very recently became so very familiar. It printed money, engaged in successive currency devaluations, borrowed more and on a mainly short-term basis, and erected still higher barriers to trade. By the late 1970s, inflation was peaking towards 100 per cent, and shortages, rationing and black markets became widespread against a backdrop of yet another balance of payments crisis, massive government debt, rising unemployment and declining economic growth. Again, the IMF, the World Bank and the OECD pressured Ankara to adopt a drastic deflationary programme in return for yet another loan package, but Turkey's coalition government baulked at the measures demanded. These included adopting free-trade practices, cutting subsidies and government spending and freeing interest rates. Eventually, in January 1980, a newly appointed economics minister, Turgut Ozal, introduced a reform programme along the lines demanded by the international financial institutions. However, it was widely opposed. In any case, and amidst worsening civil and political disorder, the military engineered another coup in September 1980.

Ozal's reforms

It had by now become evident to many that Turkey's economic problems were systemic and could not be cured by short-term rectification or stabilization measures. With other developing economies, such as India's, which had attempted to modernize by adopting economic protectionism and government controls, Turkey found that it had been bypassed by comparably placed countries that had engaged more enthusiastically with the global economy, again most notably those in the Far East. Turkish economic management had engineered a track record of repeated and chronic economic crises. The autarkic economic system that had its roots in Kemalism and nationalism had paradoxically turned Turkey into one of the world's economically most dependent states. However, the dependency was not on an integrated global economic system based on trade and increased investment flows, in which Turkey was barely a participant, but on the institutions of the post-1945 global economy and, indirectly, on Washington's commitment to Turkey's position in the global security order. Even the Turkish military had some appreciation of the extent of this failure and, having taken power, they reappointed Turgut Ozal as a 'technocrat' charged with steering the economy towards some kind of stabilization and reform.

In elections held in 1983, Ozal's newly formed ANAP emerged victorious, against the wishes of the military who now mistrusted his courtship of the same sections of the electorate that had supported the DP in the 1950s. As elected prime minister and from 1989 as president, Ozal was able to continue with the quite drastic overhaul of the country's economy on which he had embarked in 1980. Ozal was committed to Turkey's full integration into the West's economic and political system, which would include membership of the EU, which he applied to join in 1987. Perhaps the most eye-catching element of the reform programme was the achievement by 1989 of full capital account convertibility – full currency convertibility and floating exchange rates – such that 'over the course of a decade Turkey was transformed from being one of the most closed to one of the most open capital account regimes in the world' (Onis 2000: 97). However, this was a somewhat premature measure, given the weak regulatory framework and the absence of fiscal and monetary discipline. Short-term inflows of capital could now take place, but they functioned as a substitute for long-term investment, rational economic management, and measures that might address the otherwise chronic balance of payments problems.

The enhanced democracy introduced in Turkey from 1987 onwards also signalled a return to populist policies and still higher public borrowing. Ankara's tax revenue-raising capacity was, and long remained, the OECD's lowest (Onis 2000: 102–3). In 2008, only Mexico's was lower (OECD 2010). The liberalizing measures had exposed Turkey to global capital flows without giving it the resilience and state competence to benefit from them. They also removed from Turkish economic policy makers the freedom to deploy such time-honoured instruments as trade protectionism and exchange rate fixing in times of trouble. Ozal also embarked upon a liberalization of Turkey's trade policy, which involved a phasing out of import substitution and encouragement of exports via government subsidies. This eventually led to the establishment of a customs union with the EU on 1 January 1996, an important step given that the EU now accounted for over half of Turkey's trade.[1]

An important legacy of Ozal's period in office has been Turkey's emergence as a significant exporter of manufactured as well as agricultural products, especially to the EU, and the associated emergence of the so-called 'Anatolian tigers' – new, dynamic and often export-oriented companies based not in the traditional centres of economic power in Turkey such as Istanbul, Izmir and Ankara, but in the country's socially more conservative hinterland, in cities such as Bursa, Kayseri, Gaziantep, Konya and the like (Tok 2008–09). During the period 1983–98, Turkey's exports doubled, thereby signalling Turkey's increased engagement with the global economic system, although for comparable countries such as Mexico and South Korea, exports increased fourfold (Eder 2001: 191). Furthermore, and unlike the experiences of Far Eastern economies in particular, Turkey's exports were and are primarily of labour-intensive products such as textiles, iron and steel products, and foodstuffs. The country remains relatively technology deficient to this day, rendering it particularly vulnerable to the products of newly emerging economies such as China. This is compounded by the fact that educational levels and investment in education in Turkey are relatively low and unevenly distributed, with pockets of high productivity and sophistication alongside swathes of unproductive and unskilled labour. The nearly thirty per cent of the country's workforce who are employed in the agricultural sector produce less than ten per cent of its GDP (Republic of Turkey, Prime Ministry 2006: 9). Turkey's is a dual economy and a dual society (Gros 2005: 57–59), and neither Ozal's reforms nor the policies of his successors have done enough to rectify this. Indeed, it has been asserted that half of Turkey's labour force 'has essentially not yet been touched by the modern economy' (Gros 2005: 51). In 2009,

Turkey's investment in research and development amounted to 0.6 per cent of GDP, compared with an OECD average of 2.3 per cent (Foreign and Commonwealth Office 2009). This suggests that Turkey could find it difficult to move to the next stage of economic and technological development.

It is also worth noting that industry's twenty-five per cent share of the (larger) national economy did not increase between 1990 and 2004. Rather, the decline in agriculture's share was taken up by the rise of the service sector, which in 2004 accounted for over forty-five per cent of Turkey's economic output (Onis and Bakir 2007: 151) and which, according to the World Bank, accounted for sixty-nine per cent of GDP in 2009 (World Bank 2009). However, statistics on the Turkish economy must be taken with a pinch of salt for – according to Ali Babacan, then the country's economy minister – in 2005 the 'informal' part of the Turkish economy was more than one-third the size of the formal economy.[2] Perhaps this casts a different light on those statistics which suggest that, with just forty-four per cent of its working-age population actually in employment, compared with around fifty-five per cent for the EU's newest members and sixty-five per cent for the EU's first fifteen members (Gros 2005: 60), Turkey needs only to put these people to work to increase the size of its economy. In the meantime, in any case, Turkey's economy might be bigger than the official figures suggest.

During Ozal's reign, Ankara also introduced some hesitant steps towards privatizing some of the country's extensive state assets. The programme barely took off, however, and in part was a victim of the weakening of the economic reform drive by the late 1980s. There was explicit and implicit opposition and obstructionism on the part of the country's political, bureaucratic and economic elite, and a failure to establish the kind of regulatory framework necessary to supervise a more privately owned economy (Zenginobuz 2008: 476). The privatization that did occur was frequently associated with corruption, or was often approached more as a means to increase government revenues in the short term than as part of a fundamental and structural economic reform programme (Hadjit and Moxon-Browne 2005: 324). In addition, foreign investors – crucial for extensive privatization to occur – were discouraged by Turkey's opaque and arbitrary legal and administrative practices. Around half of such foreign investment as Turkey attracted was wrapped up in joint ventures with local businesses that might be able to assist foreign economic agencies to steer their way through the Turkish state's morass (Grigoriadis and Kamaras 2008: 57). Relative to the size of its economy, newly postcommunist Hungary attracted thirteen times more FDI than did Turkey in the period 1988–95. Given that FDI is typically regionally rather than globally focused, Turkey's poor FDI performance relative to central Europe's during this period was significant, as they were the main rivals in Turkey's bid to attract such funds. Turkey was similarly less successful in attracting FDI than countries such as Mexico and Argentina. This was a period of accelerated global growth in FDI, yet, in 1995, Turkey's FDI to GDP ratio was a mere 0.4 per cent compared with a two per cent average for developing and transition economies, placing Turkey in eighty-first position out of ninety-one such countries in its attractiveness to foreign investors (Hadjit and Moxon-Browne 2005: 324). Thus, 'in the first two decades, the 1980s and the 1990s, of what is commonly accepted as globalization, Turkey abstained from one of its main precepts: the acceptance and the coming into being of a substantial role for FDI' (Grigoriadis and Kamaras 2008: 58). An additional consequence was that, although greater economic growth and industrialization were undoubted successes of the Ozal years, much of this was achieved less by greater productivity resulting from the introduction of technology, and more by a simple shift from unproductive rural to more productive industrial labour (Eder 2001: 206–7).

To assist with and provide a stable platform for the reform programme, Turkey received a record five successive structural adjustment loans from the World Bank, of which Ozal was a former employee (Onis 2000: 95–97). As with its relationship with the IMF, Turkey's dependence on the World Bank has ever since been a feature of its economic evolution, and today Turkey is that institution's largest borrower in the bank's Europe and Central Asia Region (World Bank 2009). Yet the internationally backed reform programme had increased Turkey's engagement with, and exposure to, financial and economic globalization whilst denying it the means to protect itself from its full force. High public debt, high interest rates and a balance of payments gap all contributed to Turkey's severe economic vulnerability. In 1994, a reduction in interest rates and a reduced international credit rating led to yet another economic crisis requiring yet another IMF standby agreement. There was a repeat in 1998–99, when Turkey suffered from the backwash from a crisis in Russia, which had become an increasingly important trade partner for Turkey. With the IMF programme entered into in December 1999, Ankara demonstrated for the first time ever its readiness to 'accept IMF disciplines in the absence of an explicit crisis' (Onis 2009: 414). Turkey had truly become a client state of the IMF and other global financial institutions, yet it continued to resist taking the kind of measures necessary to enable it to break the cycle of crises.

The strong public–private nexus that was a legacy of the Kemalist system, and the thinking that went with it, had obstructed foreign investment, privatization and tax raising in the wake of Ozal's reforms, just as it had before them. The 1980s reforms heralded far less disruption than is sometimes imagined to the close public–private economic relationship that had for so long characterized Turkey's economic, political and social system. Corruption, clientelism, massive public debt and inflation that again reached triple digits in the mid-1990s had been the products of this uneasy cohabitation between neoliberal economic policies, a corporate state and democratization. Indeed, although populism and corruption were hardly new in Turkey, their scale in the wake of Ozal's reforms added a new twist to the country's economic dilemmas. The bureaucracy had become increasingly politicized and weak when confronted with political leaderships intent on distributing patronage and privileges to their supporters (Eder 2003; Onis 2003). Indeed, in the economic sphere at least, the Turkish state now appeared soft and weak, rather than hard and capable, in its capacity to deal with the new circumstances of the Turkish economy.

The 2000–01 crisis and its aftermath

In short, by the turn of the millennium, Turkey's now more open economy remained at least as crisis prone as it had ever been. Turkey's economic policies had changed since 1980, but the public sector and government machinery had remained largely intact. The next serious financial and economic crises to hit Turkey, in 2000 and 2001, have been seen as 'a real rupture in the history of the Turkish economy' (Onis and Bakir 2007: 147) and helped ensure that attention would now turn to the functioning of the Turkish state in a neoliberal and globalized economic system. Best seen as one economic crash in two parts, Turkey's unregulated banking system has frequently been placed at the heart of attempts to explain the crisis, although the weak commitment of a fractious coalition government to the economic programme, a particularly volatile global funds market and the 'one-size-fits-all' approach of the IMF at that time, might also share in the responsibility.[3] In any case, what began as a sudden outflow of short-term capital from Turkey in November 2000 had by February 2001 triggered a quite comprehensive economic crash affecting all sectors of society. Within a year, GNP had fallen by almost ten per cent, unemployment had risen by 1 million and average per capita incomes had dropped by around a quarter (Onis 2003: 15). The rock of Turkey's top-down, unreconstructed state system had clashed with the hard place of the Turkish economy's increased openness and vulnerability to a neoliberal globalized economic and financial system, and the 2000–01 crash suggested that Turkish society had been caught inbetween them. Even Turkey's large and increasingly internationalized conglomerates, which had for so long benefited from, and been protected by, their cosy relationship with the state, now came to realize that Turkey's approach to macroeconomic management put them at a disadvantage in their competition with their EU counterparts and with the postcommunist states of central and eastern Europe. They were also unavoidably aware that Turkey's dysfunctional economic practices constituted a serious obstacle to the EU accession they so keenly craved (Grigoriadis and Kamaras 2008: 59–60).

The results of the first election to be held in the wake of the crisis, in November 2002, suggested that Turks had come to view the system, and the political parties most associated with it, with increased scepticism. A 'new' party formed in August 2001, the AKP, won the election with thirty-four per cent of the vote, gaining 363 seats in the 550-seat TGNA. The CHP, with twenty per cent of the vote, accounted for the remainder of the seats as the only other party that reached the ten per cent threshold required by Turkish electoral law before parliamentary seats could be taken up. The parties that had formed the coalition in power at the time of the collapse lost almost forty per cent of their vote when compared with the results of the previous election in April 1999 (Carkoglu 2002). The AKP's constituency was similar to that of the DP in the 1950s – although Turkish society had changed considerably in the intervening half century – and to Ozal's in the 1980s, and consisted mainly of the new and poor immigrants to Turkey's demographically exploding urban areas, the devout, the inhabitants of rural regions and small Anatolian towns, and the new Anatolian-based small and medium business-men who had flourished as a consequence of Ozal's encouragement of private and export-oriented businesses. The party also attracted liberal reformers. The AKP had not been responsible for Turkey's economic evolution and did not necessarily share the core values of the Kemalist elite. It could be seen as presenting a challenge to the 'centre' by Turkey's 'periphery'. Furthermore, in its election campaign the AKP leadership stressed its commitment to honesty in government, economic reform and EU accession. The opportunity to form a strong single-party government – a rare event in Turkey, and one reinforced by the party's July 2007 election victory, in which the AKP won forty-seven per cent of the vote, although gaining slightly fewer seats owing to the MHP's successful hurdling of the ten per cent threshold – also held out the prospect of a more disciplined approach to the country's structural economic woes.

The international context for Turkish economic policy had also shifted, and this, too, reinforced the sense that the path Turkey had taken hitherto would no longer be indulged. The EU's Helsinki decision of December 1999 to recognize Turkey as a candidate for full membership now emerged as a gen-uine externally derived incentive for serious internal reform. The EU's December 2002 Copenhagen promise to the new government, that accession talks would indeed be opened, further strengthened this incentive while simultaneously undermining residual internal opposition to change. Further-more, the long-term nature of the EU project denied to Turkish policy makers the kind of quick-fix, superficial and temporary measures that they had been at liberty to adopt in the past. The EU would also focus on improve-ments in Turkey's democratization, transparency and governance, which most observers now believed would provide a necessary backcloth if Turkey was to successfully stabilize its economy on a more durable foundation. This reinforced the capacity of the IMF to insist on deeper structural changes to the Turkish economy. The IMF had, in any case, learned that its past insistence on capital market liberalization and its preoccupation with anti-inflationary monetary measures, unaccompanied by any comparable insistence on regulatory reform, had only served to highlight the structural weaknesses of developing countries such as Turkey. It, too, now insisted on a much more extensive and phased set of Turkish reforms in return for the support package it offered. The USA, too, had played a key role in encoura-ging the IMF to lend support to Turkey and the EU to extend membership to it, such that it is possible to identify an 'EU–US–IMF triangle' behind Turkey's re-energized economic reform drive (Onis 2009).

Due in large measure to Turkey's dependency on these external factors and the pressures and incentives they were able to apply, Turkey now had little option but to embark on the creation of a more effective and regulatory system of economic governance, one more in tune with the requirements of a modern economy located in a globalized and neoliberal economic system. This represented quite a departure from the aspirations of the republic's founders and many of those who today regard themselves as guardians of that legacy. It underscored the inconsistency inherent in simultaneously seeking both economic autarky and economic modernity and 'westernization'. Even before the 2000–01 crisis, 'there was a growing sense that the limits of clientelistic politics and populist redistribution' had been reached (Onis 2000: 112). The key was a shift in the balance between domestic sources of resistance to change on the one hand, and external realities and pressures on the other. External pressures had now gained the upper hand against internal forces of inertia. Thus, even before the AKP's 2002 electoral victory, Turkey's coalition government found itself obliged to embark on a set of measures that incorporated structural changes to the way in which the economy was managed as well as more immediate steps to address the more immediate problems. It had rationalized the social security system, improved regulation in the financial sector, and opened the country up to international arbitration of disputes arising from foreign investment in Turkey (Onis 2000). One important indication that the coalition had now recognized the seriousness of Turkey's situation (or at least that it recognized the scrutiny it was now under) was its appointment of Kemal Dervis, a former World Bank economist, as economy minister. This proved highly instrumental in Turkey's success in gaining the confidence of the world's leading financial institutions and sponsoring states.

The post-crisis reforms have involved the establishment of a more autonomous regulatory regime alongside steps to ease the government from its commanding height in the economy (Onis 2009: 420–24). Central to the regulatory measures were the 2001 laws enhancing the autonomy of the central bank, thus enabling governments to stick to their anti-inflationary path and resist populist pressures. The Bank Regulatory and Supervisory Authority (BRSA), first set up in 1999, was also granted greater autonomy and authority. This presaged a major restructuring of Turkey's traditionally risky banking sector. So successful has this been that Turkish banks survived the 2008–09 global financial crisis without needing to resort to government handouts. Other relatively independent regulatory agencies have been established in several areas, covering for example the energy and telecommunications sectors. With their separate legal personalities, they represent rather exotic and peculiar entities in the context of Turkey's unitary bureaucratic order, and the independence they enjoy is both variable and possibly contingent (Zenginobuz 2008; Sosay 2009). Nevertheless, their establishment offers a mechanism to ensure greater transparency and accountability and a revitalization of the privatization programme, which has in turn helped facilitate a reduction in the role and intrusiveness of central government in the functioning of the Turkish economy.

A further feature of the AKP's economic reform programme has been the removal of many of the administrative obstacles to FDI in Turkey, improved legal protection and a reduction in the corporate tax rate. These measures constituted elements in the 'action plan' adopted by the government, aimed at improving Turkey's attractiveness to foreign investors. This in turn followed a request made by the previous coalition government in 2001 to the Foreign Investment Agency Service (FIAS) of the World Bank to identify the factors behind Turkey's poor performance in this regard (Hadjit and Moxon-Browne 2005: 327). The result has been a remarkable increase in FDI into Turkey during the first decade of the twenty-first century, or from around 2005 at any rate. During the period 1990–2000, FDI flows into Turkey expressed as a percentage of gross fixed capital formation averaged 1.8 per cent per annum. World averages during this period were put at 8.2 per cent per annum, and for developing economies the annual average stood at 9.9 per cent. These statistics illustrate the striking degree to which FDI had passed Turkey by. In 2006 and 2007, the figures for Turkey were 17.1 and 15.6 per cent, respectively, whereas the global averages for the same years were 13.4 and 16.0 per cent. The figures for developing economies were comparable. In other words, in a remarkably short period Turkey had come to match both global and developing economy average FDI flows. With the onset of the global economic turndown in 2008, the FDI flow for Turkey dropped to 12.3 per cent, which exactly matched the much reduced global average for the same troubled year, and was only marginally below that for developing economies as a whole (UNCTAD 2009). According to this indication at least, Turkey could now and at last be said to have more fully integrated into the global economy.

However, the FDI picture remains mixed. Although 'the crisis accelerated the process of transnationalization of major Turkish conglomerates', which have considerably expanded their operations abroad (Onis 2009: 424), Turkish FDI in other countries remains low. Even with unprecedented growth, in 2008 it amounted to just 1.7 per cent of gross fixed capital formation. The outward FDI flow for developing economies as a whole was 6.1 per cent, and for the world it amounted to 13.5 per cent (UNCTAD 2009). Measured by FDI outflows, Turkish businesses have remained comparatively inward looking. Furthermore, inward FDI has helped make up for the moderately falling domestic investment in the Turkish economy, from an average twenty-four per cent of GNP in the period 1996–2000 to twenty per cent in 2005. This is partly explained by the fact that tighter banking regulations have resulted in tighter credit for the private sector, especially for small and medium firms. This could have an impact on future growth prospects and on the future dynamism of the Turkish economy (Onis 2009: 424–26). Furthermore, much of the inward FDI 'has been in the form of mergers and acquisitions rather than green field investment' and stems from the enhanced privatization programme (Onis 2009: 426). Indeed, in 2007, seventy per cent of FDI was accounted for by mergers and acquisitions, and ten per cent by land purchases. Only twenty per cent of inward investment into Turkey in 2007 created new jobs. Around forty per cent of Turkish banks, which have been a particular target of foreign investors, and seventy per cent of its stock market, fell into foreign ownership within the space of a few years.[4]

A corner turned?

'Turkey's political–economic landscape has been reshaped by the combination of domestic and external dynamics' (Onis 2009: 410), and the reforms that followed the 2000–01 crisis undoubtedly placed Turkey's economy on a surer footing. Inflation fell to single digits, growth was impressive at around six per cent per annum in the period 2002–08 and the reform of the banking sector ensured it survived the onset of the global economic downturn in 2008. Turkey's foreign exchange reserves now look healthy, and its public debt fell from a massive seventy-four per cent in 2001 to thirty-nine per cent in 2008.[5] Improved regulation and a degree of depoliticization of economic management contributed to the tighter fiscal discipline that the IMF had demanded and gave overseas investors greater confidence, with the consequent inflow of FDI funds.

Turkey's foreign trade roughly has quadrupled by volume in the decade since 2000–01, suggesting that in the trade sphere, too, Turkey is increasingly integrated into the global economy. Furthermore, with the world's seventeenth largest economy, Turkey is a member of the G20 group. Although the EU continues to account for around half of Turkey's exports, trade is now significantly more diversified, with Turkey's five biggest export markets accounting for a little over one-third of the country's exports in 2008, compared with fifty per cent just five years earlier. Much of this shift is explained by what a Turkish minister described as Turkey's 'greater Ottoman project', aimed at increasing trade relations with Turkey's near neighbours, with whom it shares 'common ties such as language, religion, culture, geography and history.' 'Thirty three countries have succeeded the Ottoman empire', he noted, and Turkey has recently invested considerable effort in expanding its trade with them. The first steps in this direction were taken by the Ecevit government in 2000, but the AKP government takes primary credit for expanding and implementing these trade enhancement strategies, which in fact have taken Turkey far beyond the confines of the former Ottoman space. To this end, Turkey put together trade and investment strategies for its immediate neighbours in 2002, for Africa in 2003, for the Asia Pacific region in 2005 and for the Americas in 2006.[6] These strategies entailed expanded participation in regional trade fairs, government-sponsored campaigns, trade delegations, ministerial visits, the establishment of direct flights by Turkey's national air carrier, Turkish Airlines, and so on. Trade with neighbouring countries such as Greece, Syria, Iran, Iraq and Bulgaria has generally shown the most spectacular growth, in some instances quadrupling in the space of a few years, such that neighbouring countries accounted for around one-third of all Turkey's exports by the end of the twenty-first century's first decade. By 2008, Turkey was exporting goods worth 1 billion dollars or more to thirty countries (Foreign and Commonwealth Office 2009).

The wave of industrialization based on the emergence of the export-oriented 'Anatolian tigers' from the Ozal period onwards has also helped diversify Turkish trade relations towards Middle Eastern, central Asian, other former Soviet state, and African markets. It has been claimed that individual Anatolian cities might export to as many as 140 different countries (Tok 2008–9: 82–83). Indeed, the collapse of the communist bloc opened up nearby regions that had been largely off limits for trade during the Cold War. Russia nudged Germany from its leading position both as Turkey's major trading partner, albeit much of it consisting of energy imports into Turkey, and as the major source of tourists (as well as the largest supplier of foreign wives to Turkish men, apparently) (Alpay 2009). Trade with Ukraine, central Asia, the Caucasus countries and the Balkans has also increased. As with the increase in FDI, trade has also been instrumental in globalizing Turkey's relationships, dependencies, interactions, perspectives and profile.

Does this suggest that Turkey has rebuilt its state capacity to better match the requirements of a globalized market economy, and that it can now look forward to sustained macroeconomic stability? The safest and truest answer is that it is too early to say. In the short to medium term, worries include the substantial current account deficit, a gap plugged by levels of FDI inflow that might not be sustained. This risk is compounded by continuing high levels of short-term capital inflows, which could dry up overnight and would be particularly vulnerable were the overvalued Turkish lira to get into exchange rate difficulties. The trade deficit is itself a reminder of Turkey's high propensity to import, especially high-technology and capital goods that it does not produce itself (Aker 2008). Ever higher dependence on energy imports also contributes, as does the impact of the lira's valuation on the cost of imports. Furthermore, Turkey's public finances still leave considerable room for improvement. Tax revenues remain low and are regressively structured, while government spending remains tied to a still unreformed social services system and an imperfectly audited defence budget. Instances of maldistributive populist spending still abound.

In terms of GNP decline, the Turkish economy was initially one of the most severely affected by the downturn that hit the global economy in 2008, with a consequently heavy impact on employment levels. The sudden decline in FDI into Turkey as a consequence of the global crisis can also be mostly attributed to factors beyond Ankara's control. These may be short-term disappointments. Structurally, the economy demonstrated an overall robustness that contrasted starkly with its 2000–01 nosedive. In fact, it emerged from the 2008 crisis as one of the world's fastest-growing economies. However, two large sets of doubts hang over the long-term future of the Turkish economy. The first set relates to the impact of external anchors on

Turkish macroeconomic management. The arrangement with the IMF expired in May 2008, and after drawn-out negotiations, the government decided it could do without further IMF assistance. The talks stumbled over the IMF's insistence on tighter fiscal control than Ankara was prepared to sign up to, and in particular to a mechanism that could independently monitor government spending. In fact, the Turkish government drew up a medium-term plan that included the imposition of limits on government spending, greater transparency, tax reform, greater efficiency in social spending programmes and more privatization. Clearly the IMF was unconvinced, and remained sceptical that the government could be trusted not to loosen the purse strings in the midst of a recession and with elections looming. Indeed, there were signs that Ankara had already relaxed its fiscal discipline and that the government was once again indulging in politically inspired populist spending programmes. A failure to control public spending could have a negative impact on the government's international credit rating.[7]

In addition to the IMF, the EU has also functioned as a longer-term sponsor of reform of the Turkish economy and of its system of governance. However, the AKP government's EU-inspired reform momentum had already lost much of its drive by 2005, while the EU's internal problems and divisions with respect to Turkish accession, combined with the continuing failure to remove the Cyprus issue functioning as a block on EU accession, meant that the capacity of the EU to serve as an anchor for Turkey's reform programme was reduced. Although Turkey's macroeconomic management had undoubtedly vastly improved since the 2000–01 crash, and although Turkey's was now a far more open economy than the one inherited by Ozal, it remains an open question whether Turkey's new arrangements will be self-sustaining and self-regulating in the absence of determined and intrusive external pressure and monitoring.[8]

Turkey's Islamic economy

The second set of doubts relates to the long-term structural, and even cultural, characteristics of the Turkish economy and the society in which it is embedded. The UN's Human Development Index (HDI) seeks to identify a population's well being beyond mere GNP indicators. It takes into account factors such as health, life expectancy, levels of poverty, standards of literacy and the like. In 2007, Turkey ranked seventy-ninth out of 182 countries, suggesting a lower HDI than its GNP would imply. Since 1980, Turkey has been located a little above, but close to, South American and Caribbean countries, and significantly behind the OECD average. This in turn raises a much bigger question, beyond the scope of this volume, about whether developing societies such as Turkey, Mexico, Brazil, China and India will ever necessarily come to resemble the world's more-developed countries in terms of their quality of governance, physical infrastructure, transparency, technological and scientific inventiveness, stability or democratization. Might Turkey and other developing countries be on the path towards an alternative modernity to that experienced by the West? (Keyman 2007).

As a Muslim country, it is not surprising that globalization has opened Turkey up to the Islamic world's economic practices and markets as well as to those of the West. It is also not surprising that it was Turgut Ozal who opened the door to this development in Turkey. In 1983, his government altered the law to enable the establishment of interest-free banks and businesses. The aim was to release the funds that had been accumulated by the mostly provincial and small-town businessmen who felt excluded by the clientelistic relationship between government and big business, and who objected to the nonreligious practices of the established financial institutions. Business and banking systems based on Islamic precepts have been growing globally since at least 1963, when they seem to have originated in Egypt (Yuce 2003). In 1985, Turkey saw the establishment of its first Islamic banking businesses, Faysal Finans and Al Baraki Finans, essentially with Saudi money, followed in 1989 by Kuwait Finans. Their example was followed by the establishment of Turkish-owned Anadolu Finans in 1991, Ihlas Finans in 1995 and Asya Finans in 1996. This latter institution grew out of the Fethullah Gulen movement, which is explored in greater detail in Chapter 12 (Yuce 2003; Maigre 2006). Both the banks and the export-oriented Muslim-owned business enterprises benefited from the free-market and free-trade policies of Ozal's government, and their interlocking relationships have in effect established a business world parallel to that of the secular sectors of the economy.

In 1990, a Muslim business association, MUSIAD,[9] was established, with branches throughout the country. In terms of membership, it has since grown to be Turkey's largest voluntary business organization (Jang 2006; Maigre 2006; Adas 2009). Seventy per cent of MUSIAD's affiliated companies were formed after 1980 and have typically been established by provincial lower-middle-class and socially conservative entrepreneurs, are rooted in Islamic networks and brotherhoods, and are mostly small concerns of fewer than 100 employees. Its members account for around ten per cent of Turkey's GNP. This contrasts markedly with the chiefly Istanbul-centred TUSIAD (*Turk Sanayici ve Isadamlari Dernigi* – Turkish Industry and Business Association),[10] formed in 1971 to represent the larger industrialists with close ties to the state apparatus. Eighty per cent of its affiliated companies were formed before 1980, and between them they represent around fifty per cent of the national economy. Another important business association is the Gulen-affiliated TUSKON (*Turkiye Isadamlari ve Sanayiciler Konfederayonu* – Turkish Confederation of Industrialists and Businessmen),[11] established in 2005. Both MUSIAD and TUSKON have sister organizations throughout central Asia, the Balkans, the Russian Federation and western Europe.

Both MUSIAD and TUSKON are associated with free-market values and a preference for a contraction of the state's role in the economy and society, but also with a preference for trade and investment in the Islamic world.

TUSIAD, by contrast, opposed Ozal's reforms, valued its cosy relationship with the state, and was generally more inward-looking. In its early years, MUSIAD's leading figures were also characterized by anti-western sentiment and an antipathy towards Turkey's EU aspirations; they insisted both on the compatibility of their business practices with Islam, and their genuine aspirations to further the Islamic cause (Maigre 2006). With the 1997 identification by the MGK of political Islam as a threat to the country's security and its Kemalist legacy, Islamic businesses found themselves subjected to blacklists, boycotts, investigations, sanctions and legal prosecutions (Jang 2006: 105; Maigre 2006). Since 2000, however, and even more so since the AKP's election victory in 2002, MUSIAD has been increasingly inclined to support Turkey's EU accession, democratization and individual liberties, as evidenced by the contents of its annual reports. TUSKON is also in favour of Turkey's free-market, pro-EU and democratizing path. Indeed, 'in Turkey [...] Islamic capitalists have been ardent free marketeers, supporters of globalization [...] and opposing the arbitrary and powerful state' (Jang 2006: 97). Since the AKP's 2002 election victory, MUSIAD has acquired a somewhat privileged status. Although it is not formally linked to the AKP, the personal relationships and overlaps are considerable. This has led to more than a whiff of the kind of clientelism and even corruption that have been associated with TUSIAD's relationship to the state (Rubin 2005a). In business, as in so much else, Turkey seems to have developed networks and structures that operate in parallel, with relatively little contact between the two sides of the divide.

Although the majority of Turkey's Islamic businesses are small, some very large multiactivity holding companies have also emerged, such as Kombassan[12] and YIMPAS.[13] Such companies have raised their capital by mobilizing the savings of hundreds of thousands of pious small savers in Turkey and within its expatriate communities in Europe and elsewhere (Adas 2009). These companies can be dubbed 'grassroots transnational corporations'. The 'transnational networks' between Turkish 'Islamic entrepreneurs and Turkish migrant workers in Europe have been critical' in their capitalization and remarkable growth (Adas 2009: 627). Informal family and social networks, regional ties and mosque and political affiliations seem to be the main determinants of the flow of these savings, and often provide the means for their transfer, which might occur electronically but which might also take the form of cash smuggled across borders. There is no legal basis for this arrangement, which is derived from the Islamic principle of *musharaka*, by which the investors are joint owners of the company and receive a share of the profits related to the scale of their investment. The relationship is based entirely on trust. The shares of such companies are not quoted on the stock exchange, as a consequence of which they are not obliged to issue financial statements. Kombassan is reckoned to have 30,000 such shareholders, YIMPAS 60,000. Overall it is estimated that 800,000 Turkish workers in Europe have invested their savings in such joint venture schemes.

As an indication of some of the risks that could be associated with unregulated economic transactions of this kind, in 2008 a German court sentenced three Turks to prison for fraud in the biggest embezzlement case in German history. It appears that around €40 million, donated by Turkish migrant workers through the German-based Deniz Feneri (Lighthouse) charity foundation, disappeared. German prosecutors have alleged that some of this money found its way to the pockets of company leaders and politically well-placed individuals, and that some was redirected for political purposes. An insight into the machinations of Turkish politics, and into the tensions between the secular and religious ends of the political spectrum, was offered by the domestic furore that accompanied the German investigation. Prime minister Erdogan took particular offence at the secular Dogan newspaper group's reporting of the affair, which the group feels was connected to a massive tax fine subsequently levied on the company by the government's taxation authorities (Kaya 2008).[14]

One conclusion might be that Turkey's openness to the economic practices and values of both the West and the Islamic world have served to intensify Turkey's political and social divisions. The country's enlarged external economic interactions seem to have been filtered through Turkey's political, economic and social culture, and to have taken on some of their distinctive Turkish colour. In the case of a country with so complex an identity as Turkey's, the conflicting cross-currents of a globalized world seem to be reflected in the country's domestic economic as well as its political evolution.

6 Turkey and the Kurdish issue

A transnationalized domestic problem

The Kurds

Turkey's approximately 15 million Kurds constitute up to twenty per cent of the country's population and account for about one half of all Kurds. Iraq's roughly 4.5 million Kurds constitute around fifteen per cent of the total Iraqi population. Iran's Kurdish population is probably a little larger than Iraq's, although a smaller percentage of the Iranian national total, while Syria is home to in excess of 1 million ethnic Kurds.[1] The traditionally and predominantly Kurdish-populated areas of Turkey, Iraq, Iran and Syria are geographically contiguous, and had formerly and for the most part been incorporated within the Ottoman empire's borders. Thus, until the decolonization and state-creation processes of the twentieth century, interaction between the largely mountain-dwelling and frequently nomadic Kurds was relatively free and open, although linguistic, tribal, regional and religious differences ensured that Kurdish society remained fragmented and fractious. Although it might be said that 'the Kurds only really began to think of themselves as an ethnic community from 1918 onwards […] for Kurdish nationalists there can be no question that the nation has existed since time immemorial, long asleep but finally aroused' (McDowall 1996: 4). In other words, the rise of Kurdish national consciousness roughly coincided with the incorporation of Kurds into the newly created states of Turkey, Iraq and Syria, as 'the Kurds found themselves separated from each other by default rather than by design' (Kirisci and Winrow 1997: 85). Unsurprisingly, therefore, the twentieth century witnessed frequent Kurdish revolts against Turkish, Iranian and Arab attempts at nation building and assimilation, and in support of the self-determination that had been denied them. In short, the Kurdish 'question' has been a transborder one since the Ottoman collapse and is rooted in the global phenomena of decolonization, state creation, nation building and the emergence of the principle of national self-determination.

Turkey's 'domestic' war: a regional and global conflict

Ataturk's early promises that the Kurds would enjoy full cultural and political rights in the new republic were soon broken. In early 1925, the Kemalist regime embarked upon a brutal repression of a tribal Kurdish rebellion. The massacres, executions, deportations, incarcerations, destruction of villages and the imposition of martial law that characterized Turkey's 1920s campaigns established a pattern that was to recur throughout the following decades. Linguistic, cultural and political expressions of Kurdish identity were banned and the very existence of Kurds as a distinct ethnic identity was increasingly denied. In a foretaste of Turkey's incursions into neighbouring Iraq in the 1990s, in 1929 Turkish forces even violated the territory of Iran in its pursuit of Kurdish rebels. Before Ataturk's death in 1938, tens of thousands of Kurds had lost their lives, their leadership was decimated, the population dispersed, and the economic infrastructure of south-eastern Turkey ruined (McDowall 1996: 184–213). Kurdish disaffection and alienation have been a persisting feature of the republic's life since its birth.

In the 1970s, a more leftist Kurdish strand emerged from that decade's heady political hothouse. For many Kurds, these leftist, more urban-based and 'detribalized' leaders gradually displaced the more traditional tribal and landowning Kurdish elites as leaders of Kurdish revolt. Radicalized still further by the harsh repression and by the tightening of general as well as specifically Kurdish political expression that followed the 1980 coup, in 1984 the leftist PKK embarked on a violent separatist war. Ankara's security elites perceived the Kurdish question as a security rather than a political issue, and again responded with uncompromising brutality. A violent conflict between the PKK and Turkish security forces has since ensued and is still ongoing, in which almost 40,000 people have lost their lives (McDowall 1996: 418–44; Barkey and Fuller 1998; Mango 2005). As a consequence, Kurdish identity in Turkey may, if anything, have been strengthened rather than weakened (Romano 2006). Fought by the security forces with little political supervision, the war against the PKK has been associated with the silencing and detention of journalists and political activists, covert assassinations, torture and scorched-earth policies that have emptied around 3000 Kurdish villages of their inhabitants. By the mid-1990s, around 300,000 Turkish troops were in occupation of Turkey's predominantly ethnically Kurdish provinces.

As a consequence of the war, rural south-eastern Turkey has increasingly become depopulated and fallen economically and socially still further behind the rest of the country. On the other hand, ethnic Kurds make up a significant and expanding portion of Turkey's growing urban poor and working class. Today, an estimated fifty per cent or more of Turkey's ethnic Kurds are thought to live outside the country's traditionally Kurdish provinces (Somer 2004: 249), often in urban ghettoes, a factor that has both encouraged assimilation and brought intercommunal tension to Turkey's cities (Ozhan and Ete 2009: 99). The conflict has also spawned a transborder refugee problem. Most notably, in excess of 10,000 Turkish Kurds fled to Iraq during the 1990s, many of them ending up in a still extant UN-administered camp at Makhmur. Other Kurdish refugees from Turkey found their way to Iran, Syria, other neighbouring states, and of course western Europe. The support and activities of this diaspora of Turkish Kurds have been crucial to the continuing struggle with Ankara, and have thus served to internationalize the conflict.

Turkey's poor human rights record is largely explained by the campaign against the PKK (Yildiz 2005) and has complicated Ankara's relationships with its western allies. In addition to the numerous damning reports by external agencies such as Amnesty International and Human Rights Watch that have drawn attention to the systematic torture, extrajudicial killings, curtailments of minority rights and other human rights abuses, 'Turkey has probably one of the worst records in the history of ECtHR (European Court of Human Rights) judgements' (Koker 2010: 62), many of which relate to the Kurdish question. In 1994, and in response to the persecution of Kurdish politicians, Germany temporarily suspended military assistance to Turkey, while the EC postponed signing the customs union with Turkey (Kirisci and Winrow 1997: 172). In December 2009, Turkey's constitutional court banned the Kurdish DTP for promoting ethnic separatism and for alleged links with the PKK. Banned DTP members promptly took the case to the ECtHR.[2]

The northern Iraq dimension of Turkey's domestic Kurdish struggle

To a degree, the PKK has owed its capacity to sustain its campaign in Turkey to the formation of the Kurdish Regional Government (KRG) in northern Iraq. The failure of the 1991 Kurdish and Shia uprisings against Saddam Hussein's regime in Iraq was followed by a flood of approximately half a million Iraqi Kurds towards the Turkish border. The resulting humanitarian crisis brought the involvement of the international community, which created safe havens for the refugees and a 'no-fly zone' – Operation Safe Haven/ Northern Watch – policed from Incirlik air base in Turkey (Altunisik 2004: 157–63). Following the withdrawal of Baghdad's forces from the area in October 1991, the self-governing KRG zone was established (Gunter 1999; Stansfield 2003; O'Leary *et al.* 2005; Yildiz 2007). As a consequence of the transborder Kurdish demography, the emergence of the KRG interlocked with Turkey's own troubles with Kurdish separatism and identity (Barkey 2005), and indeed those of Iran and Syria too. Now the PKK was able to use northern Iraq as a base for its operations against Turkey. Similarly, there was little to prevent Turkish incursions across the border in pursuit of the 3000–4000 PKK fighters believed to be based there. In addition to frequent bombing and commando raids, Ankara launched more than twenty military interventions into northern Iraq, which in 1992, 1995, 1996 and 1997 involved tens of thousands of troops. These incursions again attracted widespread international criticism, and in 1995 there were calls in the European Parliament for a military embargo to be imposed on Turkey (Kirisci and Winrow 1997: 173). Turkey also maintained a permanent troop deployment of varying strength inside northern Iraq. This enabled Ankara to carry the fight to the PKK, but also to meddle in the internal affairs of the KRG. Northern Iraq had come to resemble a Turkish protectorate of sorts, and from 1991 onwards Ankara has arguably exercised far more influence on events there than has Baghdad (Aykan 1996; Robins 2003: 312–42). Such experiences strengthened still further the Turkish tendency to blur state boundaries in its approach to the Kurdish problem.

The US-led war of 2003 against the Baghdad regime shattered these arrangements (Hale 2007). Unsurprisingly, Ankara had opposed the invasion. As early as October 2001, responding to a question on the possibility of US action against Iraq, Ecevit argued that 'Turkey cannot accept this. This operation may lead to Turkey's dismemberment. It also will disrupt all the balances in the middle east [...] We do not want any intervention against Iraq whatsoever. As I have stated, it will create many dangers.'[3] The TSK shared these concerns, although it also drew up plans to intervene in northern Iraq, possibly alongside US forces. Turkey's unease with US thinking more than survived the change of government heralded by the AKP's electoral victory in November 2002. Political and official opposition reflected Turkish public opinion, which was overwhelmingly opposed to an attack on Iraq with or without Turkish participation. Indeed, former US ambassador to Turkey Mark Parris claimed that he had 'never met a Turk who likes this idea'.[4] This led predictably, if not inexorably, to the fateful 1 March 2003 vote in the TGNA that denied US forces access to Turkish territory (Park 2003; Rubin 2005; Kapsis 2006; Hale 2007: 94–116).

US policy towards Iraq and the demands it made on Ankara, again in the prescient words of Mark Parris, were 'testing the outer limits of strategic cooperation' with Turkey (Parris 2003). Ankara's local sensitivities and interests, which on this issue were regarded by Turks as of the highest order, were in contradiction to Washington's more global considerations. Washington's strategic preoccupations appeared to blind it to the depth of Turkish opposition. Americans also failed to appreciate the extent to which their own readiness to arm, train and operate with the Iraqi Kurdish *peshmerga* (fighters) was seen as threatening to its NATO ally. Nor did the USA take sufficient note of the fact that the TSK was at best lukewarm – unless it could launch a dramatic intervention of its own in northern Iraq in order to secure Turkey's border and to maximize its ability to shape postinvasion developments (Rafaat 2007). It failed to assess the nature of the new AKP government and did not take sufficient account of the domestic political difficulties it was experiencing in its endeavours to cooperate with the USA. This conflict of perception, and US readiness to ride roughshod over, or ignore, the sensitivities of a key regional and NATO ally, have had a profound impact on the subsequent evolution of Turkish foreign policy. Most especially, it encouraged the AKP government in a bid for greater autonomy and engagement with its near neighbours, and boosted anti-American sentiment in the country. These developments have ultimately led to a debate about whether Turkey has been 'lost' as a US ally, which, if so, could be regarded as the most unanticipated and enduring ramification of post 9/11 US behaviour (Menon and Wimbush 2007).

Both as a consequence of the US presence in Iraq, and because Iraq's Kurds skilfully grasped the opportunity to entrench their self-government and ingratiate themselves with Washington, Ankara's hands were now tied. This situation proved deeply frustrating for Turkey's policy makers, both with respect to the PKK presence in northern Iraq, and in light of the deepened autonomy enjoyed by the KRG. From 1 June 2004, when the PKK called off the ceasefire it had declared unilaterally in February 2000, there was a marked increase in violent exchanges inside Turkey between Turkish security forces and PKK units conducting cross-border operations from Iraq. Turkish officials repeatedly alleged that the PKK was being armed, trained, financed and supplied by Iraq's Kurds.[5] Ankara accused Washington of turning a blind eye to the alleged collusion of Iraq's Kurdish parties with PKK activities against Turkey. Ankara wanted Erbil, Baghdad and Washington to combat the PKK in northern Iraq in Ankara's stead. Throughout this period, in both its rhetoric and its military preparations, Ankara kept alive the prospect of a Turkish invasion of northern Iraq to take on PKK forces there. The December 2006 report of the Iraq Study Group, co-chaired by former US secretary of state James Baker and former congressman Lee Hamilton, offered just one high-profile warning of this possibility (Iraq Study Group 2007).

In due course, this frustration led to an October 2007 TGNA vote, by 507 to nineteen, which authorized the Turkish government to order cross-border military operations. This forced Washington's hand, and in November 2007 the USA gave the green light to intensified Turkish military steps against the PKK, including a ground incursion across the border into northern Iraq. US president Bush referred to the PKK as 'a common enemy' of both the USA and Turkey, and an agreement was made for the USA to provide Turkey with 'actionable intelligence' on PKK movements and bases in northern Iraq and indeed in south-eastern Turkey. This has apparently included information provided by unmanned aerial vehicles (UAVs), or 'drones', reconnaissance aircraft, satellite imagery and human intelligence. In December 2007, Turkish F-16s began a bombing campaign deep into northern Iraqi territory, accompanied by limited cross-border commando raids. This was followed in February 2008 by an eight-day ground troop incursion consisting of around 1400 helicopter-borne commandos penetrating up to fifteen kilometres inside Iraq (Jenkins 2008c). Bombing raids and limited ground incursions into the KRG zone have continued ever since. So, too, have PKK attacks inside Turkey.

Turkey and the KRG

In the words of one Turkish observer, 'in Turkish security perceptions, there is no real separation between northern Iraq and south eastern Turkey: they are the geographic and ethnocultural extension of each other' (Candar 2004: 53). Put another way, 'Turkey's approach towards the Kurds of Iraq [...]

demonstrates that the traditional frontiers between foreign and domestic policy realms have gradually become blurred' (Oguzlu 2008b: 5). Iraq's future, and especially that of its Kurds, is regarded by Turks as constituting a deep-seated and core security interest. Turkey's security and territorial integrity, its domestic social and political harmony, its economic well being, and its regional and global diplomatic relationships are all regarded as at risk from Iraqi developments (Gunter 2004; Park 2005; Lundgren 2007). In particular, Ankara has worried that the emergence of an autonomous Kurdish state in northern Iraq might serve as a pole of attraction for Turkey's restive Kurds, or that it might become emboldened enough to lend them direct support. It could garner international sympathy for the idea of wider Kurdish national self-determination, which could threaten to unravel the entire region by challenging existing borders and by potentially pitting local states against each other in a struggle for influence and control.

Turkey's approach to the Kurdish issue, at least until recently, also has to be appreciated in the context of the 'Sèvres complex', whereby 'many Turks genuinely believe conspiracy theories in which the US and the EU are trying to weaken Turkey both through partition (e.g. the creation of a Kurdish state) and through instigating sufficient domestic political turmoil to ensure that the country remains weak' (Jenkins 2001: 17). Since the 2003 invasion of Iraq, the suspicion that Washington was seeking to establish an independent Kurdish state in northern Iraq became commonplace in Turkey. To be sure, the 1920 draft Treaty of Sèvres did make allowance for a Kurdish state to be carved out of Ottoman territory should the inhabitants want it. However, the British attached Mosul province to their Baghdad and Basra protectorates, not least because of the presence of oil around Kirkuk.

Ankara, on the other hand, was determined that Mosul province should become part of Turkey, in accordance with the National Pact. In a speech in 1920, Ataturk asserted that 'our national borders [...] leads [sic] to the east and comprises Mosul, Suleymaniya and Kirkuk. In fact, in the north of Kirkuk there are Turks as well as Kurds. We do not differentiate them' (Koker 2010: 55). The issue was left to an investigation by a League of Nations International Commission of Inquiry, which in 1925 awarded Mosul to Iraq. Turkey protested, but the judgement was deemed binding, and, in June 1926, Turkey and Britain signed a bilateral treaty recognizing the outcome. Iraq became independent in 1931. From time to time, Turkey's grievance at the loss of Mosul resurfaces. Thus, in 1986, Ankara apparently warned the USA and Iran that it would demand the return of Mosul and Kirkuk (in effect, the former Ottoman viliyet of Mosul) in the event of disorder in Iraq as a consequence of the Iran–Iraq war (Rabil 2002: 6). During the 1990–91 US-led war against Iraq, president Turgut Ozal had similarly mused about historic Turkish claims to the region in the event of an Iraqi collapse (Hale 1992: 691). He went on to propose that Turkey should encourage northern Iraq's economic dependency on Turkey (Robins 2003: 321–22). In May 1995, Turkish president Suleyman Demirel proposed that the border should be rectified in Turkey's favour (Pipes 1995), and in December 2003 he expressed regret that Turkey had been denied Mosul in 1923.[6] In August 2002, the far-right MHP defence minister Sabahattin Cakmakoglu remarked that Iraqi Kurdistan had been 'forcibly separated' from Turkey at the time of the republic's foundation in 1923, and that Ankara retained a protective interest in the region (Gorvett 2002: 11; Pope 2002: 11). As US-led military action against Iraq approached, Yasar Yakis, the new AKP government's foreign minister, apparently sought legal clarification of the status of Mosul and Kirkuk (Pope 2003: 14–15), whilst one of Turkey's leading commentators pointed out that Mosul and Kirkuk were ceded to Iraq, not to any Kurdish state that might subsequently emerge (Aktan 2002).

Since Saddam's overthrow, the two leading Kurdish parties of northern Iraq, the Kurdish Democratic Party (KDP) and the Patriotic Union of Kurdistan (PUK), have enjoyed *de facto* control of Kurdish-populated areas beyond the KRG zone, but to which they lay claim, such as much of Kirkuk province (Tamim) and around Mosul (International Crisis Group 2007b). Iraq's Kurds have gradually extended their control over the Kirkuk city and regional administration, including its police force and education system (International Crisis Group 2004a: 11). Kirkuk has been earmarked as the future capital of Iraqi Kurdistan, notwithstanding the Arab, Turkmen and Assyrian communities that also reside there. PUK leader Jalal Talabani has described Kirkuk as 'the Jerusalem of Kurdistan'.[7] KDP head Massoud Barzani has appeared still more obdurate on the Kirkuk issue. This claim on the city has been reinforced by the return of Kurdish refugees who had been forced out by successive 'Arabization' programmes that commenced in the 1960s (Human Rights Watch 2004). However, in addition to the forced 'Arabization' policy, the impact of the oil industry also did much to alter Kirkuk's traditional demographic make-up. Kirkuk's last census, held in 1957, had determined that the population was forty per cent Turkmen and thirty-five per cent Kurdish. Although most neutral observers now concede that the Kurds are numerically ascendant in the province, it is hardly surprising that demographic squabbles and ethnic tensions simmer (Anderson and Stansfield 2009). Turkmen as well as Kurds have sought to return to their former homes, threatening the displacement of long-resident Arabs.

Indeed, Ankara sought to deploy the Turkic card as a means to undermine the Kurdish claim to Kirkuk by insisting that Kirkuk's multiethnicity precluded an exclusively Kurdish claim to the city. Ankara's sponsorship of the Iraqi Turkmen Front (ITF), reportedly a creation of Turkey's security services in 1995 (Oguzlu 2002; International Crisis Group 2005: 9–11), caused irritation to Turkey's relations with the Iraqi Kurds, the USA and even many of Iraq's Turkmen. It appears that Turkish security forces were present in the Turkmen areas of northern Iraq since the early 1990s, and in 2001 began training and arming Turkmen fighters (Bodansky 2004: 30–31). ITF figures have been a regular presence in the corridors of power in Ankara, and Ankara and the ITF repeatedly exaggerated the size of the Turkmen population.

To Ankara's chagrin, however, Iraqi Turkmen exhibited little political unity either before or since Saddam's overthrow, partly as a consequence of their geographical dispersal around the country and high degree of urbanization, partly as a reflection of their relatively high degree of integration into Iraqi society generally, but also because around sixty per cent of Iraqi Turkmen are Shia and have politically identified themselves as such.

The KRG has emerged as a fully self-governing entity inside a federal Iraq (O'Leary *et al.* 2005; Gunter 2007; Yildiz 2007). The laws, language and security forces of Erbil take precedence over those of Baghdad. Chiefly as a consequence of Kurdish insistence, the constitutional and formal political arrangements currently in place envisage a federal Iraq, and there is little that the rest of Iraq can do about it. The formal status of Kirkuk remains unresolved, notwithstanding the much delayed (largely by the Kurds) passage of a new Iraqi electoral law in November 2009. The Kurds have also been instrumental in blocking the passage of an Iraqi oil law. Instead, they have passed their own oil law and entered into extraction and export arrangements with external oil companies. The KRG economy booms, while that of most of the rest of Iraq stagnates. Baghdad continues to struggle to form an effective government, while in contrast the leading Iraqi Kurdish parties have thus far managed to sustain their alliance and their grip on power.

Regionalization of the Kurdish issue

Concerns over developments in northern Iraq offered Turkey's AKP government an incentive to take the diplomatic lead in its immediate region. As US action against Iraq loomed, Turkey's new government began exploring the scope for a regional initiative aimed at avoiding war, or at least minimizing the regional fallout. To this end, foreign minister Gul embarked on a tour of Middle Eastern capitals in January 2003 and secured agreement for a summit to be held in Istanbul later that month, attended by Egypt, Syria, Jordan, Saudi Arabia and Iran. Ankara used the opportunity to explain its perspective on the Kurdish issue. In fact, each of these states shared Turkey's nervousness about Kurdish aspirations, Iraq's territorial integrity and the prospect of regional turmoil. Subsequent gatherings were held in Riyadh, Tehran, Damascus, Kuwait and Cairo. This loose regional alliance was subsequently incorporated into a UN Advisory Group by the UN secretary general, and has since become known as the Platform for Iraqi Neighbours. In November 2004, an enlarged meeting was held in Sharm al-Sheikh, Egypt, and included senior diplomats and foreign ministers from G8 states, senior representatives from the UN, EU, the Arab League and the OIC, and foreign ministers from other local states. With the advent of the interim Iraqi government, Iraq was brought into this round of meetings. In addition, in November 2004 an interior ministers' meeting aimed at improving security cooperation with respect to Iraq was held in Tehran at the Iranian government's suggestion.

Although some of the Arab states involved in this multilateral diplomacy continue to distrust Tehran's intentions, and suspect it of seeking to ensure a pro-Tehran and Shia regime in Iraq, around a dozen meetings of the Platform have now been held at foreign-minister level. Ankara has also cultivated the main political players inside Iraq. It befriended the country's Shia politicians, persuaded the Sunni leaderships of the wisdom of participating in the 2005 elections, and also mediated between Iraq's Sunni leaderships and the USA (Aras 2009a: 39–40). Ankara's objectives have been to maximize the prospect of a territorially intact, politically viable and stable Iraq emerging, to minimize external sponsorship of terrorism and factionalism inside Iraq and to gain sympathy for Turkey's concerns about Kurdish aspirations. In the process, it has provided a counter to Iranian influence in Iraq, won Baghdad's confidence and softened the tension between Washington and Damascus.

Ankara has been particularly keen to align its position on Iraq with those of Iran and Syria, and cultivated them intensively in the wake of Saddam's removal and with the tightening Iraqi Kurdish grip on northern Iraq. Bilateral declarations in support of Iraq's territorial integrity and against the Kurdish preference for an ethnically based Iraqi federation, border coopera-tion, agreements on the training of Iraqi security forces and government officials, and cooperation on dealing with Kurdish terrorist activities, have been just some of the fruits of this diplomacy. Furthermore, a series of inci-dents in March 2004 served as a reminder of the transborder dimensions of the Kurdish question. In Syria, Kurds constitute around nine per cent of the population, of whom tens of thousands are denied citizenship altogether. The Kurdish language is banned and place names have been 'Arabized'. On 11 March, a football match in the Kurdish town of Qameshli sparked riots and demonstrations that spread rapidly to other parts of Kurdish Syria and to Syria's cities. Security forces violently broke up an attempt to commemorate the gassing of Kurds at Halabja in Iraq. Within less than a week, clashes had resulted in at least twenty-five deaths and hundreds of Kurds injured or detained.[8] More or less simultaneously, large-scale demonstrations were held in several Iranian towns by Kurds celebrating the signing of Iraq's interim federal constitution. Discrimination against Kurds, who make up around fifteen per cent of the population, is more informal in Iran than elsewhere, and is as much aimed at their Sunni faith as at their Kurdish ethnicity, but Kurdish identity politics remains a concern to the Tehran authorities never-theless. Kurdish disaffection remains part of the political landscape of Syria and Iran, too.

The Kurdish issue had long been a thorn in the side of Turkey's relations with Syria. Although Damascus has always maintained a watchful eye on its own Kurdish minority, its readiness to offer a sanctuary and training facilities to the PKK as a lever against Ankara added substantially to the frostiness in Turkish–Syrian relations (Muslih 1996). Relations between Ankara and Damascus gradually improved in the wake of President Assad's expulsion of Abdullah Ocalan in 1998, but since March 2003 they have warmed markedly, embracing frequent official visits that have resulted in economic and cultural as well as political and diplomatic initiatives. President Bashar al-Assad's visit to Turkey in January 2004, during which he proclaimed that 'we have moved together from an atmosphere of distrust to trust' (Cagaptay 2004), was the first ever visit to Turkey by a Syrian head of state. Assad, coincidentally in Ankara again during the October 2007 crisis, expressed his support in the strongest terms for Turkey's right to conduct military operations in northern Iraq.[9] It is evident, too, that the two countries cooperate closely in Syrian attacks against Kurdish rebels inside Syria.[10]

Notwithstanding the sometimes cool, if proper, relationship between Ankara and Tehran (Eralp 1996; Cetinsaya 2003), four high-level exchanges took place during 2003, largely as a consequence of Ankara's overtures. Security issues relating to northern Iraq and the PKK provided much of the impetus behind these meetings and their content, although the wider problems of Iraq and economic relations also featured. Contacts have since intensified, and during foreign minister Gul's visit to Tehran in January 2004, the Iranian president Muhammad Khatami declared that 'Turkey's security is our own security' and that 'Turkey's enemies, terrorist groups or others, cannot harm Turkey by using Iranian territory'.[11] Prime minister Erdogan's visit to Tehran in July 2004 coincided with Iran's designation of the PKK as a proscribed terrorist organization. Subsequently, Turkish and Iranian security forces have cooperated especially closely in northern Iraq, and at the eleventh meeting of their High Security Commission in February 2006, the two neighbours renewed their counter-terrorism security pact aimed at the PKK in northern Iraq, even as the tension over Iran's weapons of mass destruction (WMD) programme was intensifying.[12] They exchange intelligence, extradite captives, support each other's fight against both internal and external Kurdish activism and have even conducted coordinated shelling of bases in northern Iraq. In the Iranian case, this has been directed towards the so-called Party of Life and Freedom (PJAK), often regarded as an Iranian Kurdish offshoot of the PKK.

Widening the reach of Turkey's diplomacy with respect to Iraq still further, at the OIC summit in Malaysia in October 2003, foreign minister Gul called for a peacekeeping force for Iraq drawn from the Islamic world. This initiative might also have been motivated in part as an attempt to deflect criticism of Turkey's offer to send 10,000 troops into Iraq, an offer subsequently withdrawn in the face of opposition from Iraq's Governing Council and particularly its Kurdish members. In fact, Turkey's suggestion received a cool response at the summit, with the Jordanian delegation arguing that parochial agendas and interests should disqualify Iraq's neighbours from participating in any peacekeeping force in Iraq. A majority of delegations took the view that an Islamic peacekeeping force for Iraq could only be put together under UN auspices.[13] Despite this apparent failure, Ankara's efforts nevertheless offer testimony to its determination to align its security considerations with those of its wider region, and indeed to 'regionalize' the Kurdish issue as an alternative to American domination of it. As one author has expressed it, 'Turkish peace building in the periphery challenges the notion that only those at the top of the power echelon of [the] international system may facilitate peace in different parts of the globe' (Aras 2009a: 41). Given the centrality of the Kurdish question to Turkey's own well being, it is not surprising that this issue has generated such an energetic approach from Ankara. It also demonstrates how a confluence of external developments and internal shifts has nudged Ankara away from its inclination to nationalize its approach to a problem that has increasingly become a regional and global issue.

The global Kurdish network

Turkey's ethnically Kurdish south-eastern region is also its poorest, and from the 1950s onwards migration from the countryside to the region's cities such as Diyarbakir and Mardin, and to those of western Turkey, has been substantial. With the intensification of violence in the region during the 1980s, Kurdish migration increased still further. Although no exact figures are available, it is probable that a majority of Turkey's Kurds no longer live in the south-east. Istanbul holds the world's biggest concentration of Kurds. However, from the 1960s onwards, many Kurds also joined the economic migration of mostly poor rural Turkish citizens to the countries of western Europe. Again, with the 1980 coup in Turkey and the intensification of the violence in the south-east, a more politicized breed of Kurdish asylum seeker began to arrive in Europe and indeed further afield – for example, north America and Australasia. Thus there is today a substantial global Kurdish diaspora. The biggest overseas community of Turkish Kurds is in Germany, where there are today reckoned to be up to three-quarters of a million ethnic Kurds, 150,000 of whom are naturalized (Ostergaard-Nielson 2003: 79). Given the intense links that have been maintained between Kurdish communities and activists in Europe and elsewhere, and their counterparts in the homeland, it might be better to think in terms of 'networks' rather than diasporas (Allievi 2003: 11–12).

Kurdish economic migrants to Europe relatively rarely express their ethnicity in highly politicized forms. However, there is a more active inner core of Kurdish lobbyists, consisting to a large degree of those who arrived as political refugees. As just one indication of this activism, in Norway – where Kurds constitute just twenty per cent of the Turkish community[14] but where, as elsewhere in Scandinavia, political refugees have been favourably regarded – there were in 2007 thirty Norwegian government-funded Kurdish organizations as against just fifteen comparable ethnically Turkish groups (Rogstad 2009: 286). This is the kind of detail that arouses Turkish suspicion of European sympathy for Kurdish separatism. Kurdish activists have been able to exploit the space afforded them by Europe's liberal regimes to organize, campaign, fundraise and broadcast. Indeed, it has been observed that 'the Kurdistan on the ground has been supplemented with a Kurdistan of the airwaves and in cyberspace, and much of the Kurdish nationalist struggle is going on in the latter' (van Bruinessen 1999).

Given the proscriptions against Kurdish identity politics in Turkey, it seems reasonable to surmise that the Kurdish 'flame' has been kept alive and has perhaps burnt more brightly still in Turkey, at least in part as a result of the activities of Kurds in Europe. The Kurdish Institute of Paris,[15] established in 1983 with the support of the then French president François Mitterrand and his wife, did much to establish a standard northern Kurdish that could be written down and disseminated. Similar institutes were established in other European and north American cities. The activities of Kurdish intellectuals such as those associated with the Kurdish Institute led to the publication of books and journals in Kurdish, many of which were smuggled into Turkey, where Kurdish language publications have been banned or are otherwise unattainable. Kurdish language courses, and sometimes Kurdish language teaching in schools, are offered in various west European locations (van Bruinessen 1999). In contrast, Kurdish language courses remained banned in Turkey until very recently, and Kurdish language school lessons remain prohibited.

Kurdish organizations in the USA, such as the American Kurdish Information Network,[16] appear to have had relatively little political impact in the host country. This may be partly a result of Washington's reluctance to put at risk its strategic relationship with Ankara, partly because of the smaller number of Kurds in the USA, and partly because the issue of Kurdish human rights does not have the immediacy in the USA that Turkey's EU aspirations give it in Europe. The impact of Kurdish lobbying in Europe has surely been augmented by Ankara's bid for EU membership, which has led to a still closer European scrutiny of Turkey's democratization and its human and minority rights record. Campaigns conducted in Europe by and on behalf of Kurds have tapped into these preoccupations (Ostergaard-Nielson 2003: 30). Kurdish groups in Europe have lobbied host-country NGOs, political parties, national parliaments and the media (Ostergaard-Nielson 2003: 80–83). They have often called for Europe's governments to adopt tough stances towards Ankara, with respect to EU accession or arms sales, for example (Ostergaard-Nielson 2003: 98). On the other hand, the Kurdish diaspora, and other marginalized Turkish groups with offshoots in Europe, frequently recognize that Turkey's eventual accession to the EU offers the surest means to achieve and protect the minority and human rights of their kinfolk in the homeland. Accession might also enhance their status as 'Europeans' in their adopted countries (Ostergaard-Nielson 2003: 125).

Although it is difficult to assess the overall impact of Europe's Kurdish lobbies and identity organizations on Turkey–European relations, it seems safe to assume both that it has been considerable, and that it has generally been to the detriment of Ankara's case. On the one hand, Turkey's EU aspirations have obliged Ankara to respond to the pressures it has been put under regarding Kurdish human and minority rights. Turkey has been more sensitive to criticisms emanating from European human rights organizations or government institutions than it has to Kurdish groups, so much so that Kurdish political parties inside Turkey have not always wanted to publicize their links with Europe's Kurdish networks and have preferred direct European support and sympathy (Ostergaard-Nielson 2003: 121). On the other hand, Ankara's perception of the homeland political allegiances of Kurds in Germany and elsewhere has frequently been at odds with European perceptions. Whereas Europeans have regarded the Kurdish plight as primarily a human and minority rights issue, Turkey has regarded these groups as associated with terrorism and as a threat to Turkey's domestic harmony and territorial integrity. Europe's tolerance of dissident activities has fed the Turkish paranoia that even its closest allies wish to weaken and dismantle the country *à la* Sèvres. Furthermore, the inclination in Turkey to regard the Kurdish problem as essentially a PKK terrorist problem has intensified Turkish anger with the indulgence shown to Kurds by EU governments and societies. Particularly in the aftermath of 9/11, Turkish officials became fond of drawing attention to their unsuccessful past endeavours to put terrorism on NATO's and the West's agenda. For the Turks, the terrorist problem has long been largely synonymous with their Kurdish problem. Overall, then, the Kurdish issue and the way it has played out within the EU have tended to underscore the mismatch between European and Turkish political culture, values and circumstances. It has also demonstrated that 'the mass migration of Kurds from their traditional habitat has resulted in the internationalization and the deterritorialization of the Kurdish question' (van Bruinessen 1999).

Of course, the PKK has been behind a great deal of Kurdish political lobbying in Europe. On this matter, EU and Turkish perceptions have moved gradually towards a closer alignment over the years. The PKK apparently despatched organizers to Europe even before Turkey's 1980 coup (van Bruinessen 1999). It was the chief mover behind the 1995 establishment in The Hague of the so-called 'Kurdistan Parliament in Exile', although the project was supported by a variety of organizations representing Turkey's Kurdish community in Europe. It was constituted under the leadership of Yasar Kaya, who had been chairman of the pro-Kurdish Democratic Labour Party (Demokratik Emek Partisi – DEP) in Turkey until its closure by the authorities in 1994. A number of other DEP politicians participated in the project (Kutschera 1995; Ibrahim and Gurbey 2000: 84–85). It later moved to Brussels, and met in a variety of European cities such as Vienna, Copenhagen, Rome, Oslo and Moscow, often hosted by regional or national parliaments or political parties. Internal tensions, and the new political situation in the wake of PKK leader Abdullah Ocalan's capture, led the 'parliament' to close itself down in 1999. In the meantime, the 'parliament's' PKK link, and the political sympathy it received, had unsurprisingly generated considerable diplomatic tension between Ankara and various European governments. Following a series of raids in Turkish cities in April 2009, which netted more than fifty suspects, including leading figures in the Democratic Security Party (DTP, successor to the banned DEP), a trial of former 'parliament in exile' figures was opened. The suspects were also indicted for membership of the PKK.[17]

The satellite television station MED-TV also appears to have been initiated by the PKK, although its output was more pluralistic than this might suggest. Licensed by the British Independent Television Commission in 1995 but broadcasting from Brussels, it could be received throughout western Europe and the Middle East, while video cassettes of its programmes enjoyed wide currency in Kurdish communities everywhere (van Bruinessen 1999). However, its licence was suspended in 1999 by its British monitors on the grounds that some of its broadcasts had incited violence. After re-establishing itself in France for a while, it was replaced in 2004 by ROJ-TV,[18] which broadcasts from Denmark – although it has been banned in Germany since 2008. The station contributed to tension in Turkish–Danish relations when, in 2005, prime minister Tayyip Erdogan cancelled a press conference during a visit to Denmark when his request that a ROJ-TV journalist be removed from the studio was rejected. The station was also a factor in Turkey's opposition to the appointment of the former Danish prime minister Fogh Rasmussen to the post of NATO secretary general.[19] Satellite TV stations such as ROJ-TV offer a good example of how technology can deterritorialize an issue and weaken the control that state authorities can exercise.

To counter these irritations, Turkey has used the various mechanisms open to it, such as NATO, EU and Council of Europe meetings, as well as bilateral lobbying to persuade host countries to control Kurdish and other dissident groups, especially those alleged to be 'fronts' for the PKK. Ankara has also directly intervened in host countries by, for example, financing and otherwise encouraging Kemalist and nationalist Turks to counter the activities and influence of Kurdish groups. State-run cable TV stations, such as TRT-INT, as well as private pro-Kemalist media outlets such as *Hurriyet*, have propagated the official political line to Turks abroad and encouraged campaigns against Turkey's critics. It is widely recognized that Turkey's intelligence agency, the *Milli Istibarat Teskilati* (MIT – National Intelligence Organization), has put dissident Kurds in Europe under surveillance. Kurds and other dissidents paying visits to Turkey are frequently detained for questioning and even arrested on the basis of their activities in their countries of residence. Indeed, in 1990, Germany expelled fifteen Turkish diplomats as a protest against such practices (Ostergaard-Nielson 2003: 114–18).

In fact, and notwithstanding intense pressure from Ankara over many years, the EU did not finally take the decision to ban the PKK until May 2002 – although Germany had banned it as early as 1993 – in the wake of the 9/11 attacks. European governments have since been much more diligent in closing down PKK front organizations, although many are still assumed to operate (Cagaptay and Fikret 2005). In any case, organizations generally regarded as legitimate, such as the Kurdish Human Rights Project[20] established in London in 1992, continue to draw attention to Turkey's human and minority rights violations against Kurdish individuals, communities and political organizations inside Turkey, and indeed throughout the Kurdish-inhabited regions of the Middle East.

Although Europe's governments remain torn between their desire for good relationships with Ankara on the one hand and their tolerance of, and sometimes sympathy for, the Kurds on the other, Kurdish groups in Europe have generally become less inclined to adopt confrontational tactics through a recognition of the deleterious impact this can have on European attitudes to the Kurdish cause. Ocalan's arrest in 1999 resulted in violent demonstrations in Germany, in which twenty-seven police officers were injured and hundreds of demonstrators were detained. This culminated in the shooting of three Kurds who stormed the Israeli consulate in Germany because of a suspicion of Israel's complicity in Ocalan's capture (Ostergaard-Nielson 2003: 72). There were similarly violent disorders throughout Europe. Such incidents did not help the Kurdish cause in Europe. Neither did the intermittent attacks on Turkish diplomats, banks and businesses located in Europe, or the occasional street clashes that have pitted Kurdish and leftist groups against their Turkish nationalist counterparts. On the other hand, it was widely suspected that the German authorities failed to execute their international arrest warrant on Ocalan when he was held in Rome for fear of Kurdish unrest on the streets of Germany (Ostergaard-Nielson 2003: 99); this in turn incurred Ankara's wrath.

Overall, the tendency for Turkey's political and social struggles to be played out in European cities has not been welcomed either in Europe or in Turkey. Nor has it invariably created a favourable impression of Turkey or its people – Turks and Kurds. The migration, asylum and integration issues that have been associated with Turkish immigration into Europe have introduced tensions between Europe's peoples and Turkey's, as well as into the relationships between Europe's capitals and Ankara. Although the complete picture is far from an entirely negative one, these experiences suggest that caution is advised when assessing the impact of transnational and globalizing processes and patterns. Interdependence can lead to discomfort and tension, contrasting value systems can be put into starker relief, and communities can draw in upon themselves as a reaction to the presence of others. Whether Turkish migration to Europe has improved Turkey's EU prospects, 'Europeanized' Turkish society and politics, or encouraged Europeans to embrace Turkey's 'Europeanness', are at best open questions. The Kurdish presence in Europe may equally have helped to destabilize Turkey, and highlighted the perceived 'non-European' character of its peoples and politics. Either way, Kurdish migration to Europe and elsewhere has undoubtedly contributed to the globalization of the Kurdish question and had an impact on Turkey's European relationships.

Turkey's Kurdish 'opening'

Alternative perspectives on Turkey's domestic Kurdish question have been dimly in evidence as far back as the Ozal era. In 1991 Ozal, who made public his own partly Kurdish origins, lifted the ban on the Kurdish language in everyday speech and in recordings. In 2001, former prime minister Mesut Yilmaz identified the country's 'national security syndrome' as a block on Turkey's democratization and, by implication, its capacity to address the Kurdish question from a political rather than a security perspective. His comments, for which he was vilified, came in the wake of the EU's 1999 Helsinki summit recognizing Turkey's candidature. However, until the EU accession process acquired more energy in the wake of the Helsinki decision, the overall picture was that Turkey's political class had generally remained inert with respect to the Kurdish issue, silenced by the securitizing perspective of the security elites that dominated the issue (Cizre 2009). In the context of the EU accession process, an alternative and less exclusively securitized perspective on the Kurdish question began to gain traction. Thus, the 2002 harmonization reform package lifted the bans on Kurdish place and personal names, and on Kurdish language lessons and broadcasting, although in practice the reforms were limited in scope and have been only partially implemented. In November 2002, the state of emergency was lifted in the two remaining south-eastern provinces that were still governed by it.

The AKP was from the outset more confident that a political approach to the question could pay dividends. Thus, in its approach to the 2002 election, the AKP appeared to believe that it could ameliorate the alienation of Turkey's Kurds by stressing the Islamic ties they shared with Turks (Yavuz and Ozcan 2006). In 2005, prime minister Erdogan acknowledged that 'the state has made mistakes about the Kurdish issue', and went on to promise substantial economic investment in the south-east. The AKP was further encouraged by its 2007 electoral success in south-eastern Turkey, where it outpolled the Kurdish DTP and won fifty parliamentary seats, although it was later chastened by the DTP's success in clawing back the Kurdish vote in the local elections of 2009. During the summer of 2009, the government announced its intention to resolve the Kurdish question by a somewhat vaguely enunciated but more democratic and progressive approach to the problem.[21] Prime minister Erdogan's televised 'Address to the Nation' of 28 August 2009 was perhaps the closest the government came to actually enunciating the approach the initiative would adopt. It was sorely lacking in specifics.[22] Variously known as the 'Kurdish opening', the 'democratic opening' and the 'national unity project', it was described by observers as an 'enigma' (Candar 2009a) and as a 'deliberative process' (Hasimi 2009), rather than a specific package of measures. It seemed to envisage a limited amnesty for some Turkish Kurds based in northern Iraq, discussions with the DTP leadership, an attempt at consultation with opposition; there were political parties, journalists, civil society organizations and the like, promises of more economic aid to the south east, an increase in the authority of local councils, an extension of minority rights, enlargement of Kurdish language rights and an improved implementation of existing measures to relax the restrictions, and legal and constitutional changes that would make the banning of political parties more difficult (Bozkurt 2009a, 2009b).[23] It also incorporated a closer embrace of the KRG, and a continuing of the military campaign against the PKK – unsurprisingly, given the increased frequency of PKK attacks during this period.

Predictably, the initiative was met by predominantly negative reactions from Turkey's more Kemalist quarters. The nationalist MHP refused the government's offers of consultation, insisting that the opening was an act of treachery that implied a victory for the PKK and that would lead to the eventual break-up of the country (Celep 2010). The CHP was only slightly more muted in its reaction (Keyman 2010). The TSK declared that it would not countenance a federal arrangement for Turkey, opposed overtures towards the PKK, insisted on the country's essential 'Turkishness', and held to its view that Turkey's elected Kurdish politicians in the form of the DTP MPs were ruled out of the process on the grounds that they remained too closely linked to the PKK.[24] The DTP's response was somewhat surly and unhelpful to the government, not least in its suggestion that Ocalan should be included in the process (Cakir 2010). In any case, the constitutional court's banning of the DTP in December 2009 hardly lent support to the initiative. PKK attacks on soldiers increased during the autumn of 2009 and into early 2010, which predictably served to generate more opposition to the initiative and added to intercommunal tensions. After a particularly bloody exchange close to Iraq's border in June 2010, in which eleven Turkish soldiers and twelve PKK fighters were killed, Erdogan himself was moved to assert that PKK militants 'would drown in their own blood' if they continued to resort to violence.[25] The ecstatic welcome given by a large crowd in the Kurdish city of Diyarbakir in October 2009 to thirty-four PKK sympathizers who had been allowed to return to Turkey further inflamed nationalist Turkish senti-ment and angered the government.[26] In any case, some of the returnees were later arrested for their alleged PKK affiliation. Although the government had not yet given up on the initiative, and although it had been commended in Europe and the USA, at the time of writing it appeared to have been rele-gated to the government's backburner. Given the fate of the initiative, there is some credence to the observation that 'Turkey swings between forces, agendas and actors of securitization and desecuritization when it comes to the Kurdish issue' (Polat 2008: 85), and that it will continue to do so.

Ankara's opening to the KRG

Alongside Ankara's initiative towards its domestic Kurdish problem, the AKP government also engineered a shift in Turkey's approach to northern Iraq. Indeed, they are twin initiatives, as they both reflect Ankara's belated realization that the cooperation of the KRG is key in the fight against the PKK. The November 2007 agreement between Washington and Ankara, which indicated US support for Turkish military incursions into northern Iraq, was recognized in Erbil as a blow to Washington's tendency to put its relationship with Ankara at risk by indulging the KRG. Thus the Iraqi Kurdish leadership, too, saw the need to grasp the nettle of its relationship with Ankara. So, in May 2008, and in stark contrast to Turkey's position hitherto of refusing to deal directly with the KRG, Erdogan's then advisor Ahmet Davutoglu met with KRG prime minister Nechirvan Barzani (Idiz 2008). Davutoglu was accompanied by Murat Ozcelik, Turkey's special envoy on Iraq, who had been instrumental in preparing the ground for the meeting. Barzani expressed the KRG's sympathy with the Turkish position that northern Iraq should not be used as a PKK base for attacks into Turkey, and promised an intensification of its efforts to thwart the PKK's activities there,[27] although Erbil continued to resist Ankara's demand that it adopt military measures against the PKK. Barzani also softened the KRG's position on its claim to Kirkuk by countenancing a power-sharing arrangement for the city and its environs, and by agreeing to seriously consider UN proposals that were being drawn up for disputed areas of northern Iraq,[28] although there are few signs that Iraq's Kurds are prepared to forego their claim to the city. For its part, Ankara reduced its support for the ITF (Barkey 2010: 3). In October 2009, foreign minister Davutoglu paid a visit to KRG president Massoud Barzani in Erbil (Zebari 2009), while in June 2010 Barzani returned the compliment with an official visit to Ankara, where he met with both Davutoglu and Erdogan (Kucukkosum 2010a). Ankara also decided to open a consulate in Erbil, as did the USA soon afterwards.

Northern Iraq had already emerged as a major market for Turkish goods and construction companies, and Ankara's embrace of Erbil encouraged this lucrative trade relationship still further. Erbil's economic interaction with Turkey has served to increase economic well being on the Turkish side of the border, too. Around fifty per cent of Turkish trade with Iraq is with the Kurdish north (Barkey 2010: 12). Approximately eighty per cent of the goods sold in northern Iraq are made in Turkey, whose construction companies have built runways, universities, hospitals and schools, and whose manufacturing companies have established factories there (Phillips 2009). It is reckoned that around 50,000 Turkish citizens work in northern Iraq.[29] More importantly, in light of Turkey's energy needs, its aspiration to emerge as a regional energy hub and the KRG's reliance on energy exports, in 2009 Turkey began directly importing oil from northern Iraq. In the continued absence of an energy law agreement with Baghdad, both Erbil and Ankara also share an impatience to develop northern Iraq's gas fields in order that they can feed gas into the Nabucco pipeline.[30] Indeed, Erbil's need of Turkey as an outlet for its energy exports, and Turkey's energy needs and aspirations, constitute in themselves a rationale for the burgeoning relationship between them.

As with the approach to Turkey's domestic Kurdish question, however, Ankara's messages towards the KRG are mixed. Ankara, and the TSK in particular, continued to express its frustration that the KRG's cooperation with Turkey with respect to the PKK does not extend to military measures. The TSK continued to insist on the need for military incursions into northern

Iraq on a scale unlikely to meet with US approval and provocative to the KRG (Kucukkosum 2010b). In July 2010, Ankara requested that Baghdad, Erbil and Washington round up around 250 PKK leaders in northern Iraq and hand them over to the Turkish authorities.[31] Public opinion appeared to view the AKP's twin initiative on the Kurdish issue as indicative of an insufficiently robust approach to Kurdish terrorism (Harvey 2010). Nor was there any sign of a shift in Turkish perspectives with respect to the KRG claim on Kirkuk. In other words, the Ankara–Erbil relationship remained fragile, dependent on the turn of events in Iraq, on the level of PKK activity in Turkey, on the willingness of the KRG leadership to moderate its position on Kirkuk and on independence, and on the restraining impact of the USA. With the summer 2010 termination of the US combat mission in Iraq and the associated drawdown of US troops in the country, US influence might wane. Furthermore, Turkey's readiness to enter into a cooperative relationship with Erbil risks strengthening the KRG administration by awarding it a degree of legitimacy and by enhancing its economic well being. It remains uncertain that it is a risk that will pay off for Ankara, and Turkey might feel freer to act on its frustrations as the US military drawdown moves towards its end state.

Turkey and the Kurds: at the confluence of conflicting pressures

Does the 'Kurdish opening' represent a genuinely new departure in Ankara's approach to the issue? One perspective is to see it as evidence of the AKP's commitment to Turkey's further democratization, hence the normative framework in which the opening was presented. The AKP's approach can also be interpreted in the context of the EU's encouragement of Turkey's democratization process. The EU's role in nudging Turkey towards reducing the military's domestic political involvement, and the deleterious impact of the Ergenekon investigation on the military's prestige in Turkey, have enabled the AKP government to assert an unprecedented degree of political primacy over the country's Kurdish policy. The battle with the TSK is also an element in the AKP's longer-term struggle for political survival, as the military is not only the vanguard of the Turkish establishment's guardianship of the Kemalist legacy of secularism, but it also benefits politically from its role in combating Turkey's persisting problem of Kurdish terrorism. Furthermore, the AKP is in an electoral competition with the political representatives of Kurdish nationalism in Turkey's south-east, in which it hopes and assumes that the appeal of ethnic identity politics can be muted by a counter-emphasis on Islam as a unifying factor and by an improvement in the region's economic prospects. An additional enabling factor behind the AKP's Kurdish opening has been the party's domestic electoral popularity, which has enhanced its political confidence and freed it from the inhibiting effect of the exigencies of Turkey's more familiar coalition politics of the past. Foreign minister Davutoglu has also been a key player, particularly in engineering the embrace of the KRG. Turkey's new approach to Iraq has been of a piece with the 'strategic depth', 'zero problems', 'soft' power, regional engagement, and strongly mercantile elements of his regional foreign policy approach more generally. It remains an open question whether, and to what extent, this approach to Iraq will survive Davutoglu's exit from office, and that of the party he represents. The initially fiercely negative reaction of Turkey's opposition parties suggests otherwise.

However, other domestic and international factors have also played their part in encouraging Ankara. On the domestic front, 'the Kurdish question has been among the principal agenda items for civil society organizations in Turkey' (Kaliber and Tocci 2010: 191), which, as we have seen (in Chapter 4), have expanded substantially in number and activity since the 1980s. Although civil society in Turkey has both challenged the leading role of the state in setting the country's security and political agenda and 'has tended to work against the illiberal features of the Turkish state' (Kaliber and Tocci 2010: 196), with respect to the Kurdish issue in particular, numerous 'establishment' groups also lobby on the issue, such as the Association of Ataturkist Thought and the Ankara Association of Martyrs' Families. These groups have served to reinforce the state's traditional securitization of the Kurdish question. Thus, although the AKP government has been able to reflect and react to the greater societal engagement with the Kurdish issue, the counter-pressures from nationalist civil society elements have ensured 'a process of political change in Turkey's Kurdish question that has been anything but linear' (Kaliber and Tocci 2010: 213). Furthermore, the uncompromising and violent strand in Kurdish nationalism itself serves to reinforce the securitization of the issue in Turkey. From 1999, the Kurdish movement in Turkey supported Turkey's EU accession process because it appreciated the role it might play in the country's democratization and in the desecuritization of the state's approach to Kurdish identity. However, the EU's sympathy with the AKP, which preferred to emphasize Islam and economic development as the answer to the problem, and the EU's readiness to proscribe the PKK in Europe and condemn its return to violence in 2004, heralded a shift in opinion against the EU amongst the PKK's leadership (Uslu 2008b).

At the international level, Ankara also had to take into account Washington's unwillingness to countenance destabilization of the KRG by Turkey. After all, Iraq's Kurds have offered Washington a welcome Iraqi hand of friendship and have presided over the most stable part of the country. The Kurds, particularly in the persons of president Jalal Talabani and foreign minister Hoshyar Zebari, have also played a key role in the political evolution of post-Saddam Baghdad. Thus Washington has sought to restrain Ankara's reaction both to the presence of the PKK in northern Iraq and to the autonomy of the KRG. On the other hand, Washington relies on Turkey for access to the Incirlik base, through which US personnel and materials pass, and as an alternative to Iran as a source of regional influence in Iraq. Indeed, countering Iranian influence serves as a motivation for Ankara too. In addition to its cultivation of all of Iraq's functions, Turkish predominance in the

Kurdish north could help balance Tehran's primary influence in the Shia south. Turks and Iraqi Kurds share an unease about the prospect of a more militantly Shi'ite Iraq, or an implosion of the country. For these reasons, the US has sought to encourage a closer relationship between Ankara and Erbil. This will become a still more vital objective in the wake of the US departure. Washington wants to leave behind a more stable Iraq and a more stable region, while for their part the Iraqi Kurds recognize that Turkey offers them their best trade outlet and regional protector. Above all, however, Ankara needs to position itself for whatever a post-US Iraq will bring. It also needs to neutralize any negative influence that Erbil might exercise in Turkey's south-east. Indeed, Erbil is now prepared to criticize the PKK's continued use of violence in Turkey, and has expressed its support for the Turkish government's efforts to resolve the domestic Kurdish issue.[32]

It has also been argued that General Ilker Basbug, the TSK chief at the time the Kurdish policy approach shifted, tacitly supported the government's approach to the Kurdish question both domestically and in Iraq (Barkey 2010: 11). If so, this reflects a wider realization both that victory has been elusive in the twenty-five-year-long armed struggle against the PKK, and that the KRG has emerged as an established fact and that its cooperation is necessary if pacification of Turkey's south-east is to be achieved. Key Turkish foreign ministry and intelligence officials have also been instrumental in levering Ankara, and not least its security establishment, towards adopting a fresh approach to the KRG. Back-channel avenues of communication have remained operative, even when Turkish rhetoric against the KRG and official unwillingness to enter into dialogue with it have been at their most trenchant (Barkey 2010: 5–6, 12). However, Basbug's successors may not always be as accommodating – he was succeeded by General Isik Kosaner in August 2010 – and the good work of diligent officials can easily be undone by rash actions, destructive turns of events and changes in the political atmosphere. The most likely outcome is that there will not be an outcome or end state as such, but that Turkish approaches towards the Kurdish question will continue to reflect both the existential threat that the issue is regarded as posing to the country's domestic harmony and territorial integrity on the one hand, and the national, regional and international realities of the Kurdish question on the other. Turkey's Kurdish question, arguably the biggest single challenge facing the country, is neither a purely national issue nor is it a self-evidently resolvable one. Yet Turkey's domestic tranquillity, its regional status, and its EU and wider global aspirations are to a very considerable degree at its mercy.

7 A new foreign policy for a globalized age?

A selective historical context

Situating Turkey geopolitically has never been easy. It can be seen as both the only European country in the Middle East and as the only Middle Eastern country in Europe, and indeed as neither, as what used to be known in European diplomacy as 'the Near East' or 'Asia Minor' or today perhaps as part of 'Eurasia'. Geographically, culturally and politically, Turkey can be seen as part of, and even an actor in, many regions, including the Middle East, but as not central to any of them. Turkey's friendships in the world have sometimes appeared, in the words of a former US ambassador to Turkey, to 'not run deep' (Abramowitz 1993: xii). However, this 'aloneness' could be seen as a blessing. In theory if not in practice, Turkey has a degree of choice in selecting both the orientation of its foreign policy alignments and their depth. That Ankara has not always chosen to maximize its options can itself be seen as a choice. The Cold War was highly instrumental in pushing Turkey towards its western security orientation. It also cut Turkey off from much of its regional hinterland, in the Balkans, the Caucasus and Eurasia. However, Turkey's approach to those parts of its 'near abroad' with which it remained free to cement closer relationships, notably the Middle East and north Africa, was left undeveloped. In time, this apparent preference for regional isolationism might come to be regarded as a curiosity or aberration.

Since the inception of the republic, its foreign policy towards the Middle East in particular has been, at least in some measure, based on a 'constructed reality' which, in retrospect, may be regarded as having artificially restricted the dimensionality of Turkey's external relationships. As we have noted (in Chapter 2), the republic's elite regarded Islam as a barrier to modernity and as a source of ignorance and backwardness. Especially after 1945, they saw Europe both as Turkey's natural destiny and as its inspiration. Furthermore, the last years of the Ottoman empire gave rise to a perception that Arabs were disloyal, treacherous and best avoided. The Arab world's view of Turkey was equally negative and perhaps equally 'constructed'. Turks were seen as barbaric and brutal, as imperialistic, and in the republic's adoption of secularism and European-style modernity were regarded as having turned their backs on their Islamic and Middle Eastern heritage. In any case, much of the Middle East remained under British and French control during the interwar period. With independence, amnesia, constructed by Kemalists in Turkey and by nationalists in the Arab world, seemed to obliterate any residual sense of a shared Ottomanism (Jung 2005). Their respective interpretations of both the past and much of the present have appeared to divide more than unite them. Yet they do share a past, and it is largely a myth that it was a predominantly negative experience either for Turks or for Arabs (Nafi 2009).

The emergence of the Cold War provided a structural or systemic reinforcement of this Turkish aloofness towards much of its immediate neighbourhood. The perceived threat of Soviet ideological subversion and territorial aggrandizement pushed Ankara towards the West, and towards NATO and the USA in particular. Thus the Turkish elite's economic, cultural and political aspiration to westernize the country merged with the apparent geostrategic imperatives of the Cold War. Turkey became almost exclusively, even excessively, focused on its western alignments. Modern Arab identity wrapped itself in anti-colonial clothing, a psyche not shared by Turks. During the Cold War, much of the Arab world leaned towards the Soviet Union in light of its professed sympathy with anti-colonialism, in its regional and global challenge to US dominance, and for such support as it offered in the Arab struggle against Israel. Diplomatically and strategically, Turkey came to be seen as a US praetorian in the region, an image reinforced by Turkey's 1952 NATO accession, by the proliferation of NATO and US military and intelligence facilities in Turkey, by Turkey's participation in the Baghdad Pact/Central Treaty Organization (CENTO, incorporating the UK, Turkey, Iraq, Iran and Pakistan) during the 1950s, and by Turkey becoming the first primarily Muslim state to recognize Israel in 1949.

At the Cold War's end

As we have noted in earlier chapters, the end of the Cold War and the crisis in neighbouring Iraq offered unprecedented opportunities and incentives for Turkey to engage more actively with the states, peoples and institutions in the various regions which Turkey abuts. Turgut Ozal, first as prime minister and then as president, is closely associated with this 'new activism' in foreign policy (Makovsky 1999), but Ismael Cem's spell as foreign minister, from 1997 until 2002, also witnessed a freshness of approach in Turkey's diplomatic engagements. The lifting of the 'iron curtain' and the series of crises that occurred in its wake opened up former Ottoman domains in the Balkans, the Black Sea and the Caucasus regions to increased Turkish engagement. Ankara was similarly drawn towards a greater involvement in Azerbaijan and in central Asia, where Turks rediscovered their long-forgotten ethnic Turkic cousin, and began to imagine the emergence of a more unified Turkic world with Anatolia at its head. An interest in gaining access to the energy resources of the former Soviet south accompanied and overlapped with Turkey's wider political, economic and cultural interest in these newly exposed and nearby regions. Much of this interaction was benign, and emphasized confidence-building 'low politics' issues such as trade, transport, communications, environmental problems, diplomatic institutionalization and the like.

An early example of Turkey's adoption of a 'soft politics' approach to regional relationships came with the establishment of the Black Sea Economic Cooperation (BSEC)[1] at Ankara's initiative. Formed in 1992, BSEC now has twelve members with the accession of Serbia in 2004, which became one of six member states that do not have a Black Sea coastline. It is headquartered in Istanbul and aims to encourage cooperation in 'low politics' confidence-building areas such as transport, combating crime, tourism, environmental protection, and trade and economic development. Turkey also took the lead in establishing the Black Sea Naval Cooperation Task Group (BLACK-SEAFOR)[2] in 2001, along with Russia, Ukraine, Georgia, Bulgaria and Romania. It aims to contribute to security, stability and maritime cooperation in the area, and in 2004 Turkey initiated a Black Sea Harmony anti-terrorist operation, which has since been joined by Russia and Ukraine. The achievements that have resulted from these initiatives have been limited, largely owing to the tensions and rivalries that exist between member states, but they nevertheless offer early indications of a relatively unfamiliar 'soft' power, cooperative approach to security on Ankara's part.

In 2006, Greece vetoed Montenegro's accession to BSEC, ostensibly in retaliation for Turkey's vetoing of Cypriot membership. This is a reminder of the limited substantive progress that has been made in another area of cooperative diplomacy on Ankara's part, that of rapprochement with Greece (Anastasakis 2007; Onis 2008a). This had its genesis during Ismael Cem's period as Turkish foreign minister and has since survived changes of government in both countries. It was given impetus by the humanitarian and rescue assistance Greece offered in the wake of Turkey's devastating 1999 earthquake, and by the embarrassment in Greece following the arrest during the same year of PKK leader Abdullah Ocalan, who was captured leaving the Greek embassy in Kenya and was in possession of Greek and (Greek) Cypriot passports (Ker-Lindsay 2007). The atmosphere of Turkey's relationship with Greece is now conciliatory and nonconfrontational and is aimed at building confidence. Technically, Greece supports Turkey's EU membership bid, and both countries have reduced their direct involvement in the search for a Cyprus settlement. In 2002 they launched a bid to jointly host the 2008 European nations football tournament, and in 2005 established a hotline between their two air forces as a crisis management measure in the face of continued mutual allegations of, and tensions over, airspace violation. They have achieved closer cooperation on tourism, environmental issues, travel between the two countries and the handling of illegal immigration across their shared borders. Their economies are more interlocked, a gas pipeline between the two countries has entered into service and military confidence-building measures have been agreed and implemented.

However, there has been little substantive progress across a whole range of issues that divide the two countries. In addition to the continuing incidence of alleged violations of air and sea space, Greece still reserves the right to extend its territorial waters in the Aegean from six to twelve miles, which Turkey still insists would be a cause of war. The scope for tension has increased as a result of the possibility that the disputed seabed might contain energy deposits (Daly 2008d). The division of Cyprus has, if anything, deepened in the wake of the 2004 referendum on the island, as has the pessimism concerning prospects for a settlement. Notwithstanding agreements on improved cooperation between the two countries and Turkey's increased successes in detaining people in transit, illegal immigration and other forms of trafficking from Turkey into Greece has continued amidst Greek and EU claims that Turkey is not diligent enough in its enforcement of measures against the trade.[3] There are also continuing differences over treatment of their respective minorities. Nevertheless, none of this should detract from the undoubted efforts on Turkey's behalf to desecuritize its relationship with Athens (Aydin and Ifantis 2004).

Overall, however, in the first decade following the Cold War's demise, Ankara's policies were for the most part reactive and opportunistic. Turkey was uncertainly and often hesitantly groping its way towards a new regional role, but remained generally reluctant to reconsider its privileging of its familiar Cold War western alignments. Furthermore, and alongside this more accommodating spirit, a coercive and heavily securitized approach to foreign policy remained a compelling feature of Turkey's behaviour, giving a somewhat dualistic flavour to Ankara's interactions with the outside world (Kirisci 2006). Even during this period, Turkey's interactions with its neighbours typically 'played into the balance of power logic' (Kirisci *et al.* 2010: 3). Thus Turkey conducted numerous military interventions into northern Iraq in pursuit of the PKK during the 1990s, and in 1998 almost went to war with neighbouring Syria over its harbouring of the PKK leader Abdullah Ocalan. In the same year, Ankara threatened a military response should Greek Cyprus agree to the deployment of Russian S-300 anti-air missiles on the island. Turkey's substantial military presence in, and political sponsorship of, the Turkish Republic of Northern Cyprus (TRNC) indicated an unwavering immobilism in Ankara's approach to the Cyprus problem. In 1996, Turkey came close to blows with Greece over an uninhabited island in the Aegean. It had also closed its border with Armenia in 1993 as a result of that country's conflict with Turkic Azerbaijan over the enclave of Nagorno-Karabahk.

Furthermore, Turkey's close association with Washington still alienated many of its neighbours, most notably in the Arab world and Iran. For all Turkey's increased interaction with a more open and accessible post-Cold War world, the country's foreign policy still retained an isolationist, suspicious strain and a decidedly zero-sum approach to security issues. The Kemalist paradigm, and the military and bureaucratic elite that adhered to it, were still dominant in Turkey's foreign and security policy. In any case, the country's domestic preoccupations concerning the Kurdish issue and the war against the PKK, the electoral fortunes of political Islam, the political role of the military, the survival of a succession of fractious coalition governments, and the performance of a troubled economy all helped curtail Ankara's capacity to pursue an imaginative, coherent, consistent and effective foreign policy. Thus, although it had shifted in response to these external developments and opportunities, Turkish foreign policy remained piecemeal and lacking in coherence or clear direction.

Ahmet Davutoglu: a foreign minister for a globalized era?

However, along with the electoral victory of the AKP in November 2002 came a relatively unknown academic, Ahmet Davutoglu, first as foreign policy advisor to prime minister Erdogan and then, from 1 May 2009, as foreign minister. Although, as we have noted, 'Turkey's attempts to broaden and deepen its ties to non western areas began well before the AKP assumed power [...] the process received new impetus' under the AKP (Larrabee 2010: 158). Much of this energy and change in direction is due to Davutoglu's influence. In the words of Bulent Aras, who himself became foreign minister Davutoglu's advisor, Davutoglu emerged as the 'intellectual architect' of the AKP government's foreign policy. Aras has credited Davutoglu with changing 'the rhetoric and practice of Turkish foreign policy' (Aras 2009b: 127). The drive, ambition and above all the vision that has characterized the AKP's foreign policy has indeed been in stark contrast to the wary, unimaginative and cautious approach that had hitherto shaped Ankara's engagement, or lack of it, with the outside world. Turkey's new foreign policy has paid particular attention to the country's immediate and overlapping neighbourhoods, although it has taken on a more global aspect too. In terms of its conduct and practice, Turkish foreign policy under Davutoglu has also been somewhat hyperactive, as if driven by a need to make up for lost time. It has consisted of a relentless round of flying visits, to one country, meeting or institution after another, generating ideas and hastily signing agreements. As one study expressed it, 'everywhere they go, the Turks tend to air new diplomatic initiatives, offer mediation, advance blueprints for new regional security regimes and, last but not least, seek to boost trade ties' (Torbakov and Ojanen 2009: 3). Davutoglu himself has commented how he sometimes longs for the time to stop and think, because 'when you run you don't think'![4] Turkish foreign policy had become 'undoubtedly far more proactive and multidimensional than at any period in Turkey's republican history' (Kirisci *et al.* 2010: 4).

As an academic, Davutoglu had laid out his foreign policy vision in a book entitled *Strategic depth* (Davutoglu 2001),[5] and he continued to explain and develop his ideas in office, in numerous speeches, interviews and journal articles. Before considering the content of his foreign policy approach, it is both necessary and possible to identify its theoretical underpinnings (Murinson 2006; Walker 2007; Davutoglu 2008, 2009; Aras 2009b; Grigoriadis 2010).

Davutoglu's guiding concept is that of 'strategic depth', which is rooted in the strain of geopolitical thinking that infuses his philosophy. As one analyst has expressed it, 'the core idea of the doctrine is that a nation's value in international relations depends on its geostrategic location' (Larrabee 2010: 159). For Davutoglu, however, 'Turkey's geography gives it a specific central country status [...] it should be seen neither as a bridge country which only connects two points, nor a frontier country' (Davutoglu 2008: 78). Thus 'Turkey is a middle eastern, Balkan, Caucasian, central Asian, Caspian, Mediterranean, Gulf, and Black Sea country' simultaneously (Davutoglu 2008: 79). This central position, in the midst of a vast Afro-Eurasian land-mass, affords Turkey the scope to manoeuvre in several regions simultaneously, and to connect and influence them. As President Abdullah Gul once expressed it, 'Turkey [...] is moving simultaneously in every direction, towards east and west, north and south' (Candar 2009b: 5). This is a reference to the multidirectionality and multidimensionality of Turkey's new foreign policy. Aras refers to this as Davutoglu's 'novel geographic imagination' (Aras 2009b: 128; Kalin 2009).

According to this new thinking, if Turkey is not to be a mere echo chamber for, and victim of, the plethora of conflicts that so routinely feature in its various neighbourhoods, it must throw off its past passivity and isolationism and diplomatically engage more actively and constructively. Its own geostrategic location both demands and enables it. Owing to its central location, Turkey is both uniquely vulnerable to regional instabilities and uniquely well placed to address them. As prime minister Erdogan has put it, 'we don't have the luxury of remaining insensitive to the problems in our neighborhood [...] because of our geographic location, our history, our civilization and our national interests'.[6] There is an element of both a 'pull' factor at play here, in that regional developments have obliged Turkey to adopt a more active diplomacy, as well as a 'push' factor rooted in the foreign policy paradigm shift that the AKP government has sought to implement – in other words, of 'reaction' as much as 'initiation' (Robins 2007b: 4). Turkey both can and must act as a catalyst and as a 'force for good' in the numerous regions of which it is part. Thus 'Turkey should make its role of a peripheral country part of its past, and appropriate a new position; one of providing security not only for itself, but also for its neighbouring regions. [...] by taking on a more active, constructive role' (Davutoglu 2008: 79).

Dialogue, engagement, confidence-building measures, dispute mediation, trade agreements, the institutionalization of diplomatic relationships, economic aid and reconstruction, and peacekeeping have all emerged as central and indispensable tools of Ankara's regional and wider policy under Davutoglu's leadership. This has gone beyond 'zero problems' with Turkey's neighbours, and extends to efforts to facilitate 'zero problems' between all neighbours in Turkey's diverse regions. Turkey's region is one of inter- and intrastate conflicts, of widespread terrorism – some of it state-sponsored – of militarization, of fears relating to the imminence of a regional WMD proliferation, of imbalances of power, and of spheres of influence and outside interference. Yet for Davutoglu, regional security is common security. This approach has been expressed as the adoption by Turkey of a Kantian approach to foreign policy. Not only does this contrast with the Hobbesian approach with which Turkey has hitherto been more familiarly associated, but it also contrasts with the Hobbesian neighbourhoods in which Turkey is located (Kirisci 2006). It might be said that Turkey has borrowed from Europe the kinds of cooperative 'security community' approaches commonplace there, and is seeking to apply them to the vastly different circumstances of Turkey's immediate neighbourhood(s).

Among the assets Turkey is able to deploy in this endeavour is its historical connection with much of its neighbourhood through a shared Ottoman past. In addition to its emphasis on the country's geographical location, Turkey's strategic depth doctrine also 'emphasizes the importance of Turkey's Ottoman past and its historical and cultural ties with the Balkans, the Middle East and central Asia [...] and is part of a larger debate in Turkey about the legacy of the Ottoman empire' (Larrabee 2010: 159). For Davutoglu, 'history too may come to constitute a country as a central country' (Davutoglu 2008: 79). This is in sharp contrast to the perspective of Turkey's earlier governing elites, who generally preferred to reject and to forget Ottomanism. In effect, the AKP's 'relative indifference to the legacy of Kemal Ataturk' (Abramowitz and Barkey 2009: 120) is freeing Turkey to rediscover its Ottoman past abroad as well as at home. This new thinking has freed Turkey to strive for its positive reintegration into regions from which either the circumstances of the Cold War, the preferences of Kemalist foreign policy, or bitter Ottoman-era legacies have hitherto excluded it. This process can be seen as a kind of 'normalization' of Turkish foreign policy, in the sense that Turkey no longer seeks to stand aside from its neighbourhood. From this perspective, it is the past 100 years of Turkish foreign policy that can appear anomalous. This is partly why Turkey's new foreign policy is also sometimes described, especially by its detractors, as a kind of 'neo-Ottomanism'. Yet other former imperial powers, such as the UK, France and Russia, have long sought to maintain their interests in, and association with, their former colonies. Today, so does Turkey. In any case, the AKP's regional foreign policy has neither been confined to former Ottoman territories, nor does it exclusively favour Turkey's Islamic partners. Ankara has also sought to establish constructive relations with its former imperial adversary, Russia, with 'Christian' Georgia, Greece, Croatia, Serbia, Ukraine, Romania and Bulgaria, and with central Asia, which never constituted part of the Ottoman empire.

Turkey's new foreign policy activism has in some measure been in 'response to structural changes in its security environment since the end of the Cold War' (Larrabee 2007: 103). However, Davutoglu's appreciation of post-Cold War structural changes goes beyond its immediate region. He also detects 'a transfer of power from a Eurocentric to an Asia centric [...] based international system' (Candar 2009b: 10). Turkey is located in Eurasia and, through their economic growth and regional and global aspirations, Asian states such as India and China are mounting a sustained challenge to western domination of the global system. Yet Davutoglu's expectation of the emerging world order also appears to look beyond the Asian challenge, and to envisage a more genuinely global distribution of economic, political, cultural and even military power. In his public addresses, Davutoglu has made much of this, and of the foreign policy implications for Turkey.[7] He certainly sees Turkey as integral to this global transformation. In its pursuit of an enhanced role in a new global order, Turkey has exhibited a 'growing interest in hitherto neglected parts of the globe' such as sub-Saharan Africa and Latin America, opening embassies and despatching trade delegations (Grigoriadis 2010: 8–9).

In this new world order, Davutoglu envisages the coexistence of more integrated regional subsystems alongside the emergence of a new globalized system of governance. Within the world's regions, a key aim should be the lowering of state boundaries, enabling a pluralistic, multicultural intermingling of peoples and the reconnection of cities with their 'natural' hinterlands. Turkish cities such as Istanbul, Edirne along the Bulgarian border, Antakya and Gaziantep in the south, and Trabzon and Rize on the Black Sea coast, have been greatly affected by the freer flows of people and goods across proximate state borders. To this end, a particular initiative of Davutoglu's has been the lifting of visa requirements for travel between Turkey and an ever growing list of countries that at the time of writing included Syria, Libya, Lebanon, Jordan, the Gulf states and Russia. At the global level, Davutoglu believes that the world is – or should be – moving towards a multipolar, interdependent, less western-centric, culturally diverse, inclusive, participatory and just order. At this level, too, territories should be denationalized and issues desecuritized. Central countries such as Turkey have a major role to play in this emerging global order because, through intensified socioeconomic interaction with their neighbours, they can assist in the integration of regional orders into globalized networks of interdependence and interaction. In other words, Turkey can link Syria and Turkmenistan with Europe, Azerbaijan with the Middle East, and so on. For Turkey, playing an enhanced role in the various regions to which it belongs might award it 'global strategic significance' (Grigoriadis 2010: 4).

Davutoglu's emphasis on regional and global transformation towards a more boundary-less and interdependent order is also both driven and enabled by Turkey's domestic transformation. Just as Islam, 'Ottomanism' and popular culture constitute elements of Turkey's 'soft' power, so too does Turkey's process of internal democratization and its economic dynamism. As Davutoglu has said, 'Turkey's most important soft power is its democracy' (Altinay 2008; Altunisik 2008; Davutoglu 2008: 80). Furthermore, the process of democratization and modernity in Turkey has led to the emergence of a new, more pious and largely Anatolian political and business elite who are more comfortable with Middle Eastern, Caucasian and central Asian cultures than are their Kemalist counterparts. It has also coincided with a weakening of the domestic power of the Turkish military. Indeed, the AKP government's success in desecuritizing Turkey's regional relationships conceivably holds out the longer-term prospect that Turkey's inflated military establishment might be reduced in size. Furthermore, given the role the EU plays in Turkey's democratization process, it is not surprising that Davutoglu and his AKP colleagues have frequently insisted that Turkey's new foreign policy is not only compatible with, but is rooted in, its EU accession project. This both increases Turkey's status in its neighbourhood and serves as a 'source of inspiration' to the region's modernizers. Turkey's economic relationship with Europe has also been instrumental in the country's emergence as its region's second largest economy after Russia's, and the seventeenth in the world. As a member of G20, Turkey regards this gathering as more representative of the new world order than the more exclusive G8. In effect, Davutoglu regards Turkey as akin to the so-called BRICS (Brazil–Russia–India–China – the newly emerging global economies). Turkey's overtures to its neighbours typically involve trade agreements, and regional trade as a percentage of Turkey's total trade has increased substantially over the past decade or so (although much of this is accounted for by the lifting of sanctions against Iraq, the Dubai construction boom, and the increase in the cost of energy). In other words, Turkey's regional initiatives are frequently closely associated with its pursuit of its expanding economic interests (Kirisci 2009). It is a mercantile approach, too, and Davutoglu frequently travels with businessmen in tow.

Turkey–Syrian relations

The international crisis over Iraq, beginning with the Gulf War of 1990–91 and culminating in the US-led invasion of Iraq and overthrow of Saddam Hussein's regime in the first part of 2003, dragged Ankara towards a far closer interaction with the politics of the Middle East and into a severe crisis in its relationship with its American ally, protector and benefactor. Under the AKP, and under Davutoglu's guidance in particular, this has been grasped as an opportunity to effect a paradigm shift in Turkey's approach to the region, from conflict to cooperation, from disengagement to engagement, and incorporating steps towards a 'desecuritization' of its hitherto troubled regional relationships (Aras and Polat 2008). Turkey's more open embrace of its Ottoman and Islamic identity has undoubtedly played a major role in this shift. So have commercial considerations, paramount for the increasingly mercantile state that Turkey has become. Ankara's disillusionment with US policies in the region, and the sense that they do not necessarily accord with, or take account of, Turkey's interests, has also undoubtedly been a factor. This paradigm shift has incorporated quite profound changes in some of Turkey's key bilateral relationships in the region, such as those with Arab Syria, Persian Iran and Israel (and with both Baghdad and the KRG, covered elsewhere in this volume). Turkey's deployment of 'soft' power – culture, trade and diplomacy – is also an expression of this shift.

Ankara's relationship with Syria has been the most troubled of all its Middle Eastern relationships, and the most unambiguous manifestation of the new direction in Turkey's foreign policy is the dramatic relaxation this has undergone (Muslih 1996; Aras and Koni 2002; Altunisik and Tur 2006). In fact, this pre-dates the advent of the AKP, and dates back to Syria's 1998 expulsion of PKK leader Abdullah Ocalan and the closure of PKK bases in the Syrian-controlled Bekaa Valley in the Lebanon, in the face of considerable pressure from Ankara, including the threat of military action (Aras, Damla 2009; Aykan 1999; Sezgin 2002). Syria's Arab nationalism, its political radicalism, its confrontation with Israel, and its Cold War leaning towards the Soviet bloc formed the backcloth for Ankara's frosty attitude towards Damascus. Syrian support for the terrorist and separatist PKK was generally tactical and aimed at creating leverage with Ankara in light of the other issues dividing these two neighbours. One such bone of contention involved Syrian and Iraqi access to the waters of the Tigris and Euphrates, which rise in Anatolia, and the flow of which is threatened by Turkey's vast GAP (*Guneydogu Anadolu Projesi* – South East Anatolian Project) (Jouejati 1996; Allen 2000; Freeman 2001). Another was Syria's continued resentment at Turkey's incorporation of Hatay province in 1939. Since the Adana agreement that was signed in the immediate aftermath of the 1998 crisis, trade, cultural, intelligence, security and diplomatic links have expanded significantly. The installation of Hatez al-Assad's son, Bashar, as Syrian president in 2000 also contributed to the improving atmosphere between the two countries.

The relationship received its major boost, however, in the wake of the AKP's November 2002 electoral victory and the US-led invasion of Iraq in March 2003. Syria was very much a partner in Ankara's initiative to coordinate the positions of Iraq's neighbours. President Bashar al-Assad's visit to Ankara in January 2004 – the first ever by a Syrian president – was followed by Turkish president Ahmet Sezer's return visit the following year. Sezer's visit took place in the face of considerable US opposition, which sought to isolate Syria for what it believed was its unhelpful meddling in Iraq and Lebanon and for its relationship with Tehran. This offered an indication of the extent to which Ankara was now prepared to pursue a foreign policy independent of US preferences. Trade also improved substantially, especially in the wake of a free-trade agreement between the two countries that was signed in 2004 and ratified in 2007. Differences over water access, which include Iraq, have been removed to the technical sphere and discussed in a more cooperative fashion. In September 2009, visa requirements were lifted between Turkey and Syria, which led to a substantial increase in border crossings and which softened still further the now largely forgotten border dispute between the two states. There are also plans to clear the border area of mines, and in 2009 Turkey and Syria instituted a series of joint military exercises. The first ministerial high-level strategic cooperation council, at which ministers from the cabinets of both countries were present, met in October 2009.[8] In December 2009 the council met again, this time co-chaired by the Turkish prime minister and the Syrian president.[9]

Forty agreements, covering 'low politics' issues such as transport, trade and the environment, as well as security, were signed, and it became evident that the diplomatic positions of the two countries had become increasingly aligned across a range of issues. This improved atmosphere of trust between Ankara and Damascus appeared to have given a fillip to Turkey's diplomatic influence. Thus, in November 2005, the then foreign minister Abdullah Gul seems to have been instrumental in persuading Damascus to hand over to a UN-appointed prosecutor the suspect in the assassination of former Lebanese prime minister Rafik Hariri (Kirisci 2006: 78). During the first half of 2008, Ankara emerged as a mediator in talks between Israel and Syria, a role that derived from Turkey's good relationships with both parties.[10] It is believed that considerable progress had been made over four rounds of talks when, without forewarning the Turkish side, Israel launched aerial attacks against Hamas positions in Gaza in December 2008. This was followed by a severe deterioration in Turkey's relations with Israel as Ankara made clear that it held Israel responsible for the breakdown of talks.

Turkey–Iranian relations

Turkey's relationship with Iran was largely unproblematic until the 1979 revolution, and even in its wake Turkey has been generally inclined towards a constructive, if wary, engagement with Islamist Iran. This approach recognized the desirability of a businesslike relationship with the largest of Turkey's Middle Eastern neighbours, was a reflection of a mutual respect and shared historical and cultural legacy between the two countries, and was also made possible by the relative absence of concrete issues to divide them. Whatever the nature of its regime, the Iranian state has long been, and will remain, an important neighbour for Turkey, a fact reflected in some of Ankara's past policy stances. For example, Ankara refused to impose US-inspired sanctions on Iran following the 1979 US embassy seizure in Tehran, and in 1985 Turkey formed the Economic Cooperation Council (ECO) with Iran and Pakistan (since expanded to include central Asian states and Afghanistan). Visa-free travel between the two countries, established before the 1979 revolution, was maintained after it. Turkey is the only country to which Iranians can travel unhindered, and over 1 million of them exploit this privilege annually. Turkish–Iranian relations have on occasion been soured by tensions over Turkish allegations of Iranian attempts to export Islamic fundamentalism (although it is far from clear that Sunni Turks are susceptible to Shi'ite Iranian overtures), by Iranian accusations of Turkish encouragement of Iran's substantial Azeri (Turkic) population, and by differences over Iraq and the Kurdish issue (Barkey 1995; Eralp 1996; Pahlavan 1996; Aras 2001). However, by the later 1990s they appear to have concurred that non-interference in each other's domestic affairs was the wisest course. Iran has not appreciated Ankara's relationships with the USA and with Israel, and in the immediate aftermath of the Cold War's end, rivalries emerged in the Caucasus and central Asia too (Kazemi and Ajdari 1998; Criss and Guner 1999; Lapidot-Firilla 2004), although they came to share a realistic assessment of Moscow's continued and substantial influence in these regions as well as their own relative limitations. Overall, their relationship has been respectful, but at least until recently they 'have shown little genuine interest in working together' (Barkey 1995: 159), at least not closely or sustainably. Nor have they seriously wanted to work against each other. In short, the stark ideological divergence after 1979 was not sufficient to pit Ankara and Tehran against each other, but it did nothing to bring them closer either.

However, as in the Syrian case, Turkey's relations with Iran have intensified in the wake of the advent of the AKP government. Turkey's refusal to allow US troops to use its territory as a base from which to attack Iraq impressed Tehran as well as much of the Arab world, as did Ankara's initiative in bringing together Iraq's neighbouring states in an attempt to regionalize the issue. Of course, Iran was also happy to see a wedge appear in the relationship between Washington and Ankara, and was keener to magnify Washington's difficulties than it was to augment Arab influence in Iraq. Turkey, Iran and Syria have certainly seen eye to eye on the undesirability of an overly autonomous Kurdish northern Iraq. In fact, Turkish–Iranian security cooperation with respect to northern Iraq precedes the advent of the AKP government, but in the wake of a February 2008 memorandum on security cooperation between the two countries, it became clear that they were sharing intelligence and even coordinating military operations against their respective Kurdish separatist movements operating in the region (Hale 2009: 154).

Another issue that has brought Ankara and Tehran closer has been energy cooperation, which has been central to the enhancement of Ankara's relationship with Tehran since 2002, again to the dismay of Washington. Iran supplies around one-third of Turkey's gas imports, and has gas reserves estimated as second only to Russia's. This trade dates back at least to the mid-1990s, but will be enhanced should two Turkish–Iranian agreements signed in July 2007 come to fruition (McCurdy 2008). One is to transport gas from Turkmenistan via Iran into Turkey and then on to Europe (the Nabucco Project). The second agreement is for the Turkish Petroleum Corporation (Turkiye Petrolleri Anonim Ortakligi – TPAO) to help develop Iran's offshore South Pars gas field. Access to Iranian energy and across its territory is crucial to Turkey's aspiration to become a regional and global energy hub. In a further assertion of Turkey's determination to pursue autonomous policies in its region, and in response to American expressions of displeasure with Turkey's energy engagement with Iran, prime minister Erdogan remarked that 'no country has the right to ask Ankara to relinquish its relations with countries that supply it with energy' (Raphaeli 2008).

Thus the AKP government's determination to engage positively with its neighbours is now added to Ankara's longer-standing preference to avoid problems in its relationship with Iran (McCurdy 2008; Breitegger 2009; Mercan 2009–10). This commitment to dialogue rather than confrontation has been most in evidence with respect to Ankara's approach to Iran's nuclear programme. Turkey has no wish to see Iran develop nuclear weapons. It believes that Tehran should comply with the resolutions of the International Atomic Energy Agency (IAEA) and permit inspection of its nuclear facilities. Indeed, it would prefer Iran to behave in such a way that its isolation from the international community could be terminated. However, Ankara also opposes either military action or the use of further sanctions against Iran. During a visit to Tehran in June 2006, foreign minister Gul offered to mediate between Iran and the West in the hope that a confrontation could be avoided (Bonab 2009). The head of Iran's Supreme National Security Council, Ali Larijani, accepted the offer. However, as the crisis intensified and the US Obama administration appeared to offer its guarded support for Ankara's efforts, Tehran eventually appeared to dismiss the idea that Turkey had a role to play.[11] The degree to which Ankara was prepared to rely on diplomacy, and indeed make itself hostage to Iran's willingness to adopt more compliant behaviour, was unmistakably signalled by its abstention in the IAEA's November 2009 resolution that condemned Iran's evasiveness and violations and called on Tehran to comply. Even Russia, China and India voted for the resolution, as did Turkey's NATO and prospective EU partners and most other members of the IAEA's Board (Schulte 2009–10).

Just as Washington's intensified diplomatic efforts to persuade the UN Security Council to adopt still tighter sanctions against Iran seemed to meet with the approval of all five permanent members, in May 2010 Turkey and fellow Security Council member Brazil negotiated an agreement with Tehran involving the depositing of some of Iran's low-enriched uranium in Turkey. In the furore that followed, both Turkey and its Brazilian partner steadfastly countered some quite severe US-led criticism of the deal, with prime minister Erdogan suggesting that all existing nuclear powers needed to disarm if their pressure on Iran were to be credible.[12] At a NATO meeting just a few weeks earlier, Davutoglu had argued that consistency on Iran required that Israel's nuclear weapons be abolished too.[13] This wrangling took place against the background of an agreement by the 189 signatories of the Non-Proliferation Treaty (NPT) to intensify efforts to achieve a nuclear-free Middle East by calling for a conference of all regional states, including Iran and Israel, to be held in 2012. Israel was called upon at the gathering to sign up to the treaty. Iran is already a signatory.[14] Turkey's position, that pressuring Iran while leaving Israel's alleged nuclear weapons arsenal unscathed was inconsistent and hypocritical, is a far from uncommon one in global politics. Nevertheless, it contributed to a further bout of criticism and worry in the USA concerning the overall direction of Turkish foreign policy.

Israel: an indicator of Turkey's foreign policy axis?

Unsurprisingly, Turkey's apparent embrace of two of the more radical Middle Eastern states has caused some conservative commentators in the USA to suspect that Turkey is being 'lost' to the West altogether (Cagaptay 2005b; Pipes 2009).[15] In the more conservative corners of the Arab world, too, there is an apprehension that a Turkey–Syria–Iran bloc might be shaping up (Winter 2009), as well as a discomfort with Iran's nuclear programme.[16] The AKP government's increasingly fraught relationship with Israel added further grist to western perceptions of an 'Islamification' of Turkey's foreign policy (International Crisis Group 2010b). Turkey has long been Israel's best friend in the Islamic world and in March 1949 became the first Muslim state to recognize Israel (Abadi 1995; Makovsky 1996; Lochery 1998; Bolukbasi 1999; Inbar 2001; Walker 2006; Bengio 2009a).

However, Ankara was frequently critical or unsupportive of Israel even before the AKP's rise to power. Thus Turkey opposed the UK/French/Israeli attack on Egypt in 1956, stayed neutral in the 1967 Arab–Israeli War by refusing to permit the use of bases in Turkey for refuelling or resupply of Israel, denied to the USA the use of the Incirlik base in the 1973 war while allowing the Soviet Union to use Turkish airspace to fly supplies to Syria, opposed Israel's annexation of East Jerusalem and Golan, allowed the PLO to open an office in Ankara in 1979, opposed Israel's 1982 incursion into Lebanon, and recognized the Palestinian National Council's declaration of a state of Palestine in 1988. In 2002, prime minister Bulent Ecevit described as 'genocidal' Israeli actions in response to the second intifada. Indeed, the Palestinian issue has repeatedly acted as a brake on Turkish–Israeli relationships, and has remained its Achilles heel throughout. Full ambassadorial relations between Turkey and Israel were not established until 1991 (simultaneously with an extension by Ankara of the same status to the Palestinian authority). Even this had been made possible chiefly as a result of the cautious improvement in Israel–PLO relations, which triggered a wider international diplomatic relaxation towards Israel.

In the mid-1990s, the bilateral relationship did become closer. Ankara seems to have made the initial overtures, driven by a range of factors. The end of the Cold War threatened to loosen Ankara's US ties, and Turkey's EU accession was stumbling. Furthermore, Turkey's western allies had proved themselves to be unreliable arms suppliers due to their human rights concerns. Israel seemed to offer a more reliable alternative source of supply. Regionally, both countries had problems with Syria, concerning its support for terrorist groups, its territorial demands and water issues. Iran and Iraq were also shared sources of concern. Both Turkey and Israel were exercised about the chronic instability of their region and the apparent rise of Islamic radicalism. Both were, and are, democratized, relatively economically developed and US-aligned states in a region where these qualities are otherwise in short supply. Their shared modernity relative to their neighbours may have meant both that Turkey's more institutionalized diplomatic approach coped imperfectly with the personalized and occasionally more emotive style of many of its neighbours, and that Turkey's diplomats have felt more at home with Israel's more recognizable political and bureaucratic system and culture

(Robins 1996: 181–82). In addition, the relationship with Israel meant that Turkey could benefit from the efforts of the US Jewish lobby in Washington on issues such as the Armenian question, relations with Greece and arms sales, while Israel took sustenance from the symbolic significance of a close relationship with a majority Muslim state and from the military access allowed by Ankara to the extensive Turkish airspace. There is also relatively little negative historical baggage between the two states and peoples. Indeed, there is much that is positive in this regard. Thus from 1996 onwards, arms deals, joint military exercises and training, intelligence cooperation, strategic dialogue, political visits, trade relations and improved political sympathy were all intensified.

Interestingly, this improvement in Turkish–Israeli relations received its boost under the coalition government led by the Islamist prime minister and Welfare (*Refah*) Party leader Necmattin Erbakan. Relations with Israel were led primarily by the TSK, and they constituted an element in Turkey's domestic political struggles. In 1997, the military inspired the so-called 'soft coup' against the Erbakan government, symbolizing an era in Turkish politics when the securitization of issues reached its apotheosis (Robins 1997). In light of the widespread public sympathy in Turkey for the plight of the Palestinians, the strongly securitized and state-to-state flavour of the Turkish–Israeli relationship perhaps always rendered it vulnerable to a change in Turkish political circumstances (Bacik 2009). For the time being, however, and from the perspective of Ankara's foreign policy elite, Turkey was at that time receiving little sympathy from its Arab and Iranian neighbours on issues such as the plight of Turkish Cypriots, the ethnic Turks of Bulgaria in the 1980s, the displaced Azeris of Nagorno-Karabakh, or even Turkey's Kurdish difficulties. For Turkey, the diplomatic costs of the embrace of Israel appeared negligible, and the gains considerable.

However, the AKP's emotional identification with the Palestinian people, and the frustration with what are seen as Israel's excesses in Gaza, have been evident since it came to power. In this, it is no more than in step with Turkish public opinion, which has long sympathized with the Palestinian people and with their core political demand for a state of their own. Until 2008, the AKP's expressions of disapproval towards Israel had mostly taken only rhetorical form, expressed most graphically by Erdogan's 2004 characterization of Israel's behaviour in the West Bank and Gaza as 'state terrorism', and when he likened Israeli persecution of Palestinians to the fifteenth-century Spanish expulsion of the Jews. His condemnations of Israel's 2006 incursion into south Lebanon were also harshly worded. These sentiments mirrored those of the Turkish public, whose opposition to Israeli policies was visibly demonstrated by the mass rallies held to oppose Israel's summer 2006 adventure in southern Lebanon. More substantive, and diplomatically no less provocative, was the AKP's January 2006 invitation to the newly elected leader of Hamas in Gaza, Khaled Mashaal, to visit Turkey. Although the AKP leadership stressed its determination to deliver the message that Israel's right to exist must be recognized and that terrorist violence should be renounced, the invitation was issued without consultation with Israel, the USA or the Turkish foreign ministry, and the move was widely interpreted as indicating a shift in Ankara's position.

Yet, even against this backdrop, Turkey–Israel relations continued to flourish. Trade grew, as did Israeli tourism to Turkey, surpassing half a million by 2008. New agreements were signed covering intelligence cooperation, joint military exercises and arms procurement. Civilian and military visits in both directions multiplied. In November 2007, president Shimon Peres became the first Israeli leader to address the TGNA. Cultural exchanges were developed, as were plans to construct energy pipelines and for the export of Turkish water to Israel. Civil society groups enjoyed a higher profile in the relationship, too. In this respect, the Ankara Forum has particular salience. Established at Turkey's initiative in April 2005 by business groups from Turkey, Israel and the Palestinian Authority, its flagship project has been the reopening of the Eraz Industrial Zone in Gaza under Turkish management.[17]

However, with the breakdown of Turkey's mediation between Israel and Syria following Israel's attacks on Gaza in late 2008, relations between the two plunged to unprecedented depths (Ayturk 2009; Bacik 2009; Bengio 2009b). At the World Economic Forum in Davos, Switzerland in January 2009, prime minister Erdogan stormed from the platform he was sharing with Peres, having shouted towards him, 'when it comes to killing, you know very well how to kill'. Erdogan subsequently suggested that Israel be expelled from the UN as punishment for ignoring that body's resolutions. The Turkish prime minister emerged as a hero amongst some Turks and in the Arab world, and numerous demonstrations took place in support of him and in protest at the Israeli attack on Gaza. Amid continued harsh rhetoric directed towards Israel's blockade of Gaza and its campaign against Hamas, in October 2009 Turkey cancelled Israeli participation in an air force military exercise to be held in Turkish airspace, prompting the other two participants, NATO partners Italy and the USA, to withdraw their participation.[18] In January 2010, Israel's deputy foreign minister caused further offence by appearing to publicly humiliate the Turkish ambassador to the country in protest at depictions of Israeli soldiers in a Turkish TV programme.[19] Then, and most dramatically of all, at the end of May 2010 a convoy of ships laden with humanitarian aid left Turkish ports with the intention of defying Israel's Gaza blockade. The blockade, first imposed by Israel in 2005 and more strictly enforced since early 2009, was designed to prevent the importation into Gaza of arms, tunnel-building equipment and any other material deemed threatening to Israel's security. It was widely believed to be more extensive in its practical application, designed rather to break the will of the residents of Gaza as well as their affiliation with Hamas, and had been declared by Amnesty International 'a flagrant violation of international law'. The flotilla was subjected to an Israeli commando raid in international waters which resulted in the loss of the lives of eight Turkish citizens and one Turkish American. Amid the international condemnation of Israel, Turkey withdrew its ambassador and relations plunged still further (Ozhan 2010).

Ankara's more confrontational stance towards Israel can be explained largely by its frustration with the fact that Israel's raid on Gaza put a sudden and unexpected end to its efforts at mediation. Ankara concluded that Israel, especially under the right-wing leadership of Benjamin Netanyahu, was not a serious peace negotiator. Davutoglu and other Turkish spokesmen continued to insist both that they did not seek to put an end to their relationship with Israel, and that Turkey remained ready to recommence its efforts at mediation. Indeed, the widespread criticism of Israel's raid on the humanitarian convoy, and the intensified criticism of Israeli policies that had already emerged as a feature of the Obama administration's approach to the problems of the Middle East, suggested that impatience with Israel was now quite widespread. Turkey's closer political and economic ties with other states in the region, most notably Syria, combined with the fact that Turkey's military and its securitizing agenda and statist approach had to some extent been eased from the country's foreign policy making, further facilitated Ankara's switch in emphasis. Time will tell how long-term and deeply entrenched Turkish estrangement from its erstwhile Israeli ally will prove to be. However, prime minister Erdogan and others in the AKP administration seem to have adopted a more essentialist anti-Israeli rhetoric. Such attitudes can be found in Turkey more generally, and they resemble those commonly found throughout the Arab world. This could have a more lasting impact and render it difficult to effect a restoration of anything like the earlier warmer relationship between Turkey and Israel.

Some observations

Although Davutoglu and his sympathizers decry the epithet 'neo-Ottoman' to describe Turkey's new foreign policy, it is clear that it is underpinned by a sense of Turkey as a significant regional player and as a more powerful state with more potential for influence than most of its neighbours. This can easily appear as arrogant or meddling, especially in the ever-sensitive Arab world. For example, Egypt and Saudi Arabia have not always welcomed Turkey's higher profile in the Arab world (Kirisci *et al.* 2010: 18). There is also a risk of overreach inherent in Turkey's diplomatic activism, so much so that it has apparently been dubbed 'the Davutoglu bluff' by a high-level European official (Barysch 2010: 6–7). Turkey, with a foreign ministry one-sixth the size of Germany's and with a bureaucratic tradition that values hierarchy and shuns lower-level initiative, simply does not have the governmental capacity to fully implement and follow through on the multiplying agreements, proposals and initiatives associated with Davutoglu, although he has appreciated this and has sought to expand his ministry's staffing levels and to enrich its recruitment base.

In any case, at least with respect to the macro-level conflicts in its neighbourhood and for all its success at micro-level mediation, 'Turkey's potential is limited' (Kirisci *et al.* 2010: 16). It 'has not yet become the global, or even the regional, player that its government declares it to be' (Abramowitz and Barkey 2009: 118). Thus, when confronted with the Russo–Georgian conflict of August 2008, Ankara could do little beyond produce yet another diplomatic proposal, this time for a Caucasus Stability Programme, which has had little, if any, impact and which was not even coordinated with its American and European allies (Barkey 2008: 41–42). By 'losing' Israel, Ankara has lost its capacity to mediate between it and the Arab world. By flirting with Armenia – without achieving the 'normalization' of relationships, which was the initial goal – Ankara upset its 'brother nation' Azerbaijan. Turkey's cultivation of Iran has borne little fruit, beyond upsetting Washington and worrying some Arab opinion. Iran has proved too politically awkward for much progress to have been achieved. There has been little substantive progress regarding the problematic issues that bedevil the relationship with Greece. Even the blossoming relationship with the KRG in northern Iraq remains at the mercy of the future status of the KRG within Iraq, and that of Kirkuk. Indeed, Turkey's diplomatic agenda is replete with potentially insoluble problems. US engagement remains crucial if real progress is to be made across a range of issues in Turkey's vicinity, and a US 'green light' is frequently essential for Turkey's diplomatic initiatives to gain traction. Indeed, Turkey might yet discover – or rediscover – that, although it overlaps with many regions, it is ultimately not central to any of them. The pull and influence of the EU and Russia in the Balkans and Mediterranean regions and the former Soviet space, respectively, the internal preoccupations of the Arab world, and the political and economic presence of the USA specifically and the West generally, might ultimately overwhelm Turkey's efforts to assert itself. Turkey might find that, rather than emerge as the central player that binds its regions together in a dense web of interactions and interdependencies, it might for all its efforts remain as a country with an (albeit) improved set of bilateral relationships with states and regions that nevertheless primarily look elsewhere for their economic, cultural, political and strategic connectivity.

There is little doubt, though, that Turkey now conducts an altogether more autonomous foreign policy than hitherto. It can no longer be taken for granted by the USA and the EU, if it ever could, and is increasingly a player in its own right (Kirisci *et al.* 2010). There is perhaps a strain of Turkish 'Gaullism' in the country's new foreign policy direction. However, de Gaulle's France was firmly anchored within the EU and, although its foreign policies were irritating to transatlanticists, France had nowhere else to go in terms of its political and ideological alignments. This is less the case with Turkey – or, rather, its leaders might believe themselves to have diplomatic alternatives to alignment with the West. Of course, Turkey's regional initiatives need not necessarily contradict and might even complement western policies and interests. Turkey's overtures to Syria might help reduce that country's attachment to Tehran, and its efforts towards resolving the stand-off over Iran's nuclear programme might yet give western diplomats a breathing space and enable Iran to compromise without appearing to back down. Given the AKP government's efforts to join the EU, its professed commitment to its western alliances, and its continued cooperation with the USA in Iraq, Afghanistan and elsewhere, the argument that Turkey is undergoing a 'change of axis' in its external alignments can seem a little far-fetched. Yet the sometimes inconsistent and unhelpful stances exhibited by the emotional intensity of Ankara's verbal attacks on Israel, the welcome afforded to the Hamas leadership, the apparent embrace of Sudan's president Bashir, the determined pursuit of good relationships with Iran and Syria even in the face of Washington's unease, and the opposition to Rasmussen's appointment as NATO secretary general because, as a Danish minister, he could be associated with the controversial publication in a Danish newspaper of cartoons ridiculing the Prophet, have given some western observers pause for thought. In this context, the very essence of Davutoglu's foreign policy thinking, which serves to relegate the EU to just one of Turkey's priorities, contains a risk. It is in Turkey's interest to cultivate and befriend its near neighbours, to assist in the resolution of local differences and to widen its economic relationships. It is less clear that worrying moderate Arab opinion, irritating the USA and Europe, risking Israel's friendship and alienating Azerbaijan serve Turkey's interest. There is a balance to be struck, and Ankara might still be struggling to locate where that balance lies. Turkey is not India or China. It does not possess their capacity, nor is it blessed with their geography. It is a middle power, not a great power in waiting.

One final set of questions regarding the new direction in Turkish foreign policy relates to the future of the AKP government in general, and of Davutoglu in particular. At the time of writing, the AKP's dominance of Turkey's domestic political scene looks complete. The opposition remains in disarray. The CHP in particular, which, as we have seen (in Chapter 5), has never attained the electoral popularity recently enjoyed by the AKP, is struggling to embrace the realities of Turkey's more brazen embrace of its Islamic roots, of the openness to external influences and challenges that accompany globalization in general and the EU accession process more specifically, of the weakening of the domestic political role of the TSK, and of the ever increasing complexity of the Kurdish issue. Yet the AKP, too, has its problems. It is essentially a coalition of more hardened Islamists, Islamic pragmatists and modernizers, and relatively liberal reformers. Furthermore, personalities can be key in Turkish party politics, and this is true for the AKP too. Who succeeds Erdogan and Gul is a crucial question to which no obvious answer presents itself. The party could become more Islamist or at least 'Muslimist', drawn increasingly towards an emotional attachment to the East and an accompanying anti-westernism. On the other hand, progress in its EU venture and the realities of Turkey's concrete diplomatic alignments and trading patterns might tilt the country back towards its more traditional western friendships. Also, the emergence of a virulent, aggressive nationalism can never be discounted as an option in Turkish politics, whether it is wrapped in the emblems of the CHP, the AKP or the MHP, or takes some other shape. Predicting the future of Turkish politics is a risky business. Suffice it to say that, if the future consists of a continuing dominance of the domestic political scene by an AKP constructed along its present lines, then Turkey will truly have turned a corner in its political evolution.

Another possibility is that, whoever is in charge of Turkey's foreign policy, exhaustion and an awareness of overreach could set in. After all, and notwithstanding Davutoglu's Herculean efforts, Turkey has made little substantive progress with respect to its Aegean differences with Greece, Cyprus remains divided and unresolved, Turkey remains outside the EU, and relations with Armenia are still frozen. It is hard to see Ankara's relationship with Israel returning to its earlier warmer basis so long as Erdogan and indeed Davutoglu are in office, which means that Turkey has lost the opportunity to act as mediator between Israel on one hand and Syria or the Palestinians on the other. Turkey's undoubtedly improved relationships with Syria and Iran have further aroused US and Israeli suspicion, and that of some parts of the Arab world too. The differences between Russia and Georgia, and Turkey's overtures towards Armenia, have somewhat cooled the attitude of Tbilisi and Baku towards Ankara. The future of Iraq, and of Ankara's approach to the KRG, is still at the mercy of forces it cannot really control or predict. None of this is to decry the improvement in the atmosphere surrounding Turkey's regional diplomacy, but in due course Ankara's policy makers might conclude that the costs and efforts have been high given the relatively minimal substantive progress that has been achieved. They might also conclude that Turkey's interests demand a more careful cultivation of its western ties.

8   Turkey between East and West
A bridge or afloat?

A bridge between two banks?

Although the idea that the 'Christian' and 'Muslim' worlds were in a civilizational clash can be dated back to the 1920s, if not before (Balci 2009), Turkey's predicament as an echo chamber for conflicts in its environment was made manifest by the post-9/11 'war on terror' and the renewed spectre of civilizational conflict between the Muslim and western worlds to which it gave rise. These developments were deeply compromising for Turkey, which was described by Samuel Huntington as 'the most obvious and prototypical torn country', straddling these two apparently contending civilizations (Huntington 1993: 141; Huntington 1996; Cornell and Karaveli 2008; Kosebalaban 2008). The November 2002 electoral victory of the Islam-inspired AKP government further emphasized the uniqueness of Turkey's status as a socially Islamic but politically and diplomatically West-leaning country. This 'torn' or hybrid personality directed a spotlight towards Turkey's possible role in the post-9/11 world. It was thought that as a consequence of a kind of 'Middle Easternization' or 're-Islamification' of Turkish society under the new government, Turkey could perhaps more fully emerge as a kind of bridge or interlocutor between these two worlds.

For the USA especially, the idea that Turkey could function as a bridge between East and West has long had a strongly geopolitical aspect associated with Turkey's location (Vali 1971: 42–48), as well as, or more than, an ideological aspect. This potential Turkish role gained a fresh impetus with the end of the Cold War (Lesser 1992, 2006). Indeed, as the 2003 invasion of Iraq approached, Washington seemed to regard Turkey's geography as offering a military 'bridgehead' from which neighbouring countries could be attacked (Park 2002). Alternatively, in the post-9/11 world especially, some were inclined to cast Turkey as a barrier or insulator between the European and the Islamic Middle East's respective regional security complexes, with potential implications for the country's EU prospects (Buzan and Diez 1999). Then again, Turkey might be pressured, or inclined, to align more unambiguously with one side or the other, or again to be unwittingly 'relocated' according to the whims and behaviour of others. Indeed, one US analyst asserted that, with its invasion of Iraq, the USA had 'in one bold stroke managed to push Turkey back into the Middle East' (Barkey 2008: 31). This observation has more than a grain of truth in it, as the invasion of Iraq did indeed encourage Ankara to find common cause with its near neighbours, given that the Iraq invasion had highlighted the absence of a shared understanding of regional dynamics and of regional stakes between these two NATO allies. So the Cold War's end, the 9/11 attack, the AKP election victory, and the sequence of events immediately preceding and following the 2003 Iraq invasion undoubtedly encouraged Turkish foreign policy to become more attentive to its neighbourhood. As a consequence of this shift of emphasis, and particularly in the wake of Ahmet Davutoglu's appointment as foreign minister in May 2009, a debate emerged over the extent to which Turkey was shifting its foreign policy axis away from the West and towards the East (Oguzlu 2008a; International Crisis Group 2010a; Oguzlu and Kibaroglu 2009).[1] However, to function effectively, a bridge must reach both banks. The attempt to combine a domestic transformation that moved the country away from the farther reaches of Kemalist secularism with a more regionally oriented foreign policy has proved difficult to achieve without raising fundamental questions about the direction Turkey is taking. Furthermore, the prospect that Turkey might increasingly be perceived either as essentially western, or as essentially eastern and Islamic, carried possibly divisive implications for Turkey's domestic politics.

The Turkish model

The idea that Turkish experience provided a model that other Muslim majority states might adopt proved particularly attractive with the break-up of the Soviet Union, when it was seen as potentially applicable to the former Soviet Turkic states of central Asia and the Caspian region (Mango 1993; Bal 2000: 1–6). This perspective was a not entirely novel feature of US policy, and can even be traced back to the early Cold War years (Jacobs 2006). In Washington's thinking, and to some extent in Ankara's too, the Turkish model offered an alternative to a feared rise in fundamentalist, anti-western and Iranian influence in the region and a counter to the residual Russian presence there. In the first year or two of their independence, the leaders of the newly independent central Asian states, eager to deepen their autonomy from Russia, to engage with the West and to attract economic aid, appeared to welcome the Turkish example (Bal 2000: 144–82), although 'with differing degrees of enthusiasm' (Bal 2000: 181–82). For its part, and notwithstanding a more cautious foreign ministry, Turkish society and political leaders were euphoric following their rediscovery of this wider Turkic world, and some even began entertaining long-dormant pan-Turkic hopes and dreams. The entry of central Asia and Azerbaijan into the global political arena seemed to offer an end to that element of isolation that stemmed from Turkey's peripheral relationship to the regional complexes around it;

from its Ottoman historical legacy as oppressor; as Europe's 'other'; from its incomplete process of westernization; and from its ethnic distinctiveness. Now, Turks had discovered a world to which they might truly belong (Fuller 1993; Robins 1993; Sayari 1994; Swietochowski 1994; Carley 1995; Winrow 1995).

Thus Turkey was the first state to recognize Azerbaijan's independence and to open embassies in the central Asian republics. Economic and cultural agreements followed as Ankara established student programmes, TV channels, training schemes for civil servants, and despatched trade delegations. In 1992, Ankara established the Turkish International Cooperation and Development Agency (TIKA),[2] tasked to provide and coordinate development assistance of various kinds to the Turkic republics. Indeed, Ankara was driven more by pan-Turkic aspirations than by any desire to offer itself as a model. In any case, this uncharacteristically adventurous approach petered out on both fronts. As a model, Turkey was itself found wanting and not invariably attractive. The leaderships of the new republics were not necessarily seeking to democratize and, if they were, Turkey obviously suffered from deficiencies in this area. Economically and culturally, they were not in all respects always so far behind anything Turkey had to offer. Turkey did not have the resources to deliver on its aid promises, and in any case the new states sought to establish relationships directly with potential western donors. Furthermore, Russian influence in the former Soviet south had far from evaporated. The West, too, soon lost interest in advocating Turkey's virtues once it became evident both that Iran did not present much of a threat, and also that the region remained very much in Russia's backyard. As for Ankara's Turkic enthusiasm, although Turkish economic and cultural influence and associated pan-Turkic sentiment may yet develop and grow (Aras 2008), in these early post-Cold War years the cultural, linguistic and historical distance between Turkey and the newly independent Turkic republics came to appear more compelling than did their proximity. Another consideration was that the post-Soviet Turkic republics were not keen to exchange an overbearing Russia for an equally overbearing Turkey. In short, Turkey for a brief period had entertained 'inflated hopes and unrealistic expectations' (Winrow 1995: 3) in its attempt to embrace and lead a pan-Turkic world, and found instead that it 'was not yet ready for the role it wanted to play' (Bal 2000: 206). Even so, in October 2009 the first Turkic summit for four years was held in Nakhchivan, Azerbaijan. Attended by Gul and other Turkic heads of state (although Uzbekistan chose not to send a delegation), it agreed to institutionalize the forum by the creation of a Turkic Council (Kaya 2009). This development indicates that the dream of a more unified Turkic world remains alive, even if the reality remains less impressive.

Despite these early post-Cold War disappointments, the propagation of Turkey as a pro-western, developmental, secular and democratic model again made an appearance in US policy in the context of the Bush administration's post-9/11 aspiration to democratize the Middle East as a means of stabilizing it. Washington laid the Islamic extremism that was seen as the root cause of the 9/11 attacks at the door of the autocracy, corruption and economically and intellectually stagnant atmosphere that seemed pervasive throughout much of the Islamic world. The contrast with Turkey's evolution seemed quite striking. Thus, in March 2002, the Turcophile deputy defence secretary Paul Wolfowitz referred to Turkey as 'a model for those in the Muslim world who have aspirations for democratic progress and prosperity' (Wolfowitz 2002). National security advisor Condoleezza Rice described Turkey as 'an excellent model, a ninety nine percent Muslim country that has great importance as an alternative to radical Islam', while Bush himself suggested that Turkey 'provided Muslims around the world with a hopeful model of a modern and secular democracy' (Peterson 2002). Undersecretary of state Nicholas Burns declared that 'Turkey can be a strong force for democratic reform, economic development, interethnic and interreligious tolerance in the broader Middle East, north Africa, and central Asia' (Burns 2005). Washington's ambition to reform the Middle East eventually shaped up as the Broader Middle East and North Africa Initiative, adopted at a G8 summit in June 2004 (Gordon 2003; International Crisis Group 2004b).

Turkey cosponsored, with Yemen and Italy, the initiative's Democracy Assistance Dialogue, and generally presented itself as a key partner in the project. The AKP government proved notably keen to contribute to the debate over Islam and modernization. Indeed, both as foreign minister and as president, Abdullah Gul – whilst at all times insistent that any reforms must emanate from within the region and not be imposed from outside, and generally at pains to avoid using the word 'model' – repeatedly expressed sympathy for the broad content of the Bush administration's Broader Middle East Initiative and insisted on the need for regional transformation.[3] Gul first outlined what he dubbed 'the Turkish vision' for the Middle East region at the OIC foreign minister's conference in Tehran in May 2003, a year before the G8 initiative emerged, where he argued that the Muslim world needed 'to determine the issues and shortcomings that continue to hamper our progress', and that it needed to put its own house in order (Gul 2003). He identified corruption, instability and economic irrationality as among the problems facing Muslim societies, and called for the Muslim world to strive towards better governance, transparency, accountability, gender equality, and improved human rights and freedoms. There was a need to engender a 'sense of ownership on the part of the people of the systems they live in'. In an interview with the *International Herald Tribune* towards the end of 2003, he asserted that 'Turkey is living proof that a Muslim society can be governed in a democratic, accountable and transparent manner in accordance with European norms [...] Turkey testifies to the fact that European values indeed transcend geography, religion and cultures'.[4] Gul has also argued that, due to its unique cross-cultural nature and its broad experience of multilateral and regional diplomacy, Turkey is well placed to mobilize 'the dynamics of multilateral regional cooperation in the Middle East' (Gul 2004: 7).

In a speech he delivered at the American Enterprise Institute (AEI) in January 2004, prime minister Erdogan referred to Turkey's role in contributing to the development and dissemination to the Islamic world of universal values such as human rights, the rule of law and good governance. He noted, however, that 'Turkey's democratization was a self-imposed process. Turkey's experience is not a model that can be implemented identically in all other Muslim societies. Each Muslim society will have to find its own solutions, and each country should determine for itself both the method and the pacing by which this will occur'.[5] Ahmet Davutoglu, then serving as Erdogan's advisor, exhibited a similar coyness in recommending Turkey's practices to its neighbours, but otherwise continued in a similar vein. He, with the Turkish secretary general of the OIC Ekmeleddin Ihsanoglu, was instrumental in persuading the organization to undergo a process of structural reform, and to adopt a new ten-year action plan and a new charter. As Davutoglu noted in his speech at the OIC's foreign ministers' meeting in May 2009, 'this guiding document embraces shared values and principles that uphold peace, transparent, accountable and democratic good governance, the rule of law, the rights of women, respect for human rights and human dignity'.[6] In an article published in *The Irish Times* in March 2010, he asserted that 'Turkey's liberalizing and democratizing policies over recent years have turned the country into a beacon of hope for millions of people in the region who wish to emulate the Turkish experience and embrace modernity'.[7] Over the years, 'source of inspiration' rather than 'model' emerged as the preferred Turkish term.[8]

Turkey's secular elite has not invariably appreciated Washington's inclination to dwell on Turkey's relevance for the Islamic world, as they prefer to stress Turkey's politically secular arrangements and its western identity rather than its Islamic heritage and culture. Furthermore, critical analyses of the 'Turkish model' have tended to draw attention to the top-down imposition of secularism, the tutelage of the military over the country's politics, the unconsolidated democracy and the unresolved issue of 'Kurdishness' in Turkish society (Taspinar 2003; Ugur 2004; Altunisik 2005). US attachment to the 'Turkish model' has sometimes been inclined to overlook these imperfections. The Pakistani military, which has in the past exhibited authoritarianism and secularism, has arguably been more drawn towards Kemalist Turkey than most (Taspinar 2003: 39). In so far as Turkey can be presented as democratic, this has sometimes appeared threatening to those autocratic regimes which have otherwise been happy to align themselves diplomatically and strategically with the USA. Thus political considerations have often muted US championing of the Turkish model. More relevantly, a Turkey characterized by an enforced secularism, and by excessive pro-American and pro-Israeli leanings, was unlikely to generate much emulation in the Middle East, before or since 9/11.

Of course, many observers doubt that there is much of a market for democratization in the Middle East in any case. Reformers are relatively small in number throughout the region and lack influence. The small bourgeoisie of Arab societies are subordinated to autocratic, patrimonialist 'security state' regimes, with which they share a fear that Islamism could be the main victor of any democratization process. The preoccupation with Israel, the impact of oil wealth, and the colonial legacy of artificial state boundaries and imposed royal dynasties have also served to limit the scope for Arab democratization (Candar 2005; Erdogan 2005; McCabe 2007; Mohapatra 2008). Notwithstanding such doubts, for Turkey to emerge as a model for the Islamic world's reformers, two developments are necessary. One is that Turkey must achieve a harmonious balance between its secularism and modernity, on the one hand, and the Islamic faith of its people on the other. The impulses represented by the AKP government have a much greater chance of evolving towards this outcome, assuming the wilder excesses of both the country's Kemalist elite and the AKP's Islamic zealots can be sufficiently tamed. As one seasoned observer has expressed it, 'By accommodating rather than suppressing Islamist expression of many popular grievances, Turkey has set important precedents for the Islamic world' (Fuller 2004: 55). However, as Washington gradually came to appreciate that democracy in the Middle East might lead to the triumph of political Islam in its various but invariably anti-American forms, its enthusiasm for the 'Broader Middle East' project atrophied. Turkey's has not, although Ankara remains unwilling to allow its regional relationships to hinge on the domestic political practices of its neighbours.

The second requirement for the 'Turkish model' to become more marketable in the Middle East demands that Ankara distance itself from the USA and Israel in its regional policies. Turkey's pro-western stance has often been a hindrance to the development of closer regional relationships (Noureddine 2009), an observation that Washington might do well to ponder. The March 2003 TGNA vote came as a pleasant surprise to many Arab and Iranian observers, and the subsequent diplomatic positioning by the AKP government in the region has broadly added to this favourable impression. The crisis provoked by the May 2010 Israeli commando raid on a Turkish-flagged ship carrying aid to Gaza (Ozhan 2010), which followed quickly on the heels of Turkey's nuclear swap understanding with Iran, was arrived at in some defiance of Washington. It was emphasized still further when Turkey cast its Security Council vote against imposing further sanctions on Iran (Ustun 2010). Whether this pleased the 'Arab street' more than it did its governments is a moot point, and it is worth noting that Syria's president Assad regretfully but pointedly observed that, with the downturn in its relationship with Israel, Turkey was no longer in a position to mediate Middle East peace talks.[9] What these developments in Turkish regional behaviour do suggest is that, were the region to adopt the Turkish model of democratization to any significant degree, it would not necessarily lead to foreign policies that Washington would welcome. In any case, as many in Washington appreciate, democratization in the Middle East could lead to greater Islamification and anti-western sentiment in the region rather than more secularism at home and pro-western policies abroad. As some fear, this observation could apply to Turkey, too. Either way, reform in the Middle East will be a drawn-out process, should it occur at all. Pursuit of the Turkish model does not constitute a 'quick fix' solution to the region's problems, any more than it has for Turkey itself. Nor need it put an end to such civilizational conflict as exists between the West and the Muslim world.

Alliance of civilizations

In his January 2004 address at the AEI, referred to above, prime minister Erdogan said that, 'as one of the historical cradles of cross cultural interaction, Turkey remains ready to do its share to help establish a harmony of Islamic and western civilizations'. He also argued that Turkey's inclusion in the EU would 'demonstrate that a Muslim society can find acceptance by predominantly Christian societies when they share common universal and democratic values'. Within two months of this speech, an al Qaeda terrorist attack on the Madrid transport network resulted in the deaths of almost 200 victims. This led the Spanish prime minister to propose to the UN the creation of an 'Alliance of Civilizations between the western and the Arab and Muslim worlds'. The idea that civilizations needed to establish dialogue was not an original one, and indeed a Dialogue among Civilizations had been proposed to a receptive UN General Assembly in 1998 by the reformist president of Iran, Mohammad Khatami. Khatami's initiative addressed itself to all 'civilizations', and among the eminent persons appointed by the UN secretary general were representatives from the Sino world, Africa, India and Japan as well as from western and Muslim countries, but no Turkish representative.[10] Even before the accession to power of the AKP, in February 2002 Ankara had organized and hosted an EU/OIC inter-civilization conference as a response to the divisive impact of the 9/11 incidents and in an attempt to counter the 'clash of civilizations' thesis that appeared to be gaining credence at that time. An EU–OIC troika emerged from the 2002 forum and continues to meet.

At UN secretary general Kofi Annan's suggestion, Turkey was invited to co-sponsor the Spanish initiative. Turkey accepted, and the Alliance of Civilizations (AoC) initiative was formally launched in July 2005,[11] amidst great fanfare in Turkey in particular, and just one week after the 7 July terrorist attacks in London. Its first forum was held in Madrid in January 2008, the second in Istanbul in April 2009.[12] The AoC launched a number of programmes involving such diverse matters as youth employment, media initiatives, philanthropy and interreligious and cultural dialogue of various kinds (Kose 2009). A number of (mainly non-Muslim) affiliated countries adopted national plans to advance the aims of the AoC. In fact Turkey, and prime minister Erdogan in particular, became the chief protagonist for the AoC. Spanish interest waned with the passage of time and once its withdrawal from Iraq had been achieved. With its central involvement in the initiative, Turkey hoped to augment its international standing, enhance its EU prospects and increase its influence in the Islamic world (Kilinc 2009). In the context of this role, Erdogan repeatedly returned to the theme that his country's EU inclusion would be seen as proof that such an 'alliance' was possible, and frequently expressed his impatience both at the failure of some western states to appreciate Turkey's accession process from an intercivilization perspective, and at their more general lack of enthusiasm for the AoC project (Balci and Mis 2008). The USA did not join until May 2010, the hundredth country to do so. However, Muslim countries have, if anything, shown still less interest in the idea.

'Civilizations' are not global actors. Yet, although many of the problems confronting western and Islamic countries in their mutual relationships have been regarded as micro or political rather than macro and religious, an element of mutual antipathy has undoubtedly been at work. A succession of events and incidents that hinted at persisting 'civilizational' tension between the West and the Muslim world, and involving acts of terrorism, military interventions, armed clashes, statements by religious leaders, racist political movements and intercommunal strife, have served to intensify scepticism on all sides rather than lend support to the call for tolerance, understanding and harmony propagated by the AoC. Indeed, Turkey's policies – or, as is often the case, Erdogan's rash statements – have also been perceived in some quarters to highlight rather than negate the idea of a 'clash of civilizations'. For example, in April 2009 Turkey's objections to the appointment of former Danish prime minister Anders Fogh Rassmusen as the NATO secretary general – reportedly because of his right of free speech defence of the Danish cartoonists who had three years earlier caused a global uproar for satirizing the Prophet – created considerable irritation in Europe and led to allegations that Ankara was behaving as the Islamic world's representative in NATO. In fact, Erdogan was not supported in his stance by others in the Turkish government. In any case, his position owed much to his objection to Denmark's hosting of the Kurdish TV station ROJ-TV, and to an apprehension that Rasmussen's appointment might be misrepresented or misconstrued in the Muslim world. Even so, the incident made Turkey appear as an uncooperative alliance member that was at best only half-heartedly committed to media freedoms as understood elsewhere in NATO.[13]

On occasion, Turkish rhetoric could easily be construed as being more concerned with Islamophobia in the West than with the mistreatment of Christians and others in the East, and with mistreatment of Muslims than mistreatment by them (Balci and Mis 2008: 396–97). This could appear both hypocritical and unconducive to civilization harmony. The EU continues to identify failings in Turkey's treatment of its religious minorities, both Christian and Muslim, and in its handling of the Ecumenical patriarchate and Halki Seminary issues, against a backdrop of Turkish attacks against Europe's alleged Islamophobia.[14] Turkey has embraced Hamas and denied it is a terrorist organization, whilst continuing the fight against the PKK and banning its own elected Kurdish political party. Erdogan has proved able to claim simultaneously that Muslims do not kill Muslims, embrace the repressive Sudanese and Iranian leaderships and condemn Israel's behaviour in Gaza. The list of contradictions and alleged hypocrisies is a long one, and Turkish analysts and pundits have not been slow in pointing them out (Dereli 2009/2010). Overall, it is a moot point whether the content of the AKP's foreign policy, and the rhetoric that has frequently accompanied it, has calmed intercivilization misperception more than it has augmented it.

Turkey's sponsorship of the AoC reflects its desire to raise its own profile and can be linked to its EU aspirations. It might also be seen as part of the AKP's domestic tussle with its secularist opponents (Kilinc 2009). However, the project fits uneasily with the determination Ankara otherwise shows to deny the existence of civilization fault lines. Under the AKP, Turkey's position has been that universal values unite humanity, and that Turkey in its very nature is a repository and expression of universal values. As a hybrid state, it seeks to deny the existence of opposing civilizations. Yet, in seeking to overcome a clash between civilizations, the AoC is predicated on the assumption that distinct civilizations exist and that there must be tolerance, dialogue and harmony between them (Balci 2009). In engaging with this civilization conflict, and as 'Christian' Spain's 'Muslim' partner, Turkey has in effect recognized the existence of these two worlds, and in the process has drawn yet more attention to the question of its own identity. The AoC, an honourable attempt to minimize global tension, may have served only to underscore the very complexity, even invidiousness, of Turkey's position. Which 'side' is Turkey on? Is Turkey – can Turkey be – both and/or neither at one and the same time? Does Turkey's behaviour confirm its membership of one civilization more than the other? Is it a 'bridge' between East and West in the sense of being a kind of hybrid of the two? Or is it a 'bridge' between East and West in the sense of bringing them into contact, but perhaps not truly belonging to either? Or, is Turkey's very nature, and its potential both as a 'model' for the Muslim world and as an EU member state, an affront to the very notion that there is necessarily an East and a West? The very notion of distinct civilizations implies 'a hardness of edge and an internal consistency' (Findley 2005: 3) that both Turkey's history and its contemporary circumstances arguably rebut.

Turkey and the OIC

Turkey's relationship to the rest of the Islamic world has followed a quite remarkable trajectory. With the Ottoman conquest of Arab lands in 1517, the title of Caliph – which incorporated both temporal and religious authority over, and leadership of, the entire Islamic world – was transferred from the Mamluks of Egypt to the Ottoman sultans. There it remained until the

Turkish republic's unilateral abolition of the caliphate in 1924. Since that time, there has been no overall leadership of the Islamic world. Although the abolition was greeted with disquiet, Turkey's relations with Muslim countries in the early decades of the republic were not invariably bad or distant, and with Iran, Iraq and Afghanistan were quite good, as reflected by the 1937 Sadabad Pact between them. Turkey also attended the Islamic world's second international conference, held in Cairo in 1926. After the Second World War and the emergence of the Cold War, and notwithstanding its 1947 UN vote against the partition of Palestine and such diplomatic ventures as the 1955 Baghdad Pact, Turkey became surely the most estranged from global Islam of all Muslim states. When the OIC was formed in 1969, Turkey agreed to participate, but refused to sign the organization's charter on the grounds that it contravened both Turkey's secular constitution and its western political alignment (Aykan 1994). After all, the charter aimed 'to preserve Islamic spiritual, ethnic, social and economic values' and 'to promote Islamic solidarity among member states'.[15] Consequently, Turkey did not participate in the more religiously oriented organs of the organization, such as the International Islamic Court of Justice or the Islamic Jurisprudence Academy. In practice, Turkey's political stance on many issues often overlapped with that of the majority of OIC members. For example, Ankara joined other OIC states in opposing Israel's 1980 declaration of Jerusalem as its capital, condemned Israel's 1981 bombing of Iraq's Osirak reactor, opposed Washington's attempts to isolate Iran and Libya, and condemned the US bombing of Libya in 1986. However, Ankara also frequently reserved its position on OIC resolutions relating to Zionism or Israel's right to exist, and withstood the Arab demands that it break relations with Israel. Indeed, in 1997 president Demirel walked out of an OIC summit in Tehran in protest at Arab attacks on Turkey's relationship with Israel.

Notwithstanding its semi-detached and frequently uncomfortable status, Turkey evolved into a quite active and influential OIC member. In 1974 it agreed to contribute to the OIC's budget, joined its Islamic Development Bank in 1975, participated – for the first time at foreign-minister level – at the Jeddah foreign ministers' meeting in the same year, and hosted the OIC foreign ministers' meeting in Istanbul in 1976, as well as the meetings in 1991 and 2004. At the 1976 gathering and at Turkey's initiative, the OIC agreed to the establishment of the Research Centre for Islamic History, Art and Culture and the Statistical, Economic, Social Research and Training Centre, in Istanbul and Ankara respectively. Turkey still hosts these two bodies. In 1981, Turkey was for the first time represented at the OIC's summit (its third) by the prime minister. In 1984, Turkey agreed to chair the OIC's Standing Committee on Economic and Commercial Cooperation (COMCEC), which is to this day chaired by the Turkish president. This formed one plank in a more general Turkish economic opening to Islamic states during the 1970s and 1980s, in response to the 1973 oil price hike and in keeping with the wider liberalization of the Turkish economy in the 1980s.

Turkish trade with other Islamic countries rose from around a quarter to almost a half of all Turkish trade by the middle of the 1980s, only to fall away again as the decade came to an end. A 1983 law permitted Islamic finance houses to open for business in Turkey, and flows of funds into Turkey from especially the oil-rich Gulf states followed. The globalization of the Turkish economy opened up the country to Islamic trade and business practices as well as to those of the West. However, trade between Islamic states remained undeveloped and could not offer an alternative to Turkey's European trade relationships.

Ankara also sought to interest the OIC in political issues close to its own heart, notably in the immediate post-Cold War years. It successfully lobbied for inclusion of the Turkic states of the former Soviet Union; brought the crisis in Bosnia-Herzegovina to the attention of the OIC, not least as a way to force the West to pay attention to the plight of the Bosnian Muslims (Hale 2000: 262); and gained a modicum of support for the plight of ethnic Turks in Bulgaria (Hale 2000: 169) and in Greek Thrace, and for Azerbaijan in its conflict with Armenia over Nagorno–Karabakh. On the other hand, Ankara disappointingly failed to achieve recognition of the TRNC within the Islamic world, and it enjoys only observer status within the OIC. More broadly, the OIC remained preoccupied with the Palestinian issue and with Arab affairs generally, and its readiness to focus on issues of greater concern to Ankara has been patchy at best. Mutual Turkish–Arab mistrust, Arab support for Syria and Iraq over their water differences with Turkey, the political fragmentation of and rivalries within the Muslim world, and the limited scope for the development of deeper economic relationships between its members all served to restrict Turkey's investment and faith in the OIC. From Ankara's perspective, the OIC offered a platform, enabled it to enhance its relationships with other Muslim majority states, and dovetailed with the 'bridging' role that both Ankara and the West have aspired for Turkey to play. A strong example of this was the EU–OIC forum organized by Turkey and held in Istanbul in 2002. But it has not offered a diplomatic orientation either alternative to, or comparable with, that which Turkey has achieved with the West. For most of its history, the OIC failed to help Ankara overcome the distance between itself and the rest of the Islamic world.

With the election of the AKP government, followed by the 1 January 2005 elevation of a Turkish citizen, Ekmeleddin Ihsanoglu, as OIC secretary general in the first-ever election for that office, Turkey's influence within the OIC increased in line with its more active diplomacy towards the Islamic world. Ankara has made additional voluntary contributions to the OIC, and Ihsanoglu has spearheaded a reform effort aimed at extending the remit of the OIC, intensifying its focus on, and embrace of, global issues such as women's and human rights, and tightening the political relationships between its members. Overall, the objective has been to make the OIC more action-oriented and less attached to predominantly rhetorical stances. In 2005, a blueprint was laid down for a ten-year plan of action aimed at the 'promotion of tolerance and moderation, modernization, extensive reforms in all spheres of activities including science and technology, education, trade enhancement, emphasizes good governance and promotion of human rights in the Muslim world, especially with regard to rights of children, women and the elderly and the family values enshrined by Islam'.[16] In 2008, the organization adopted an updated charter which incorporated, among other innovations, an OIC human rights commission. The OIC's first women's rights' meeting was held in Cairo in 2006. Turkey also fought hard to establish an OIC-wide trade preference system, not least because the percentage of Turkey's total trade conducted with OIC members has grown from around seventeen per cent in 2006 to almost a quarter of Turkish trade in 2008.[17] Under the AKP, Turkey has also persisted in using the OIC as a forum where it could lobby on behalf of issues in which it had a political stake. As these increasingly dovetailed with the perspectives of the wider OIC membership, Ankara's efforts met with more success than had earlier been the case. This was most notably so in the wake of the 31 May 2010 Israeli commando raid on a Turkish-registered ship carrying aid to Gaza. An extraordinary OIC meeting was held in Jeddah, which expressed its appreciation of Turkey's stance and adopted a resolution exactly mirroring Turkey's diplomatic position.[18]

However, and notwithstanding these valiant Turkish efforts, in its resolutions and debates the OIC remains far more virulent in its rhetoric against the West for its alleged Islamophobia and in the face of any perceived aggression against Muslim states and peoples than it does when confronted with terrorist attacks carried out by Muslims, or the internal governance and human rights failings of Islamic states, or conflictual relationships between OIC members. In fact, in 2007 the OIC set up an Islamophobia Observatory. The OIC's fifty-seven members incorporate some of the world's worst human rights offenders, its most corrupt governments and its most religiously intolerant. Its membership includes some of the world's richest and some of its poorest societies, but there is no effective OIC mechanism for addressing this. Little is done by the OIC to address conflict between or within its member states. It includes some of the worst available instances of the repression of women that the world has to offer. In short, OIC states for the most part bear little economic, social or political resemblance to the EU states that Ankara wishes to join, and the OIC remains ineffective as a body that might contribute towards closing this gap. Turkey may have moved close to the OIC, but it is less evident that the OIC or its member states have moved closer to Turkey. Turkey's cultivation of its status within the OIC certainly puts the eastern leg of the bridge on firmer foundations, but it is less clear that it does anything to negate the need for a bridge. Indeed, some of Ankara's investment in its role within the OIC could be seen by some as weakening the bridge's western foundations.

Turkey's multilateralism: peacekeeping in the Balkans

In what became Turkey's first deployment abroad of military forces since the republic's inception, in 1950 Ankara offered to contribute a brigade of soldiers to support the US-led UN force that was despatched to the Korean peninsula to resist aggression from the communist north. Turkey evolved into the coalition's fourth largest military contributor and retained its force deployment to the peninsula until 1966. Turkey's leaders were concerned at the rise of Soviet power and the menace it posed to Turkey directly, and they saw in the north Korean attack a globalization of the communist menace. However, their chief motivation in offering troops was to convince a doubting NATO of the merits of Turkey's inclusion in the alliance (Vander Lippe 2000; Brown 2008). Having achieved its aim in 1952, during the Cold War, Turkey had little reason, nor was it presented with opportunities, to make further contributions to multilateral peacekeeping efforts. However, with the Cold War's demise and the removal of the Soviet threat, Ankara again needed to reassure its western allies of its strategic utility and that it could be a security 'provider' in the new world order that was taking shape. This pressure became still more intense after 9/11, when Turkey felt it had a particular obligation and interest in preventing the tensions between the Islamic world and the West from escalating.

However, there were additional factors at play too. Turkey found itself geographically located in the eye of a storm of post-Cold War disorders, in the Balkans, the Caucasus and the Middle East. Furthermore, with the removal of the Cold War's overlay, Turks were again reconnected to former Ottoman or Turkic provinces with which they felt empathy or in which they again began to identify interests. These new circumstances provided space for the appearance, or re-emergence, of the phenomenon known as neo-Ottomanism (Yavuz 1998). Furthermore, in response to the changed global conditions, NATO embarked on its transformation from a primarily regionally based collective defence alliance towards a more global, interventionist 'force for good'. The EU, too, began to aspire to play a role as a more active agent of global security. As a member of one and an aspirant for membership of the other, Ankara had incentives to engage with this new thinking and the roles that went with it (Gruen 2006; Oguzlu and Gungor 2006; Ibas 2007). With the shift in Turkey's foreign and security policy prioritization that was prompted by both the US-led Iraq invasion of 2003 and the AKP's electoral victory in November 2002, Ankara also began to more fully internalize the value of multilateral approaches to regional and global security problems, especially in those theatres where its own identity issues were brought into play. It also began to grasp that, with the removal of the iron curtain and the greater diplomatic fluidity of the post-Cold War era, it had the scope and the incentive to emerge as a truly multiregional actor (Fuller and Lesser 1993; Mastny and Nation 1996; Candar and Fuller 2001; Rubin and Kirisci 2001).

The first test and opportunity for a new Turkish stance came with the Yugoslav crisis (Lesser 2000; Sayari 2000; Calis 2001; Robins 2003: 343–78). Initially, Ankara's position mirrored that of the EU and the USA, which was that Yugoslavia's territorial integrity should be preserved. Ankara had generally enjoyed a friendly relationship with Yugoslavia, which also served as a major transit route for Turkish trade with Europe. Ankara was nervous that a crisis there could generate a major humanitarian and refugee problem, as well as tensions between the neighbouring Balkan states. Furthermore, Turkey had generally shied away from revisionism since the republic's inception. However, once the EU recognized the independence of Slovenia and Croatia, it was evident both that the days of Yugoslavia were numbered and that Serbian policies were threatening further destabilization. Turkey was also subjected to lobbying by both the Bosnian and the Macedonian authorities. Ankara now swung emphatically towards a championing of the Muslim population of Bosnia (known as Bosniaks) on both humanitarian and identity grounds. Indeed, it is estimated that between ten and twenty per cent of Turks have Balkan antecedents, and this added to the widespread fellow feeling in Turkey for the plight of Bosnia's Muslims (Calis 2001: 146; Robins 2003: 345). In February 1992, Turkey became only the second state after Bulgaria to extend diplomatic recognition to Bosnia and Macedonia, and as the killing mounted Turks began to share with other Muslims around the world the sense that the West's inaction masked a bias towards the Christian Serbs and against the Bosniaks. Ankara sought to drum up support for their plight at the OIC, without much practical success, and also began secretly to arm the increasingly beleaguered Bosniaks in defiance of a UN arms embargo. Iran also sent arms, and it is reckoned that up to 4000 mostly Afghan-trained Islamic fighters entered the fray on the Bosniak side.

In August 1992, Ankara submitted an action plan both to the UN Security Council and to the London conference on Yugoslavia. This called for UN-sanctioned air raids against Serb forces and a ground-force intervention into the region. In November 1992, Turkey hosted a Balkans conference in Istanbul, boycotted by Athens, which called for general recognition of Macedonia, in stark contrast to the Greek position. Turkey also began sending aid to Bosnia and receiving Bosniak refugees. By early 1993, there were in excess of 200,000 such refugees in Turkey, many of them staying at the homes of Turkish relatives. Ankara's diplomacy had by now run well ahead of that of its more cautious western allies. That Turkey had little more capacity to act unilaterally did not prevent some Turks from turning on the government for subordinating its own heady inclinations to the slower-moving multilateral diplomatic effort. This was indeed a frustrating moment for Turkish diplomacy, as both its limited influence and the fact that its western allies did not share its perspective were abundantly apparent. However, Turkish diplomacy also appears to have had the effect of keeping the issue from domination by the more radical edge of the Islamic world's spectrum. It may also have helped galvanize the West's eventual response. Certainly the US swung progressively towards support for the Bosniaks.

As the UN moved to intervene more actively in the crisis, Turkey pursued two additional lines of approach. One was to present itself as mediator between the Bosniak and Croat forces in Bosnia. Both parties encouraged Ankara in this role, as did Brussels and Washington. The result was the Washington Agreement of 1994 establishing the Croat–Bosnian Federation, as well as the enduring friendship towards Turkey of both Croatia and Bosnia. The other approach was to make its security forces available for UN, NATO and indeed EU peacekeeping missions in former Yugoslavia. Ankara had declared its readiness to contribute to a UN-led peace force in Bosnia as early as December 1992, and in April 1993 Turkey provided eighteen F-16s to NATO's 'Operation Clear Skies', designed to impose a no-fly zone. Around a year later, it was agreed that Turkey should contribute around 1500 troops to the UN Protection Force (UNPROFOR)[19] to help maintain the peace between the Croatian and Bosniak communities of Zeneca in central Bosnia. This signalled that the unease concerning the deployment of troops, associated in some minds with those of the former imperial Ottoman power, had finally been stilled. In 1995, UNPROFOR became the NATO-led Implementation Force (IFOR), which a year later became the Stabilization Force (SFOR). The Turkish deployment was generally regarded as a considerable success, not least as a result of the contribution the Turks made to educational, health and other facilities in their area of operations. Ankara also contributed police officers to Bosnia, and its navy participated in Operation Sharp Guard, designed to enforce a naval blockade against the participants in the Bosnian conflict. In 2004, the UN authorized the EU to take over responsibility for peacekeeping in Bosnia from the NATO-led SFOR. The force now became known as the EU Force (EUFOR-ALTHEA).[20] Turkey contributed troops, police officers and observers to the force, which at the time of writing number almost 300 Turkish personnel.

Since its involvement in the Bosnian crisis, Turkey has emerged as a regular contributor to multilateral peacekeeping efforts in the Balkans. It has contributed soldiers, ships, aircraft and police units to the NATO-led Kosovo Force (KFOR), and to NATO- and EU-led forces in Macedonia and Albania. At the time of writing, there are in excess of 1000 uniformed Turkish personnel on peacekeeping missions in the Balkans, mostly in Kosovo.[21] Ankara's relations with Bosnia in particular, but also Albania, Macedonia and Kosovo, are particularly close. Turkey has been quite heavily involved in training the armed forces of its Balkan friends, largely under the umbrella of the NATO Partnership for Peace (PfP) programme,[22] which has also afforded Turkey a platform for the training of forces from the Caucasus and central Asia. With its 2005 opening in Ankara of both a training centre and a counter-terrorism centre, and its 2006 opening in Konya of a tactical air training centre, NATO's PfP programme and its peacekeeping activities have emerged as a significant vehicle for Turkish military and diplomatic outreach.

Multilateralism and 'neo-Ottomanism': Turkish diplomacy in the Balkans

Along with its European neighbours to its immediate west and north, Turkey participated in the February 1988 launch of the Balkan Multilateral Cooperation Process, the first Balkan regional gathering since 1945. However, given the contrasting economic and political systems and diplomatic alignments of the participating states, and the Yugoslav crisis that broke out shortly afterwards, little progress was made, although a follow-up meeting did take place in 1990. The initiative was resurrected in 1996 as the South East European Cooperation Process (SEECP) (Cevikoz 1997–98). In other words, Ankara was quick to re-engage in the region as soon as political conditions there were ripe. There are some interesting observations to draw from the way in which Turkey's involvement in post-Cold War Balkan politics have evolved. There can be little doubt that Ankara was drawn into the region's affairs as a result of its historical legacy there, and particularly through its empathy with the region's Muslims (Bulut 2004). The flight of over of 300,000 ethnic Turks from Bulgaria in 1989 following an official campaign of discrimination and harassment by the authorities in Sofia had served as a reminder of the Ottoman legacy of 'outer Turkish' communities that remained scattered throughout the region, and of how the plight of the region's Muslim minorities could affect Turkey's relationships with its Balkan neighbours (Petkova 2002). At the outset of the Yugoslav crises, Ankara's rhetoric was often heady, passionate and infused with an identity-based approach. The plight of the region's Muslims aroused considerable passion on Turkey's streets too. In this, it found itself out of step with, or ahead of, its western allies, and turned to the Islamic world in a bid to garner support. Turkey was also quick to recognize Kosovo's independence and remains one of its firmest champions (Eralp 2010). Yet in its actions Ankara also chose not to stray far from its western allies, nor from the pace of international diplomacy as it worked its way through at the UN. Ankara was confronted not only with its own limitations, but also with the necessity, and indeed the virtues, of multilateralism.

Notwithstanding the fact that its relations with the region's majority Muslim states – Albania, Kosovo and Bosnia – are generally warmer and more developed, Turkey has been diplomatically active in the search for resolutions to the region's myriad differences, most notably since Davutoglu entered the corridors of power. In particular, Davutoglu has offered Turkey's mediation to help overcome the differences between Croatia, Serbia and Bosnia, often under the auspices of SEECP. These efforts produced the Istanbul Declaration of April 2010 between Turkey, Serbia and Bosnia, which recognizes the territorial integrity and sovereignty of Bosnia, records a number of confidence-building measures that have been agreed, and welcomes Serbia's declaration of regret for the Srebenica atrocities – a declaration which Ankara was instrumental in encouraging.[23] Ankara's relationship with Croatia is following a similar trajectory. In addition to the mutually supportive diplomatic understanding between the two states, an initiative between Turkey, Croatia and Bosnia is focusing on infrastructure projects and reconstruction in the region.[24] Turkey has actively sought reconciliation between Serbia and Kosovo on the basis that only this will produce a lasting peace in the region and ensure Kosovo's security. It also offers a means to bring Serbia in from the cold. Turkey has sought, and generally achieved, friendship with all countries in the Balkans, including Serbia, with whom it has free trade, defence cooperation and visa-waiving agreements.[25] President Gul visited Serbia in October 2009, followed by prime minister Erdogan in July 2010. Needless to say, the Turkish economic stake in the region is also increasing significantly (Alic 2010).

This activity arguably does warrant the epithet 'neo-Ottomanism' in the sense that Turkey is rebuilding its relationships with former imperial domains, and perhaps also in the sense that it is reasserting its developing economic and political power. This is expressed in benign and constructive rather than atavistic forms, however. Furthermore, although there is an element of Islamic identity politics behind Ankara's Balkan diplomacy, this is far from exclusively so. Ankara's Balkan overtures also qualify or even undermine the suspicion that Turkey is favouring the East over the West. Rather, the evidence offered by its Balkan diplomacy and presence more readily suggests that it is endeavouring to restore its relationships with all of its neighbours – that its approach is as multidirectional as Davutoglu claims it is.

Turkey's multilateralism: Afghanistan and Lebanon

The October 2001 US-led attack against the Taliban regime and al Qaeda in Afghanistan led rapidly to the overthrow of the Taliban and the establishment of the UN-mandated International Security Assistance Force (ISAF)[26] in December 2001. Although the invasion was unpopular in Turkey, Ankara was quick to offer troops to the force 'as a country with deep historical ties and a particular bond of friendship with Afghanistan and in line with her responsibilities within NATO',[27] and was one of just eighteen NATO and PfP countries that contributed in this initial phase. In fact, leadership of ISAF did not pass to NATO until August 2003, by which time Turkey had already undertaken its first command of the twenty-two-nation-strong ISAF during the period June 2002 until February 2003, and had deployed 1400 troops to Afghanistan. Between February and August 2005, Turkey again commanded ISAF, the only country to have undertaken the role twice. At the time of writing, Turkey heads the Kabul Regional Command and has around 1700 troops in the country (Erdagi 2005; Cetin 2007; Guney 2007; Ibas 2007; Weitz 2010). In 2003, former Turkish foreign minister Hikmet Cetin was appointed as NATO's first senior civilian representative in Afghanistan. In November 2006, Ankara established its own civilian-led Provincial Reconstruction Team (PRT) in Wardak province. Its 130 operatives are engaged in health and education programmes, economic and infrastructure reconstruction and the training of officials. In July 2010, Turkey opened a second PRT at Jowzan in the north of the country (Dogan 2010). Turkey's aid and reconstruction efforts in Afghanistan are funded chiefly by TIKA, and have resulted in the building or refurbishment of around seventy schools, a sports complex, numerous hospitals and clinics, the award of hundreds of educational scholarships, and the restoration of roads, bridges and other buildings. From the outset, Turkish troops in Afghanistan have not engaged in counter-insurgency operations, as Ankara does not wish to associate with something that is regarded by some Afghans as an invasion force, although it is engaged in the training of Afghan soldiers for such roles.

The Turkish presence in Afghanistan reflects to some degree the long-established friendship between the two countries that dates back to the Ottoman era and that is given extra weight by the Turkic ethnicity of the northern Afghan people. The 1921 treaty of friendship between them, signed during Turkey's ongoing war of independence, made Afghanistan only the second state after the Soviet Union to recognize the new Turkish republic. In 1928 this treaty was strengthened, and Kabul even adopted a constitution based on the Kemalist model. The 1937 Saadabad Pact of non-aggression between Turkey, Afghanistan, Iraq and Iran was a further indication of their close relationship, as was the training of Afghan military officers in Turkey. Turkey's relations with Kabul remained warm until the Soviet intervention in December 1979, and Ankara retained close contacts with elements of the Afghan Northern Alliance during the Afghan civil wars of the 1990s. Although Turkey's engagement with Afghanistan since the Taliban's overthrow has been conducted in a multilateral and essentially NATO context, it has also reflected a deeper sense of goodwill, kinship and responsibility for the Afghan people. As a former Turkish special coordinator for Afghan affairs has insisted, Turkey's role in the country has long been based on the exercise of 'soft power' (Erman 2010). Thus Ankara has been keen to distance itself from the US-led war against the Taliban in the south of the country. Indeed, the AKP government has taken the view that elements of the Taliban need to be brought into the political process, and that Afghanistan cannot be pacified without improved cooperation between Kabul and Islamabad. To that end, Turkey has hosted annual meetings between the Afghan and Pakistani heads of state since 2007, and has brought together intelligence and military officials. In January 2010, it also brought them together with neighbouring and other interested countries such as China, Iran, the central Asian states and the UK (Dogan 2010; Weitz 2010).[28] Overall, Ankara's inclinations are towards 'Afghanization' and 'regionalization' of the approach to that country's travails.

Since 2006, Turkey has contributed to the UN Interim Force in Lebanon (UNIFIL), first established in 1978 but enhanced in 2006 in order to provide an effective security buffer between Israeli forces and those of Lebanon's Hezbollah in the wake of their summer conflict.[29] European states, and especially France and Italy, lobbied hard for UNIFIL's enhancement and they have since provided the lion's share of the assets. Germany commands the maritime element, and the initial EU contribution numbered around 7000 personnel. Turkey's contribution consists primarily of maritime assets, but it also provides an army engineering unit, numbering around 1000 personnel in total. Ankara has also made air bases and ports available to UNIFIL's contributors.[30] Typically, Turkey has also been keen to provide humanitarian assistance, infrastructure repair and other welcome services to the local population. Turkey's participation was, and in some quarters still is, a domestically sensitive issue which was opposed by public opinion, president Sezer and most of the parliamentary opposition.

Ankara needed reassurance that the force would not be used to disarm Hezbollah, and many critics in Turkey believed the deployment would be both dangerous and futile. Some even saw it as a western occupation force acting in the interests of Israel, as did Lebanon's Hezbollah – at least rhetorically. Turks were also aware that their country's contribution was regarded as particularly desirable by the West in order to give the force a Muslim component (Kardas 2009a, 2009b). In fact predominantly Islamic countries such as Brunei, Qatar, Indonesia, Malaysia and Bangladesh have also contributed. According to foreign minister Davutoglu, Turkey's participation in UNIFIL forms part of his government's wider engagement with Lebanon and with the region as a whole. Thus in comments to Turkey's parliament in June 2009 he claimed that 'preserving peace in Lebanon is one of Turkey's responsibilities as part of our country's historical obligations', and that Turkey's participation in UNIFIL should not be assessed as having 'solely military value but should be considered as a reflection of Turkey's stance in the region' (Kasapoglu 2009).

Turkey's multilateralism: between East and West

Turkey's engagement with Afghanistan through its membership of the western alliance, and its participation in a largely EU-staffed force in Lebanon, reflect its embrace of the West's shift towards 'out of area' interventions aimed at projecting stability and emphasizing crisis management and peacebuilding missions (Guney 2007; Gonul 2010). Thus, 'when the west started to see peacekeeping operations through a new perspective, Turkey's interest in such operations also developed' (Oguzlu and Gungor 2006: 479). Turkey's Defence White Paper 2000 introduced crisis management and crisis interventions as new military roles,[31] and a significant portion of the Turkish military now undergo specialized training for peacekeeping missions. With the military's now considerable peacekeeping experience, including that of working alongside the militaries of other states, a raft of Turkish soldiers has emerged with an altogether more internationalized outlook and professional identity than is traditionally associated with the Turkish military. The Turkish experience is indeed considerable, and the impact on Turkey's armed forces as well as the country's global image could in time be transformative. Turkey contributed to UN Iraq–Iran and Iraq–Kuwait observer missions between 1998 and 2003; put 300 troops at the disposal of the UN operation in Somalia 1993–94, which Turkey also commanded for a period; and has provided observers and monitors (often police officials) to various UN missions in Georgia since 1994, and also in Burundi, the Central African Republic and Chad, Haiti, the Ivory Coast, Congo, Liberia, East Timor and Sudan. In 2009, and in the wake of a number of pirate raids on Turkish merchant vessels, Ankara also decided to contribute to one of the four international maritime operations against Somalian pirates operating in the Gulf of Aden (Uslu 2009c).

Ankara thus appears simultaneously to share in the West's embrace of far-flung crisis management and peacebuilding missions, but to also be driven by motivations at some variance with those of its NATO and EU allies. Turkey's participation in multilateral peacebuilding missions has metamorphosed into a vehicle for the pursuit of some of its wider foreign policy objectives and approaches. It is a means of augmenting its influence and raising its profile in the host countries and regions, and of reconnecting with its non-western or former Ottoman spheres of interest and identity. In Afghanistan and Lebanon in particular, there has been considerable focus on the 'hearts and minds' aspects of the mission, and a determination to avoid confrontations with local populations and forces. It is regarded as part of Turkey's new emphasis on a 'soft' power approach to diplomacy. Ankara's participation has been espe-cially welcomed by its western partners, who appreciate the impact Turkish forces can have on the way in which an external force is perceived by the local population. Ankara has also used the opportunities presented by its physical investment in some of the world's conflict zones to engage in diplomatic mediation, including between the factions in Lebanon. Yet Turkey is also compromised. Peacebuilding interventions are invariably western-initiated and led, and are frequently directed towards predominantly Islamic conflict zones. Islamic governments are often incapable or disinclined to participate, even where it is their co-religionists that are in need of help. Public opinion, and that of much of Turkey's elite, has sometimes exhibited a degree of sus-picion of western intentions comparable with that found in the wider Muslim world. Yet Turkey has nevertheless progressively carved out something of a foreign policy niche for the country, as one of the very few fully active peacebuilders of the Islamic world. In this respect, it is a leader in the Islamic world, but has yet to recruit committed followers.

9 Between consumers and producers

Turkey as an energy bridge?

Introduction: the globalization of energy politics

The increased world demand for, and trade in, energy resources offers one of the most dramatic illustrations of globalization. Industrialization, urbanization, population growth, rising material living standards and expectations, and world trade, travel and communications have all contributed to the global rise in demand for energy. Indeed, the (uneven) global economic development of the twentieth century and the material comforts and ease of travel associated with it would not have been possible without the ready availability of relatively cheap supplies of traded energy products, primarily oil. The scale of this demand has meant that few economically developed states are now able to meet their energy requirements from domestic resources. To take the USA as an illustrative example, from the mid-nineteenth century until the Second World War it was the world's leading oil producer, and throughout the period was largely self-sufficient in, and indeed an exporter of, oil. Since the late 1940s, US reliance on imported oil has steadily risen as needs have grown, and imports now account for well over half of domestic oil consumption. Furthermore, by 1972 domestic production had entered into an irreversible decline (Klare 2004: 7–18). European and Japanese dependence on imported oil is greater still.

In recent years, newly industrializing and demographically expanding states in the developing world, notably China and India, have accounted for most of the global increase in demand for oil. Furthermore, gas is increasingly joining oil as a globally sought-after energy resource, although its transportation over long distances is more problematic. This explosive growth in demand for energy has led to an intensifying search for new sources of supply, a trend that is amplified by the fact that the extraction of additional supplies from the world's existing oil fields is increasingly costly and technologically challenging. Indeed, many analysts contend that the world economy has reached, or is approaching, so-called 'peak oil', the turning point at which oil extraction reaches its maximum level and enters a period of terminal decline (Deffeyes 2001, 2005; Hirsch 2005; Roberts 2005; Energy Watch Group 2008). Although the imminence and seriousness of 'peak oil' are bathed in some controversy, the logic that the gap will widen as consumption increases and non-renewable resources deplete seems inexorable. The discovery and exploitation of new energy fields, and increased investment in extraction and transportation of energy from existing fields, can surely only delay the arrival of this critical point, or slow the widening of the gap between supply and demand. In the meantime, the search for new fields, and the exploitation and transportation of their output, is and will continue to be intensely competitive. Furthermore, the mismatch between the geographical distribution of the world's reserves of non-renewable energy supplies, and the major centres of demand for it, is and will remain striking. The world's oil and gas reserves are disproportionately located in the industrially undeveloped and sometimes politically unstable or problematic corners of the globe. They are also generally remote from the main centres of demand. This geopolitical and geostrategic fact intensifies the globalization of the energy industry, and adds to the tension and scope for conflict generated by the scramble for access to the world's energy resources (Klare 2001, 2008; Pascual and Elkind 2010).

It has also opened up an opportunity for Turkey to emerge as a player in global energy politics. This involves the construction of a pipeline network that would criss-cross Turkish territory. Again, it is Turkey's geographical location that is key to this development. However, pipeline politics are enormously complicated (Hill 2004; Bacik 2006; Fink 2006; Babali 2009, 2010; Saivetz 2009). The energy business is a quintessentially globalized and transnational one. There are multiple players – governments, extraction companies, energy transportation and pipeline construction companies, financial institutions. There are also mixed motives, and a wide range of complex legal, technical, financial, environmental, physical and political factors that come into play. Negotiations are complex, and plans and agreements made do not always come to fruition, or are put on hold until difficulties and differences can be resolved. This chapter aims only to offer an overview of the prospects, problems and progress thus far in Turkey's bid to become a serious player in the energy business. It will note how Turkey's distinctive approach seems at times to be an obstacle to, or a drag on, rather than a facilitator of, the further expansion and liberalization of the world's energy markets.

Turkey's energy needs

From the 1960s onwards, Turkey's expanding economy, rapid urbanization and demographic growth have ensured that the country has mirrored the global growth in demand for energy (Hill 2004: 212). Indeed, its energy consumption profile more closely resembles those of India and Brazil than it does those of western Europe and other established developed states. Although Turkey has significant reserves of environmentally problematic lignite and a relatively unexploited hydroelectric energy capacity, its small coal deposits are typically deep underground and both difficult and expensive to extract. Turkey is believed to have relatively little in the way of exploitable oil reserves and even less gas. Its oil is mainly to be found scattered in small pockets throughout the politically uncertain ethnically Kurdish south-east of the country. Indeed, domestic oil production has decreased since 1991 as the country's consumption soared, more than doubling since 1980. Extensive exploration of what could be significant reserves under the Aegean has been limited by the unresolved dispute with Greece over the sovereignty of those waters (Daly 2008d). There are also hopes of finding oil and gas off Turkey's Black Sea coastline.[1] However, since the 1970s Turkey has had little option but to become dependent on large-scale energy importation as a consequence of its growing energy shortfall. In 2007, the country supplied only a quarter of its energy needs from domestic sources, and of that over half was accounted for by coal and lignite. Furthermore, in the five years to 2009, Turkish energy consumption rose by forty-three per cent.[2]

For this reason alone, Turkey has been drawn inexorably into the global energy market. Turkey's geographical location, relatively close to some of the world's major oil and gas reserves, has meant that its energy dependence is primarily on its proximate neighbours. Before 1990, Iraq was Turkey's chief source of imported oil. Turkey also benefited from the transit and storage fees earned from the export of one-third of Iraq's oil via Turkey. However, the war over Kuwait, the subsequent UN sanctions on Iraq, infrastructure decay, and sabotage in the wake of the 2003 invasion of Iraq obliged Turkey to turn to alternative sources of supply (Hill 2004: 212; Williams and Tekin 2008: 384). Iran soon took over from Iraq, and by 2007 Russia, which began exporting oil to Turkey in 1987, had emerged as Turkey's second biggest source of oil after Iran, supplying around one-third of its needs. Around two-thirds of Turkey's gas also emanates from Russia (Ediger and Bagdadi 2010), much of it via the Blue Stream pipeline that runs beneath the Black Sea to Samsun. Much of the remainder of Turkey's imported gas comes from Iran and, via the recently completed South Caucasus (or Baku–Tbilisi–Erzerum) pipeline, from Azerbaijan. Thus Iran and Russia are currently Turkey's major energy suppliers. Turkey's overall gas imports have risen more quickly than those of oil, and Ankara has signed additional gas importation deals not only with Russia, Azerbaijan and Iran, but also with Algeria, Egypt, Iraq, Kazakhstan, Turkmenistan, Uzbekistan, Qatar, Yemen and Nigeria (Hill 2004: 213). Even so, Turkey remains heavily dependent on Russia for its importation of gas. Even non-Russian gas from the Caspian basin states is largely pipelined into the Russian network and on to Turkey and elsewhere. Thus a key pillar of Turkey's energy strategy must be 'to ensure diversified, reliable, and cost effective supplies for domestic consumption' (Babali 2009). This is proving easier to aspire to than to achieve.

Turkey as an energy 'bridge'

However, it is geographical location rather than domestic energy needs that has raised Turkey's profile as a significant factor in the evolving globalized energy market, for the country sits between the energy-producing regions to its north, east and south on the one hand, and the energy-consuming countries of Europe to its west. This location became truly significant only with the collapse of the Soviet Union, which opened up the prospect that the substantial oil and gas reserves of Russia and of the Caucasus and Caspian regions, stretching from Azerbaijan to the borders of China, could be better exploited and made more available to the growing world energy markets. As the Turkish foreign ministry's 2009 energy strategy document expressed it, 'Turkey is geographically located in close proximity to seventy two percent of the world's proven gas and seventy three percent of oil reserves, in particular those in the Middle East and the Caspian basin. It thus forms a natural energy bridge between the source countries and consumer markets and stands as a key country in ensuring energy security through diversification of supply sources and routes' (Republic of Turkey, Ministry of Foreign Affairs 2009). Once again, Turkey's geographical location is serving to elevate its significance in global political developments.

As is so often the case, however, Turkey's geography can also be its curse. Turkey's role as a significant energy transit country posed a clear risk of a further augmentation of the passage of shipping through the already congested Bosphorus. This narrow choke point runs right through the middle of Istanbul, millions of whose inhabitants perilously cross it by ferry and small vessel on a daily basis (Hill 2004: 215–17; Daly 2008a). The Bosphorus already carries around 50,000 cargo ships per annum, at least half of which carry crude oil and liquefied natural gas (LNG). Almost four per cent of the world's oil consumption passes through the Turkish straits, and around fifty per cent of Russian oil is already exported via this route. These figures would rise still further were increased quantities of Russian and Caspian energy also to transit the straits. With the rise in traffic has come an increased risk of accident, putting the inhabitants of Istanbul, as well as the environment and trade, at risk. Responding to these pressures, since 1994 Turkey has imposed tightening restrictions on traffic transiting the strait, including restrictions on night-time passage and the request that ships carrying hazardous materials report to Turkey's environmental protection ministry. Turkey has also introduced a radar and vessel control system. However, its powers are limited by the 1936 Montreux Convention, which delineates the straits as international waterways. This prevents Turkey from levying transit tariffs and gives shipping the right of free passage. Most do not declare their cargo, and only around half request pilotage (Adams 2004: 97–101). These considerations have added to Ankara's determination to encourage the construction of a pipeline network as the preferred method of moving energy across its territory.

Turkey was initially advantaged in its post-Cold War quest to put itself on the global energy map by the willingness of Washington to support its ambitions (Page 2004). Wider US policies in the region included challenging Russia's sway in the Caucasus and central Asia, and the containment and weakening of Iran. These geopolitical and geostrategic drivers melded with the narrower but no less significant concern that the West's energy security should not become overreliant on the more developed and largely Soviet-era pipeline network transiting Russia from the Caucasus and central Asia, or on any development of the shorter and more logical Iranian route from the Caspian to the Gulf. As an interested actor, but one external to the region, the USA was very happy to sponsor Turkey as an alternative energy transit route to Russia and to Iran. By the mid- to late-1990s the idea of an 'east–west' or 'Silk Road' energy corridor had emerged out of this confluence of interests, in which Turkey would play the part of a major transit route for gas and oil from the Caucasus and central Asia towards Europe. The EU, too, began to take an interest in diversifying its energy supply, not least so that it might lessen its dependence on imported Russian gas in light of the 2006 and 2009 Moscow–Kiev crises regarding gas transportation across Ukraine. This would require the 'development of a southern gas corridor for supply from Caspian and Middle Eastern sources and possibly other countries in the longer term' (European Union 2008). Thus Brussels, too, swung its support behind the development of Turkey as an energy pipeline crossroads.

By the late 1990s, Turkey and the USA had formed a 'strategic energy alliance' based around the construction of energy pipelines to and through Turkey and onwards to western Europe. Its early centrepiece was the Baku–Tbilisi–Ceyhan (BTC) pipeline project (Erdemir 2009). The project grew out of the so-called 'contract of the century' of September 1994 between the Azerbaijan International Oil Company (AIOC), an international consortium made up of US, European, Russian (Lukoil) and Japanese companies along with the Turkish State Petroleum Company (*Turkiye Petrolleri Anonim Ortakligi* – TPAO)[3] and the State Oil Company of Azerbaijan (SOCAR). This provided for increased investment in, and exploitation of, Azerbaijan's Caspian oil resources. The Ankara Declaration of 1998, signed by Turkey, Georgia, Azerbaijan, Kazakhstan and Uzbekistan and strongly supported by Washington, gave the project added impetus. Although commercial interests remained wary, and instability in Georgia and south-eastern Turkey and the unresolved dispute between Azerbaijan and Armenia all added to these reservations, geostrategically the BTC route's advantage was that it bypassed Russia, Iran and (for Turkey) Armenia.

Thus, with determined US and Turkish lobbying, and with significant financial support from publicly funded agencies such as the World Bank's International Finance Corporation (IFC), the European Bank for Reconstruction and Development (EBRD) and seven national export credit agencies, as well as the commercial backing of banks led by the US-based Citicorp, the Dutch ABN Amro, Japan's Mizuho and Société Générale of France, along with German, Italian, Belgian and British banks, the BTC company was finally established in 2002 and pipeline construction commenced in 2003. In fact, bank loans accounted for seventy per cent of the

BTC's costs, and oil company equity the remaining thirty per cent. The BTC company itself is BP-led, with SOCAR as its second biggest shareholder, and oil companies from the USA, Norway, Italy, France, Japan and Saudi Arabia also participating, as well as TPAO, which holds a 6.5 per cent share.[4] Turkey's state-owned Petroleum Pipeline Corporation (Boru Hatlari ile Petrol Tasima – BOTAS) constructed the Turkish section of the line.[5] This interlocking complex of financing, ownership and development is itself testimony to the globalization of the energy industry in Turkey and elsewhere.

The first oil pumped through the pipeline reached Ceyhan on Turkey's Mediterranean coast in May 2006. Ceyhan was already the destination of oil pipelined from northern Iraq. Also in 2006, Kazakhstan agreed to export oil through the BTC pipeline from its western fields by shipping oil by tanker across the Caspian to Baku, pending the construction of a trans-Caspian oil pipeline. Many believe that the long-term viability of BTC hinges on its use as an export route by Kazakhstan (Daly 2008c). In the meantime, the BTC already appears to have cut tanker traffic in the Bosphorus (Daly 2008a). As for Ceyhan, the quantity of oil it handles is projected to double between 2008 and 2015, and it 'will be turned into an integrated energy terminal where […] crude oil may be offered for international markets, and where a refinery, petrochemicals facilities and liquefied natural gas (LNG) exportation terminal will be available' (Republic of Turkey, Ministry of Energy and Natural Resources, undated: 31). The facilities at Ceyhan will be crucial for Turkey's ambition to emerge as a fully fledged energy hub. In fact, Turkey's oil refining capacity has not grown substantially, and the growth of trade in LNG, which can be shipped from any location where the necessary facilities are installed, potentially offers a longer-term threat to Turkey's gas pipeline network strategy (Dereli 2010).

The BTC is just the first element in the projected development of an east–west energy corridor, a range of pipeline route proposals and projects which have Turkey at their heart and which are designed to bring oil and gas from the Caucasus and Caspian regions to Europe, bypassing Russia and, as far as Washington is concerned at least, Iran too (Fink 2006). The frequently sabotaged oil pipeline from Kirkuk to Ceyhan, although established in 1977 and Turkey's oldest energy pipeline, can also be regarded as an element in the overall corridor. Russia's series of spats over energy pricing with Ukraine, across which eighty per cent of Russia's gas and much of its oil exports to Europe transit, cast doubt on both the reliability of Russia as an energy partner and the advisability of dependence on too few energy routes. Moscow's punitive behaviour towards Georgia in 2008 added to the doubts (Tsereteli 2009). Although the BTC pipeline was not subject to direct attack during the conflict, pipeline traffic through Georgia was suspended. Azeri oil was diverted via Russia and Iran (Daly 2008b). The crisis served as a brutal reminder that attempts to develop energy transit networks bypassing Russia remained at Moscow's mercy as a consequence of its readiness to use military force, as well as through its continued control over transportation networks in the former Soviet space, its commercial involvement even in many of the alternative routes (such as the BTC), its manipulation of existing levels of dependence by suppliers and consumers alike, and its energetic championing of new routes over which it could retain control. Turkey found itself treading a tightrope between Tbilisi and Moscow, both countries with which it enjoyed constructive relationships, and between Moscow and the USA over the issue of transit through the Bosphorus of US ships carrying aid to Georgia (Torbakov 2008). All in all, Turkey's potential emergence as an energy bridge is inextricably bound up with its overall relationship with Moscow.

Turkey's heavy reliance on Russian gas is fed by the Blue Stream pipeline, completed in 2003. In 2005, President Vladmir Putin and Erdogan discussed the possibility that it could be extended into south-eastern Europe and beyond, simultaneously reflecting both Russia's search for alternative transit routes to the Ukraine on the one hand, and Turkey's energy hub ambitions on the other. The possibility of an augmentation of the line's carrying capacity remains, raising the prospect of Turkey becoming a transit country for the export of Russian gas to the Middle East. So has the possibility that Russian gas could be fed via Turkey into the proposed Nabucco pipeline network. Russia and Turkey have also revived the so-called Blue Stream Two project, which could carry gas from Russia across Turkey and onwards to the Middle East and south-eastern Europe (Socor 2009a). Projects such as these undermine the search for energy routes that avoid Russian territory, such as the proposed Nabucco pipeline (Socor 2009b), and undermine Turkey's expressed desire to reduce dependence on Russia. Clearly there is a strongly cooperative element to Turkish–Russian energy relationships which means that Ankara cannot be relied upon to fit in with western aspirations to reduce dependence on Russia. As has been noted, 'by the beginning of the second post-Soviet decade, the competition between Russia, Iran and Turkey to secure a share in the hydrocarbon wealth of the Caspian was largely over. All three had acquired a slice of the Caspian pie' (Bolukbasi 2004: 227). Ultimately, Turkey's approach to energy issues has meant that Ankara has cultivated a close energy relationship with Russia.

Part of the explanation for this development has been that Turkey has sought to emerge as a centrepiece for a 'north–south energy corridor' too. This has not always sat easily with at least some of Turkey's western allies. In October 2009, Turkey, Russia and Italy signed an agreement to construct a Samsun–Ceyhan pipeline to carry mainly Kazakh oil shipped from Novorossiysk on Russia's Black Sea coast. Russian and Caspian oil could also be tankered to Samsun from other Black Sea ports such as Odessa in Ukraine and Supsa in Georgia, where a BP-owned pipeline from Baku terminates. In other words, once this pipeline is constructed, then some of the oil reaching Ceyhan will also have first transited Russia. This will further underscore Kazakh dependence on Moscow for its oil exports, and undermine the case for alternative pipelines – for example, across the Caspian – that avoid transiting Russia. Worse still, Russia seemed to agree to the Samsun–Ceyhan oil pipeline project in return for Turkey's support for a South Stream gas pipeline that will carry gas originating in Russia and the Caspian basin to south-eastern Europe under the Black Sea, utilizing Turkey's exclusive economic zone.

Turkey's mixed motives

In a globalized world, and in light of Turkey's complex foreign policy agenda, Ankara also saw an opportunity to bring together a number of interlocking issues and agendas (Laciner 2009; Babali 2010). By developing as a key component in the supply of energy to Europe and beyond, Ankara's decision makers could once again exploit the country's geographical location to function as a bridge between East and West and thereby raise, or retain, a strategic significance that was in danger of eroding with the Cold War's demise. Becoming an energy transit route might also strengthen its bid for membership of the EU (Barysch 2007). Given the ethnically, linguistically and culturally Turkic make-up of Azerbaijan and the energy-rich central Asian states, Turkey's energy politics also dovetailed with its ambition to develop and lead a Turkic world that was just emerging from its Soviet-era isolation. With the advent of the AKP government, Turkey's energy policies could simultaneously reinforce, and be reinforced by, its policy of closer engagement with its Middle Eastern neighbours, notably Iran. The opportunities offered by the world's energy requirements seemed to support Ankara's desire to diversify its international relationships, perhaps reduce what many Turks perceived as its overdependence on the West, and strengthen its overall diplomatic, strategic and economic position in the world. Turkey's energy policy has both driven, and been driven by, its broader foreign policy goal to establish itself as a central rather than peripheral country.

Turkey's readiness to countenance a close energy relationship with Iran has been a particularly negative factor in Turkish–US relations (Kardas 2010b). Iran is Turkey's second biggest supplier of gas and possesses the world's third largest reserves. In addition to its existing imports of oil and gas from Iran, of Turkmen gas via Iran, and of the joint construction of natural gas power stations, in 2007 Turkey also signed a memorandum of understanding (MoU) with Tehran to jointly develop a section of Iran's offshore Caspian South Pars gas field. The agreement incorporates the proposed construction of pipelines to Turkey carrying gas intended in equal measure for the Turkish domestic market and for transit to more distant consumers. Iranian gas would certainly rescue the Nabucco project from the feared gas supply shortfall, but Turkey's relationship with Tehran has upset a US administration trying to internationally isolate Tehran in an attempt to halt its nuclear programme. US grumblings about Turkish policy produced a sharp response from prime minister Erdogan and no discernible shift in Turkish policy. On the other hand, Ankara has not found Tehran to be an easy partner, and cuts in supplies of Iranian gas to Turkey during the harsh winters of 2007 and 2008 have induced caution.

Nabucco

On the other hand, Turkey has itself pinned great hopes on the proposed Nabucco gas pipeline project,[6] notwithstanding its simultaneous support for projects that appear to undermine its viability. This is an EU-sponsored project, backed by the USA, to bring gas to Europe from a range of potential sources, transiting Turkey (via Erzerum), Bulgaria, Romania and Hungary on the way to its Austrian terminal. Azerbaijan is expected to be the biggest provider of gas, but Turkmenistan, Kazakhstan, Iraq, even Egypt and possibly Iran might also eventually contribute. Again, the obstacles to the project's realization have been legion. It requires painstakingly constructed arrangements between supplier, transit and consumer countries. In addition to the enormous technical, economic and security aspects of the project, which have induced considerable commercial caution, as with the trans-Caspian pipeline proposals there have been doubts about whether sufficient gas would be made available by the supplier states to warrant such a large-scale and costly enterprise. Washington and some European governments have been uneasy about the prospect that the pipeline could evolve as a key outlet for Iranian gas, although Turkey is relaxed about this outcome. Turkmenistan's considerable gas supplies would also have to enter the network via Iran or indeed Russia unless, at least until, a trans-Caspian pipeline is constructed. Notwithstanding these considerable doubts, the eventual construction of the Nabucco pipeline cannot at all be ruled out (Socor 2010).

The proposed construction of pipelines on the Caspian seabed would give still greater substance to the 'east–west corridor' idea in general, and the Nabucco project in particular. Interest in such projects was rekindled in 2006 in the wake of the Russo–Ukrainian dispute. They would enable oil and gas from Kazakhstan and Turkmenistan to reach western markets via Azerbaijan, and onwards to Turkey via the recently built lines. Currently, most central Asian energy, of which Kazahkstan provides most of the oil and Turkmenistan most of the gas, is exported via Russia. Some Turkmen gas is also exported to Iran via a pipeline completed in 1997. The fact that trans-Caspian pipelines would be built in order to bypass them constitutes just one reason why Russia and Iran, both of which border the Caspian, have been unhappy with their proposed construction. Russia in particular is currently able to operate very much as an energy hub, buying up oil and gas from central Asia and transporting it at a profit through its largely Soviet-era pipeline network on to Europe or, for oil, to world markets via the Bosphorus.

In any case, the geological, technical, economic and environmental problems of laying pipelines under the Caspian are formidable. Added to these are the legal uncertainties surrounding the sovereignty over portions of the Caspian. To classify the Caspian as a 'lake' would render it jointly owned. As a 'sea', on the other hand, it would be divided into five sectors, the delineations between which would be disputed. Either way, and certainly for the foreseeable future, it is difficult to arrive at an agreement without the consent of all five Caspian littoral states – Russia, Iran, Azerbaijan, Turkmenistan and Kazakhstan (Granmayeli 2004). This, too, enables Moscow and Tehran to obstruct progress. Investors also have to take into account the possibility that Russia will remain the preferred route for the export of energy from the Caspian area, even with the construction of new pipeline alternatives, and that a geographically well-placed, needy and single-minded China will capture an increasing share of central Asian energy exports. Nevertheless, in light of doubts about Russian reliability as an energy partner, Washington's desire to weaken dependence on Russia and Iran, and the aspirations by the Caspian states themselves to maximize both income and independence, the eventual construction of Caspian pipelines cannot be ruled out.

Turkey's energy ambitions rely considerably on its relationship with its Turkic 'brother nation' Azerbaijan, as does the fate of the Nabucco project. However, it is far from clear that Azerbaijan and other producer countries are prepared to sell their energy to Turkey at significantly lower prices than those Turkey could then charge on world markets (although this is indeed what Russia practises with respect to central Asian energy). In July 2007, the first gas arrived in Turkey through the South Caucasus (or BTE – Baku–Tbilisi–Erzerum) gas pipeline, another BP-led project.[7] This runs from the Shah Deniz field in Azerbaijan's section of the Caspian,[8] and follows the BTC route via Georgia to Erzerum in Turkey. There are future plans to expand its capacity. Largely to enable the export of Azeri gas to Europe, a pipeline transporting gas to Greece from Turkey was completed in 2007, which in due course will be extended to Italy and also connected to the western Balkans and Bulgaria. However, Ankara's tussle with Baku over gas prices appeared to delay the development of phase two of Azerbaijan's Shah Deniz field, a development that is essential if Azerbaijan is going to be able to produce enough gas to warrant the construction of the Nabucco pipeline. Turkey has also sought to negotiate agreements that would enable it to take for its own use a percentage of the gas transiting its territory at reduced prices. Azerbaijan has become wary of Turkey as an energy partner (Kardas 2010a). Azerbaijan, with Turkmenistan, has also been ready to enter into discussions with Moscow to continue to export gas through Russian-controlled pipelines, thereby undermining confidence in Nabucco's viability. Turkey's 2009 attempt to normalize relations with Armenia disappointed Azerbaijan, while the 2008 Russian conflict with Georgia caused Baku to reconsider the viability of alternative export routes to those already established in Russia. Azerbaijan emerged from these shocks as seemingly more willing to export its gas via the Russian pipeline network (Baev 2010), although Baku's uncertainty about the southern route might not last.

In any case, consensus on energy policy within Europe has been somewhat elusive, notwithstanding the EU commitment to the Nabucco project. Readiness to upset Russia has been unevenly distributed in the EU, as has the willingness to arrive at agreements to purchase energy from Russia via routes other than Nabucco. In other words, EU countries have themselves undermined the viability of the Nabucco project. Thus, in addition to Turkey, potential Nabucco transit states such as Bulgaria and Hungary, and the EU itself, have also exhibited a strong interest in Russia's plan to construct a rival South Stream project to build a pipeline under the Black Sea to Bulgaria, and from there transport gas both to west central Europe via Serbia, and to Italy via Greece. Interestingly, this project was not only widely interpreted as a Russian attempt to rival Nabucco and perhaps derail it altogether, but simultaneously had the virtue from Russia's perspective of enabling it to avoid its own troubled dependence on Ukraine as its main export transit country to western Europe. The EU and some of its key members, such as Germany, have also lent support for the Nord Stream project, currently under construction and designed to bring gas from Russia to western Europe via pipelines under the Baltic Sea.[9]

Turkey as an energy 'hub'

EU states initially envisaged Turkey's role in Europe's energy security as amounting to little more than as a transit country. However, Turkey began to see itself as not simply a transit route from which the country could earn fees, but also a fully fledged energy-trading hub. Properly understood, this would involve Turkey importing more energy than it needs, storing and refining or otherwise processing it, and so liberalizing its market that it becomes a 'price formation centre', or 'spot market' (Bilgin 2010; Roberts 2010). An energy hub is a location at which energy can be sold on at prices higher than those paid to the supplier countries. Both supplier and consumer countries might be discomforted by this. Turkey's prospect of developing further as an energy hub depends in large measure on diversifying the source of supplies into the country, especially of gas. For Turkey to become an energy-trading hub in gas depends on the development of the Nabucco pipeline network that could bring gas from a variety of sources to Europe via Turkey (Ogutcu 2010: 72–73).

This means that a number of countries might be required to enter into agreements to export gas to Turkey, yet leave Ankara free to negotiate higher prices to consumers. It would also require consumer countries and companies to invest in developing Caspian fields and building pipelines, yet have considerably less than full control over the eventual price at which they receive the gas from Turkey, or even its destination. Ankara's politicians and diplomats have occasionally made things worse by a nationalist and statist rhetoric that suggests neither partnership nor market orientation. Thus in January 2009, prime minister Erdogan threatened to withdraw from the Nabucco project unless Brussels lifted obstacles to the country's EU accession talks. Statements such as that by the country's energy minister that, with respect to its energy role, 'Turkey already understands its power. The entire world has seen that there is no choice without Turkey' (Roberts 2010: 48) do not create the impression that Turkey would be a more reliable energy partner than Russia. In any case, Turkey would need to advance the liberalization of its energy businesses if it is to develop as a trading hub rather than pursue a state-directed energy policy. TPAO and BOTAS are state-owned and control the majority of Turkey's oil and gas importation, transport and processing. Thus far, progress has been slow (Dereli 2010: 6; Roberts 2010: 45), and this too induces concerns that Ankara might regard its position in the world's energy network as an asset to be manipulated for the state's ends.

Turkey as a player in the energy game?

Turkey's domestic energy needs, its geographical location, and its own economic and regional aspirations have caused it to increase its profile in the global energy business, but have not ensured that its relationships either with energy suppliers or with other energy consumers have invariably been smooth. Ankara has been willing to exploit widespread unease concerning energy dependence on Russia, but has simultaneously offered Russia an additional outlet for its energy exports. It has also been prepared to accept a high level of dependence on Russian energy for itself. Energy issues have introduced tension as well as cooperation into Ankara's relationship with the USA. Furthermore, Turkey has discovered that its ambition to establish itself as a significant energy transport hub depends on an array of complications largely beyond its direct control (Fink 2006; Baykal 2009; Saivetz 2009; Winrow 2009). Thus globalization affects Turkish energy policies and prospects not only as a consequence of the nature of the world energy market, but also because of the interlocking nature of diverse issues in a globalized international system. Other governments need to cooperate with each other and with Turkey if pipelines are to be constructed. Commercial interests need to be persuaded of the technical, economic and political feasibility of exploration, extraction and pipeline projects before they prove ready to invest. Poor governance and corruption in some key post-Soviet energy-rich states have slowed progress. Technical, geological and legal issues, too, must be overcome, such as the disputes over the territorial status of the Caspian. Furthermore, fluctuating energy prices and the global economic downturn that set in during 2008 complicated matters still further, as have progressively downward revisions of estimates of the scale of Caucasian and central Asian energy reserves.

The region's myriad intrastate conflicts and instabilities – in south-eastern Turkey, northern Iraq, Nagorno-Karabakh, Georgia, Chechnya and elsewhere – also have to be taken into account. Rivalries such as those between

Armenia and Azerbaijan (and Turkey), Russia and Georgia, Russia and Ukraine, the USA and Iran, and Erbil and Baghdad, have to be ameliorated or bypassed. In particular, Ankara found that its pursuit of a diplomatic opening with Armenia put at risk its relationship with Azerbaijan, which interpreted Ankara's initiative as an indication that Turkey was cooling in its hitherto stalwart support of Baku in the Nagorno-Karabakh conflict. Turkey's energy relationship with Tehran has attracted US criticism. The complexity of the region's Kurdish issue also served as a complicating factor in Ankara's energy aspirations. The future of Iraq, let alone of its energy exports, remains unclear, while in August 2008 a terrorist attack on the Turkish section of the BTC pipeline took place, for which the PKK claimed responsibility (Jenkins 2008a). The operation of the line was temporarily suspended at considerable financial cost to Turkey, and seemed to vindicate those who had initially queried the advisability of the BTC's construction on the basis of the conflict-prone regions through which it passes.

Indeed, given the transnational nature of the BTC and of energy security issues more generally, the three countries conduct regular pipeline protection exercises – in addition to the general military training that Turkey has extended to Georgia and Azerbaijan. BP had already arranged for the training, equipping and funding of a 700-strong strategic pipeline protection department in Georgia (Petersen 2006). US Special Forces have trained around 2000 Georgian soldiers in counter-terrorism and pipeline protection. An antiterrorism centre was established in Georgia, and radar antennae granted to Azerbaijan. Local security corps have already been granted training from other NATO member countries. A Georgian special state protection service and Azerbaijani pipeline security service have been trained by American security company Equity International, whereas the Turkish *gendarmerie* received training from Northern Ireland security forces. In addition to this, the three governments have established jointly with BP field security teams a special area patrolling force along the route of BTC and BTE.

Yet, for all the concerns and uncertainties, Turkey will clearly play a more important role in global energy politics in the future. The Nabucco and trans-Caspian pipelines may or may not be constructed. Regional conflicts might slow progress. Turkey and the EU might continue simultaneously to fret over their dependence on Russia and enable it to continue and grow. The energy-rich countries of the Caspian basin might diversify their export routes to a greater or lesser extent, or indeed be found to be less energy rich than was originally hoped. Iran could remain isolated or could, in time, rejoin the diplomatic mainstream. The future of Kurdish northern Iraq could take any one of a number of different directions. Whatever happens in these and a whole range of other issues in the region, the supply of energy from producer to consumer nations will increase in diversity, complexity and importance, and Turkey will be a significant part of that range of intertwining equations that make up the world's energy politics. Yet Turkey's future as a hub is also dependent on its own behaviour. It will need to find the wherewithal to invest and modernize, to construct its foreign policy positions with sensitivity and care and to present to actual and potential energy partners a less statist and menacing, and a more open and reliable, face. There remains much for Ankara to do.

10 The Armenian genocide

A foreign policy problem in a globalized world

The 'events'

During the First World War, hundreds of thousands of Ottoman Armenians were force-marched towards Syria from their homes in eastern Anatolia. Hundreds of thousands died. The exact figure is disputed, and in any case cannot be verified with precision, but Ataturk himself, who reportedly referred to the killings as a 'shameful act' (Akcam 2007: xxii), also apparently cited a figure of 800,000 dead, as did a 1928 Turkish General Staff publication (Akcam 2007: 200). A more commonly cited figure is 1.5 million. Many who were not killed were forcibly converted, especially women married off to Muslim men and children adopted by Muslim families. Armenians and many historians regard what happened as genocide, which, according to the 1948 UN Convention on the Prevention and Punishment of the Crime of Genocide, means acts committed with 'the intent to destroy, in whole or in part, a national, ethnic, racial or religious group'.[1] In 2003, the International Centre for Transitional Justice, an NGO specializing in identifying culpability for mass atrocities and human rights abuses, concluded that genocide of Armenians did indeed take place.[2] The Turkish republic and some historians accept that many deaths occurred, but contest that what occurred constituted genocide. They point to the thousands of Muslims who also died, and stress both the intercommunal dimensions of the killing and the widespread starvation, disease and exhaustion that afflicted the entire Anatolian population during this period. Furthermore, the substantial Armenian communities residing in cities such as Istanbul, Izmir and Aleppo were left largely intact, and a small Armenian community resides in Istanbul to this day.

The main point at issue is whether a physical eradication of the Armenian population was intended and centrally planned, and thus warrants being termed genocide, or whether what happened was an unintended or spontaneous, rather than planned, by-product of a war measure. There are also differences of view concerning the extent to which culpability lies with regular Ottoman forces or was primarily the work of irregular, often Kurdish, bands; and whether the Ottoman authorities can be deemed responsible, or whether the deportations were essentially the brainchild of a relatively small number of

CUP leaders acting independently through the highly secretive 'special organization'. There are also differences of view concerning the accessibility, reliability and utility of documentation relating to the events. These debates are not merely one more example of those that habitually occur between professional historians. The Armenian genocide issue arouses deep and violent passions amongst Turks and Armenians. The chief protagonists are the Turkish government and the globally distributed Armenian diaspora,[3] but the Armenian government and Turkish society are also highly engaged with the issue. Few who venture into the debate escape the wrath of one side or the other. This chapter does not concern itself primarily with these debates, but instead focuses on the way in which globalization processes have kept the issue alive and affected Turkey's foreign relations. It will also seek to offer an insight into how Turkish society has responded to these external pressures. Data, propaganda and detailed historical analyses concerning the fate of Anatolia's Armenians are available elsewhere (Bloxham 2005; Lewy 2005; European Stability Initiative 2009).

The impetus behind the deportations and resettlements, as the Turkish side of the debate prefers to characterize the events, stemmed ostensibly from doubts about Armenian fidelity to the Ottoman regime. The empire's Armenian subjects had in the past been regarded as the 'loyal community' (*millet-i-Sadika*) (Gunter 1990: 2). However, towards the latter half of the nineteenth century, and along with other Christian minorities in the Ottoman sphere, the Armenians began to demand self-determination. The Christian communities of the empire – Greeks, Bulgarians, Serbs and so on – had been championed by the European powers, keen to present themselves as protectors of the empire's Christian subjects. By 1914, the empire had lost its Balkan territories, many of which had been Ottoman domains for five centuries, and most of its Christian subjects. The Armenians were cultivated by the Russian empire in particular, which had established an Armenian entity on its territory in 1827, and which regarded itself as the protector of eastern Christians residing within the Ottoman sphere. External interest in the fate of Ottoman Armenians was internationally legitimized by the 1878 Treaty of Berlin, which followed in the wake of the 1877–78 Russo–Ottoman war. This also coincided with the empire being left with a clear Muslim majority for the first time in its history (Findley 2005: 164).

However, Armenian settlements were scattered throughout eastern Anatolia, with substantial communities in Istanbul, Izmir and other cities, and along the southern coastline. They nowhere constituted a clear majority, and their struggle for self-determination led increasingly to clashes with their ethnically Turkish and Kurdish Muslim neighbours. These intercommunal clashes had already resulted in the deaths of up to a quarter of a million Armenians during the period 1894–96 and again on the south coast in 1909. They were accompanied by a kind of 'Islamification' of the Ottoman empire's ethos, or what has been described as a 'transition from Ottomanism to Turkism' (Akcam 2007: 73). This increased prioritization and privileging of the Muslim population was also a response to the arrival and settlement of the millions of Muslims who had fled to Anatolia from the Balkans and Caucasus during the last decades of the nineteenth century and the early years of the twentieth, fleeing the discrimination and brutality of triumphant Christian nations. Indeed, there is a less-well-known movement for the recognition of the genocide of Caucasian (or 'Circassian') people by Russia during the nineteenth century. Many of the Caucasians fled to Anatolia.[4] European support for the creation of an Armenian homeland covering substantial swathes of Anatolian territory threatened further displacement of Muslim communities, this time in Anatolia itself. Unsurprisingly, the empire's Muslims belatedly began to acquire the nationalist impulses that had infected its Christian subjects, while the Ottoman authorities became ever more mistrustful of the Christian communities scattered throughout Anatolia. Thus, and in addition to the exigencies of war, a broader Ottoman aspiration to secure the Anatolian heartland for its loyal Muslim subjects can also be regarded as one of the impulses behind the deportations. Indeed, the Assyrian Christian community was also largely purged from the region (Travis 2006), as were hundreds of thousands of Greeks. Armenia today hosts a small community of adherents to the syncretic Yezidi faith, who fled Anatolia with the Armenians during the First World War.[5]

With the onset of the First World War, the Ottoman and Russian empires again found themselves contesting for control over the Caucasus and eastern Anatolia. Ottoman doubts about Armenian fealty were fed both by Russian overtures to the Armenians and by the inclination of the latter to respond positively to them. Armenian units fought alongside Russian forces, and irregular Armenian gangs sometimes engaged in ethnic cleansing of Muslim populations. In any case, the Ottoman authorities initially preferred to conscript its Armenian subjects into labour battalions rather than into the Ottoman fighting corps. Thousands of these conscripted labourers died of exhaustion, brutality and starvation. On 24 April 1915 – the date that is today commemorated as Armenian Memorial Day – there were large-scale arrests of Armenians in Istanbul. Many of the detained were executed, many deported. Soon deportations and killing of Armenians escalated throughout Anatolia, and their forced removal to the Syrian desert commenced. Starvation, disease, exhaustion and murder ensured that most failed to arrive at their purported destination, and even those who did mostly died through lack of water, food or shelter. The bulk of Anatolia's Armenian population had been removed by 1917, but intercommunal killings continued until 1922, not least as a by-product of the return of Armenians to Anatolia under European protection.

After the war, the Ottoman regime, under pressure from the occupying allies and wishing to distance itself from and weaken the CUP, put the culprits on trial for war crimes, the first instance in which a state's war crimes were to be punished under its national law. Indeed, the case that genocide took place derives in part from the court archives of this period. The Ottoman courts even passed death sentences on some of the accused, who were either in exile or held in detention in Malta by the allies. The trials were, in due course, suspended and the alleged ringleaders of the genocide escaped justice. This outcome was the by-product of a number of factors, including the declining legitimacy and efficacy of the Ottoman regime; the disinclination of Ataturk's alternative nationalist government in Ankara to prosecute fellow CUP comrades, particularly at the behest of the occupying allied governments; the evolving reluctance of some of the allied powers to fall out with Ataturk's nationalist movement; and a general feeling amongst nationalists that the killings had been necessary as part of the war effort and to secure Anatolia for the Muslims (Akcam 2007: 393–424). The last of the alleged perpetrators of the massacres were released from Malta in October 1921. Some went on to become leading members of the nationalist government and the republican regime that was established in 1923. Some were honoured by having street names, neighbourhoods and schools named after them. In 1926, a law was passed giving pensions and other privileges to the families of alleged ringleaders of the massacres and to those who had subsequently fallen victim to Armenian revenge killings. From the very outset, the newly established Turkish republic showed little remorse or regret over the deaths of so many non-Muslim Ottoman subjects.

The emergence of 'genocide' as a global issue

The revenge killings of alleged perpetrators, such as the 1921 assassination in Berlin of Talat Pasha by an Armenian survivor, offer early instances of the Armenian community's capacity and desire to ensure that the massacre of Armenians should remain in the global public's eye. Yet for half a century, the Armenian tragedy was largely forgotten by the international community. Interest appears to have been rekindled alongside a growing international interest in, and concern with, the phenomenon of genocide more generally. No doubt the fact of the Jewish holocaust has been a major contributor to this phenomenon, and even the 1943 coining of the word 'genocide' by a Polish Jewish lawyer, Raphael Lemkin, largely with the Armenian issue in mind,[6] may have functioned as an 'organizing principle' around which international thinking about the issue could develop. Certainly, this led to the adoption of the 1948 UN Convention on the Prevention and Punishment of the Crime of Genocide. Since then, but more especially during the past two or three decades, academic courses, scholarly studies, specialist journals, court cases and official declarations have blossomed. In 1997, an International Association of Genocide Scholars[7] was founded, which in the same year affirmed its belief that the Armenian people of Anatolia had been subjected to genocide. In 2005, the Association penned an open letter to prime minister Erdogan calling on Turkey to recognize Ottoman responsibility for genocide of its Armenian subjects.[8] This explosion of interest in genocide is not exclusively focused on the Armenian case, but has highlighted events as diverse as the Jewish holocaust, the fate of north America's native Indians and Australasia's aborigines, the Ukraine under Stalin, the tragedies in Cambodia, former Yugoslavia and Rwanda, and so on (European Stability Initiative 2009: 15–19).

The Armenian diaspora, formed with the expulsion and flight of Armenians from Anatolia in the early twentieth century, was also both less active and barely influential until relatively recently. It was internally divided and its main arm, the transnational Armenian Revolutionary Federation (ARF), or 'Dashnaks', which dates back to the 1880s and which has re-established itself as a major force in the domestic politics of the Armenian republic since independence in 1991, focused its efforts primarily on the fate of Armenians under Soviet rule. Nationwide Armenian associations with explicitly political agendas, such as the Armenian Assembly of America (AAA),[9] did not start to appear in the USA until the 1970s. The AAA in turn did not launch the Armenian National Institute as a repository of genocide material 'dedicated to the study, research and affirmation of the Armenian genocide' until 1997,[10] or help establish the Congressional Caucus on Armenian issues until 1995. The Armenian Library and Museum of America[11] did not open its doors until 1971, and university-based Armenian research centres, such as those at the University of Michigan-Dearborn or California State University, did not appear until the 1970s and 1980s. In other words, the delayed emergence of an Armenian genocide 'lobby', as distinct from individual and private or family memories, seems to be explained by, and to have accompanied the wider emergence of, lobby politics, identity politics and improved communications in democratic societies. The lobby is a manifestation of globalization as much as it is a response to the events of 1915.

In the 1970s violence re-emerged, after a fifty-year absence, as a tool of embittered elements within the global Armenian diaspora (Gunter 1990). Although essentially nationalistic in its ideology and spawned by the ARF, the Justice Commandos of the Armenian Genocide (JCAG) was influenced by the third-world 'liberation' and terrorist movements that were globally current at that time. The JCAG began its campaign of attacks against Turkish state facilities and representatives abroad with the 1975 assassination of the Turkish ambassador to Austria. Renamed the Armenian Revolutionary Army (ARA) in 1983, by the time it called a halt to its campaign of violence in 1985, it had been responsible for the deaths of twenty Turkish diplomats or their family members. The Turkish foreign ministry website continues to list the names of its fallen. An opposing Marxist group calling itself the Armenian Secret Army for the Liberation of Armenia (ASALA) also made an appearance in the mid-1970s, and was responsible for less discriminating attacks against a World Council of Churches office in Lebanon, the Turkish consulate in Paris, the airports in Ankara and at Orly, Paris, and the Istanbul bazaar. It, too, ceased operations in the mid-1980s, partly as a consequence of its removal from Beirut to the Bekaa Valley in the wake of Israel's 1982 invasion of Lebanon. It then fell increasingly under Syrian control.

In addition to the security threat they posed to Turkish citizens, officials and businesses abroad, these campaigns served to draw the world's attention to the Armenian cause and to Ankara's policy of genocide denial, galvanized and deepened the identity of the Armenian diaspora, and offered Turkey's foes, such as Syria and Greece, a handy stick with which to embarrass Turkey. The 1981 seizure by ASALA of the Turkish consulate in Paris seems to have galvanized the large French Armenian community, who from that date began to turn up in far larger numbers to commemorate the dead, to learn the Armenian language, and so on (Gunter 1990: 22–23).

The existence of an active global Armenian diaspora and its adoption of a more peaceful campaigning strategy have proved a more effective means of generating global awareness and sympathy, and of imposing a foreign policy headache on Ankara. The exact size of the Armenian diaspora is impossible to establish definitively, but it probably amounts to around one-third of all those who might be regarded as Armenians. The republic of Armenia, which gained independence in 1991, has a population of 3 million. Today there are reckoned to be just 60,000 or so Armenian citizens in Turkey, although it has been estimated that up to 2 million of today's 'Turkish' population have an Armenian grandparent who was forcibly or otherwise converted to Islam to avoid their fate. One Turkish author, Fethiye Cetin, has written movingly of her discovery of her 'Turkish' grandmother's Armenian roots (Cetin 2008). That the book, first published in Turkey in 2004, is now in its seventh reprint there is an indication of the widespread interest in Turkey's Armenian past that is now evident. So, too, is the publication and success of a novel on a similar theme by Elif Shafak (Shafak 2007). Shafak was charged under Turkey's Article 301 for 'insulting Turkishness' in the book by mentioning the Armenian genocide. Her acquittal was welcomed by Turkey's prime minister Tayyip Erdogan. There are thought to be at least 1 million ethnic Armenian citizens of Russia, in excess of 1 million people of Armenian descent in the USA, perhaps 400,000 in France, around 200,000 in Lebanon, a similar figure in Syria, and around half that in Iran. Smaller communities can be found in places such as Argentina, Brazil, Uruguay, Canada, Australia, Greece, Bulgaria and Jordan.[12] Furthermore, these dispersed Armenian communities are often relatively wealthy and educated, and have been able to make use of the opportunities available to them to organize and to lobby.

This has been especially so in the USA, where there are thought to be in excess of 400 Armenian groups presided over by the AAA. Especially since the 1970s, the USA's Armenian lobbies have campaigned for global and indeed Turkish recognition that what happened to Ottoman Armenians should be understood as genocide, that reparations are due, and that there should be a restoration of 'Armenian' lands taken by the Turks. They have also lobbied on behalf of issues relating to the Armenian republic, most notably with respect to its conflict with Azerbaijan over the disputed territory of Nagorno-Karabakh. Far more numerous and active than the USA's Turkish lobby, they have been predisposed to side against Turkey generally, whether on human rights, arms sales, Kurdish or Greek and Greek Cypriot issues. Indeed, they often coalesce with the similarly formidable American Greek lobby. Formed in 1995, the bipartisan Congressional Caucus on Armenian Issues today boasts 148 members in the House of Representatives.[13] Over forty American states have affirmed that genocide took place and commemorate 24 April as Armenian Memorial Day. The governments or parliaments of around twenty sovereign states globally, beginning with Uruguay in 1965, have passed resolutions or laws or issued declarations affirming the view that Turkey bears responsibility for the mass murders, even though the word genocide is not used in all instances. Some of these states are EU members, notably France. Indeed, in the latest of a succession of similar resolutions dating back to 1987, the European Parliament in 2005 not only again called on Turkey to recognize the genocide, but also 'considers this recognition to be a prerequisite for accession to the European Union',[14] a position not formally adopted by the EU, but one favoured by a number of European, notably French, politicians, including the current French president Nikolas Sarkozy.

The genocide lobby's impact

The Armenian genocide issue as a global phenomenon is more than a mere source of embarrassment to Ankara, even though it has been argued that all that has been achieved by the campaign has been 'symbolic resolutions of sympathy' (Gunter 1990: 30). It has, and continues to, put at risk Turkey's relationships even with its European and north American allies, and it threatens any attempt to normalize relationships with the neighbouring state of Armenia (European Stability Initiative 2009). However, the genocide issue is such not simply because Armenians have made it so, but also as a consequence of the manner in which Turkey has responded. As one prominent Turkish American has put it, even Turkey's friends are 'frustrated with Turkey's intransigence' and feel that Ankara, without necessarily conceding genocide, could 'express more empathy for the fact that hundreds of thousands of Armenians died as a result of the Ottoman government policy to deport Armenians' (Bengur 2009: 46). The allegations, and Ankara's response to them, combine to generate a sense that even Turkey's closest friends sometimes approach their relationship with Ankara holding their noses, and bedevil attempts by the country's diplomats to create closer relationships and ensure a more sympathetic hearing (Bengur 2009).

Of Turkey's European partners, France has by far the largest Armenian population and has been the most vociferous critic of Ankara's genocide denial. Yet the impact of the French stance on its relationship with Ankara goes a long way towards explaining why, despite the weight of historical opinion, most states have shied away from confronting Turkey with this issue. In 1984, in an address to a largely French Armenian community, president François Mitterrand followed a number of his ministers and earlier incumbents of political offices in France (Gunter 1990: 29) in referring openly to the genocide.[15] In 2001, France approved a bill that simply asserted that 'France publicly recognizes the Armenian genocide of 1915', without mentioning Turkey. Ankara, which had long been threatening Paris with dire consequences should the bill be adopted, responded by recalling its ambassador and issuing a statement declaring that passage of the bill 'will cause serious and lasting harm to Turkish–French relations'. Ankara also suspended military cooperation and cancelled trade contracts and negotiations. French companies and sports events were boycotted. The Turkish media were in uproar, calling for boycotts of French products, and French exports to Turkey temporarily plummeted (Peuch 2001a, 2001b).[16]

Undeterred, in 2006 the French lower house passed a bill that would make denial of the Armenian genocide a crime in French law, a position already adopted by Switzerland. In fact the French government opposed passage of the bill, it has not been passed into law, and the European Commission declared it 'unhelpful'. Even so, Turkey's reaction was again fierce. Its foreign ministry issued a statement declaring that 'Turkish–French relations, which have been meticulously developed over the centuries, took a severe blow today through the irresponsible initiatives of some short sighted French politicians, based on unfounded allegations'.[17] Military relations were completely suspended, including port visits, arms sales and guaranteed overflight rights. As of January 2008, overflight rights had yet to be restored, which complicated the French contribution to the NATO operation in Afghanistan.[18] French commercial participation in a number of public contracts and privatization projects were blocked. Talks with Gaz de France (GDF) over its participation in the Nabucco pipeline project were suspended (Vaisse 2008: 17–18). In early 2008, GDF decided to withdraw from the project in the face of this 'silent economic embargo'.[19] Again, the Turkish media was in uproar, and there were again widespread calls for boycotts of French products, which contributed to another subsequent fall in French exports to Turkey. France, at the level both of its political class and public opinion, has emerged as one of the EU's leading opponents of Turkey's EU accession. It was not always the case. It is hard to assess what role the Armenian genocide issue, or rather the way Turkey handles it, has had on the overall French and wider European perception of Turkey, but it can hardly have helped.

As we have noted, interest in the fate of the Armenians frequently stems from the emergence of genocide as a global focus of interest, rather than as a direct result of the successful lobbying of the Armenian diaspora. Thus states such as the Netherlands, with no Armenian lobby to speak of and with a strong record of support for Turkey's EU accession, have also declared their sympathy with the fate of the Ottoman empire's Armenian subjects. Germany, which has fully recognized its responsibility for the Jewish holocaust, occupies a particularly sensitive place in this issue area. Thus the German Bundestag's resolution of 15 June 2005, which was sponsored by groups ranging across the entire German parliamentary spectrum, perhaps most perfectly illustrates the flavour of the global concern with genocide. The resolution does not use the term genocide, but it 'deplores the deeds of the Young Turkish government in the Ottoman empire which have resulted in the almost total annihilation of the Armenians in Anatolia'. In recognizing the involvement of some German officers in the Armenian killings, 'the German Bundestag is painfully aware from its own national experience how hard it is for every people to face the dark sides of its past. But it also believes that facing one's own history fairly and squarely is necessary and constitutes an important basis for reconciliation'. Expressing its support for Turkish–Armenian reconciliation, the resolution nevertheless 'deplores the fact that a full discussion of these events of the past in the Ottoman empire is still not possible today in Turkey and that scientists and writers who wish to deal with this aspect of Turkish history are being prosecuted and exposed to public defamation'. In a hint at the difficulties Ankara's approach to the issue poses to its EU prospects, the resolution goes on to assert that 'the true extent of the massacres and deportations is still belittled and largely disputed in Turkey today. This Turkish attitude stands in opposition to the idea of reconciliation which guides the common values of the European Union'.[20]

It is indeed the case that at both the official level, and for great swathes of Turkish public opinion, the extent of the massacres is belittled and disputed in Turkey. Notwithstanding the generally sensitive and conciliatory wording adopted in the German Bundestag's resolution and the well-known support of a number of its sponsors for Turkey's EU accession, Turkey's ambassador to Germany managed to accuse the sponsors of acting as 'spokespersons of fanatic Armenian nationalism, which is using organized terror around the world'. Turkey's parliamentary speaker Bulent Arinc described the resolution as a 'one-sided decision', while the Turkish foreign ministry regretted that none of its 'warnings' was heeded by the Bundestag. To quote Cem Ozdemir, himself of Turkish origin and a prominent German Green politician, 'with state propaganda, which has worked far too long in a closed society, you cannot continue in an international debate' (European Stability Initiative 2009: 19–20). There is considerable revulsion in Europe at Turkey's inability to address its past in a calmer and more considered fashion.

On the other hand it is necessary to factor in the observation that, despite the occasional furore, Turkish–French and wider Turkish–European relations have demonstrated a tendency to return to some 'normalcy' after each troubled interval. A similar argument applies to the impact of the Armenian genocide issue on Turkish–US relations. Although, as we have noted, a majority of US states have acknowledged the Armenian fate, successive US governments have blocked a series of congressional attempts to adopt genocide resolutions. In 2000, the particularly pro-Turkey administration of Bill Clinton had an especially difficult fight on its hands to block the passage of such a resolution. US energy and arms companies were threatened with sanctions, Turkey's much prized military cooperation was put under threat, TSK chief General Huseyin Kivrikoglu canceled a scheduled visit to

Washington, and the US embassy was picketed (McKeeby 2000). As a NATO member and host to the important air base at Incirlik, Ankara has been able to play on Turkey's strategic utility to the USA by threatening to rupture or reduce military cooperation. Thus, when congressional passage of a genocide resolution again loomed in 2007, Ankara withdrew its ambassador and warned Washington that use of the Incirlik air base in eastern Turkey as its main supply route and troop-rotation hub for US forces in Iraq could be put at risk should the resolution pass. Furthermore, the then TSK chief General Yasar Buyukanit pronounced that 'our military ties with the US will never be the same again' if the resolution were to pass.[21]

The resolution was withdrawn, but the issue was only to reappear again with the presidential election victory of Barack Obama. Obama, his secretary of state Hillary Clinton and his vice-president Joe Biden had all expressed their belief that the Armenian people had been the victims of genocide. Indeed, Senator Biden had in the past sponsored genocide resolutions. Obama's presidential campaign website had stated that 'the Armenian genocide is not an allegation, a personal opinion, or a point of view, but rather a widely documented fact supported by an overwhelming body of historical evidence'. Once in office, however, reasons of state again took over, not least as Washington would be relying on access to the Incirlik base to facilitate its troop withdrawals from Iraq. Obama also wished to improve Washington's relationship with Turkey after the difficulties of the Bush presidency, and to encourage an opening of the relationship between Turkey and Armenia. Thus, although in his address to the TGNA on 6 April 2009, Obama referred to 'the terrible events of 1915',[22] and in his commemoration statement of 24 April, Obama referred to the 1.5 million Armenians who were 'massacred or marched to their death', he then used the term Armenians use, '*Meds Yeghern*', to refer to these deaths. Thus Obama used language that does not carry the legal implications of declaring it to have been genocide.[23] All US presidents are obliged to offer their remarks on Armenian Remembrance Day, and it is clear from their texts that, although all but President Reagan have avoided using the word genocide, they recognize these tragic events as just that.

In his speech to the TGNA, Obama also commented that 'each country must work through its past. And reckoning with the past can help us seize a better future.' In any case, Obama subsequently made it clear that he had not changed his mind as to whether or not genocide took place. Out of consideration for Obama's presidency, Democrat house speaker Nancy Pelosi chose not to reintroduce a genocide resolution. However, in March 2010 the House Foreign Affairs Committee again voted for a resolution calling on Obama to recognize the Armenian 'genocide', leading again to a recall to Ankara of the Turkish ambassador (Whittell 2010). Again, the White House was able to deflect the pressure, but there can be little doubt that in future more resolutions will appear, and there can be no guarantee that all future US presidents will choose the path taken by Obama and his predecessors.

Browbeating US administrations into avoiding use of the term genocide has become a regular and routine sport, but Turkey's victories are no more than tactical, or 'pyrrhic', as one US-based Turkish analyst has expressed it (Taspinar 2008). Many Americans, like their European counterparts, believe that the mass killing of Armenians was deliberate, whether or not it is described as genocide, and they will not cease to declare that belief. Only Turkey's friendship with, and utility to, the USA has ensured that, unlike Canada, Washington has not yet formally recognized that genocide occurred. This is a stance that is very much at the mercy of the condition of the Turkish–US relationship.

The Armenian 'genocide' and Turkish society and politics

In the early republican years, the preference was to forget what had happened. Some of the nationalists who now found themselves occupying high office had participated directly in, or profited from, the removal of Armenians from Anatolia, and in any case the massacres could be put down to a few CUP members of the Ottoman regime acting independently. The new Turkish government was content to inherit a largely Muslim population because it promised to ease the new state's nation-building project. Its objective was to weld together a unified and Muslim population and in turn to weld that population to the territory it had inherited. This entailed simply ignoring the centuries of substantial Armenian presence in Anatolia rather than explaining what had happened to it. Indeed, Turkey's educational system has subsequently been so silent that it has left many Turkish citizens largely ignorant of the fate of the Ottoman Armenian population. There are monuments commemorating the thousands of Muslims who undoubtedly died at the hands of Armenian separatists and brigands, but none to Ottoman Armenian subjects. Streets and neighbourhoods have been named after some of the CUP nationalists who are most closely associated with the fate of the Armenians, but Armenian churches have been almost entirely neglected – at least until very recently. For their part, the European powers preferred to establish a working relationship with the new Turkish state. Furthermore, and as we have seen, there was at this time little international pressure to pursue the Armenian case. As Hitler rationalized in 1939 when justifying his proposed removal of the Polish population so as to create *lebensraum* in the east in which Germans could be settled, 'who, after all, speaks today of the annihilation of the Armenians?'

Since the emergence of the Armenian genocide issue as a global concern, the Kemalist state apparatus has invested enormous effort in countering Armenian claims or juxtaposing them with counter-allegations of Armenian atrocities. It has even been claimed that seventy per cent of Turkey's US embassy staff's time is spent combating the genocide issue (Bengur 2009: 45). In addition to the Turkish foreign ministry and TSK, nationalist organizations established by, or that are close to, the Turkish state, such as the Turkish

Historical Society, the Association for Kemalist Thought, the Patriotic Forces United Movement and the Talat Pasa Committee, have all campaigned against the Armenian allegations. The state has not been content simply to deny that what occurred can properly be regarded as genocide. After all, this remains a subject for a debate of sorts, even for historians. Rather, it has preferred to inhibit any debate on the subject of the massacres and to downplay their extent. Lawyers from the Great Union of Jurists have been instrumental in prosecuting authors such as Orhan Pamuk and Elif Shafak and the ethnic Armenian journalist Hrant Dink, victim of a still largely unexplained assassination in January 2007,[24] for daring to raise the issue publicly.

The role of the TSK is particularly interesting, as it takes a lead role – perhaps the lead role – in propagating Turkey's official version of the events. It has uploaded onto its website seven vast volumes of archive material detailing the excesses and deceits of Armenians and the measures Turkish forces took to ensure the safety of the relocated and deported Armenian subjects. The website also contains an entire volume consisting of the accounts of a Russian officer who witnessed Armenian atrocities against Muslims, and other material aimed to cast a shadow over Armenian behaviour at the time. The TSK also distributes these publications, unsolicited, as gifts to foreign guests to its establishments.[25] All this material is in English as well as Turkish. Leading TSK officers are invariably at the forefront of Ankara's violent reactions to any external recognition or commemoration of the Armenian deaths. There are many indications that swathes of Turkish society have internalized the official line.

These reactions could indeed all be a reflection of the extent to which Turkey has been a relatively closed society, as the German Green Cem Ozdemir suggested. It could also be seen as an expression of a defensive – or aggressive – nationalism soaked in the Sèvres complex that is deeply entrenched in Turkish politics and society (see Chapter 3), and that resents what it perceives as external interference and criticism. In any case, Turkey's approach to this issue has won it little goodwill, either in Washington or in Europe. Indeed, the sheer ferocity and emotionalism of Turkey's behaviour may have been as, or more, instrumental in keeping the issue alive as any amount of external lobbying. However, there are signs that some elements within Turkish society have now come to recognize the substance behind the alternative narratives and perceptions that have infiltrated Turkish society from outside, and that have bubbled up from inside Turkey too. The impact of this fresh thinking seems to have been to further deepen divisions within Turkish society, which have been a consequence of so many other forms of external influence and pressure on Turkey in recent years.

Thus, in addition to the outspoken comments of a few high-profile individuals such as Halil Berktay, Murat Belge and Gengiz Candar (European Stability Initiative 2009), and a greater readiness to discuss the issue openly, in September 2005 a conference was held at Bilgi University to discuss the fate of Ottoman Armenians. Further conferences on Turkish–Armenian issues have subsequently been held at the university. On the other hand, the September 2005 Bilgi event had been moved there from Bogazici University as a ruse to avoid a last-minute court ban. Bogazici had initially intended to hold the conference in May 2005 but had been legally blocked from doing so. Furthermore, the justice minister Cemil Cicek had described the very idea of holding such a conference as 'stabbing the Turkish nation in the back', although other ministers, including Turkey's prime minister, president and chief EU negotiator, disapproved of the court's judgements and defended the right of the conference to go ahead.[26] The EU enlargement commissioner condemned the court's decision as an 'attempt to prevent the Turkish society from discussing its history'. The Bilgi conference was held against a backdrop of demonstrations and some lurid media commentary, and was followed in November 2005 by a counter-conference held at Gazi University (Aktan 2005a, 2005b; Kiniklioglu 2005; Soylemez 2005).[27] In another indication that some sectors of Turkish society no longer accepted the official line, in December 2008 over 200 Turkish intellectuals launched an online signature campaign with the text: 'My conscience does not accept the insensitivity showed to and the denial of the great catastrophe that the Ottoman Armenians were subjected to in 1915. I reject this injustice and for my share, I empathize with the feelings and pain of my Armenian brothers and sisters. I apologize to them.'[28] Although roundly condemned by the TSK, nationalist political leaders and retired diplomats, and in much of the media, the campaign has attracted 30,000 signatures. It also attracted a counter-campaign online calling on Armenians to apologize, and a counter-declaration signed by 146 retired ambassadors declaring that 'Today, Armenian terror has completed its mission. We are aware that the second phase of the plan includes an apology and the next step will be demands for land and compensation.' In fact, the possibility that Armenia might demand a border revision, or that individual Armenians will demand compensation from Turkey should Ankara concede that genocide occurred, are among the material reasons for Turkey to deny the allegation.

The assassination of the Turkish Armenian journalist Hrant Dink in January 2007 in Istanbul was greeted both by a funeral procession in which thousands of Turks took part, and by newspaper columns declaring him to have been an enemy of Turkey, the fate of anyone who queries Ankara's official position on the massacres. In 2010, a play-park named after Dink was opened on one of Istanbul's Princes' Islands. Even more remarkably, its opening was supported by both the ruling AKP and the CHP opposition parties.[29] However, the state continues to obstruct attempts by the Dink family lawyers and others to access information that might point to negligence or even complicity in the assassination. As with so many issues, Turkey's absorption of external pressures has been met with a nationalistic and defensive reaction, or with the continued obduracy of those elements of the state or Turkish society that remain impervious to global and transnational influences.

The AKP government has demonstrated a little more movement on the issue than has normally been associated with Ankara. In 2005, prime minister Erdogan suggested that Turkish and Armenian archives be made available to a joint commission of experts from both countries and abroad in order to investigate the events of 1915. Armenia turned down the offer, but it was left on the table. In July 2008, Yusuf Halicoglu, head of the Turkish Historical Society since 1993 and one of the country's most outspoken, and most insensitive, critics of the genocide allegation, was dismissed by the AKP government, presumably to help clear the way for an opening of diplomatic relationships with Armenia. However, Erdogan and others in the government have continued to deny that genocide occurred.

The relationship with Armenia

One of the many factors that persuaded Obama to desist from uttering the word 'genocide' was the hope that Turkey's relations with Armenia could be unblocked. Relations had been frozen since the conflict between Armenians and Azerbaijanis over the ethnically Armenian enclave of Nagorno-Karabakh in the early 1990s, which left Armenians in control of the enclave and its surrounding territory, thus enabling the creation of a buffer zone linking it to Armenia proper. Its declaration of independence is formally not even recognized by Yerevan, and there are still around 1 million displaced Azeri refugees. In response to the Armenian victory in the enclave, Turkey and Azerbaijan closed their borders with Armenia, which had supported the Armenians of Nagorno-Karabakh. This has left Armenia landlocked, which has caused it considerable economic distress. Clashes between Armenian and Azeri forces occur from time to time, and the somewhat desultory efforts of the Minsk Group, co-chaired by Russia, France and the USA under the Organization for Security and Cooperation in Europe (OSCE) umbrella, have made little headway. The USA would prefer to give Armenia the opportunity to wean itself from its dependence on Moscow, and would also like to see Armenia's territory be made available for the burgeoning pipeline network of the region.

During 2008, relations between Armenia and Azerbaijan, and between Armenia and Turkey, began to thaw a little. With US encouragement, this resulted in the October 2009 signing by both Ankara and Yerevan of a set of protocols envisaging the eventual establishment of diplomatic relations and the founding of an intergovernmental commission to address all issues between the two countries, including a subcommission on history. However, the Armenian constitutional court declared the protocols incompatible with the country's constitution, which contains a clause insisting on the recognition of the genocide. In any case, prime minister Erdogan had earlier insisted that there could be no opening of borders and re-establishment of diplomatic relations until the Armenian 'occupation' of Nagorno-Karabakh was ended. The Turkish foreign ministry also served notice that it rejected what it regarded as a 'precondition' laid down by the Armenian court. The protocols remained unratified by either side and opposed by nationalists on all sides, and the 'normalization' process petered out (European Stability Initiative 2009; International Crisis Group 2009; Idiz 2010). The two sides have since continued to discuss 'low politics' issues of common interest, such as tourism. With Davutoglu at the helm, Turkey's preference is still to minimize its foreign policy differences with all its neighbours, and to exploit its 'soft' power possibilities. However, there is little sign that Turkey is ready to accept the demand that it recognize the 'genocide', or that the Armenians of Nagorno-Karabakh can be persuaded to give up their hold over the territory they have occupied. The only way forward seems to be for Ankara and Yerevan to normalize their relationship in the absence of a prior resolution of these differences. At the time of writing, that appears unlikely. It appears just as unlikely that global pressure on Turkey to recognize the Armenian 'genocide' will abate. Indeed, it seems more likely to intensify, and again pit the peculiarities of Turkish politics and society against the norms and behaviours of the global system.

11 Migration, Turkey and Turks

Migration as a global phenomenon

Migration has been part of the human experience for centuries. The attachment of nomadic peoples in particular to specific and defined territorialities is weak or absent, but opportunity, conflict and need have encouraged millions of people to migrate, as individuals or as whole communities. The Turkic peoples offer one of the prime examples of the phenomenon, but many other examples abound. For example, the origin of the Hungarian or Magyar people is much disputed and dates from a distant historical epoch, but most agree that it is to be found in semi-nomadic tribes from the Ural Mountains or even from central Asia. More formal empires have frequently deposited peoples far from their original homelands. The decline of the Roman empire did not necessarily entail the departure of its soldiers and administrators – many of whom did not, in any case, hail from the Italian peninsula – from its imperial outposts. A wonderful example is afforded by the Iazgyians, an Iranian-speaking Black Sea people, 5500 of whom were shipped by the Romans to northern Britain to serve as horsemen. They stayed after the empire collapsed, and settled in the Preston area of western Lancashire (Ascherson 1996: 236–37). More familiar residues of imperial expansion are the Russians of eastern Siberia, Hispanics throughout the Americas, and people of British stock in southern Africa, north America and Australasia. Viking warriors and mercenaries from Scandinavia settled in the British Isles, in Normandy in France, in Iceland and Greenland, deep into Russia, eastern Europe and elsewhere. The history of the Jewish people is largely one of migration. Chinese communities are scattered throughout the world's cities. Africans suffered forced migration, and were transported as slaves to the Caribbean and throughout north and south America. Throughout history, there have been millions of individual migrant stories, through marriage for example, or as seamen, traders and the like. Many settled in locations in which they were initially transient. Societies such as those of the USA, Canada, Argentina, Australia and New Zealand have been composed almost entirely of migrants.

Notwithstanding the long and rich history of human migration, it is nevertheless commonly perceived as a defining feature of modern-day globalization. Part of the explanation is offered by the International Organization for Migration (IOM), established in 1951 and itself an institutional expression of globalization:

'Migration is considered one of the defining global issues of the early twenty first century, as more and more people are on the move today than at any other point in human history. There are now about 192 million people living outside their place of birth, which is about three per cent of the world's population. This means that roughly one of every thirty five persons in the world is a migrant. Between 1965 and 1990, the number of international migrants increased by 45 million – an annual growth rate of about 2.1 percent. The current annual growth rate is about 2.9 percent.'[1]

The context in which global migration takes place today is one of established sovereign-state borders. The policing and porosity of these inter-state boundaries is variable, and cross-border nomadism is not yet entirely dead. There is also a good deal of relatively informal and unregulated migration across contiguous borders in some of the less-well-policed regions of the world, such as in sub-Saharan Africa. Wars and instability sometimes prompt floods of people to cross neighbouring borders, frequently resulting in permanent or semi-permanent migrations, such as happened from Afghanistan into Pakistan and Iran. However, it is the large-scale migration, whether sanctioned or illegal, into the more developed parts of the world from its poorer regions that has grabbed most attention. This is particularly so in the case of western Europe, where, in the space of a half-century, the ethnic make-up of many cities has been massively transformed by immigration. Societies whose self-perception has long been based on race and culture have had to adjust in a very short space of time to the realities generated by the arrival of people from quite distant and different cultural backgrounds. Furthermore, the ease of human movement and communication in the modern, globalized world has meant that migration now raises a quite new set of issues.

Migration to and through Turkey

Since its establishment in 1923, the Turkish republic has absorbed over 1.5 million immigrants, chiefly from the Balkans and from amongst the Turkic peoples of the Soviet Union. Around two-thirds of the 300,000 or so Pomaks (Bulgarian Turks) who fled Bulgaria in 1989 remained and acquired Turkish citizenship. These immigrants accorded with a 1934 Law on Settlement which restricted immigration to people of 'Turkish descent and culture'. Since the end of the Cold War there has also been substantial irregular migration from the former Soviet Union, some of it as a result of trafficking in women for the sex trade, but also consisting of people entering the country legally and then choosing to remain, finding work as agricultural and construction-site labourers, domestic servants and so on. Estimates of this group of people vary from 150,000 to 1 million or more (Kirisci 2003), and they include Moldovans, Russians and Ukrainians as well as Kyrgyz, Azerbaijanis and other Muslim and Turkic people.

Since the early 1990s, wars, human rights abuses, the availability of means of transport and communications, and the economic discrepancies between the developed and underdeveloped world, have all contributed to the rise of irregular migration from poor and troubled countries to the rich West. Given its geography, forming a bridge between a developed and stable Europe and an undeveloped and strife-prone Middle East and Asia, Turkey has become a major transit route for such migration, such that between 2000 and 2006 alone, around half a million irregular migrants were apprehended in Turkey. The main sources of these migrants were Iran, Iraq, Afghanistan, Pakistan and Bangladesh (IOM 2008: 11). They are usually heading towards western Europe via Greece (Icduygu 2004b) and Bulgaria. Many of those who are apprehended are not returned to their country of origin, and either 'go underground' in Turkey or attempt to continue their westward-bound journey. It is difficult to estimate what proportion of irregular migrants are apprehended in Turkey or at the borders, but the EC's *Turkey 2010 Progress Report*, with its predecessors, expressed some doubt as to the capacity of Turkey's border-policing and migrant-processing systems and with regard to the implementation of its own legislation and of the various bilateral readmission agreements it has entered into (European Commission 2010: 80–86). The report also notes that in the past couple of years, the flow of illegal migrants from Turkey into Greece and Bulgaria appears to have dropped. With respect to human trafficking, which typically applies to prostitution or forced labour, the US State Department's annual reports have also found wanting Turkey's policing of human trafficking and treatment of its victims (US Department of State 2010).

Turkey's EU accession process obliges it to align its asylum regulations and its treatment of apprehended irregular migrants with the EU *acquis*. It also requires Turkey to improve both its border policing and its cooperation with EU neighbours. With regard to asylum, since 1951 Turkey has been prepared to grant refugee status only to asylum seekers coming from Europe. This has applied mainly to people fleeing the communist regimes of the Cold War, most of whom were then settled in the West. The EU is far less restrictive in its application of refugee and asylum regulations, and has engaged in extensive negotiations and agreements with Turkey relating to this issue (Biehl 2009). Ankara's difficulty is, first, that it fears that with EU membership it would become the point of entry for irregular migrants into the EU, and it seeks reassurance that other EU countries would take their 'fair share' of asylum seekers. Second, and more sensitively, widening the geographical net of its refugee and asylum policies would challenge Turkey's approach to nation building, which, as we have seen, has been based on people of 'Turkish descent and culture' who might be integrated more readily (Kirisci 2003).

Global smuggling: the Turkish contribution

Almost all those arrested smuggling irregular migrants into, through and onwards from Turkey have been Turkish nationals (European Commission 2010: 82). This does not necessarily mean that Turks control the entire smuggling network of irregular migrants passing through the country. It appears more likely that 'locally operating independent, individual groups comprise the essential foundation for human trafficking and smuggling in the region' (Icduygu and Toktas 2002: 25). This involves agents and recruiters from the source countries, drivers and shippers from all transit countries involved, corrupt officials along the entire route, providers of safe houses along the way, agents arranging for reception in the final destination, and financiers, forgers and recruiters from a range of countries, all forming an informal transborder network. Similar structures might function with respect to drug smuggling, too. However, it is clear that Turkish (and ethnically Kurdish) groups have been and are heavily involved in smuggling of people and drugs into Europe from Asia. The EU recognizes the importance of Turkey as a major illicit drug transit country for entry into Europe (European Commission 2010: 86). In 2006, an ethnically Kurdish London-based gang leader originating from Turkey, Abdullah Baybasin, was sentenced to prison for his role in smuggling heroin into the UK. Around eighty per cent of the heroin entering the UK market was believed to have been smuggled by Turkish gangs. Baybasin's gang had been responsible for most of it. Much of it originates in Afghanistan.[2] Although other gangs, notably from Albania, appeared to have muscled into the trade, Turkish groups remain significant players in the people- and drug-smuggling business. Drug-related turf wars between Turkish smuggling gangs continue to break out in London and other European cities.[3] A factor that has enabled Turkish criminal gangs to emerge as significant players in the trade in people and drugs into Europe has been the emergence of host communities located in the countries of destination.

Turkish migration

In recent decades, Turks too have joined this wave of global migration. Although there was considerable emigration of non-Muslim Ottoman subjects, such as Armenians, Greeks and Jews, few of the Ottoman empire's Muslims chose to leave its protection, although many moved around within its boundaries. Thus from 1820 onwards, only a very small number of largely rural, illiterate and unskilled Muslims from Anatolia ventured to the USA, and most of those returned with the 1923 establishment of the Turkish Republic (Akcapar 2009: 167–70). This contrasted significantly with the flood of people to north America from most other parts of Europe during that period. It also contrasts with Turkish emigration since the 1960s. Although the figures can vary a little depending on the source, there are now reckoned to be more than 3 million Turkish citizens resident in EU countries, with an additional 1 million having been naturalized. We can add to that figure around 300,000 Turks in north America (Akcapar 2009: 172–73), around half that figure in Australia, 200,000 in the Middle East, and over 80,000 in the Russian Federation (Akcapar and Yurdakul 2009: 139). There are said to be around 50,000 Turkish citizens living and working in other Commonwealth of Independent States (CIS) countries, chiefly in central Asia (Icduygu 2004a). These figures suggest that around six per cent of Turkey's population is living abroad at any one time, and that many of those residing in Turkey will at some time have lived and worked elsewhere.

In short, Turkey has emerged as a country of emigration, a development that flows into a broader global phenomenon. In the context of globalization and transnationalism, this Turkish experience raises a number of questions. What economic, social and political impact have Turkish emigrants had on Turkey itself? What issues are raised in the host countries by the presence of significant communities of people originating from Turkey? What impact has the phenomenon had on state-to-state relations between Turkey and the receiving countries? Such questions are made all the more compelling by the ethnic, social, political and religious diversity that characterizes the pool of Turkish emigrants. Most obviously, many of them are ethnically not Turks at all, but Kurds.[4] Some are secular, some are conservative Sunni Muslims, some are more radically Islamist, and others are adherents to Alevism. Some have integrated and even assimilated with their host populations, or have otherwise acquired economic and social status; others remain largely isolated from their host neighbours, ghettoized and towards the bottom end of the social, educational and economic pecking order. Some retain strong links with their country of origin and largely derive their identity from it, others less so. Questions relating to the impact of Turkish emigration also spill over into Turkey's bid for EU accession, and into Europe's response to 9/11 and fears for its own social and political cohesion.

Large-scale Turkish emigration to Europe dates back to a 1961 bilateral agreement between Turkey and the German Federal Republic, which aimed to provide the booming West German economy with unskilled labour. Ankara signed similar agreements with Austria, Belgium, the Netherlands, France and Sweden. Initially, the expectation was that their stay would be temporary, that they were merely 'guestworkers'. As such, the early waves of Turkish migrants were largely male. With the 1973 oil price hike and the economic downturn it induced, European countries ended their 'guestworker' programmes. By this time, around 1 million Turks had emigrated to Germany alone (International Crisis Group 2007a: 4). However, most elected to stay and were increasingly joined by their families or by new spouses from their home countries. This, in turn, led to an increase in the number of children born to Turks in Europe, such that in Germany, for example, around half Germany's Turkish-origin population is in fact German-born (International Crisis Group 2007a: 5). The profile of Turks in Europe was further altered in the wake of Turkey's 1980 military coup and with the intensification of its internal conflict with the PKK, when large numbers of ethnic Turks and Kurds applied for and obtained political asylum. Germany alone received 370,000 political asylum applications in the two decades after 1980 (Ostergaard-Nielson 2003: 33). These were often more educated and urbanized than the earlier mainly rural and unskilled labourers. Even today, up to 50,000 Turks migrate to Europe each year (Kirisci 2007: 92), increasingly made up of professionals and students. Turkish emigration to north America has long been characterized by a predominance of the educated and skilled (Akcapar 2009; Ozcurumez 2009).

Turks abroad or Europeanized Turks?

Such diversity suggests that caution should be exercised in generalizing about the behaviour of Turkish residents abroad. Furthermore, Turks – as with all immigrant groups – appear to behave differently in different host contexts, and the 'opportunity' approach suggests that issues such as 'migrant identity and belonging are very much affected by different legal and political integration policies adopted by host countries' (Akcapar and Yurdakul 2009: 140). The USA is a country of immigration, and its relatively small number of mainly skilled Turkish immigrants seem to be less oriented towards Turkey than their counterparts in Europe (Akcapar 2009: 180). On the other hand, seventy-five per cent of all Turks abroad reside in Germany (International Crisis Group 2007a: 7), and of these, fewer than twenty per cent were naturalized (Ostergaard-Nielson 2003: 3) until Germany eased its naturalization laws in 2000 and granted the right of citizenship to German-born children of resident foreigners. Even today, only around 1 million of Europe's resident Turks have been naturalized (Kirisci 2007: 92). Although in societies such as the Netherlands there has been greater emphasis on integration – and although there are numerous individual examples of Turkish integration with, and even assimilation into, the host population – the predominant European picture is of a Turkish emigrant population that disproportionately suffers high unemployment, low pay and low levels of educational attainment. Intermarriage with the host population is relatively rare, and there is a quite high degree of urban ghettoization (Avci 2006; Sohn and Ozcan 2006; Wets 2006). It was phenomena such as these that led the German chancellor Angela Merkel to declare in October 2010 that her country had failed to build a functioning multicultural society.[5]

Furthermore, Europe's Turkish migrants maintain high levels of contact with their country of origin via telephone calls, return visits, the purchase of property, the sending of letters, the opening of businesses and the like. They might return to Turkey to vote in elections there. They often contribute towards a fund to ensure they will be buried in Turkey (Yurdakul and Yukleyen 2009: 228). Remittances back to the homeland have made Turkey the world's third largest receiver of migrant remittances (Ostergaard-Nielson 2003: 5), in the 1980s amounting to as much as 2.5 per cent of Turkey's GNP and equivalent to sixty-five per cent of the country's trade deficit (Icduygu 2006: 4). Informal and unrecorded transfers have probably augmented these figures. Turkish migrants often socialize more or less exclusively with fellow Turks. In Germany, almost all Turkish-origin residents read Turkish newspapers and most watch Turkish television stations, around half of them exclusively so (Ostergaard-Nielson 2003: 34). This could imply the emergence of 'localized cosmopolites', truly transnational communities of people with attachment to two or more countries at the same time. It could equally be seen as a paradox of globalization that the ease of communications enabled by the internet, satellite broadcasting, cellular telephones, electronic banking and cheap air travel may help sustain or reinforce ties to the country of origin and serve to complicate or undermine integration or assimilation (Avci 2006: 80). It has been argued that 'median spaces' have been created that do not correspond to a specific territory, and that these lead to 'networks' rather than what might more usually be understood as diasporas (Allievi 2003: 10–12). Indeed, given Turkey's provincialism on the one hand and the urban concentrations of Europe's Turkish migrants on the other, the ties are often between two localities rather than two countries. The concept of *hemserilik*, which involves large-scale migrations of whole village or rural communities to specific destinations abroad – or even to narrowly defined neighbourhoods in Turkey's growing cities – transforms transnational ties into translocal ones. Thus most Belgian Turks originate from the district of Emirdag in Afyon province, in western Turkey. The majority of houses in Emirdag, which has a population of 20,000, are owned by people living in western Europe. So are many of its businesses. Most families in the region have, or have had, close relatives living in western Europe, and benefit substantially from their remittances. Much of the remaining population continues to aspire to emigrate, and many will achieve this aspiration via 'arranged' marriage to local emigrants (Timmerman 2006: 132).

Organizations and associations, of which there are a very large number, can also constitute a mechanism by which Turkish emigrants maintain links with their country of origin, thereby creating transnational links between the host country and Turkey. Of course, many of these focus primarily on the status of migrants in their host countries, and as such might contribute to their integration. Others are more focused on homeland politics and issues, such that Turkish organizations in Europe can often be reflective of political circumstances in the home country. Indeed, it has been claimed that Germany's Turks 'are still more interested in Turkish politics than in German politics' (Ostergaard-Nielson 2003: 90). As a consequence, Turkey's instability and its tendency towards left–right, secular–religious, Sunni–Alevi or Turk–Kurd polarization is often played out in western Europe. The scale of Germany's Turkish community in particular, and the relative freedoms to be enjoyed there, has converted Germany and other west European states into a kind of 'transnational free space for political socialization of Turks' (LeVine 2003: 109). Movements banned in Turkey have been able to flourish in

Germany and elsewhere in Europe. These greater freedoms to debate, to organize and to lobby seem also to have resulted in more exaggerated and even confrontational forms of identity and political expression than have usually been possible in Turkey (Odmalm 2009: 159). Furthermore, these transnational links and the activities with which they are associated constitute an important factor in the political relationships between Turkey and Germany in particular. It is certainly the case that German political parties follow Turkish developments relatively closely as a result of the large Turkish presence in Germany (Ostergaard-Nielson 2003: 86).

Europe's Turks and religion

Religious associations have always been popular among Turkish immigrants in Germany in particular, and in Europe more widely. *Diyanet*[6] (Directorate of Religious Affairs) is the largest Turkish religious organization in Europe. It was established in the newly formed Turkish republic in 1924 to control the mosques and train and appoint *imams*. It is an arm of the Turkish state and an instrument of its policies, and adheres to the Kemalist idea that religion should be a private matter (Avci 2005; International Crisis Group 2007a: 6–11; Yurdakul and Yukleyen 2009). It did not establish itself in Europe, however, until the early 1980s, partly in an attempt to counter the influence there of the Sufi orders such as the *Suleymancilar* and of other Islamist movements deemed threatening by the Turkish state. It is guided by the Turkish foreign ministry's missions in Europe, and rarely actively engages in public debates that might break out in host countries on contentious issues, such as headscarf-wearing or the right to religious education, although there are indications that this position is shifting with the advent of the AKP government in Turkey. It is responsible for 800 mosques in Germany, 140 in the Netherlands and numerous others wherever sizeable Turkish communities are to be found. *Diyanet* appoints state-trained and -paid *imams*, who typically have little or no knowledge of host-country languages or customs. It also organizes religious, sociocultural and educational activities for the Turkish community, and is disproportionately favoured by older and first-generation Turkish migrants. Although it is rhetorically committed to integration and tends to be the preferred dialogue partner for host-country governments, its close ties to the Turkish government, and the somewhat closed and intensely Turkish nature of many of its activities and personnel, cast a shadow over this claim. *Diyanet*'s official ties have sometimes aroused mistrust in Europe as, in effect, it serves as an arm of the Turkish state operating freely on the territory of Europe's host states, and it can appear to obstruct assimilation and even integration.

Diyanet's chief rival in Europe, and the main reason for its establishment there in the wake of the 1980 coup in Turkey, is *Milli Gorus* (National Vision). This movement emerged in the 1970s as an offshoot of Necemettin Erbakan's National Salvation Party and its subsequent reincarnation as the

Refah (Welfare), *Fazilet* (Virtue) and the still extant *Saadet* (Felicity) parties. Given the successive banning of these parties in Turkey because of the challenge they were deemed to mount to the country's state-controlled version of Islam, *Milli Gorus* was able to organize, recruit and raise funds in Europe even when proscribed in the homeland. Indeed, Turkish communities in Europe not only raised substantial sums of money for *Milli Gorus* electioneering campaigns in Turkey – a practice explicitly denounced by Turkey's MGK in 1997, the year of the 'soft coup' against the Erbakan-led coalition government there (Amiraux 2003: 157) – but Europe has also served as the political testing ground for a number of significant Islamist politicians in Turkey who have returned 'home' to become city mayors, MPs and the like. It is not surprising that Erbakan has been a frequent visitor to Germany since the mid-1970s (Amiraux 2003: 162–66; Ostergaard-Nielson 2003: 56), and it has even been claimed that *Refah* (and, by extension, its successor parties, including the AKP) 'has drawn benefit from the expatriation of part of its structure in Germany' and that it 'succeeded in using migration as a space for its reconquest of politics in Turkey' (Amiraux 2003: 148, 166).

In the aftermath of 9/11, a general radicalization of Muslims has been identified across Europe. With respect to Europe's Turkish populations, this is in part explained by 'a sense of social exclusion and marginalization (that) makes Turkish youth, in particular, turn to more radical forms of Turkish nationalism or Islam' (Ostergaard-Nielson 2003: 20). However, Germany's Sunni Turkish population more widely also seems to have been 're-Islamicized' since the 1980s (Ostergaard-Nielson 2003: 55), a development that appears to parallel what has happened in Turkey itself. *Milli Gorus* has been a significant beneficiary of this shift amongst Germany's Turks and, as we have seen, has been able to transfer some of the impact to Turkey's domestic politics. *Milli Gorus* followers in Europe tend to be younger than those of *Diyanet* and, if anything, more likely to be born in, and speak the language of, the host country. Although the movement also declares its commitment to integration, its understanding of this takes the form of a multiculturalism that would permit a kind of 'separate development' and parallel existence for Europe's Turkish communities. Thus in Germany it has campaigned actively for the right of Muslim women to wear headscarves in the public sphere, including the classroom; the right to religious education; the right to ritual slaughter; the right to burial according to Muslim rituals; the right to be granted leave from work for daily prayer and Muslim religious holidays, and so on (Ostergaard-Nielson 2003: 255). These campaigns have not always endeared *Milli Gorus* to indigenous populations, and have sometimes reinforced the disinclination of the authorities to engage positively with it. Given the banning of the political parties in Turkey with which it has been associated, Europe's cold shouldering of the movement has generally been welcomed by Ankara. Furthermore, *Milli Gorus* has been under surveillance by the German security agencies, who have suspected it of Islamist and anti-constitutional activities (International Crisis Group 2007a: 11). Thus '*Milli Gorus* is a contentious issue in transnational political relations between Germany and Turkey', although this might shift as more *Milli Gorus* activists and supporters in Europe develop sympathies with the AKP in Turkey (Yurdakul and Yukleyen 2009: 228).

Alevis abroad and the rise of Alevi identity

Around thirty per cent of Turkish migrants to Europe are Turkish and Kurdish Alevis, a disproportionate number given that they probably amount to between fifteen and twenty per cent of Turkey's population (Ozyurek 2009).[7] It is difficult to pin down the essence of what is an eclectic and traditionally orally transmitted faith, and in any case the roots of Alevism are disputed. Theologically it can be regarded as an offshoot of Shia Islam, but with an admixture of pre-Islamic shamanism, even Christianity, and a strongly mystical flavour. Alevi men and women worship together in their *cemevi* (prayer houses), the women do not wear headscarves, and drinking and dancing are not at all frowned upon (Zeidan 1999; Massicard 2003; Shankland 2003; White and Jongerden 2003). Although they constitute an almost exclusively Turkish phenomenon, the position of Alevis in Turkish society and politics is complex and ambiguous. Although usually politically secular and therefore generally supportive of the Kemalist order, although increasingly leftist in orientation since the 1960s, they remain quite marginalized and have often been disinclined to admit to their faith (Kehl-Bodrogi 2003).

They have not benefited from the post-1980 increase in state funding for religious establishments in Turkey, and teaching about Alevism has remained absent from the educational curricula. Thus there has been no state support for the construction of Alevi *cemevi*, and no state training of Alevi religious teachers, or *dedes*. The Sunni majority regards them with suspicion, as not truly Muslim, and they were generally suppressed for their presumed unreliability during the Ottoman era. Alevis have been particularly uncomfortable with the recent re-emergence of Islamic politics in Turkey. Outbreaks of tension and even violence between Sunnis and Alevis have occurred from time to time. For example, in 1993 in the south-eastern Turkish town of Sivas, also the scene of violence in 1978, thirty-three Alevi intellectuals died in a fire started deliberately by a Sunni mob, possibly with the connivance of the local police. Also in 1978, Kurdish Alevis were attacked by largely fellow-Kurdish Sunnis in Kahramanmaras, there was violence in Corum in 1980, and in 1995 there was an outbreak of intercommunal Alevi–Sunni violence in the predominantly Alevi Gazi district of Istanbul, widely suspected of having been provoked by elements of Turkey's so-called 'deep state'. Kurdish Alevis, centred in Tunceli province, have frequently been at the forefront of the Kurdish struggle in Turkey. As recently as 2002, an Alevi cultural association in Ankara was banned by the country's judiciary (Peuch 2002).

Alevis are traditionally largely poor and rural, but recent decades have seen large-scale migration to Turkey's cities and abroad. The absence of headscarves and of frequent prayer rituals, the greater equality of Alevi women, and the Alevi inclination towards secularism have all helped render Europe's Alevi community more palatable to their host populations, and their integration has been smoother than that of Turkey's Sunni Muslims. Alevis in Germany appear to have disproportionately naturalized (Poyraz 2006: 8). Alevi migrants have progressively become socially and organizationally distinct from other Turkish migrant communities, such that they have been criticized by fellow Turks for their divisiveness. More to the point, Alevi migrants in Europe have been able to use the freedoms available to them to develop and articulate the hitherto barely articulated source of their distinctive identity, encouraged by a European Parliament decision in 1986 to subsidize groups engaged in the promotion of immigrant cultures and identities. Some German local authorities have recognized Alevism as a distinct religion and permit its teaching in schools (Ozyurek 2009: 239–41). The space afforded Alevis in Europe has had the consequence that 'a rural, remote, diverse, private, largely oral Islamic society has become urban, public, active, secular' (Shankland 2003: 13). This increasing self-awareness culminated in the 1989 production in Germany of the Alevi Manifesto. Published in Turkey the following year, it calls on the Turkish state and society to grant recognition, equal representation, better access to education and to the media and financial assistance to Alevis on a par with that made available to Sunni Islam. Thus 'Alevis who organized in Europe financially and ideologically supported their networks in Turkey', and Alevi returnees frequently provided leadership (Ozyurek 2009: 240). Amongst leading Alevi associations inside Turkey, the Pir Sultan Adbal Association was founded only in 1988, and the Cem Foundation in 1995. Repatriated Alevi money has often been used for the purposes of rural and urban *cemevi* restoration and building, which the Turkish state still fails to fund. Especially with the arrival of numerous leftist Alevis as political refugees in the wake of Turkey's 1980 coup, Alevis in Europe became more politically sophisticated and this had an impact on Alevi politics in Turkey. In 2008, the French Alevi Federation celebrated its tenth anniversary by inviting, among others, leading Alevis from Turkey.[8]

Mainstream Turkish society and politics have not always reacted favourably to intensified Alevi activism and sharpened identity, essentially because in the Turkish context, the very idea of a minority is deemed divisive (Poyraz 2006: 7–10; Ozyurek 2009: 244–45), a status reserved exclusively (and constitutionally) for non-Muslims. On the other hand, there is now an intensified awareness of, and debate surrounding, Alevism in Turkey (Erman and Goker 2000). Interestingly, Alevis in Turkey often express their discomfort with the idea of minority status, and instead insist on religious equality with Sunni Turks. In Europe, on the other hand, it is precisely their distinct status as a minority that has been exploited. Alevi community leaders have not only lobbied for minority status in the European context, but have also lobbied host governments and the EC in order to highlight the Alevi plight in Turkey (Ozyurek 2009: 244). After all, the first of the Copenhagen criteria to which all prospective EU members are required to adhere includes 'respect for and protection of minorities'. Largely as a consequence of the efforts of Europe-based Alevis, and to the irritation of Turkey's politicians, EC progress reports on Turkey since 1998 have made critical mention of the unfair treatment of Alevis when compared with the state-funded construction of mosques and training of Sunni *imams*.

The 2008 report (European Commission 2008) illustrated the tenor of Europe's approach to the Alevi issue in Turkey and the nature of Turkey's response. It also illustrated the extent to which the Alevi issue has become a factor in Turkey–EU relations, as well as some of the problems Turkey has in adjusting to European expectations of the accession process. It demonstrated, too, that pressures originating from the opportunities enjoyed by Europe-based Alevis to define their identity are having an impact inside Turkey. Thus, and on a positive note, the report noted that 'as regards the Alevis, the government announced an initiative aimed at improving dialogue with this community and addressing its concerns.' This was a reference to prime minister Erdogan's so-called 'Alevi opening', which involved appointing an AKP Alevi MP, Reha Camuroglu, as his special advisor for Alevi affairs, and accepting an invitation to an Alevi *itfar* (fast-breaking) dinner, a quite unprecedented event in Turkey.[9] In what was noted as a first decision of its kind in the country, a municipal council recognized a *cemivi* house as a place of worship and applied mosque tariffs to its water charges.[10]

'However', the report notes, 'the government's initiative has not been followed through. Overall, Alevis continue to face the same problems as before, in particular as regards education and places of worship' (European Commission 2008: 17). This is illustrated by the fact that in 2007, Camuroglu and the Alevi Cem Foundation demanded that *cemevis* be afforded similar status to mosques – that, for example, they be tax-exempted – and that, like Sunni *imams*, Alevi *dedes* should be state-employed. The demand was thrown out (Ozyurek 2009: 246). In frustration at the general lack of progress, Camuroglu later resigned his position as advisor though he retained his AKP parliamentary seat and membership.[11] The report observed that Turkey's Council of State had declared that Alevi children could be exempted from religious education classes in Turkish schools,[12] but also that cases were still occurring of local authorities in Turkey refusing permission for the construction of *cemevi*. There are persisting allegations that the Sunni bias of the ruling AKP has led to discrimination against Alevis,[13] but there are also indications that greater recognition is being paid to the rights of the Alevi community. In short, the picture is mixed. The emergence of an Alevi identity has led to some movement on the issue inside Turkey, but the Sunni bias of the ruling AKP – itself a beneficiary of the scope to keep the flame of political Islam alive in Europe – and Turkey's perennial difficulty with the very concept of a 'minority' have meant that the existence of this interfaith conflict has been brought into clearer relief as a result of the impact of Turkey's various migrant communities (Uslu 2008c).

12 The Fethullah Gulen movement (and Turkish Al Qaeda) as transnational phenomena

Introduction

Recent years have witnessed an upsurge of curiosity about the Turkish Sufi scholar Fethullah Gulen and his legion of followers, known as *Fethullahci*, both in his native country and abroad. One factor contributing to this attention was Gulen's summer 2008 election as the world's leading intellectual in a poll organized jointly by the British *Prospect* magazine and the US publication *Foreign Policy*, in which over half a million votes were registered for a candidate who had hitherto been unknown to *Prospect*'s editor (Tait 2008). *Prospect*'s analysis of the poll identified in Gulen's victory the emergence of a new kind of intellectual, 'one whose influence is expressed through a personal network, aided by the internet, rather than publications or institutions' (Nuttall 2008). *Prospect* additionally noted how votes for Gulen mounted in the wake of publicity for the poll in the Gulen-inspired Turkish newspaper *Zaman* and a host of other Gulen websites. This appeared to testify to the legendary 'efficiency and discipline' and 'organizational ability' of the *Fethullahci*.

These observations offered an insight into the mechanisms of Gulen's influence and the nature of the Gulen movement, and into the way in which it is sometimes regarded. There is a hint of something sinister in this interpretation of Gulen's victory, implying as it does central direction rather than spontaneity. Secular Turks share such suspicions, and conspiracy theories abound in Turkey concerning both the source and level of the movement's funding and the nature of its ultimate ambitions. Indeed, both are obscure. A trawl of the web reveals allegations that the Gulen movement receives funding, either alternatively or simultaneously, from the CIA, Saudi Arabia, Iran and the Turkish state, and from Bill Gates and Walmart.[1] Certainly the financial resources at the movement's disposal are considerable. Many would probably concur with *The Economist*, which has noted that the West's security services 'have not detected any hidden ties with extremism' and that the Gulen movement generally receives a good reception in Europe and the USA.[2] On the other hand, according to the American neo-conservative Michael Rubin, if Gulen does return to Turkey 'Istanbul 2008 may very well look like Tehran 1979' (Rubin 2008). Rubin anticipates millions turning out to greet Gulen on his return to Turkey, his issuing of *fatwas* designed to distance Turkey from its official secularism, the restoration of the caliphate, and the subversion of the rule of law 'to an imam's conception of God'. Similar alarm has been expressed, albeit in more measured fashion, by Hakan Yavuz, a US-based Turkish scholar of Islam in Turkey, who has been quoted as asserting that the Gulen movement is 'the most powerful movement right now in the country [...] The point where they are today scares me. There is no other movement to balance them in society' (Hudson 2008).

Clearly, Gulen and the *Fethullahci* are divisive domestically, but they were also described by the same article in *The Economist* as 'one of the most powerful and best connected of the networks that are competing to influence Muslims round the globe'. However, the movement's activities abroad also arouse suspicions (Park 2007). For example, the Russian authorities, fearful of any indications of Islamic or pan-Turkic revivalism within their borders, have closed down Gulen schools as part of a wider campaign against the movement's activities and influences, a campaign that has included bans on the works of the Sufi teacher Said Nursi, from whom Gulen draws much of his inspiration (Fagan 2007).[3] Unease concerning the proliferation of 'Turkish schools' has been recorded in Georgia,[4] central Asia (Najibullah 2009) and elsewhere. In the USA, the newly formed (in 2010) and Gulen-inspired Assembly of Turkic American Federations (ATAF) appears to aim at lobbying for Turkish interests (as interpreted by the Gulen movement) in Washington.[5] It is too early to assess its impact, but the signs are that it will be politically active and seek to lobby US political circles and influence US policies towards Turkey. It will be interesting to see how the American reaction to this evolves.

Gulen's thinking

Before addressing more fully the global activities and transnational character of the Gulen movement, it is first necessary to offer a sketch of the man, the ideas, and the emergence of the movement in Turkey. Gulen himself has lived in somewhat hermit-like exile in Pennsylvania since 1998, ostensibly due to ill health, but also as a consequence of fears for his freedom should he return to Turkey. He was charged in 1999 for 'establishing an illegal organization in order to change the secular structure of the state and to establish a state based on religious rules' (Ozdalga 2005: 439–40). Although he was acquitted in 2006, the judgment was appealed, and it was not until June 2008 that the acquittal was finally upheld, thus clearing the way for his safe return to Turkey.[6] He has chosen to remain in the USA.

Although Fethullah Gulen's thinking continues to evolve (Yavuz 2003b: 45), it is rooted both in Turkish Ottoman experience and in the 'folk Islam' and Sufism, or spirituality, of Anatolian Turkish Islam (Saritoprak 2003; Yavuz 2004; Michel 2005; Gokcek 2006). Specifically, Gulen derives inspiration from the writings of the prominent Kurdish religious authority Said Nursi (1877–1961). The *Nur* (Light) or *Nurci* movement that Said inspired was distinguished by its advocacy of reason, progress and tolerance, and by its shunning of direct political involvement. Added to this is Gulen's observation that the 'top-down' imposition of the sometimes anti-religious secular dogma associated with Turkey's Kemalist state has only served to distance its citizens from the governing elite. Gulen's preference is for the Ottoman rather than the republican model of state–society relationships. The Ottoman system of governance was not directly theocratic. Public laws were formulated on the basis of the state's needs rather than in accordance with Islamic law (*Shari'a*). Indeed, Gulen's thinking is quite distinctly state-centric. For Gulen, the state has a functionally secular role to provide internal and external security and stability for its citizens. It is desirable, however, that a state's rulers, as well as its citizens, are guided by faith.

Thus Gulen is not in favour of the political implementation of *Shari'a*, and he is opposed to 'political Islam' as such. Indeed, he sympathized with the 1997 'postmodern coup' that removed Erbakan's Welfare Party from power, although Gulen was himself caught up in the crackdown on religious activity that came in its wake. Gulen sympathized with the 1980 coup too, regarding it as appropriate and necessary that the state protect itself and its citizens against the chaos and violence that was threatening to engulf Turkish society. According to Gulen, Turkish Islam's more flexible, adaptable, spiritual and less doctrinal traditions have enabled republican Turkey and Turkish society more broadly to incorporate aspects of modernity to an extent barely found elsewhere in the Muslim world. Thus Gulen sees no contradiction between Islam and modernity. Indeed, he insists on the desirability of Islam's embrace of science, reason, democratization and tolerance. Religion should not become a dogma, but can be adaptive, open, flexible, rational and tolerant, and not closed and shielded from other faiths, other ideas, and from scientific and technological progress.

Thus the roots of the Gulen movement are in some respects quintessentially Turkish, located in Turkey's historical baggage and its domestic political circumstances, and in a version of Islam that arguably has more currency in Turkey than elsewhere – although some would dispute the particularity of Turkish Islam (Ozdalga 2006). Modern Turkish society is also intensely nationalistic, and some of this flavour, too, has been absorbed by the Gulen movement. The movement's philosophy fuses its brand of Islam with Turkish nationalism. After all, its theological and cultural roots, as well as its key personnel and resource base, lie in Turkish practice and experience. Its 'Turkish' quality endows this globally engaged movement with a paradoxical and sometimes quixotic character. The Gulen movement offers an example of a transnational phenomenon that nevertheless retains, and indeed lauds, its national flavour. This conscious 'Turkishness' has encouraged the movement to engage far more actively with the Turkic world than anywhere else. Gulen followers were swept up in Turkey's enthusiastic response to the post-1991

Soviet collapse, which opened the way for an extension of its activities into Turkic central Asia and Azerbaijan, purportedly Turkic republics and regions of the Russian Federation such as Dagestan, Karachai-Cherkessiya, Tatarstan and Bashkortostan, other former Soviet states containing Turkic minorities such as Ukraine, Georgia and Moldova, and into the Balkans. The full-scale emergence of the Gulen movement as a transnational educational community is rooted in this period and these regions. Thus the Gulen movement can be said to have thrived largely as a response to international, as well as domestic, 'opportunity structures' that presented themselves (Kuru 2005). However, the movement's continued growth has also extended its presence into Turkish diasporic communities in western Europe and elsewhere, and into regions of the world where few Turks, and even few Muslims, live.

The origins and nature of the Gulen movement in Turkey

In the wake of Gulen's 1966 appointment as a state-employed religious preacher in Izmir, a loose network of students, teachers, professionals, businessmen and the like began to gather around him and to coalesce as a seemingly spontaneous social movement inspired by Gulen's teaching. Its first venture into the wider propagation of its philosophy came in the form of summer schools, from which it progressed to the establishment of teaching centres (*dershane*), often with dormitories, to prepare religious students for university admission. These remain an important element in the inculcation of Gulen's values, not least through a 'mentoring' system found throughout the movement's educational establishments and its wider 'structure'. The *dershane* are also a prime source of recruits. As it blossomed, so it attracted the attention of Turkey's secularist state establishment. Gulen himself served a seven-month spell in prison in the early 1970s for propagating religion, and again attracted uncomfortable attention both during the 1980s and, as already noted, in the late 1990s. The network did not openly blossom as a major educational, social and religious movement until the early 1980s, when, in the wake of the military coup of 1980, the space for religious activity was expanded, inspired by the so-called 'Turkish–Islamic synthesis', which advocated a fusion between Turkish national identity and the Islamic faith.

As we have already noted, Turkey's increased pluralism and democratization have enabled its more devout and conservative provincial hinterland to challenge the Kemalist, secular, 'westernizing' and urban centre. The Gulen movement has emerged as a major beneficiary of this post-1980 liberalization, which created a space for its media, educational and financial activities free from the control of the statist secular establishment. Initially benefiting from some protective cover from prime minister Turgut Ozal, reckoned to be a sympathizer, the movement has since gone on to open hundreds of schools in Turkey since it was established in 1982; universities such as Fatih in Istanbul; hospitals; charities; a television channel (Samanyolu TV) which transmits programmes to a variety of Balkan, central Asian, south-east Asian and other countries and now has plans to broadcast to the Turkish community in Germany and into the Arab world;[7] a radio station (Burc FM); a mass-circulation daily newspaper (*Zaman*) which, in addition to its online English-language edition, also publishes elsewhere in the Turkic world – for example, Azerbaijan, Kyrgyzstan, Turkmenistan and Bashkortostan in the Russian Federation; and several other periodicals. In 1996 it established a bank, Asya Finans, operating on the basis of Islamic principles such as interest-free banking and initially tasked to raise investment funds for the newly independent Turkic republics. Its activities are now extensive and global. The network also spawned a Journalists and Writers Foundation,[8] largely to facilitate dialogue activities, and a Teachers Foundation, each of which publishes journals and organizes symposiums and conferences, frequently abroad, and provides an umbrella for a host of dialogue groups and charitable organizations.

Cooperation between, and overlapping membership of, these various institutions is extensive, and confusing – largely because Gulen-inspired institutions rarely own up to that fact. The websites of its schools, universities, media outlets, charities and dialogue groups almost never directly refer to Gulen's inspiration. To offer just a few examples, one searches in vain for any sign either of Gulen's inspiration or of any notable religious focus on the website of the Dialogue Society[9] that hosted this author in Istanbul, or of *Zaman* newspaper, or of Fatih University in Istanbul,[10] or of the Confederation of Businessmen and Industrialists in Turkey (*Turkiye Isadamlari ve Sanayiciler Konferasyonu* – TUSKON),[11] or of charities such as Is Anybody There? (*Kimse Yok Mu*).[12] Yet all are part of the Gulen network. This explains why estimates of the number of financial institutions, think tanks, media outlets, hospitals, charities, schools and other educational institutions run by the movement can vary, though it undoubtedly runs into the thousands, inside Turkey and beyond.

At first glance, the movement appears loosely structured and decentralized, and each of its ventures is individually financed (and usually self-financing), and run on a voluntary basis by members and sympathizers. Yet the various businesses, businessmen's associations, education trusts, charities, media outlets, think tanks and the like are also closely enmeshed. They advertise with, patronize, sponsor and provide facilities for each other. These links are informal and hard to trace, and seem to be facilitated by middle-men or mentors, a kind of hierarchy of activists. Nor does the movement have a membership as such, and *Fethullahci* are often loath to openly declare themselves. Furthermore, the distinction between members, followers, sympathizers and collaborators is blurred, and the movement is coy about revealing its scale – which, in any case, it might not accurately know. As a consequence, estimates of the movement's 'membership' vary considerably. One source suggested a figure anywhere between 200,000 and 4 million Turks (Aras and Caha 2000: 33). More recently, *Prospect* offered a figure of 5 million. This 'structure', or lack of it, raises the question of whether so devolved, publicity-shy, extensive, variegated and voluntaristic a movement can exhibit the sense of purpose and discipline sometimes attributed to it, but it also adds to the suspicion with which it is regarded. It is an internet-connected, informal and word-of-mouth set of overlapping networks, which is more social movement than organization. It fuses faith with practical activity in a way that empirical and material analyses of it struggle to grasp.

Turkey's 'new' class of businessmen, professionals, teachers and intellectuals form the core of the *Fethullahci*. This middle-class profile is not quite coincident with the newly urbanized working class and the rural poor who provide the backbone of the AKP's electoral support, nor is the movement quite coincident with the AKP. Their relationship has been described as 'an alliance of convenience', and some have speculated about tensions existing within the relationship (Dogru 2010; Ulsever 2010). In power, the AKP offers a vehicle enabling the appointment of Gulen sympathizers to positions of power, while the movement is a valuable source of funds for the party (Jane's 2009). Gulen followers range from extremely pious individuals – often teachers and preachers and those engaged in the movement's dialogue activities, who are inspired by the Islamic principle of *hizmet* (service), and whose lives are dedicated to the propagation of the values and ideas of Fethullah Gulen – to the more occasional and more pragmatic members and sympathizers such as businessmen, politicians, journalists and, increasingly, even officials of the supposedly secular Kemalist state. The movement's pious and dedicated activists are inclined towards constant and somewhat uncritical reference to Gulen's writings. Such 'true believers' can convey the impression of 'cultism' (Cetin 2007), and can perhaps be likened to early Christian sects, both in their motivation and their voluntarism.

There seems little reason to doubt the debt of the movement's business backers to Gulen's philosophy, the sincerity of their Islamic approach to their wider social and moral obligations, their desire to please God, and their voluntarism. *Zakat* is one of the five pillars of Islam, and obliges Muslims to donate 2.5 per cent of their wealth to worthy causes. *Sadaqa*, voluntary charity, can inspire the wealthy to donate in excess of this minimum. Many rich Gulen sympathizers do indeed donate a large percentage of their personal wealth as an expression of their commitment. Businessmen, typically forming tightly knit circles drawn from a particular town or locality and whose relationships rely heavily on mutual trust, donate – in money or in kind – to the building of schools and the like as acts of Islamic charity. Such 'giving' might also bring a commercial return in the form of contracts or 'profits' from a venture's revenue-raising capacity (Ebaugh and Koc 2007), although the general principle is that ventures should be self-financing and that any surplus funds be ploughed back.

There is a growing belief that the Gulen movement is gradually but inexorably extending its tentacles and control throughout Turkish society and its institutions, most notably the police (Jane's 2009; Sharon-Krespin 2009). A Turkish interior minister once suggested that as many as seventy per cent of the nation's police force are Gulen sympathizers.[13] Indeed, in 2010 a former police chief of Eskisehir, Hanefi Avci, himself once a Gulen sympathizer, published a book alleging precisely that. In September of the same year, he was arrested as part of the Ergenekon investigation into the 'deep state'. For Gulen's opponents, this arrest, and even the investigation as a whole, serve as testimony to the power and pervasiveness of the movement and its emergence as a kind of fifth estate or third power in Turkey. Gulen denied any such penetration of the state by his followers, of course.[14] However, the movement is undoubtedly massively well resourced, interconnected, effective and extensive, with tentacles throughout society and sympathizers within the political and bureaucratic elite. Gulen sympathizers can increasingly be found in government service. This development aggravates Turkey's secularists. After all, the judicial case against Gulen in the late 1990s was based on a tape in which he seemed to be urging his followers to take over the state by stealth. This chimes with the mission with which Gulen's 'golden generation' is tasked – to re-Islamize society from below. Overall, the impression is of a parallel structure and society that sit uneasily alongside Turkey's officially secular state institutions and ruling elite, providing a silent, amorphous, ungraspable but increasingly irresistible challenge to Turkey's traditional ordering.

The movement's transnationalism

'Islam was 'transnational' [...] long before there were nations' (Vertovec 2003: 324), and the notion of a global Muslim *umma* (community) has continued to provide a source of resistance to the territorialization and nationalization of global politics. The kind of radical Islam associated with the al Qaeda network is additionally seen as resistant to globalization understood as Americanization or westernization, although it is simultaneously enabled by globalization via its exploitation of the modern media, the internet, international travel and emigration. The Gulen movement, or network (Aras and Caha 2000; Yavuz and Esposito 2003; Hunt and Aslandogan 2006; West 2006; Park 2008a; Ebaugh 2010),[15] is actively engaged in disseminating to a world beyond Turkey's state boundaries, as well as within them, an approach to Islam and to its relationship to politics and other faiths that is quite at odds with that propagated by Islamic fundamentalism. The movement is in effect a participant in a global contestation over what Islam is and what role it should play, and its message could hardly be more at odds with that brand of Islam typically dubbed 'fundamentalist' (Hendrick 2006). Specifically, it qualifies to be considered as a transnational phenomenon, and as contributing to and manifesting the spirit of globalization, via both its geographically dispersed educational activities and its commitment to dialogue with other faiths. Each of these areas of activity will be discussed below.

Robert O. Keohane and Joseph S. Nye famously defined transnational relations as 'contacts, coalitions and interactions across state boundaries that are not controlled by the central foreign policy organs of government'

(Keohane and Nye 1973: xi). One possible outcome of the activities of transnational agencies might be the creation of transnational networks of individuals and groups that interact, where possible, without direct reference to state authorities or territorial boundaries. These new social formations might have an impact on the power structures, values and ultimately state policies of both 'sending' and 'receiving' societies. Another outcome might be the generation of blurred, multiple, shared or shifting identities and value systems amongst individuals and groups that by their very existence offset the territorialization of global politics and might even consciously resist it. This might take the form of a loosely constructed, transnationally shared ideational consciousness, or a much tighter, emulative cultural reproduction or hybridity. It is hard to assess which of these two best describes the essence of the Gulen movement abroad, because its secrecy renders it difficult to trace the interactions, ties and influences linking Gulen-inspired individuals, groups and institutions across state boundaries. However, the former seems more likely where the raw material for the transmission of Gulen's Turkish Islam is absent, as in the West; the latter where it is present, as in central Asia.

In any case, the impact and significance of transnational phenomena cannot readily be measured or even defined with precision. When considering the Gulen movement's transnational activities, or indeed those of any comparable phenomena, we must also guard against the risk of slipping into an unexamined assumption that transnational activities are necessarily welcome, especially in 'receiving' countries. Transnational phenomena might be simultaneously transcending in their impact, and perceived as competitive by receiving states and societies. Existing social values and institutional structures might generate defensive reactions to unwelcome externally derived intrusions and challenges. The more transnational phenomena are seen as intrusive, as imports from one state, society or value system into another, the more they might generate nationalist or otherwise culturally protective forms of resistance. Transnational interactions can just as easily highlight differences, and attachments to such differences, as they can create new, transformative and shared social formations. They might also be broadly neutral in impact. In our exploration of the Gulen movement's impact, we must open our minds to the possibility of reactions, outcomes and consequences such as these.

The Gulen movement's transnational educational activities: the Turkic world

Gulen propagates a kind of 'educational Islamism' as opposed to a 'political Islamism' (Agai 2003: 50). Although education curricula should emphasize science and technology rather than faith teaching as such, Gulen also advocates the transmission of spiritual, moral and behavioural values (Agai 2003; Michel 2003; Aslandogan and Cetin 2006). Through the Gulen-inspired

spiritual transformation of individuals will emerge a wider social transformation and a (re-)'Islamification' of modernity. Thus politics in Turkey, and
perhaps in other Islamic societies in which the movement operates, should be
'Islamized' only via a bottom-up process and indirectly, in which people and
state are reunited in a kind of organic way. In this sense, the Gulen movement's mission in the Islamic societies in which it operates can be said to be a
political project, but one that aspires to achieve its goals indirectly. People of
faith as well as learning, a 'golden generation', should be cultivated and
encouraged to dedicate their lives to the service (*hizmet*) of the people. It is an
approach that resembles a kind of 'long march through the institutions', and
Turkey's secular establishment, and secularists and those of different religious
persuasion outside Turkey, are occasionally unsettled by it.

That overt religious teaching, and even explicit mention of Fethullah
Gulen, is generally absent from Gulen educational establishments, is partly
but not entirely explained by the need to tread carefully in the presence
of political authorities suspicious of religious or foreign activities within their
borders. This delicacy about the movement's nature raises a question of
whether the Gulen movement's educational establishments, especially beyond
Turkey or the wider Turkic world, should be seen as anything other than a
commercially based transnational educational foundation. It simultaneously
raises concerns that there might be more sinister purposes behind the movement's activities. For example, one searches in vain for any sign either
of Gulen's inspiration or of any notable religious focus on the website of
the Gulen-sourced Virginia International University in the USA,[16] yet in the
USA the risks of transparency would appear to be limited.

The Gulen movement's external activities were initially concentrated
in Turkic central Asia and Azerbaijan, and the Gulen presence throughout
the Turkic world remains substantial (Muzalevsky 2009). There are half a
dozen or more Gulen-sponsored universities in central Asia, and numerous
other educational, welfare and economic institutions and activities. One can
readily see why the movement might have assumed that in Turkic central Asia
and Azerbaijan, the likely receptivity to its overtures would be high. The
region shares a linguistic and ethnic root with Turkey, and a 'folk Islam' that,
as in Turkey, incorporates numerous Sufi sects and has absorbed pre-Islamic
traditions, beliefs and rituals. Furthermore, modern Turkish interest in
this 'diaspora' can be seen as a resuscitation of the earlier global interconnectedness and shared history of the Turkic peoples. Additionally, the
Soviet era left behind a legacy of secular education and a commitment to
science, progress and modernity that broadly corresponds with the Gulen
movement's aspirations (Yavuz 2003b: 39–40). Together, these factors suggest
some scope for cultural reproduction in the region, whereby the Gulen network's central Asian elites could, in time, take on the forms of their Turkish
counterparts, blending to generate a new, distinct and perhaps deterritor-
ialized transnational social formation. In the longer term, this could have
important ramifications and lend support to the emergence of a pan-Turkic

world linked by overlapping and fused identities. This could, in turn, ease the development of economic interactions and even encourage closer state-to-state relationships. Such an evolution would not quite accord with the adoption of the 'Turkish model' that Ankara's secularists and some of its western advocates had hoped for, but it might dovetail with the aspirations of pan-Turkic nationalist elements in Turkey.

In the Turkic territories of central Asia and elsewhere, much of the push behind the network's penetration of the region came from devout and conservative Turkish businessmen who were willing to finance educational activities 'because of their commitment to Gulen's Turko-Islamic worldview' (Yavuz 2003b: 39). Furthermore, these business groups have frequently fused their commercial ventures with their support for the Gulen network's activities in central Asia (Balci 2003a: 154–55; Peuch 2004a). As an illustration of the form the Turkish presence in the region can take, in Kazakhstan the most important location for the Gulen network's activities, the Kazakh–Turkish Education Foundation (KATEV) in Almaty, functions as a cornerstone of the resident Turkish community, and is supported and frequented by Turkish business and charitable groups often associated with the Gulen network (Turam 2003: 188–89). This kind of presence has, in turn, generated a close working relationship with Turkish embassies in the region, whose staff have become progressively more willing to facilitate the activities of businesses and other institutions associated with the Gulen network (Balci 2003b). The Gulen network's transnationalist activities might in this way be furthering Turkey's economic interests abroad and furthering its 'soft diplomacy'. Certainly a great deal of Turkey's expanding economic interaction, in central Asia and beyond, piggy-backs on the wider Gulenist presence in locations around the globe.

The pan-Turkic strain that sometimes runs through the Gulen movement's approach stresses the shared ethnic and cultural origins of the Turkic people. As one observer has expressed it, 'the followers of the Gulen community aspire to reconnect central Asians with their Turkic origins by spreading Turkish Muslim culture and morality to that region' (Turam 2003: 187). It appears that the movement's Turkish activists in the region typically regard central Asians as their Turkic blood brothers, and aspire to create individuals oriented towards Turkey and 'Turkishness' as well towards Islamic progress and enlightenment. Indeed, there may have been a greater receptivity to 'Turkism' than to Islam in the region (Balci 2003a: 153; Turam 2004). However, there are indications that a shared Turkic ethnic and linguistic root might not be sufficient to remove all barriers to a fuller interpenetration and blending. The movement's educational establishments in the region are frequently referred to simply as 'Turkish schools', and at least initially some inhabitants of central Asia seem to have resented the speed with which Turkish institutions replaced Soviet/Russian ones after 1991 (Peuch 2004b). Furthermore, there have been indications of a Turkish chauvinism towards the Turkic peoples of the region, whether intentional or not. Students in the movement's schools abroad might be expected to sing the Turkish national anthem and raise the Turkish national flag as well as their own (Peuch 2004b). Instruction is chiefly in English, but Turkish is also extensively used in addition to local languages where necessary. Furthermore, the overwhelming majority of the teachers and administrators in the movement's institutions abroad are Turks from Turkey rather than locals (Balci 2003b). This sense of a 'foreign' and intrusive penetration has occasionally combined with a dislike of the perceived religious and missionary self-righteousness of the movement's teachers, whose piety and dedication can grate with more secular, perhaps non-believing, locals. They can even seem to be imbued with a distasteful 'big brother' attitude (Miller 2003).

Additionally, the determined and autocratic secularity of the region's political leaderships, and their post-Soviet prickly sensitivity to anything they perceive as external meddling in their affairs, put the Gulen movement's reception in the Turkic world very much at the mercy of the region's governments. In 1994 and again four years later, Uzbek president Islam Karimov cracked down on the movement's activities in his country, including a ban on the distribution of *Zaman*, such that the movement has minimal presence there today. It is unclear whether this was a reaction to the presence in his country of a religious group that he did not control, or whether it indicated retaliation against the Turkish state's harbouring of Uzbek opposition leaders (Aras and Caha 2000: 28; Balci 2003a: 155–57; Peuch 2004b). In 2005, Turkish teaching staff at the Islamic theology school at a university in Turkmenistan were sacked by the country's autocratic leader Saparmurat Niazov, apparently reflecting unease about both the pan-Turkic and the Islamic ideology of the Gulen network in the country (IWPR 2005). Beyond former Soviet central Asia, the Taliban regime closed down the Gulen movement's activities in Afghanistan in the late 1990s, disapproving both of its brand of Islam and of external interference in the country (Kuru 2005: 262), and the movement was denied permission to open a school in an Azeri (Turkic) region of Iran through Tehran's suspicion of its pan-Turkic aspirations (Kosebalaban 2003: 179–80). In fact, it appears that not a single school has been opened in Iran (Bilici 2010). Such incidents constitute examples of how the non-state activities of transnational enterprises can nevertheless become entangled with state-to-state interactions, and can as easily reinforce negative tendencies in such relationships as help overcome them by transcending them.

An additional source of resentment at the activities of the movement in central Asia is its elitist nature, a notable feature of its activities in Turkey too. In this sense, the movement's activities can be seen as 'translocal' rather than transnational, as a vehicle for relatively exclusive and restricted interpenetration by narrow sectors of societies rather than more mass-based, transborder interactions. It is relatively rare for children of the disadvantaged, even if devout, to gain entry into Gulen schools. The fees and entrance requirements are high, and the good reputations the schools have acquired for the quality of their technical education, their use of English as a language of instruction, and the high behavioural standards they set have combined to ensure that places are at a premium. Typically, successful applicants in central Asia and elsewhere in the post-communist world are the children either of the wealthy or of government officials (Balci 2003a: 164–65; Miller 2003). This has to be appreciated against the background of a collapsed educational, social and economic infrastructure throughout much of the region. State spending on education has plummeted throughout central Asia in particular, leading to school closures, a shortage of teachers, a degradation of the physical infrastructure and widespread corruption surrounding school and college admissions and test results (Silova *et al.* 2007).

The Gulen movement's transnational educational activities: the non-Turkic world

However, we should be wary of excessive generalization concerning the nature and impact of the Gulen movement's activities abroad. Largely as a consequence of its devolved and voluntaristic nature, the precise characteristics of each establishment might differ, just as the motives behind their establishment can vary (Peuch 2004b). It might also be that from the mid-1990s onwards the movement, or at any rate Gulen's own thinking, shifted from a chauvinistic Turkish Islamic identity towards 'global educational activities that encourage the national identities of the countries in which it is operating' (Agai 2003: 63). In this context, it is worth noting that the movement has a presence in the form of a variety of educational institutions in over 100 countries, and now supervises as many or more schools abroad as it does in Turkey – although the unstructured nature of the movement again means that no precise figure can be given. Gulen schools and other educational and media establishments are globally far-flung, and can be found in such places as northern Iraq, the Balkans (notably Bosnia), Armenia, Georgia, the USA, Australia, China, Cambodia, sub-Saharan Africa and India, and in western countries where Turkish minorities are located, such as Germany, France, the Netherlands and the UK. Indeed, in western Europe the movement's schools have served to reinforce or preserve Turkish and Muslim identities otherwise vulnerable to dilution and distortion as a result of interaction with host societies, although the simultaneous commitment to accommodation and tolerance of host-country customs is strong (Bilir 2004; Irvine 2006). Belatedly, the network is now venturing into the Arab world, with projects such as the Salahaldin International School in Cairo, opened in 2009. There are schools in Jordan, Yemen and Tunisia too. In 2005, the movement launched an Arabic journal, *Hira*, which generally and advisedly steers well clear of politics (Heck 2007).[17]

A quite different assessment might be made of a Gulen educational initiative in a non-Turkic location such as the Philippines. Here, in an area where the denominational split between Muslims and Christians is roughly half and half, a Gulen school employs many Filipino teachers (some of whom are Christian) and admits many Christian students. Furthermore, and in keeping with the movement's commitment to interfaith dialogue, healthy links are maintained with nearby Christian institutions. Even in central Asia, non-Muslim students might be granted admission to Gulen establishments (Michel 2003). Interestingly, even in decidedly non-Turkic countries such as India and Kenya, portraits of Ataturk are on show, Turkish is taught, and the Turkish national anthem sung. The Turkishness of Gulen schools is frequently far more evident than their Islamism. This emphasis on Turkish language and culture has even won over some of the usually suspicious representatives of Turkey's secularist political class.[18] Wherever they are found, Gulen educational establishments abide by local curricula requirements. They do not directly propagate Islam, but rather emphasize virtues such as respect for elders, politeness, modesty and hard work. In other words, they teach by example. As elsewhere, this approach accounts for the popularity of Gulen schools in Africa, where there are scores of Turkish schools in over thirty countries, many of them in largely Christian sub-Saharan Africa.[19] It is difficult to assess, however, what the ultimate impact might be of a globally scattered body of well-behaved, hard-working, well-educated individuals with a knowledge of, and sympathy with, Turkish culture. It is hardly likely to do harm to Turkey's image and interests abroad, or to the more general cause of global understanding and tolerance. On the other hand, the relative scale of the Gulen movement's presence is so small, and Turkey's footprint in such regions otherwise so light, that it is hard to see what measurable good it might do either.

An especially interesting and curious case, in equal measure, are the educational activities of the Gulen network in the USA, where there are relatively very few ethnic Turks and Muslims but around 100 Gulen network schools (Schwartz 2010). The mainly charter schools are run by nominally distinct, but in fact interconnected, trusts, organized largely on a state basis and with names such as 'Daisy', 'Beehive' and 'Harmony'. They emphasize science teaching and good behaviour, and attract aspiring and generally middle-income parents who value the high educational and behavioural standards with which the schools are associated. The pupils are offered classes in the Turkish language and trips to Turkey, and are inculcated in aspects of Turkish culture. They also appear to serve as a vehicle for enabling Turkish immigration into the USA, as at least one-third of the teaching and administrative staff are Turkish, about which questions have been raised.[20]

Gulen's educational ventures: an impact assessment

Is it possible to assess the contribution the Gulen movement's educational activities are making to Islam, to Turkey's interests and image, and to global dialogue and tolerance? As we have noted, we would surely be well advised to differentiate in our assessments and to avoid conclusiveness. It is too early to tell, and too difficult to estimate. This is especially so with respect to the movement's ventures in non-Turkic and non-Muslim locations. In any case, their role in the Turkic world looms larger and is conceivably more portentous. *Fethullahci* schools represent a minority of central Asia's education system (Peuch 2004b), albeit a share disproportionately patronized by the region's economic, intellectual and social elite. It could be that, in a tacit partnership with the Turkish state, the movement's activities will, over the longer term, intensify the emotive and material bonds between Turkic peoples – or their elites – and states (Balci 2003a: 166–67). As one observer has expressed it, the Gulen movement has 'an ethnic agenda, which calls for the realization of Turkic homogeneity in central Asia. It is this ethnic politics that makes Gulen an effective international actor' (Turam 2003: 192).

Alternatively, if its activities serve to 'encourage the national identities of the countries in which it is operating' (Agai 2003: 63), and perhaps also assist the survival of local variants of the Islamic faith, it might simultaneously help generate local bulwarks against a denationalized Islamic fundamentalism and increase belief in the viability of a Turkish-style fusion of modernity and Islam. There is scope for differences of view as to which of these two propositions is closest to reality, but both might contain elements of truth. Even in the face of opposition, unease or ambivalence from Turkey's Kemalist elite, the movement could in time have a transformative impact on the Turkic region and even the wider Islamic world – although we should be wary of looking for an 'arrival' at, rather than a potential journey towards, a more 'Turkish Islamic' future.

Furthermore, the Gulen message, with its heady and promising combination of faith, identity, material progress, democratization and dialogue, might offer a model more attractive to, and more worthy of emulation by, Muslim states and societies struggling to orient themselves towards a more dynamic and open future. For this reason, an increased presence of the Gulen movement in those parts of the Islamic world seemingly prone to take a quite different course, such as parts of the Arab world and Iran, would be especially interesting. Yet the movement initially shunned involvement in the Arab world and remains absent in Iran. This is partly explained by its occasionally dismissive attitude towards the role and practice of Islam in these countries, and by Iran's Shia character (West 2006: 292). Today, however, overtures to the Arab world occur, and are intensifying. Thus the twelfth meeting of the network's Journalists and Writers Foundation, the Abant Platform – its first anywhere in the Muslim world outside Turkey – was held in Cairo in February 2007.[21] In such guises, the movement has already emerged as an element in Turkey's 'soft' power, whether the state appreciates it or not. It forms part of a more general challenge to Kemalist power and tenets, both in domestic Turkish politics and society, and in the face Turkey turns towards the outside world.

Still more difficult to assess are the network's educational activities in non-Turkic and non-Islamic locations. To a degree, the activities of Gulen schools in underdeveloped regions, such as sub-Saharan Africa, have gone hand-in-hand with valiant attempts to increase Turkish trade in such regions. However, the trade volumes remain generally very small, and the non-trade Turkish footprint is sparse. Can this really be an early manifestation of a very long-term bid to enhance Turkey's (or the Gulen movement's) economic, political and cultural influence, even in some rather unlikely locations? What can possibly be the wider impact of Turkish schools in the USA? The network is growing rapidly there. Again, is there any long-term strategy behind this phenomenon, or anything sinister? Or should the schools be seen as little more than profitable educational ventures, with a little bit of Turkish emigration thrown in?

Interfaith dialogue

In its sponsorship and support for interfaith and intercivilizational dialogue, the Gulen movement seeks both to counter the impact of the more violent fundamentalist strains in modern Islam and to undermine wherever it can Huntington's 'clash of civilizations' thesis (see Chapter 8). These are transnational activities, but are global in their reach and potential impact. Fethullah Gulen's championing of interfaith dialogue has complex roots. In part it springs from a profound recognition and embrace of the shared theological origins of Islam, Christianity and Judaism – although, in his appeal for interfaith dialogue and tolerance, Gulen incorporates Buddhism and Hinduism too – and the Prophet's injunction to respect the 'people of the book'. The transcendental quality of faith itself is for Gulen a unifying force that outweighs theological differences. His commitment to dialogue with the western or Judaeo-Christian world is also related to his admiration for western modernity, liberalism, and technological and economic prowess, and his belief that the Islamic world can and should adopt elements of the West's dynamism. Gulen's explicit references to the 'global village' express an assumption that the phenomena of globalization have so bound together the fates of peoples that conflict between them serves no-one's interests. Characteristically, he draws upon the multifaith and multicultural example of the Ottoman empire, which he adduces as evidence of, and inspiration for, the capacity of diverse peoples to live together harmoniously and fruitfully. The empire was officially tolerant towards its non-Muslim subjects and sought to incorporate many western practices, such as female education, the rule of law and constitutionalism, in addition to its technology. Gulenists seek to transpose these perspectives onto a global stage.

Tracing the range of interfaith activities of the Gulen movement is difficult, given its devolved nature and its coy approach to self-publicity. The movement has sponsored or contributed to a confusing diversity of often overlapping interfaith organizations that operate both at the global or transnational and at the local, intrasocietal level. Unsurprisingly, the Gulen movement is seen by many non-Muslims as a particularly congenial Islamic dialogue partner. The movement takes the credit for organizing the Inter-Civilization Dialogue Conference in 1997, and in 1998 it initiated the annual Eurasian Meetings focusing on central Asia and Russia. It also claims to have provided the inspiration for the EU–OIC summit in Istanbul in 2002, in the wake of the 9/11 attacks (Kosebalaban 2003: 181–82). Inside Turkey, it has brought together leaders of the three Abrahamic religious communities (Kuru 2005: 263). Gulen himself met with Patriarch Bartholomeos, head of the Greek Orthodox Fener patriarchate in Istanbul, the former Chief Rabbi of Turkey's Jewish community David Aseo, and with numerous other high-profile Jewish and Christian figures.[22] He also met with Pope John Paul II in Rome in 1998. In 2007, the movement organized a panel in Turkey aimed at encouraging dialogue between the Sunni majority and the Alevi minority, and it has initiated dialogue with Kurds. Its activists and offices in Turkey have been subjected to threats and violent attacks in reaction to such endeavours. Another method adopted by the movement as a means of interfaith dialogue is the so-called *Iftar* (fast-breaking) meal, which brings together people of different faiths and communities. These enable a more low-key and localized approach to interfaith and intercommunal understanding, not least to address the more local ramifications of global interfaith tension.

Since its formation in 2006, the Intercultural Dialogue Platform (*Kuİturler Arasi Diyalog Platformu* – KADIP)[23] has functioned as a kind of clearing house for much of the movement's dialogue activity. It brings together a range of other dialogue platforms, such as the Abant Platform of the Journalists and Writers Foundations, the Intercultural Dialogue Platform and the Dialogue Eurasia Platform. In its various meetings, conferences, panels, publications and other fora, these platforms seek to propagate Gulen's advocacy of tolerance and modernity, and bring together intellectuals, writers, activists and others to discuss a wide range of current issues, some of them domestic. On the global stage, the movement's interfaith platforms are disproportionately US-based, perhaps owing partly to the considerable market for interfaith dialogue among segments of the large actively Christian section of the US population and to the deeper impact there of the 9/11 attacks. Amongst the numerous US-based Gulen organizations are the Institute of Interfaith Dialog[24] and the InterFaith Cultural Organization.[25] In the UK, the Dialogue Society[26] (which this author serves as an advisor) is Gulen-inspired. The first of the Abant Platform's annual meetings to take place abroad was held in Washington, DC in 2004, followed by Brussels and Paris. It was not until February 2007 that it held its first international meeting in the Islamic world, in Egypt. This can be interpreted in a number of ways, but it can appear to reinforce the impression that the movement has, at least until recently, been inclined to turn its back somewhat on the non-Turkic Islamic world in its dialogue as well as its educational ventures.

Interfaith dialogue is a growth area. There are over 250 interfaith groups, councils and fora in the UK alone. At both local and national levels in the West (although less so in most of the Muslim world and anywhere else where civil society is less developed), and at a transnational level globally, religious representatives and thinkers find themselves engaged in a constant round of initiatives, conferences, panels and the like. Websites, publications and fora proliferate. This is a truly transnational phenomenon, and has created a transnational consciousness among its participants. Members of the Gulen movement are at the heart of much of this activity, and have come to be seen by many who are not of the Muslim faith as inhabiting a place very much towards the more accessible end of the spectrum of Muslim opinion. However, it is hard to avoid the observation that those engaged in interfaith dialogue are, after all, preaching largely to the converted – to each other. It is not at all clear that the fruits of this intense activity spill over into areas of society or consciousness that are unsympathetic. Intense interfaith activity at the transnational level should not too readily be assumed to convert into expanded transnational understanding. In a battle for hearts and minds, it is those not yet won that need to be reached, and the Gulen movement makes little attempt to engage with its more militant Muslim co-religionists, at home or abroad.

In its very nature, interfaith dialogue is more about the dissemination of ideas and the battle for hearts and minds than it is an institutional power struggle. This is a process, not an event that produces winners and losers. As such, it is not, and may never be, possible definitively to assess the impact of the Gulen movement's transnational interfaith engagement. Nevertheless, and particularly in light of the international atmosphere in the wake of the 9/11 events, any initiative that seeks to reduce the suspicion, hostility and misunderstanding between the Islamic and other worlds will be welcomed in most quarters. This is true not only at the macro or global level, but also on a more local scale, where intercommunal and interfaith relations have sometimes been threatened by the ripple effects of 9/11 and its aftermath.

Gulen: an element in Turkey's 'soft' power?

The Gulen movement's Islamic inspiration combines with its Turkic identity to serve as a reminder that transnationalism is not at all a recent phenomenon. Historically, neither religions nor ethnic groups and cultures have been great respecters of artificially constructed politico-geographical boundaries. Yet, if transnationalism isn't new, more recent historical developments have intensified and expanded its scope. Both the capacity of the Gulen movement to grow in its country of origin, Turkey, and the opportunity it has exploited to expand its activities and influence on such a global scale, even into regions of the world long kept secluded, are testimony to the increased interconnectedness and transparency of the modern world. It is evident that the Gulen movement is a transnational actor on a major scale, through both its educational and its interfaith programmes. Its non-state nature is clear and its global reach substantial. It stands to play a significant role in the evolution of the Turkic world in terms of its cultural unity, its modernity and the role Islam assumes in the region. It has become part of Turkey's face abroad, and an expression of Turkey's 'soft power' in particular. In this respect, it could offer to much of the Islamic world a more digestible and accessible model for development and democratization than that usually associated with Turkey's ardently secular republic.

However, its educational elitism and cultural Turkishness leave many untouched, both inside and beyond Turkey. Its interfaith dialogue, too, focuses largely on the cultivation of those (mostly in the West) who share its commitment to such activities. Its activities in non-Turkic and largely non-Islamic parts of the world might be likened to the work of the cultural agencies of the major globally active western powers such as the USA, the UK and France. They are unlikely to harm Turkey's economic prospects and diplomatic image, and are indeed likely to benefit them. Yet in the relative absence of so many of the other attributes of power possessed and disseminated by the major powers – military, political, technological, cultural and economic – it is hard to calculate just how much direct advantage will accrue to Turkey and its people as a spillover from the movement's activities abroad. There is perhaps insufficient Turkish political, technological and economic presence and 'follow-up' to the Gulen movement's activities for Turkish influence to take root fully and have a truly lasting impact. Consider, by contrast, the substantial cultural, economic, political, linguistic and even religious interpenetration between the UK and France and the Anglophone and Francophone worlds, respectively. On the other hand, through Turkey's large diaspora; through its writers, artists and film-makers; and as a consequence of its economic output and of its more transparent social and political system, non-Turks – especially in the West – are acquiring a more nuanced and sophisticated appreciation of the complexities of Turkish society than that traditionally afforded by the Kemalist regime. In understanding Turkey differently, external expectations of, and policies towards, Turkish domestic developments might gradually alter. The Gulen movement is centrally involved in this global dissemination of knowledge of, insight into, and familiarity with Turkey and its people and culture.

Turkish al Qaeda?

The very fact that Turks are Muslims renders it unsurprising that a few have been drawn to violent extremism, as has been the case with most Muslim societies. Numerous individual Turkish militants are believed to have fought in Bosnia, Chechnya and Iraq, and in Afghanistan against the Soviets (Kaya 2001) as well as more recently, although the Turkish jihadists in Bosnia and Chechnya appear to have been drawn by ethnic and Ottoman affiliations as much as by the pull of global jihad (William 2005a). The country has produced a number of violent Islamic groups going back to the 1980s and even earlier (Cakir 2007; Uslu 2007; Jenkins 2008b: 183–211; Steinberg 2009). The most prominent of these has been the so-called 'Kurdish Hizbollah' (KH), formed in the 1980s and initially containing an extremely violent faction. However, KH suffered a serious blow in 2000 when its leader, Huseyin Velioglu, was killed and over 3000 of its activists were detained during major police raids throughout Turkey (Nugent 2004). In fact the PKK had been KH's chief target and it was responsible for as many as 500 PKK deaths during the 1980s and 1990s, as well as those of a number of businessmen and prominent secular intellectuals. However, KH has since revived, has for the moment adopted a peaceful path, and seems quite well supported (Cagaptay 2005a). It has even entered into a competition with the Gulen movement for hearts and minds in south-eastern Turkey (Uslu 2009a). This reinforces the assessment that KH is more a part of the struggle for the hearts and minds of Turkey's Kurds than it is part of any global jihad. There is also an ethnically Turkish and rather nationalistic group known as The Great Eastern Islamic Raiders Front (*Islami Buyukdogu Akincilar Cephesi* – IBDA-C). Small and poorly resourced, it did in 2005 launch an online journal called *Kaide* declaring its support for the wider al Qaeda network (William 2005b).[27]

There are indications of a degree of overlap between each of these organizations and an offshoot of al Qaeda with roots in Turkey. Al Qaeda in Turkey was found responsible for the two sets of suicide bombings in Istanbul in November 2003 which killed sixty-three people, including the British consul general. In 2007, seven of its adherents, all but one of whom were Turkish citizens of Kurdish ethnicity (the other was a Syrian), were found guilty of carrying out the bombings. There have since been a number of police raids against al Qaeda cells in Turkey, which have netted hundreds of suspects. Although these raids appeared to have weakened the al Qaeda network inside Turkey (Uslu 2009b), in recent years there have been indications of an increasing number of Turks who are attracted to global jihad, and that although the roots of Turkish jihadism have been ethnic and national, 'Turkish Islamist groups have developed into parts of larger transnational networks, increasingly transcending national affiliations' (Steinberg 2009). An Uzbek jihadist group, the Islamic Jihad Union (IJU), seems to have functioned as a Turkic vehicle facilitating the incorporation of Turks into global jihad, especially in Afghanistan and Pakistan, where Turks have trained in Uzbek camps and fought alongside Uzbek jihadists. Many, possibly most, of those attracted to the IJU as a vehicle to join the international jihad are German-born (Steinberg 2008a, 2008b). At the moment, the numbers of Turks involved in al Qaeda affiliates appear small, but most analysts of this murky world seem convinced that the trend is upwards. If so, then the image of Turkish Islam abroad that is propagated by the Gulen movement could find itself facing serious competition.

13 Concluding thoughts

One hesitates to draw firm conclusions about the impact of globalization on the Turkish state, its people and its foreign policy. As noted in the introduction to this volume, it is sometimes difficult to be certain that forces of globalization constitute the major explanatory factor behind shifts in political behaviour and policies, as opposed to more organically indigenous and internal pressures. In any case, processes of globalization, in all their variety, weave into and become integral to how we think and act, and what we think and act about. Thus a heavy dose of ultimately subjective assessment has to be involved, and indeed has been involved, in the preparation of this work. On the other hand, it is evident that the environment, the opportunities and the problems that states and societies face have shifted substantially owing to profound changes in the international system. This volume has sought to identify the key shifts in the operating environment of the Turkish state and society, to explore whether and how those shifts have altered that state and society, and to trace the consequent adaptations made by Turkey, not least in its foreign policy. It has also offered observation and analysis of how forces emanating from within Turkey – ideas, people, products, activities – have themselves contributed to the wider river of globalization processes beyond Turkey's borders.

The circumstances and cognitive mindset of the founders of the Turkish republic enabled them to embark on an experiment in social and political engineering. They had a vision of how Turkey should evolve, and imagined they could shape the state and society they inherited with little interference, obstruction or, indeed, popular participation. Whenever they met with internal resistance, notably from Islam or dissatisfied Kurds, they acted as if they could simply remove, or at any rate control, the source of friction. Few beyond Turkey's borders took much interest in this Turkish laboratory. The republic's founders genuinely believed they could achieve a kind of ideological and political as well as an economic self-sufficiency. However, global developments marched on. The Turkish republic was born into a world far different from the one in which it must today make its way. In particular, in 1923 much of Europe was only uncertainly or not at all democratic, and the continent was rife with conflict rather than bent on integration. Furthermore,

Europe was then rather distant from Turkey. There was relatively little inter-action between Turkey and Europe of any kind in either direction beyond the machinations of Europe's imperial diplomats.

Given the destiny laid down by the republic's founders, European develop-ments have been crucial to Turkey's evolving fate. The post-1945 European story has been a remarkable one. It reaches far beyond its institutionalization in the form of the EU and other bodies. Democratization, transparency and the emergence of shared norms are key features of modern Europe. Europe is at the forefront of a mostly 'soft power' campaign to spread 'western' norms – of human and minority rights, freedom of thought and worship, the rule of law – throughout the world. Turkey aspires to, and is expected to embrace, these norms, and ultimately to join the EU. However, the emergence of this increasingly norm-based international political environment, especially in Europe, was not and could not have been fully anticipated by the republic's founders in 1923. In any case, throughout Europe's transformation Ataturk's followers remained faithful to his vision for Turkey – or, rather, the vision they regarded him as having had – and many still are. Remarkably, they somehow contrived to overlook or discount the fact that Europe had changed profoundly and had become both a major driver behind, and a manifestation of, forces of globalization that in so many ways were eliminat-ing the scope for self-sufficiency and autonomy that Ankara still sought to exploit.

Today, millions of Turks live in Europe, thousands of Europeans visit Turkey, around half of Turkey's trade is with EU states, the EU is the biggest source of inward investment into Turkey, and modern forms of communica-tion have led to an explosion in the interactions between Turkish and European societies, and indeed those of the wider world. Turks have surely become more 'Europeanized' than could have been imagined in 1923, yet what 'being European' consists of has altered profoundly, and continues to shift. Turkey may have changed dramatically, but so has Europe. The result is that a gap remains in place. Turkey's level of economic development, and its attachment to human rights, the rule of law, democratization and civilian control of the military are less than what its European partners would wish. Furthermore, Turkey's Islamic root is regarded in some quarters as a dis-qualification for membership of the European family, and is even sometimes suspected of being part of the explanation for Turkey's tardy political and economic development relative to that of most of Europe. The Turkish relationship to Europe does raise a number of bigger questions of relevance to Turkey, Europe and beyond. Are the West's 'globalized' values in fact western rather than universal, and rooted in specifically western culture and historical evolution – its Christian roots, or the Renaissance, for example? Is Islam compatible with democracy and modernity in their fuller senses? Is Europe, too, in its cautious approach to Turkey, more constrained in its embrace of a globalized world than many of its inhabitants would be pre-pared to admit?

At the global level, in 1923 decolonization had not yet taken hold in the world, and Turkey was one of a very few 'underdeveloped' societies that enjoyed sovereignty – most of the rest were located in Latin America. Decolonization profoundly altered the wider world and Turkey's immediate environment, yet Turkey's own history as an imperial power, and the Kemalist ideology of westernization and modernization, discouraged Turkey from identifying too closely with its newly decolonized neighbours and with politically, economically and socially similarly placed states and societies. The Kemalist preference to minimize the role played by Islam in Turkish political life and identity further obstructed Turkey's identification with societies with whom in fact it shared so much. The advent of the Cold War ensured that the USA, which had retreated to isolationism in the post-1918 era, now displaced Europe's major states as the world's greatest power. With the rise of the Soviet Union, a global power balance unimaginable in 1923 had emerged. This generated a quite different and unfamiliar set of diplomatic and security concerns and opportunities for Ankara to contend with. The Cold War also drew attention both to Turkey's geostrategic significance and, via its ideological dimensions, to Turkey's domestic political arrangements. These developments served to encourage Turkey on its chosen path of westernization, whilst simultaneously highlighting the fact that it remained a poor fit with the new Europe that now emerged.

The Cold War has come and gone and has taken the Soviet Union with it, thus profoundly reshaping Turkey's regional context. It opened up the Turkic world, enabled a reconnection with the post-communist and former Ottoman possessions in the Balkans and Black Sea regions, and offered unprecedented opportunities for greater diplomatic fluidity and for the diversification of trade patterns. Few states have such a wide range of foreign policy spheres, let alone a set of regions that are simultaneously as overlapping, distinct, interconnected, and indeed conflictual as Turkey's. In fact, Turkey's location tells its own story, for in spatially abutting Europe, the Middle East and the Black Sea region, Turkey culturally, economically and politically abuts, absorbs, reflects and links these diverse worlds. In its foreign policy problems, opportunities and aspirations it is a part of Europe, but it is also a part of the Islamic and Middle Eastern worlds, the developing world, the Turkic world, and the former Ottoman space. As a consequence of both decolonization and the Cold War's demise, in its diplomatic alignments Turkey now has greater options than at any time in its history. Few countries are beset, blessed or confronted by an array of foreign policy choices and problems as diverse or as complex. This is one of the factors making Turkey so fascinating, and so germane to the evolution of regional and global politics.

Ordinary Turks, too, have choices that could not have been imagined in 1923. Then, few Turks left Turkey or enjoyed any means of communicating with, or learning about, the world beyond their very immediate environment. Ataturk's context was not one in which people, goods, news and ideas travelled with the immediacy and universality that they do today.

Global communications have become infinitely faster, more ubiquitous and more varied, and Turks and Turkey have frequently engaged enthusiastically with this brave new world. Today, millions of Turks live or regularly travel abroad, and they are one of the most wired-up of the world's populations. Their country is wide open to influences and pressures of all kinds from all quarters, and not just from the West, via trade, the media, inward and outward foreign travel, and so on. English and other European languages are widely spoken, even beyond the educated elite. Turkey's democratization, partly a condition of the European destiny laid out by its founders, has, along with the opening up of its neighbourhoods, paradoxically enabled Turks to express their more complex identities as a Turkic, Muslim, Middle Eastern, post-Ottoman as well as a European people and society. In any case, many Turks had never fully bought into the vision that had been laid out for them by the republic's founders, and they became increasingly impatient and increasingly able to find expression for their dissatisfactions. The AKP is a beneficiary of these dissatisfactions and suppressed identities. As such, it embraces, or is seeking to adapt to, so much of what an earlier Turkey rejected, and ignores or downplays so many elements of the vision that was laid out in 1923. Yet it is, simultaneously, a uniquely Turkish phenomenon. The approach of Turkey's current AKP government also reflects a truly remarkable alteration in the cognitive mindset of the country's leaders. It is seeking, in sometimes novel ways, to grapple with the opportunities, crises and problems that the domestic and global systems have presented to it.

Ankara's unwillingness to fully adapt to and embrace the changed domestic and external environment became unsustainable and, many came to believe, even undesirable. The AKP benefited from this too. Turkey's geographical location, its frustrations at the continued failure to achieve its European vision, the end of the Cold War, and the global issues and tensions raised by the events of 9/11 all encouraged Turkey to embrace more adaptive behaviour. Its diplomacy, economic interactions, cultural openness and communications with the outside world exploded. From being one of the world's more sealed-off societies, it has become one of its more open and penetrated. There are signs that Turkey is now reconsidering the distance it has traditionally kept between itself and much of the rest of the developing and post-imperial world. As it cultivates its Middle Eastern, African, Asian and south and central American relationships, so Turkey seems at last to be more fulsomely embracing states and societies that are arguably more similar to itself than those of western Europe. Turkey is thus open to, and a participant in, regional and global patterns of trade and economic interaction, energy transportation, migration, democratization and the globalization of norms. It is also susceptible to trends and currents in the Islamic world, and to the emergence of a pan-Turkic identity.

Yet Turkey simultaneously houses strong residues of the Kemalist laboratory as well as of the Ottoman era that preceded it. Elements of Turkish society and of its political life have retained a powerful attachment to the legacy of Ataturk and to the vision he had for the country. Others feel a closer attachment to the Muslim world. External pressures and influences have tapped into, and in some ways intensified, the struggles and divisions inside Turkey, and inside the heads of many individual Turks, over which direction the country should take. Turkey is as remarkable for the enthusiasm and alacrity with which it has laid itself open to external influences as it is for the stubbornness and determination with which it has resisted them. Europeanization, Eurasianism, Kemalism, Ottomanism, Islamism, Turkism, orientalism and a whole host of other mindsets, perspectives, ideologies and values that have been imported or absorbed from, exported to, or overlap with the rest of the world now jostle for the light in an increasingly noisy Turkish domestic social and political marketplace. This complexity and fluidity have become particularly manifest under the leadership of the AKP, which exhibits in both its foreign and domestic policies a more complex and diversified set of Turkish identities. Those who make it their business to study and comment on Turkey might do well to look at the entire picture, rather than draw far-reaching conclusions from developments in just one of Turkey's many conflicting dimensions.

In the globalized, hybridized world that has emerged, Turkey has a special place. This is more than a simple consequence of geographical location. Globalization in all its forms and variety has demonstrated, and intensified, how truly hybrid Turkey is. It is both European and Asian; secular and devout; a westernized Islamic society; a democratized autocracy; a developing society closely linked to, and seeking to join, a collection of the world's most developed and prosperous states; a formerly imperial state seemingly moving ever closer to many of the governments of its former colonial territories; and a member of a US-led political and military alliance with which it appears increasingly at odds. Turkish society is similarly multifaceted. It is vulnerable to, and impinged upon by, the political, economic, social and cultural trends in each of these contrasting regions and global subsets. Turkey's peculiarities have rendered it open to a more complex and variegated range of external influences and internal trends than is the case for most other societies. Forces, choices, identities, novelties and pressures are both battering at Turkey's door, and also seeping under it.

The case studies offered in this volume serve to highlight just some of the complex characteristics of Turkey's rich circumstances. Thus the Kurdish issue drags Turkey into the maelstrom of Middle Eastern politics, and simultaneously encourages and obstructs steps towards the further democratization of the country. The Armenian genocide lobby is repeatedly able to unveil the country's discomfort with its own past, its resistance to free speech, and its stubborn suspicions of precisely those parts of the world it has for so long most wanted to emulate. Turkey's reaction to it can appear as if it would prefer to return to the self-sufficient and insular place it enjoyed in the early years of its existence. However, the Armenian issue has also prompted a fierce internal and foundational debate about the origins and nature of the republic. In 1923, energy was nowhere near as in demand, as exploited and as traded as it is in today's world. Today, Turkey finds itself located close to the source of the majority of this energy, especially oil, and actually or potentially along the route by which it is, or will increasingly be, traded. This could place Turkey at a veritable epicentre of the global order. The activities of the Gulen movement, and its very nature, can demonstrate both how 'non-European' and indeed uniquely 'Turkish' Turkey can be, but it can also throw down a gauntlet to those parts of the Islamic world that seek to deny the universality of 'western' values. The movement is also a reminder, should one be needed, that state borders are no longer effective boundaries in today's world.

In its G20 membership and remarkable economic growth, in its overtures to its Islamic, Turkic and Eurasian neighbours and beyond, in its sometimes strident resistance and hostility to western pressures and expectations, Turkey is as much a part of the emerging global challenge to western political, economic, diplomatic, cultural and military dominance as it is a part of that hitherto dominant West. Is it then possible to assert, as many have done, that Turkey does or could function as a bridge across divides, as a potential unifier in a divided world? In truth, the bridge analogy has never worked as well as some would have wished. Many in Turkey's elite have in the past been uninterested in, or hostile to, the eastern side of the 'bridge', and many of Turkey's policy inclinations alienated its Middle Eastern neighbours. Washington was, and sometimes still is, in any case more interested in Turkey as a 'bridgehead', a launching pad for attacks against, or containment of, regional adversaries. Furthermore, Turkey's internal differences mean that its actual or potential role and position in global politics has been, and is, contested. Turkish society can sometimes appear scarcely less torn, confused or simply hybridized where identity issues are concerned than the world in which it is located. Nor can bridges easily be built across divides that are too wide. Sometimes Turkey appears buffeted by, or a contributor to, regional and global sores rather than a balm to them. Its identity is disputed and challenged by others, as evidenced by the US reaction to Ankara's recent supposed axis tilt away from the West and by persisting suspicion in the Islamic world that Turkey has in some way forsaken its 'true' heritage. Turkey is sometimes expected to lean either eastwards or westwards and can be vilified from any direction if it appears to comply.

But what if Turkey is, in fact, not quite defined by either or any of the categories it is put into or asserts for itself? It is as easy for Turkey to upset all parties as to bring them together. Just as a globalized world is fractious, sometimes inchoate, contested, disharmonious, hybridized, imperfect, yet nevertheless forms a whole, so the same is true of Turkey. Turkey is perhaps better perceived less as a bridge across divides, but rather as a vessel that contains or reflects those divides, and in both external policy and internal arrangements the divides are not always easy to bridge. For these reasons, it is in the future bound – even doomed – to play a higher-profile role in the evolving regional and world (dis)order.

In any case, Turks of all persuasions are probably less able to control their future than they imagine or would be comfortable with. In this, at least, they are perhaps like everyone else. Globalization can be seen as a 'seat of the pants' adventure, a roller coaster that defies attempts to shape and direct it. No-one could have envisaged that the UK's early industrialization would, in time, lead to the interconnected, interdependent, fast-moving and high-technology world that has since evolved. Equally, no-one can say where today's global cacophony of political and social pressures, economic trends, technological developments, intellectual exchanges, shifting military balances and contested identities is taking us. What we can say is that Turkey and its people have emerged as significant contributors to, and vessels for, this cacophony, and that they have now joined the ride with a more open mind than hitherto about where it might take them.

This volume has endeavoured to explore some of Turkey's efforts to adjust to, resist, participate in, deflect, ignore, defend against and interpose itself into the world that has evolved since 1923. This remarkable journey is still ongoing. Of course the 'journey' analogy can be applied to any state or institution endeavouring to steer its way through its cluttered, surprising, obstacle-strewn environment. All states and societies are faced with both the need to adjust to, and the temptation to resist, the pressures upon them. They prosper or not depending on the choices they make. However, Turkey's route is quite unique, as is Turkey itself. There are many reasons and perspectives from which to doubt or object to the path the country has taken, and it is not difficult to identify shortcomings. Yet it has been, and still is, an impressive journey. Turkey's geography, its historical and cultural starting point, and its ambitions have all made it particularly susceptible to the world beyond its borders. Yet its internal narratives have provided the bases for a great deal of resistance to those pressures. Turkey is indeed an echo chamber, but one that has never quite let go of a strong inclination to manipulate the apertures through which sound penetrates the interior of the chamber. In Turkey's case, the internal arrangements are sensitive, and the impact of external inputs can be varied, unique, uneven, unexpected and divisive. This volume has sought to demonstrate and explain that fact.

Notes

Chapter 2: The Kemalist legacy: cult, ideology and political practice

1 Official figures for the Turkish economy are available from the State Planning Organization at www.dpt.gov.tr and the State Statistical Institute at www.turkstat. gov.tr.
2 'Secret Kurdish plan unveiled in Ecevit archives', www.hurriyetdailynews.com, 23 January 2008.
3 Just a few years ago, a senior – in both senses – representative of the Turkish establishment explained to this author how the English county name 'Kent' offered proof of the Turkish roots of the English language and possibly of its people. In Turkish 'kent' means town or city.

Chapter 3: Kemalism and state security

1 'Giscard predicts "end of EU" if Turkey joins', *The Independent*, 9 November 2002.

Chapter 4: Turkey's Europeanization: a journey without an arrival?

1 An expression used by a senior Turkish foreign ministry official in an interview with the author, Ankara, 24 May 1999.
2 http://ec.europa.eu/enlargement/enlargement_process/accession_process/criteria/ index_ en.htm.
3 Quoted in *Turkish Daily News*, 16 December 1999.
4 Quoted in *Turkish Daily News*, 16 December 1999.
5 'Erdogan meets with Turkey's Roma community in historic gathering', www. hurriyetdailynews.com, 14 March 2010.
6 www1.umn.edu/humanrts/instree/z1afchar.htm.
7 www.oic-oci.org/english/article/human.htm.
8 http://law.hku.hk/lawgovtsociety/Bangkok%20Declaration.htm.
9 For the text of the Convention see www.coe.int/t/dghl/monitoring/minorities/ 1_AtGlance/FCNM_Texts_en.asp.
10 For the full text see www.europarl.europa.eu/charter/pdf/text_en.pdf.
11 For the full text of the treaty see http://eur-lex.europa.eu/JOHtml.do?uri=OJ: C:2007:306:SOM:EN:HTML.
12 www.coalitionfortheicc.org/?mod=urc1006& idudctp = 21.

13 At a conference at St Antony's College, Oxford in May 2010, at which this author was present, foreign minister Ahmet Davutoglu was still insisting that Turkey's membership of the ICC was under consideration.

14 For an update on international human rights instruments which Turkey signed or ratified from June 2003, see www.turkishembassy.com/ii/O/InternationalHuman RightsUpdate.htm.

15 For the full text see www2.ohchr.org/english/law/ccpr.htm.

16 www.treaties.un.org/pages/ViewDetails.aspx?src=TREATY&mtdsg_no=IV-4& chapter=4& lang=en#EndDec.

17 For the full text see www2.ohchr.org/english/law/minorities.htm.

18 For the full text see www.anayasa.gov.tr/images/loaded/pdf_dosyalari/THE_ CONSTITUTION_OF_THE_REPUBLIC_OF_TURKEY.pdf.

19 For the full text see wwwi.lib.byu.edu/index.php/Treaty_of_Lausanne.

20 Indeed, at a conference in Antakya, Turkey, in November 2010, this author's reference to the Kurdish minority in Turkey prompted a passionate intervention by a retired Turkish diplomat with whom he shared the platform. It was a 'mistake', he declared, to use the term 'minority' to describe Turkey's Kurds. His declaration that there is no Kurdish minority in Turkey was met with enthusiastic applause from many of the Turkish academics, military officers, NGO representatives and officials in the audience.

21 www.hrw.org/europecentral-asia/turkey.

22 www.amnesty.org/en/region/turkey.

23 https://wcd.coe.int/ViewDoc.jsp?id=1511197&   Site   =   CommDH&   Back-ColorInternet = FEC65B& BackColorIntranet = FEC65B&BackColorL.

24 See www.freedomhouse.org for annual reports and tables on global media freedom.

25 http://fr.rsf.org.

Chapter 5: From autarky to globalization: Turkey's economic transition

1 Official figures for the Turkish economy are available from the State Planning Organization at www.dpt.gov.tr and the State Statistical Institute at www.turkstat. gov.tr.

2 'A promising start', *The Economist,* 17 March 2005.

3 See the special issue of *Turkish Studies,* 4(2), Summer 2003, 'The Turkish economy in crisis', for a range of analyses of the crisis.

4 'Mixed signals', *The Economist,* 6 March 2008.

5 'In need of an anchor', *The Economist,* 23 October 2008.

6 'Turkey's foreign trade strategy: Turkish state minister Kursat Tuzmen', interview, *Insight Turkey,* 7(1), January/March 2005: 30–35.

7 'Rating agency moody on Turkey', www.hurriyetdailynews.com, 11 November 2009.

8 'Anchors aweigh', *The Economist,* 21 October 2010.

9 www.musiad.org.tr

10 www.tusiad.org.tr

11 www.tuskon.org

12 www.kombassan.com.tr

13 www.yimpas.com.tr

14 Both the Lighthouse investigation and the Dogan tax row have been widely reported in the Turkish press, including the English language versions of *Today's Zaman* (www.todayszaman.com) and *Hurriyet Daily News* (www.hurriyetdaily news.com, a Dogan group newspaper). See their archives. Also see 'Less than white?', *The Economist,* 18 September 2008.

Chapter 6: Turkey and the Kurdish issue: a transnationalized domestic problem

1 All figures for Kurdish populations are approximate for a variety of reasons: the absence of recent or reliable census figures, ethnically insensitive data gathering, dispersal, intermarriage, assimilation and registration of Kurds as other nationalities.
2 'Banned pro-Kurdish DTP appeals to European court', www.todayszaman.com, 21 January 2010.
3 Quoted in Cengiz Candar, 'Regime change in Iraq; repercussions for Turkey', July 2002, www.patrides.com/july02/enregime.htm; Bulent Aliriza, CSIS Turkey Update, 21 December 2001, http://csis.org.
4 Quoted in *Turkish Daily News*, 'Washington Post: Turks would be a reluctant ally against Washington', 10 September 2002.
5 For example, see 'PKK uses northern Iraq as arsenal, says official report', www. todayszaman.com, 17 September 2007.
6 'If Turkey had kept Mosul, there would be no N. Iraq issue, says Demirel', *Turkish Daily News*, 19 December 2003.
7 'Talabani: Kirkuk is Kurds' Jerusalem', *Turkish Daily News*, 31 December 2004.
8 'Kurds "killed" in Syria clashes', 16 March 2004; 'Syria urged to free riot Kurds', 7 April 2004, http://news.bbc.co.uk/1/hi/world/middle_east/3607059.stm., www.news. bbc.co.uk/1/hi/world/middle_east/3517848.stm.
9 'Syrian president expresses support for incursion into N. Iraq', www.todayszaman. com, 18 October 2007.
10 'PKK hit hard with simultaneous operations in Syria', *Sabah English Edition*, 1 July 2010, http://english.sabah.com.tr.
11 'Iran reassures Turkey on border security', *Turkish Daily News*, 12 January 2004.
12 'Turkey, Iran agree on active cooperation against terrorism', *The New Anatolian*, 27 February 2006.
13 'Malaysia urges Muslim peacekeeping force in Iraq under UN', *Washington Post*, 10 October 2003; 'Turkey faces tough task in getting OIC support for Iraq mission', *Turkish Daily News*, 13 October 2004; 'Turkey calls for Islamic peacekeeping call for Iraq', *Turkish Daily News*, 14 October 2004.
14 Defined here as 'from Turkey'.
15 www.institutkurde.org
16 www.kurdistan.org
17 'Trial of Kurdish parliament in exile to begin in Ankara', www.todayszaman.com, 22 April 2009.
18 www.roj.tv
19 'Fogh in the Aegean', *The Economist*, 10 September 2009.
20 www.khrp.org
21 'Turkish government vows more democracy to solve Kurdish issue', www. hurriyetdailynews.com, 29 July 2009.
22 The speech was published in *Today's Zaman* on 30 August 2009 as 'We want democracy as a national unity project', www.todayszaman.com.
23 'Turkish opposition leaders speak out against Kurdish initiative', www.hurriyet dailynews.com, 13 November 2009.
24 'Military outlines its "red lines" on Kurdish move', www.hurriyetdailynews.com, 25 August 2010.
25 'Turkey's prime minister vows Kurdish rebels will "drown in their own blood"', *The Guardian*, 20 June 2010.
26 'Rift develops over PKK group's welcome', www.hurriyetdailynews.com, 22 October 2009.
27 'Local Kurdish prime minister extends warm message to Turkey', www.hurriyet dailynews.com, 23 May 2008.

28 'Iraq Kurd prime minister says ready for power sharing in Kirkuk', www.hurriyet dailynews.com, 4 June 2008.

29 'Turkey, northern Iraq: economic allies with political obstacles to be overcome', www.sundayszaman.com, 9 August 2009.

30 'Northern Iraq looks to export gas via Turkey and Nabucco', www.hurriyetdaily news.com, 5 July 2010.

31 'Turkey asks Iraq, US to hand over PKK members', www.hurriyetdailynews.com, 10 July 2010.

32 'Barzani says PKK's decision to end cease fire is wrong', www.hurriyetdailynews. com, 5 June 2010.

Chapter 7: A new foreign policy for a globalized age?

1 www.bsec-organization.org.

2 www.blackseafor.org.

3 'Turkey frets over EU's illegal immigrations stance', www.todayszaman.com, 30 October 2009.

4 Comments made in his opening address to a conference organized by the Turkish foreign ministry on 'Turkish diplomacy and regional/global order', held in Istanbul 15–16 May 2010 and attended by this author.

5 At the time of writing this book had not yet been translated into English.

6 'PM says Turkey to pursue active foreign policy', www.hurriyetdailynews.com, 5 January 2005.

7 For example, at the May 2010 Istanbul conference noted above, and at a conference on 'Turkey's foreign policy in a changing world: old alignments and new neighbourhoods', held at St Antony's College, Oxford on 30 April–2 May 2010, organized by South East European Studies at Oxford (SEESOX). This author attended both conferences.

8 'Turkey confident to intensify military ties with Syria', www.hurriyetdailynews. com, 14 October 2009.

9 'Turkish government to up middle east diplomacy efforts', www.hurriyetdailynews. com, 21 December 2009.

10 'Israel, Syria launch peace talks through Turkey', www.hurriyetdailynews.com, 22 May 2008.

11 'Iran rejects Turkish role in nuclear talks', www.hurriyetdailynews.com, 8 December 2009.

12 'Iran inks deal to send low enriched uranium to Turkey', 17 May 2010; 'Turkey urges west to be flexible with Iran', 18 May 2010; 'US announces deal with Russia, China on new Iran sanctions', 19 May 2010; 'Iran notifies UN nuclear watchdog of nuclear fuel swap plan', 24 May 2010; 'Ahmadinejad urges Obama to adopt nuke swap deal', 26 May 2010; 'Turkey says nuclear powers should disarm as rift within UN deepens', 28 May 2010, all www.hurriyetdailynews.com.

13 'Turkey brings Israel's nukes to NATO's attention', www.hurriyetdailynews.com, 26 April 2010.

14 'UN talks back conference on nuclear free Middle East', www.bbc.co.uk/news/ 10185256, 29 May 2010; 'Ban welcomes outcome of month long nuclear treaty review conference', www.un.org/apps/news/story.asp?NewsID=34852& Cr = npt& Cr1 = .

15 Soner Cagaptay at the Washington Institute for Near East Policy (www. washingtoninstitute.org) has been a particularly prolific critic of Turkey's foreign policy direction under the AKP, and his newspaper articles, transcripts, policy briefs and testimonies can be accessed at their website. As one example, see his 'As Turkey pulls away', *Jerusalem Post*, 5 December 2009.

16 'Egyptian foreign minister Ahmad Abu al-Gheit warns that a nuclear Iran would force the Arabs to join the nuclear race', report no. 2929, 30 April 2010, www. memri.org/report/en/0/0/0/0/0/0/807/4124.htm.

17 The Economic Policy Research Foundation of Turkey (TEPAV) website is a good source of information on this project: www.tepav.org.tr.

18 'US chides Turkey for excluding Israel from NATO drills', www.hurriyetdailynews. com, 14 October 2009.

19 'Diplomatic tensions escalate after Israel snubs Turkish ambassador', www. hurriyetdailynews.com, 12 January 2010.

Chapter 8: Turkey between East and West: a bridge or afloat?

1 Soner Cagaptay, director of the Turkish research programme at the Washington Institute for Near East Policy, has been particularly active in this debate. See his various papers, editorials and policy briefs, and a transcript of his July 2010 testimony to the House Committee of Foreign Affairs, at www.washingtoninstitute.org.

2 www.tika.gov.tr.

3 For example, see 'Gul backs US-led Middle East initiative, says it complies with Turkey's vision', www.hurriyetdailynews.com, 6 March 2006.

4 www.tccb.gov.tr/sayfa/konusma_aciklama_mesajlar/kitap/79.pdf.

5 Erdogan's speech was entitled 'Conservative democracy and the globalization of freedom', www.aei.org/event/735#tpt.

6 www.mfa.gov.tr/statement-by-h_e–ahmet-davutoglu–at-the-36th-session-of-the-oic-council-of-foreign-ministers.en.mfa.

7 www.mfa.gov.tr/article-by-h_e–ahmet-davutoglu-published-in-irish-times–news-paper–ireland–on-9-march-2010.en.mfa.

8 See, for example, the remarks by Turkey's EU negotiator Egemen Bagis, 'Turkey can be a source of inspiration for Islamic countries, state[s] minister Bagis', www. todayszaman.com, 5 March 2009.

9 'Israel–Syria talks moving ahead without Turkey', www.hurriyetdailynews.com, 11 July 2010.

10 www.un.org/Dialogue.

11 For the work of the AoC, see www.unaoc.org.

12 For the Istanbul Forum, see www.unaoc.org/docs/AoC_Istanbul-09web.pdf.

13 'Turkey approves Rasmussen as the head of NATO', *The Journal of Turkish Weekly,* 4 April 2009.

14 In opposition to the position of the Greek Orthodox Church and in the face of international criticism, Turkey refuses to accept the ecumenical nature of Istanbul s Greek Patriarch. It also refuses to reopen the Halki Seminary, which means it is impossible to train new Orthodox priests in Turkey.

15 See www.oic-oci.org for the charter, which was amended in 2008. This also describes the OIC's activities.

16 www.oic-oci.org/ex-summit/english/10-years-plan.htm.

17 'Gul calls on OIC to approve preferential trade agreement to boost cooperation', 10 November 2009; 'Trade preference programme for OIC members on the way', 6 November 2009; 'Turkey backs economic integration between OIC members', 11 May 2010; 'Turkey turns to OIC as its EU trade ebbs', 15 December 2008, all at www.todayszaman.com.

18 www.oic-oci.org/english/conf/exec/fc_execom_9_3_PAL_en.pdf.

19 www.un.org/en/peacekeeping/missions/past/unprofor.htm.

20 www.euforbih.org.

21 www.mfa.gov.tr/nato.en.mfa#II.

22 www.nato.int/cps/en/natolive/topics_50349.htm.

23 www.seecp-turkey.org/icerik.php?no=60.
24 'Turkey is rediscovering Balkans, says Croatia envoy', www.hurriyetdailynews.com, 6 May 2010.
25 'Exit, pursued by a Turk', *The Economist,* 15 July 2010; 'Turkey, Serbia, expand cooperation with visa deal', www.todayszaman.com, 13 July 2010.
26 www.isaf.nato.int.
27 According to the Turkish Foreign Ministry website; see www.mfa.gov.tr/nato.en. mfa#II.
28 For the communiqué, see 'Istanbul summit on friendship and cooperation in the heart of Asia', www.mfa.gov.tr/istanbul-statement-on-friendship-and-cooperation-in-the–heart-of-asia_.en.mfa.
29 http://unifil.unmissions.org.
30 www.tsk.tr/eng/uluslararasi/BM_UNIFIL.htm.
31 http://merln.ndu.edu/whitepapers/Turkey_English2000.pdf.

Chapter 9: Between consumers and producers: Turkey as an energy bridge?

1 'Black Sea oil exploration costs top $4 billion', www.todayszaman.com, 23 April 2010.
2 'Expert warns of Turkish dependency on foreign energy resources', www.hurriyet dailynews.com, 10 November 2009.
3 www.tpao.gov.tr
4 Information on the BTC project can be found at www.bakuceyhan.org.uk, a website formed by a consortium of NGOs opposed to the project. See also the section of BP's website dedicated to its interests in the Caspian region, at www.bp.com/ genericsection.do?categoryId=6071& contentId = 7014288.
5 www.botas.gov.tr.
6 www.nabucco-pipeline.com.
7 www.bp.com/sectiongenericarticle.do?categoryId=9006670& contentId = 7015095.
8 www.bp.com/sectiongenericarticle.do?categoryId=9006668& contentId = 7015092.
9 www.nord-stream.com.

Chapter 10: The Armenian genocide: a foreign policy problem in a globalized world

1 www.un.org/millennium/law/iv-1.htm.
2 *The Applicability of the United Nations Convention on the Prevention and Punishment of the Crime of Genocide to Events which Occurred During the Early Twentieth Century,* legal analysis prepared for the International Center for Transitional Justice, February 2003, www.ictj.org/images/content/7/5/759.pdf.
3 For the Armenian position, shared by both the diaspora and the Armenian government, see the website of the US-based Armenian National Institute, which offers a rich resource base of eye-witness accounts, official statements and resolutions, photographs and the like, at www.armenian-genocide.org. The official position of the Turkish Republic can be obtained at the websites of the Turkish General Staff at www.tsk.tr/eng/ermeni_sorunu_salonu/armenianissues_index.htm and the Turkish Ministry of Foreign Affairs at www.mfa.gov.tr/sub.en.mfa? c4aa6758-dde9–477c-98c6–335c94c2fe18.
4 http://circassiangenocide.org.
5 'Tiny ethnic minority disputes "common" error', www.hurriyetdailynews.com, 4 October 2009.

6 www.preventgenocide.org/lemkin.
7 www.genocidescholars.org.
8 www.genocidescholars.org/images/OpenLetterTurkishPMreArmenia6-13-05.pdf.
9 www.aaainc.org.
10 www.armenian-genocide.org.
11 www.almainc.org.
12 www.armeniadiaspora.com/population.html.
13 See www.aaainc.org for information on this.
14 www.europa-eu-un.org/articles/en/article_5068_en.htm.
15 www.armenian-genocide.org/Affirmation.1/current_category.1/affirmation_detail.
   html.
16 'Armenia: Turkey recalls ambassador from France over genocide bill', 18 January
   2001, www.rferl.org/content/article/1095539.html.
17 'French in Armenia "genocide" row', www.news.bbc.co.uk/1/hi/6043730.stm,
   12 October 2006.
18 'France and Turkey negotiate flying rights', www.hurriyetdailynews.com, 28 March
   2007.
19 'French GDF pulls out of Nabucco project as a result of Ankara's "silent economic embargo"', 21 February 2008; 'France seeks economic thaw against political
   chill', 20 February 2008, both at www.hurriyetdailynews.com.
20 Taken from the US-based Armenian National Institute website at www.armenian-
   genocide.org/Affirmation.339/current_category.7/affirmation_detail.html.
21 'Turkish General sees US ties at risk', *Washington Post*, 15 October 2007.
22 www.whitehouse.gov/the_press_office/Remarks-By-President-Obama-To-The-Turk-
   ish-Parliament.
23 www.whitehouse.gov/the_press_office/Statement-of-President-Barack-Obama-on-
   Armenian-Remembrance-Day.
24 'Hrant Dink murder trial – where are the state's records?', http://en.rsf.org/turquie-
   hrant-dink-murder-trial-where-are-19-07-2010,37978.html, 19 July 2010.
25 This author is in possession of this material as a result of one such visit.
26 'Government rattled by court move against Armenian conference', www.hurriyet
   dailynews.com, 24 September 2005.
27 'Turks protest at Armenian forum', www.news.bbc.co.uk/1/hi/world/europe/
   4277262.stm, 24 September 2005.
28 For the campaign's website, see www.ozurdiliyoruz.com.
29 'Park on Istanbul's islands named in slain journalist Dink's honour', www.hur-
   riyetdailynews.com, 12 September 2010.

Chapter 11: Migration, Turkey and Turks

1 www.iom.int.
2 'Turkish family "controls UK drugs business"', *The Guardian*, 25 October 1999;
   'Turkey at the drugs crossroads', http://news.bbc.co.uk/1/hi/4305692.stm; 'Drug
   godfather's reign of terror ends', *The Times*, 11 February 2006; 'Violent Turkish
   gangs on London streets', *Police News*, 25 October 2009.
3 'Gun murders in north London linked to Turkish gangs in heroin war', *The Times*,
   10 October 2010.
4 Kurdish transborder migrants were discussed in Chapter 6 of this volume. In this
   chapter, unless otherwise made clear, the term 'Turks' will henceforward be used to
   refer to emigrants from the Turkish republic, regardless of their ethnicity or any
   other affiliation or identity they might have.
5 'Germany has "utterly failed" to build multicultural society', *The Telegraph*,
   17 October 2010.

6 www.diyanet.gov.tr.
7 A useful Alevi website is www.alevibektasi.org.
8 'Seeking unity – the Alevis of the world', www.hurriyetdailynews.com, 13 June 2008.
9 'Alevi demand rejected despite warm messages', www.hurriyetdailynews.com, 14 January 2008.
10 'Cemevis given status of worship houses in Kusadasi', www.hurriyetdailynews.com, 5 September 2008.
11 'Alevi origins deputy resigns from office', www.hurriyetdailynews.com, 13 June 2008.
12 'Religious education should not be compulsory, says top court', www.hurriyet dailynews.com, 5 March 2008.
13 'Alevis charge AKP with double standards', www.hurriyetdailynews.com, 14 June 2008.

Chapter 12: The Fethullah Gulen movement (and Turkish Al Qaeda) as transnational phenomena

1 For example, see 'Court documents shed light on CIA illegal operations in central Asia using Islam and madrassas', www.libertyforum.org/showflat.php?Cat=& Board = news_news& Number = 296370649.
2 'Global muslim networks: how far they have travelled', *The Economist*, 8 March 2008.
3 'St. Petersburg Turkish college wins case, resumes services', www.todayszaman. com, 24 August 2008.
4 'Georgian Labour party protests opening of Turkish schools', *Trend*, 27 April 2010, http://en.trend.az/news/politics/foreign/1676685.html.
5 http://turkicamericanassembly.org. See Ilhan Tanir, 'The Gulen movement play big in Washington', www.hurriyetdailynews.com, 14 May 2010. Note the use of 'Turkic' rather than 'Turkish' in the federation's naming.
6 'Court of Appeals clears Gulen of all allegations', www.todayszaman.com, 26 June 2008.
7 'Samanyolu TV increasingly popular outside Turkey', www.todayszaman.com, 21 March 2010.
8 www.gyv.org.tr.
9 www.dialoguesociety.org.
10 www.fatih.edu.tr.
11 www.tuskon.org.
12 www.kimseyokmu.org.tr.
13 'A farm boy on the world stage', *The Economist*, 8 *March* 2008.
14 'Gulen: citizens do not infiltrate "state" posts', www.todayszaman.com, 12 October 2010.
15 Articles, speeches, interviews, etc. by Fethullah Gulen can be found at the movement's website at www.fgulen.com. See also *The Muslim World*, 95(3), July 2005: Special Issue.
16 www.viu.edu.
17 www.hiramagazine.com.
18 'CHP deputies: Turkish schools abroad are a source of pride', www.todayszaman. com, 21 March 2007.
19 'What are Gulen's missionaries after?', http://english.sabah.com.tr, 19 February 2007.
20 Tom Stellar of the *Arizona Star* has conducted an investigation into the activities of Gulen schools in Arizona and elsewhere in the USA, and has opened a blog on the issue: http://azstarnet.com.

21 'Abant meeting in Muslim state for the first time', www.hurriyetdailynews.com, 26 February 2007.
22 Fethullah Gulen's website contains transcripts of speeches and interviews in which he outlines his reasoning on interfaith dialogue. See also Saritoprak and Griffith 2005; Weller 2006.
23 www.kadip.org.tr.
24 www.interfaithdialog.org.
25 www.uga.edu/ifco.org.
26 http://dialoguesociety.org.
27 '"Kaide" ("al Qaeda") magazine published openly in Turkey', *Middle East Media Research Institute*, special dispatch 951, 7 August 2005, www.memri.org.

Bibliography

The English language online newspapers *Hurriyet Daily News* and *Today's Zaman* have been used as sources throughout this book. Rather than give the full title of these publications in each instance, only the websites www.hurriyetdailynews.com and www.todayszaman.com are given. Each website contains a full archive enabling entries cited in this book to be traced.

Abadi, Jacob (1995) 'Israel and Turkey: from covert to overt relations', *Journal of Conflict Studies* XV(2): 104–28.

Abramowitz, Morton (1993) 'Foreword', vii–xii, in Fuller, Graham E. and Lesser, Ian O. (eds) *Turkey's new geopolitics: from the Balkans to western China*, Boulder, Colorado: Westview/RAND.

Abramowitz, Morton and Barkey, Henri J. (2009) 'Turkey's transformers: the AKP sees big', *Foreign Affairs* 88(6): 118–28.

Adams, Terence (2004) 'Caspian energy developments', 90–106, in Akiner, Shirin (ed.) *The Caspian: politics, energy and security*, London and New York: Routledge.

Adas, Emin Baki (2009) 'Production of trust and distrust: transnational networks, Islamic holding companies and the state in Turkey', *Middle Eastern Studies* 45(4): 625–36.

Ademi, Adam (2010) 'Turkey makes tangible steps on the right track? Or just a jaunt?', *Decade of Roma inclusion 2005–2015*, www.romadecade.org/tangible_steps, 19 April.

Agai, Bekim (2003) 'The Gulen movement's Islamic ethic of education', 48–68, in Yavuz, M. Hakan and Esposito, John L. (eds) *Turkish Islam and the secular state: the Gulen movement*, Syracuse, New York: Syracuse University Press.

Akcam, Taner (2007) *A shameful act: the Armenian genocide and the question of Turkish responsibility*, London: Constable.

Akcapar, Sebnem Koser (2009) 'Turkish associations in the United States: towards building a transnational identity', *Turkish Studies* 10(2): 165–93.

Akcapar, Sebnem Koser and Yurdakul, Gokce (2009) 'Turkish identity formation and political mobilization in western Europe and north America', *Turkish Studies* 10(2): 139–47.

Aker, Sule L. (2008) 'Major determinants of imports in Turkey', *Turkish Studies* 9(1): 131–45.

Akkoyunlu, Karabekir (2007) *Military reform and democratization: Turkish and Indonesian experiences at the turn of the century*, Adelphi Papers 392, London and Oxford: International Institute for Strategic Studies.

Aktan, Gunduz (2002) 'If Iraq operation takes place', *Turkish Daily News*, 20 November.
—— (2005a) 'Genocide: new developments (I)', www.hurriyetdailynews.com, 1 November.
—— (2005b) 'The return game (i)', www.hurriyetdailynews.com, 29 November.
Aktay, Yasin (2003) 'Diaspora and stability: constitutive elements in a body of knowledge', 131–55, in Yavuz, M. Hakan and Esposito, John L. (eds) *Turkish Islam and the secular state: the Gulen movement*, Syracuse, New York: Syracuse University Press.
Akyol, Mustafa (2010) 'Ahmet Davutoglu: yet another crypto Armenian?', www. hurriyetdailynews.com, 8 January.
Alaranta, Toni (2008) 'Mustafa Kemal Ataturk's six day speech of 1927: defining the official historical view of the foundation of the Turkish republic', *Turkish Studies* 9(1): 115–29.
Alic, Anes (2010) 'Turkey's growing influence in the Balkans', http://oilprice.com/Geo-Politics/Europe/Turkeys-Growing-Influence-in-the-Balkans.html, 9 June.
Allen, Tony (2000) *The Middle East water question: hydropolitics and the global economy*, London: I.B. Tauris.
Allievi, Stefano (2003) 'Islam in the public space: social networks, media, and neo-communities', 1–27, in Allievi, Stefano and Nielson, Jorgen (eds) *Muslim networks and transnational communities in and across Europe*, Leiden, the Netherlands and Boston: Brill.
Alpay, Sahin (2009) 'Is Russia Turkey's alternative to the EU?', www.todayszaman. com, 17 August.
Altinay, Hakan (2008) 'Turkey's soft power: an unpolished gem or an elusive mirage?', *Insight Turkey* 10(2): 55–66.
Altug, Sumru, Filiztekin, Alpay and Pamuk, Sevket (2008) 'Sources of long term economic growth for Turkey 1880–2005', *European Review of Economic History* 12 (3): 393–430.
Altunisik, Meliha Benli (2004) 'Turkish–American security relations; the Middle East dimension', 151–80, in Aydin, Mustafa and Erhan, Cagri (eds) *Turkish–American relations: past, present and future*, London and New York: Routledge.
—— (2005) 'The Turkish model and democratization in the Middle East', *Arab Studies Quarterly* 27(1–2): 45–63.
—— (2008) 'The possibilities and limits of Turkey's soft power in the Middle East', *Insight Turkey* 10(2): 41–54.
—— (2009) 'Worldviews and Turkish foreign policy in the Middle East', *New Perspectives on Turkey* 40: 171–94.
Altunisik, Meliha Benli and Tur, Ozlem (2006) 'From distant neighbours to partners? Changing Syrian–Turkish relations', *Security Dialogue* 37(2): 229–48.
Amiraux, Valerie (2003) 'Turkish political Islam and Europe: story of an opportunistic intimacy', 146–69, in Allievi, Stefano and Nielson, Jorgen (eds) *Muslim networks and transnational communities in and across Europe*, Leiden, the Netherlands and Boston: Brill.
Anastasakis, Othon (2007) 'Power and interdependence: uncertainties of Greek–Turkish rapprochement', *Harvard International Review*, http://hir.harvard.edu/big-ideas/turkeys-road-to-europe, 16 April.
Anderson, Benedict (1991) *Imagined communities: reflections on the origin and spread of nationalism*, London: Verso.

Anderson, Liam and Stansfield, Gareth (2009) *Crisis in Kirkuk: the ethnopolitics of conflict and compromise*, Philadelphia, Pennsylvania: University of Pennsylvania Press.

Anderson, Perry (2008) 'Kemalism', 3–12, *London Review of Books*, 11 September.

Anheier, Helmut, Glasius, Marlies and Kaldor, Mary (eds) (2001) *Global civil society 2001*, Oxford: Oxford University Press.

Aral, Berdal (1997) 'Turkey's insecure identity from the perspective of nationalism', *Mediterranean Quarterly* 8(1): 77–91.

Aras, Bulent (2001) 'Turkish foreign policy towards Iran: ideology and foreign policy in flux', *Journal of Third World Studies*, 18(1): 105–24.

—— (2008) *Turkish policy towards central Asia*, SETA (Siyaset, Ekonomi ve Toplum Arastirmalari Vakfi; Foundation for Political, Economic and Social Research) Policy Brief 12, Ankara. Available at www.setadc.org/pdfs/SETA_Policy_Brief_No_12_Bulent_Aras.pdf.

—— (2009a) 'Turkey's rise in the greater Middle East: peacebuilding in the periphery', *Journal of Balkan and Near Eastern Studies* 11(1): 29–41.

—— (2009b) 'The Davutoglu era in Turkish foreign policy', *Insight Turkey* 11(3): 127–42.

Aras, Bulent and Caha, Omer (2000) 'Fethullah Gulen and his liberal "Turkish Islam" movement', *Middle East Review of International Affairs* 4(4): 30–42.

Aras, Bulent and Koni, Hasan (2002) 'Turkish–Syrian relations revisited', *Arab Studies Quarterly* 24(4): 47–60.

Aras, Bulent and Polat, Rabia Karakaya (2008) 'From conflict to cooperation: desecuritization of Turkey's relations with Syria and Iran', *Security Dialogue* 39(5): 495–515.

Aras, Damla (2009) 'The role of motivation in the success of coercive diplomacy: the 1998 Turkish–Syrian crisis as a case study', *Defence Studies*, 9(2): 207–23.

Arkman, Ceren (2006) 'The launching of the Turkish thesis of history: a close textual analysis', unpublished graduate paper, Sabanci University, www.turklib.com/engine/includes/print.php?category=general_history-science-lingo&altname=the_launching_of_the_turkish_thesis_of_history_a_close_textual_analysis_-_2006.

Arnett, David L. (2006) 'The heart of the matter: the importance of emotion in Turkish–American relations', *Turkish Policy Quarterly* 5(4): 31–40.

Ascherson, Neal (1996) *Black Sea: the birthplace of civilization and barbarism*, London: Vintage Books.

Aslandogan, Yuksel A. and Cetin, Muhammed (2006) 'The educational philosophy of Gulen in thought and practice', 31–54, in Hunt, Robert A. and Aslandogan, Yuksel A. (eds) *Muslim citizens of the globalized world: contributions of the Gulen movement*, Somerset, New Jersey: The Light, Inc. and IID Press.

Atay, Tayfun (2010) '"Ethnicity within ethnicity" among the Turkish speaking immigrants in London', *Insight Turkey* 12(1): 123–38.

Athanassopoulou, E. (1998) 'Western defence developments and Turkey's search for security in 1948', 77–108, in Kedourie, Sylvia (ed.) *Turkey: identity, democracy and politics*, London and Portland, Oregon: Frank Cass.

Avci, Gamze (2003) 'Turkey's slow EU candidacy: insurmountable hurdles to membership, or simple Euroscepticism?', *Turkish Studies* 4(1): 149–70.

—— (2005) 'Religion, transnationalism and Turks in Europe', *Turkish Studies* 6(2): 201–13.

—— (2006) 'Comparing integration policies and outcomes: Turks in the Netherlands and Germany', *Turkish Studies* 7(1): 67–84.

Aydin, Mustafa and Ifantis, Kostas (eds) (2004) *Turkish–Greek relations: the security dilemma in the Aegean*, London and New York: Routledge.

Aydinli, Ersel, Ozcan, Nihat Ali and Akyaz, Dogan (2006) 'The Turkish military's march towards Europe', *Foreign Affairs* 85(1): 77–90.

Aykan, Mahmut B. (1994) *Turkey's role in the Organization of the Islamic Conference: 1960–1992; the nature of deviation from the Kemalist heritage*, New York: Vantage Press.

—— (1996) 'Turkey's policy in northern Iraq, 1991–95', *Middle Eastern Studies*, 32(4): 343–66.

—— (1999) 'The Turkish–Syrian crisis of 1998: a Turkish view', *Middle East Policy*, 6(4): 174–91.

Aytac, Onder (2010) 'The democratic initiative and the Kurdish issue in Turkey since 2009', *Turkish Political Quarterly* 9(1): 101–16.

Ayturk, Ilker (2009) 'Between crises and cooperation: the future of Turkish–Israeli relations', *Insight Turkey* 11(2): 57–74.

Babali, Tuncay (2009) 'Turkey at the energy crossroads', *Middle East Quarterly*, XVI(2), www.meforum.org/2108/turkey-at-the-energy-crossroad.

—— (2010) 'Regional energy equations and Turkish foreign policy: the Middle East and the CIS', *Insight Turkey* 12(3): 147–68.

Bacik, Gokhan (2006) 'Turkey and pipeline politics', *Turkish Studies* 7(2): 293–306.

—— (2009) 'Turkish–Israeli relations after Davos: a view from Turkey', *Insight Turkey* 11(2): 31–41.

Baev, Pavel K. (2010) 'Medvedev reenergizes Russian Caspian policy in Baku', *Eurasia Daily Monitor* 7(159), Jamestown Foundation, Washington, DC, www.jamestown.org.

Bal, Idris (2000) *Turkey's relations with the west and the Turkic republics: the rise and fall of the 'Turkish model'*, Aldershot: Ashgate.

Balci, Ali (2009) 'The alliance of civilizations: the poverty of the clash/alliance dichotomy?', *Insight Turkey* 11(3): 95–108.

Balci, Ali and Mis, Nebi (2008) 'Turkey's role in the alliance of civilizations: a new perspective in Turkish foreign policy?', *Turkish Studies* 9(3): 387–406.

Balci, Bayram (2003a) 'Fethullah Gulen's missionary schools in central Asia and their role in the spreading of Turkism and Islam', *Religion, State and Society* 31(2): 151–77.

—— (2003b) 'Central Asia: Fethullah Gulen's missionary schools', *ISIM Newsletter* 9/02, www.religioscope.com/info/articles/007_fetulluhci.htm, 11 April.

Balkir, Canan (2007) 'The July 2007 election in Turkey: a test for democracy', *Mediterranean Politics* 12(3): 415–22.

Barkey, Henri J. (1995) 'Iran and Turkey: confrontation across an ideological divide', 147–68, in Rubinstein, Alvin Z. and Smolansky, Oleg M. (eds) *Regional power rivalries in the new Eurasia: Russia, Turkey and Iran*, London and New York: M.E. Sharpe.

—— (2005) *Turkey and Iraq: the perils (and prospects) of proximity*, Special Report 141, Washington, DC: United States Institute of Peace.

—— (2008) 'The effect of US policy in the Middle East on EU–Turkey relations', *The International Spectator* 43(4): 31–44.

—— (2010) *Turkey's new engagement in Iraq: embracing Iraqi Kurdistan*, Special Report 237, Washington, DC: United States Institute of Peace.

Barkey, Henri J. and Fuller, Graham E. (1998) *Turkey's Kurdish question*, Lanham, Maryland: Rowman and Littlefield.

Barysch, Katinka (2007) *Turkey's role in European energy security*, Centre for European Policy Reform, www.cer.org.uk/pdf/essay_turkey_energy_12dec07.pdf.

—— (2010) *Can Turkey combine EU accession and regional leadership?* Centre for European Policy Reform, www.cer.org.uk/pdf/pb_barysch_turkey_25jan10.pdf.

Baykal, Arda (2009) *Turkey's energy politics*, International Affairs and Defence Section, House of Commons Library, SN/IA/5301, www.parliament.uk/briefingpapers/commons/lib/research/briefings/SNIA-05301.pdf.

Baylis, John and Smith, Steve (2001) 'Introduction', in Baylis, John and Smith, Steve (eds) *The globalization of world politics: an introduction to international relations*, Oxford: Oxford University Press, 2nd edn.

Beckwith, Christopher I. (2009) *Empires of the Silk Road: a history of central Eurasia from the bronze age to the present*, Princeton, New Jersey and Oxford: Princeton University Press.

de Bellaigue, Christopher (2009) *Rebel land: among Turkey's forgotten people*, London: Bloomsbury.

Bengio, Ofra (2009a) *The Turkish–Israeli relationship: changing ties of Middle Eastern outsiders*, New York: Palgrave Macmillan.

—— (2009b) 'Altercating interests and orientations between Israel and Turkey: a view from Israel', *Insight Turkey* 11(2): 43–55.

Bengur, Osman (2009) 'Turkey's image and the Armenian question', *Turkish Policy Quarterly* 8(1): 43–48.

Biehl, Kristen (2009) *Migration 'securitization' and its everyday implications: an examination of Turkish asylum policy and practice*, Euro Mediterranean Consortium for Applied Research on International Migration (CARIM) Summer School, Badia Fiesolana, Italy: European University Institute, Robert Schuman Centre for Advanced Studies, http://cadmus.eui.eu/bitstream/handle/1814/11761/CARIM_SS_IV_Essay_2009_01.pdf?sequence=1.

Bilge, Suat (1975) 'The Cyprus conflict and Turkey', 135–85, in Karpat, Kemal H. (ed.) *Turkey's foreign policy in transition, 1950–74*, Leiden, the Netherlands: E.J. Brill.

Bilgin, Mert (2010) *Turkey's energy strategy: what difference does it make to become an energy transit corridor, hub or centre?*, UNISCI Discussion Paper 23, Madrid: Research Unit on International Security and Cooperation, Complutense University of Madrid.

Bilgin, Pinar (2005) 'Turkey's changing security discourses: the challenge of globalization', *European Journal of Political Research* 44(1): 175–201.

—— (2007) '"Only strong states can survive in Turkey's geography", the uses of "geopolitical truths" in Turkey', *Political Geography* 26(7): 740–56.

—— (2008) 'The securityness of secularism? The case of Turkey', *Security Dialogue* 39(6): 593–614.

Bilici, Abdulhamit (2010) 'Strategic defamation', www.todayszaman.com, 2 September.

Bilir, Unal (2004) '"Turkey–Islam", recipe for success or hindrance to the integration of the Turkish diaspora community in Germany?', *Journal of Muslim Minority Affairs* 24(2): 259–83.

Birand, Mehmet Ali (1996) 'Is there a new role for Turkey in the Middle East?', 171–78, in Barkey, Henri J. (ed.) *Reluctant neighbour: Turkey's role in the Middle East*, Washington, DC: United States Institute of Peace Press.

Bloxham, David (2005) *The great game of genocide: imperialism, nationalism, and the destruction of Ottoman Armenians*, Oxford: Oxford University Press.

Bodansky, Yossef (2004) *The secret history*, New York: Regan Books.

Bolme, Selin M. (2007) 'The politics of Incirlik air base', *Insight Turkey* 9(3): 82–91.

Bolukbasi, Suha (1999) 'Behind the Turkish–Israeli alliance', *Journal of Palestine Studies* 29(1): 21–35.

—— (2004) 'Jockeying for power in the Caspian basin: Turkey versus Russia and Iran', 219–29, in Akiner, Shirin (ed.) *The Caspian: politics, energy and security,* London and New York: Routledge.

Bonab, Rahman G. (2009) 'Turkey's emerging role as a mediator on Iran's nuclear activities', *Insight Turkey* 11(3): 161–75.

Borowiez, Andrew (2000) *Cyprus: a troubled island,* Westport: Praeger.

Bozkurt, Goksel (2009a) 'Details of Kurdish opening get clearer', www.hurriyetdailynews.com, 31 July.

—— (2009b) 'Gov't road map includes "more democracy, more freedom"', www.hurriyetdailynews.com, 23 September.

Breitegger, Andrea (2009) 'Turkish–Iranian relations: a reality check', *Turkish Policy Quarterly* 8(3): 109–23.

Brown, Cameron S. (2008) 'The one coalition they craved to join: Turkey in the Korean war', *Review of International Studies* 34: 89–108.

van Bruinessen, Martin (1999) 'The Kurds in movement: migrations, mobilizations, communications and the globalization of the Kurdish question', www.hum.uu.nl/medewerkers/m.vanbruinessen/publications/Kurds_in_movement.htm.

Bulut, Esra (2004) 'The role of religion in Turkish reactions to Balkan conflicts', *Turkish Policy Quarterly* 3(1): 1–13.

Burns, R. Nicholas (2005) 'The U.S.–Turkish relationship beyond Iraq: common values, common agenda', Turgut Ozal Memorial Lecture, Washington Institute for Near East Policy, www.washingtoninstitute.org/templateC07.php?CID=247.

Buzan, Barry and Diez, Thomas (1999) 'The European Union and Turkey', *Survival* 41(1): 41–57.

Buzan, Barry and Weaver, Ole (2003) *Regions and powers: the structure of international security,* Cambridge: Cambridge University Press.

Cagaptay, Soner (2002) 'Reconfiguring the Turkish nation in the 1930s', *Nationalism and Ethnic Politics* 8(2): 67–82.

—— (2004) 'A Turkish rapprochement with Middle East rogue states?' *Policy Watch* 825, Washington Institute for Near East Policy, www.washingtoninstitute.org/templateC05.php?CID=1703.

—— (2005a) 'Hizballah in Turkey revives: al Qaeda's bridge between Turkey and Iraq?' *Policy Watch* 946, Washington Institute for Near East Policy, www.washingtoninstitute.org/templateC05.php?CID=2240.

—— (2005b) 'Turkey at the crossroads: preserving Ankara's western orientation', *Policy Focus* 48, Washington Institute for Near East Policy, www.washingtoninstitute.org/pubPDFs/CagaptayBookWeb.pdf.

Cagaptay, Soner and Fikret, Cem S. (2005) 'Europe's terror problem: PKK fronts inside the EU', *Policy Watch* 1057, Washington Institute for Near East Policy, www.washingtoninstitute.org/templateC05.php?CID=2413.

Cakir, Rusen (2007) 'The re-emergence of Hizbollah in Turkey', *Policy Focus* 74, Washington Institute for Near East Policy, www.washingtoninstitute.org/pubPDFs/PolicyFocus74initial.pdf.

—— (2010) 'The Kurdish political movement and the "democratic opening"', *Insight Turkey* 12(2): 179–92.

Cakmak, Cenap (2005) 'Turkey's foreign policy, the European Union and the International Criminal Court', *Insight Turkey* 7(4): 111–25.

Calis, Saban (2001) 'Turkey's Balkan policy in the early 1990s', *Turkish Studies* 2(1): 135–46.

Candar, Cengiz (2004) 'Turkish foreign policy and the war on Iraq', 47–60, in Martin, Lenore G. and Keridis, Dimitris (eds) *The future of Turkish foreign policy*, Cambridge, Massachusetts: MIT Press.

—— (2005) 'Democracy in the greater Middle East: inevitable', *Turkish Policy Quarterly* 4(2): 81–101.

—— (2009a) 'The Kurdish question: the reasons and fortunes of the "opening"', *Insight Turkey*, 11(4): 13–19.

—— (2009b) *Turkey's 'soft power' strategy: a new vision for a multipolar world*, SETA Policy Brief 38, Ankara. Available at www.setadc.org/pdfs/SETA_Policy_Brief_No_38_Turkeys_Soft_Power_Strategy_Candar.pdf.

Candar, Cengiz and Fuller, Graham (2001) 'Grand geopolitics for a new Turkey', *Mediterranean Quarterly* 12(1): 22–38.

Carkoglu, Ali (2002) 'Turkey's November 2002 elections: a new beginning?', *Middle East Review of International Affairs* 6(4): 30–41.

Carley, Patricia M. (1995) 'Turkey and central Asia: reality comes calling', 169–97, in Rubinstein, Alvin Z. and Smolansky, Oleg M. (eds) *Regional power rivalries in the new Eurasia: Russia, Turkey and Iran*, London and New York: M.E. Sharpe.

—— (1996), 'Turkey's place in the modern world', 3–12, in Barkey, Henri J. (ed.) *Reluctant neighbour: Turkey's role in the Middle East*, Washington, DC: United States Institute of Peace Press.

Catherwood, Christopher (2004) *Winston's folly: imperialism and the creation of modern Iraq*, London: Constable and Robinson.

Celenk, Ayse Aslihan (2009) 'Europeanization and administrative reform: the case of Turkey', *Mediterranean Politics* 14(1): 41–60.

Celep, Odul (2010) 'Turkey's radical right and the Kurdish issue: the MHP's reaction to the "democratic opening"', *Insight Turkey* 12(2): 125–42.

Celikpala, M. (2006) 'From immigrants to diaspora: influence of the north Caucasian diaspora in Turkey', *Middle Eastern Studies* 42(3): 423–46.

Cetin, Fethiye (2008) *My grandmother: a memoir*, London: Verso.

Cetin, Hikmet (2007) 'Turkey's role in Afghanistan', *Turkish Policy Quarterly* 6(2): 13–17.

Cetin, Muhammed (2007) 'The Gulen movement: its nature and identity', 377–90, in Cantori, Louis J., Hermansen, Marcia K. and Capes, David B. (eds) *Muslim world in transition: contributions of the Gulen movement*, Leeds: Leeds Metropolitan University Press.

Cetinsaya, Gokhan (2003) 'Essential friends and natural enemies: the historic roots of Turkish–Iranian relations', *Middle East Review of International Affairs* 7(3): 116–32.

Cevikoz, Unal (1997–98) 'European integration and regional cooperation in southeast Europe', *Perceptions* 2(4), www.sam.gov.tr/perceptions/Volume2/December1997–February1998/cevik%C3%B6z.PDF.

Chase, Robert, Hill, Emily and Kennedy, Paul M. (1999) *The pivotal state: a new framework for US policy in the developing world*, New York: W.W. Norton and Co.

Cilinger, Sevgi (2010) 'Identity and integration among Turkish Sunni Muslims in Britain', *Insight Turkey* 12(1): 103–22.

CIVICUS Civil Society Index Report for Turkey (undated) *Civil society in Turkey: an era of transition*, www.civicus.org/new/media/CSI_Turkey_Executive_Summary.pdf.

Cizre, Umit (2003) 'Demythologizing the national security concept: the case of Turkey', *Middle East Journal* 57(2): 213–29.

—— (2009) 'The emergence of the government's perspective on the Kurdish issue', *Insight Turkey* 11(4): 1–12.

Clark, Ian (2001) 'Globalization and the post-Cold War order', 634–47, in Baylis, John and Smith, Steve, *The globalization of world politics: an introduction to international relations*, Oxford: Oxford University Press, 2nd edn.

Cornell, Svante E. and Karaveli, Halil Magnus (2008) *Prospects for a 'torn' Turkey: a secular and unitary future?* Johns Hopkins University and Institute for Security and Development Policy, Central Asia-Caucasus Institute and Silk Road Studies Program, Silk Road Paper, Washington, DC and Stockholm. Available at www.silkroadstudies.org/new/docs/silkroadpapers/0810Turkey.pdf.

Council of Europe (2009) *Freedom of religion and other human rights for non Muslim minorities in Turkey and for the Muslim minority in Thrace*, Parliamentary Assembly Report Doc 11860, 21 April, www.assembly.coe.int/Main.asp?link=/Documents/WorkingDocs/Doc09/EDOC11860.htm.

Criss, Nur Bilge and Guner, Serdar (1999) 'Geopolitical configuration: the Russia–Turkey–Iran triangle', *Security Dialogue* 30(3): 365–76.

Daly, John C. K. (2008a) 'Tankers, pipelines and the Turkish straits', *Eurasia Daily Monitor* 5(122), Jamestown Foundation, Washington, DC, www.jamestown.org.

—— (2008b) 'Iran gains from Georgia confrontation', *Eurasia Daily Monitor* 5(199), Jamestown Foundation, Washington, DC, www.jamestown.org.

—— (2008c) 'Turkey courts central Asia', *Eurasia Daily Monitor* 5(202), Jamestown Foundation, Washington, DC, www.jamestown.org.

—— (2008d) 'Greece and Turkey spar over offshore oil exploration', *Eurasia Daily Monitor* 5(222), Jamestown Foundation, Washington, DC, www.jamestown.org.

Davutoglu, Ahmet (2001) *Stratejik derinlik: Turkiye'nin uluslararasi konumu*, Istanbul: Kure Yayinlari.

—— (2008) 'Turkey's foreign policy vision: an assessment of 2007', *Insight Turkey* 10(1): 77–96.

—— (2009) 'Turkish foreign policy and the EU', *Turkish Policy Quarterly*, 8 (1): 11–17.

Deffeyes, Kenneth S. (2001) *Hubbert's peak: the impending world oil shortage*, Princeton, New Jersey: Princeton University Press.

—— (2005) *Beyond oil: the view from Hubbert's peak*, New York: Hill and Wang.

Demirel, Tanel (2003) 'Civil–military relations in Turkey: two patterns of civilian behaviour towards the military', *Turkish Studies* 4(3): 1–25.

—— (2005) 'Lessons of military regimes and democracy: the Turkish case in comparative perspective', *Armed Forces and Society* 31(2): 245–71.

Dereli, Zeynep (2009/2010) 'A movement for change: forging a bright future on firm principles', *Turkish Political Quarterly* 8(4): 27–39.

—— (2010) 'Towards a grander Turkish energy strategy', London: Foreign Policy Centre, http://fpc.org.uk/fsblob/1231.pdf.

Diez, Thomas (2005) 'Turkey, the European Union and security complexes revisited', *Mediterranean Politics* 10(2): 167–80.

Dodd, Clement (2010) *The history and politics of the Cyprus conflict*, Basingstoke: Palgrave Macmillan.

Dogan, Salih (2010) 'Turkey's presence and importance in Afghanistan', www.hurriyetdailynews.com, 22 August.

Dogru, Emre (2010) 'Turkey: an emerging AKP–Gulenist split?', www.hurriyetdailynews.com, 31 August.

Drorian, Sevgi (2005) 'Rethinking European security: the interregional dimension and the Turkish nexus', *European Security* 14(4): 421–41.

Duncker, Anne K. (2006/07) 'Human rights are what NGOs make of it: the diversity of human rights and the influence of the European process', *Turkish Policy Quarterly* 5(4): 51–61.

Ebaugh, Helen Rose (2010) *The Gulen movement: a sociological analysis of a civic movement rooted in moderate Islam*, Dordrecht, Heidelberg, London and New York: Springer.

Ebaugh, Helen Rose and Koc, Dogan (2007) 'Funding Gulen inspired good works: demonstrating and generating commitment to the movement', 539–51, in Cantori, Louis J., Hermansen, Marcia K. and Capes, David B. (eds) *Muslim world in transition: contributions of the Gulen movement*, Leeds: Leeds Metropolitan University Press.

Eder, Mine (2001) 'The challenge of globalization and Turkey's changing political economy', 189–215, in Rubin, Barry and Kirisci, Kemal (eds) *Turkey in world politics: an emerging multiregional power*, Boulder, Colorado and London: Lynne Rienner.

—— (2003) 'Implementing economic criteria of EU membership: how difficult is it for Turkey?', *Turkish Studies* 4(1): 219–44.

Ediger, Volkan S. and Bagdadi, Itir (2010) 'Turkey–Russia energy relations: same old story, new actors', *Insight Turkey* 12(3): 221–36.

Energy Watch Group (2008) *Crude oil: the supply outlook*, Berlin: Energy Watch Group/Ludwig-Boelkow-Foundation, revised edn. Available at www.energy watchgroup.org/fileadmin/global/pdf/2008–02_EWG_Oil_Report_updated.pdf.

Eralp, Atila (1996) 'Facing the challenge: post revolutionary relations with Iran', 93–112, in Barkey, Henri J. (ed.) *Reluctant neighbour: Turkey's role in the Middle East*, Washington, DC: US Institute of Peace Press.

Eralp, Dogu Ulas (2010) *Kosovo and Turkey: what lies ahead?*, SETA, Policy Brief 50, Ankara. Available at http://setadc.org/pdfs/SETA_Policy_Brief_No_50_Kosovo_Turkey_Doga_Ulas_Eralp.pdf.

Erdagi, Lt Gen. Ethem (2005) 'The ISAF mission and Turkey's role in rebuilding the Afghan state', *Policy Watch* 1052, Washington Institute for Near East Policy, www.washingtoninstitute.org/templateC05.php?CID=2403.

Erdemir, Halil (2009) 'The policies around the BTC pipeline', *Alternatives* 8(4): 20–44.

Erdogan, Emre (2005) 'A fourth alternative for Turkey: a democratic Middle East', *Turkish Policy Quarterly* 4(2): 139–58.

Erman, Aydemir (2010) 'How Turkey can help NATO in Afghanistan', *Christian Science Monitor*, www.csmonitor.com/Commentary/Opinion/2010/0209/How-Turkey-can-help-NATO-in-Afghanistan, 9 February.

Erman, Tahire and Goker, E. (2000) 'Alevi politics in contemporary Turkey', *Middle Eastern Studies* 36(4): 99–118.

Ertugal, Ebru (2005) 'Strategies for regional development: challenges facing Turkey on the road to EU membership', *Turkish Policy Quarterly* 4(3): 63–86.

European Commission (2007) *Turkey 2007 Progress Report*, Brussels: Commission of the European Communities, http://ec.europa.eu/enlargement/pdf/key_documents/2007/nov/turkey_progress_reports_en.pdf.

—— (2008) *Turkey 2008 Progress Report*, Brussels: Commission of the European Communities, http://ec.europa.eu/enlargement/pdf/press_corner/key-documents/reports_nov_2008/turkey_progress_report_en.pdf.

—— (2009) *Turkey 2009 Progress Report*, Brussels: Commission of the European Communities, http://ec.europa.eu/enlargement/pdf/key_documents/2009/tr_rapport_2009_en.pdf.

—— (2010) *Turkey 2010 Progress Report*, Brussels: Commission of the European Communities, http://ec.europa.eu/enlargement/pdf/key_documents/2010/package/tr_rapport_2010_en.pdf.

—— (undated) 'Enlargement: accession criteria', http://ec.europa.eu/enlargement/enlargement_process/accession_process/criteria/index_en.htm.

European Stability Initiative (2009) *Noah's dove returns: Armenia, Turkey and the debate on genocide*, www.esiweb.org, 21 April.

European Union (2008) 'Energy security and solidarity action plan: second strategic energy review', 13 November, Memo/08/703, Brussels: European Union, http://europa.eu/rapid/pressReleasesAction.do?reference=MEMO/08/703& format = HTML& aged = 0& language = en& guiLanguage = en.

Fagan, Geraldine (2007) 'Russia: Said Nursi ban brands moderate Muslims as extremist', *Forum* 18, reproduced in *World Wide ReligiousNews (WWRN)*, http://wwrn.org/articles/25508, 27 June.

Findley, Carter Vaughn (2005) *The Turks in world history*, Oxford: Oxford University Press.

Finer, Samuel E. (2002) *The man on horseback: the role of the military in politics*, New Brunswick, New Jersey: Transaction Publishers.

Fink, Daniel (2006) *Assessing Turkey's future as an energy transit country*, Research Note 11, Washington Institute for Near East Policy, www.washingtoninstitute.org/pubPDFs/ResearchNote11.pdf.

Foreign and Commonwealth Office (2009) 'Turkey: global competitiveness: making the grade', London: Foreign and Commonwealth Office.

Freeman, Kevin (2001) 'Water wars? Inequalities in the Tigris–Euphrates river basin', *Geopolitics* 6(2): 127–40.

Fuller, Graham E. (1993) 'Turkey's new eastern orientation', 37–97, in Fuller, Graham E. and Lesser, Ian O. (eds) *Turkey's new geopolitics: from the Balkans to western China*, Boulder, Colorado: Westview/RAND.

—— (2004) 'Turkey's strategic model: myths and realities', *Washington Quarterly*, 27(3): 51–64.

Fuller, Graham E. and Lesser, Ian O. (eds) (1993) *Turkey's new geopolitics: from the Balkans to western China*, Boulder, Colorado: Westview/RAND.

Genis, Serife and Maynard, Kelly Lynne (2009) 'Formation of a diasporic community: the history of migration and resettlement of Muslim Albanians in the Black Sea region of Turkey', *Government and Opposition* 45(4): 553–69.

Gokalp, Deniz and Unsar, Seda (2008) 'From the myth of European Union accession to disillusion: implications for religious and ethnic polarization in Turkey', *Middle East Journal* 62(1): 93–116.

Gokcek, Mustafa (2006) 'Fethullah Gulen and Sufism: a historical perspective', 165–75, in Hunt, Robert A. and Aslandogan, Yuksel A. (eds) *Muslim citizens of the globalized world: contributions of the Gulen movement*, Somerset, New Jersey: The Light, Inc. and IID Press.

Golden, Peter B. (2005) 'The Turks: a historical view'; 18–31, in Roxburgh, David J. (ed.) *Turks: a journey of a thousand years, 600–1600*, London: Royal Academy of Arts.

Gonlubol, Mehmet (1975) 'NATO, USA and Turkey', 13–50, in Karpat, Kemal H. (ed.) *Turkey's foreign policy in transition, 1950–1974*, Leiden, the Netherlands: E.J. Brill.

Gonul, Vecdi (2010) 'Turkey–NATO relations and NATO's new strategic concept', *Turkish Policy Quarterly* 9(1): 15–21.

Gordon, Philip H. (2003) 'Bush's Middle East vision', *Survival* 45(1): 155–65.

Gorvett, Jan (2002) 'A hugely unpopular war', *The Middle East*, November: 328.

Granmayeli, Ali (2004) 'Legal history of the Caspian Sea', 17–47, in Akiner, Shirin (ed.) *The Caspian: politics, energy and security*, London and New York: Routledge.

Grigoriadis, Ioannis N. (2008) 'On the Europeanization of minority rights protection: comparing the cases of Greece and Turkey', *Mediterranean Politics* 13(1): 23–41.

—— (2009) *Trials of Europeanization: Turkish political culture and the European Union*, New York and Basingstoke: Palgrave Macmillan.

—— (2010) *The Davutoglu doctrine and Turkish foreign policy*, Working Paper 8, Hellenic Foundation for European and Foreign Policy (ELIAMEP), www.eliamep.gr.

Grigoriadis, Ioannis N. and Kamaras, Antonis (2008) 'Foreign direct investment in Turkey: historical constraints and the AKP success story', *Middle Eastern Studies* 44(1): 53–68.

Gros, David (2005) 'Economic aspects of Turkey's quest for EU membership', *Insight Turkey* 7(1): 50–63.

Gruen, George E. (2006) 'Turkey's role in peacekeeping missions', *American Foreign Policy Interests* 28(6): 435–49.

Guida, Michelangelo (2008) 'The Sevres syndrome and "Komplo" theories in the Islamist and secular press', *Turkish Studies* 9(1): 37–52.

Gul, Abdullah (2003) www.tccb.gov.tr/sayfa/konusma_aciklama_mesajlar/kitap/79.pdf.

—— (2004) 'Turkey's role in a changing Middle East environment', *Mediterranean Quarterly* 15(1): 1–7.

Guney, Aylin and Karatekelioglu, Petek (2005) 'Turkey's EU candidacy and civil–military relations: challenges and prospects', *Armed Forces and Society* 31(3): 439–62.

Guney, Cengiz (2006–07) 'Flags against fears and uncertainties', *Turkish Policy Quarterly* 5(4): 19–30.

Guney, Nursin Atesoglu (2007) 'The new security environment and Turkey's ISAF experience', 177–89, in Guney, Nursin Atesoglu (ed.) *Contentious issues of security and the future of Turkey*, Aldershot, UK and Burlington VT: Ashgate.

Gunter, Michael M. (1990) *Transnational Armenian activism*, Conflict Studies no. 229, London: Research Institute for the Study of Conflict and Terrorism.

—— (1999) *The Kurdish predicament in Iraq: a political analysis*, London: Macmillan.

—— (2004) 'The consequences of a failed Iraqi state: an independent Kurdish state in northern Iraq?', *Journal of South Asian and Middle Eastern Studies* XXVII(3): 1–11.

—— (2007) *The Kurds ascending; the evolving solution to the Kurdish problem in Iraq and Turkey*, Basingstoke and New York, Palgrave Macmillan.

Hadjit, Assia and Moxon-Browne, Edward (2005) 'Foreign direct investment in Turkey: the implications of EU accession', *Turkish Studies* 6(3): 321–40.

Hale, William (1981) *The political and economic development of modern Turkey*, London: Croom Helm.

—— (1992) 'Turkey, the Middle East, and the Gulf crisis', *International Affairs* 68(4): 679–92.

—— (2000) *Turkish foreign policy, 1774–2000*, London and Portland, Oregon: Frank Cass.

—— (2007) *Turkey, the US and Iraq*, London: SAQI.

—— (2009) 'Turkey and the Middle East in the "new era"', *Insight Turkey* 11(3): 143–59.

Halliday, Fred (2001) 'Nationalism', 440–55, in Baylis, John and Smith, Steve (eds) *The globalization of world politics: an introduction to international relations*, Oxford: Oxford University Press, 2nd edn.

Hanke, Steve H. (2001) 'Turkey: here we go again', Cato Institute, www.cato.org/pub_display.php?pub_id=3965, 9 July.

Hannay, David (2005) *Cyprus: the search for a solution*, London: I.B. Tauris.

Harris, George S. (1975) 'Turkey and the United States', 51–72, in Karput, Kemal H. (ed.) *Turkey's foreign policy in transition, 1950–1974*, Leiden, the Netherlands: E.J. Brill.

Harvey, Benjamin (2010) 'Kurdish issue turns into Turkish PM Erdogan's achilles' heel', www.hurriyetdailynews.com, 9 July.

Hasimi, Cemalettin (2009) 'Mapping the pathways: public perception and the Kurdish question', *Insight Turkey* 11(4): 21–27.

Hay, Colin and Marsh, David (eds) (2000) *Demystifying globalization*, Basingstoke: Palgrave.

Heck, Paul L. (2007) 'Turkish in the language of the Qur'an: HIRA', 643–9, in Cantori, Louis J., Hermansen, Marcia K. and Capes, David B. (eds) *Muslim world in transition: contributions of the Gulen movement*, Leeds: Leeds Metropolitan University Press.

Hendrick, Joshua D. (2006) 'The regulated potential of kinetic Islam: antitheses in global Islamic activism', 11–29, in Hunt, Robert A. and Aslandogan, Yuksel A. (eds) *Muslim citizens of the globalized world: contributions of the Gulen movement*, Somerset, New Jersey: The Light, Inc. and IID Press.

Hershlag, Zvi Yehuda (1968) *Turkey: the challenge of growth*, Leiden, the Netherlands: E.J. Brill.

Hill, Christopher (2003) *The changing politics of foreign policy*, Basingstoke: Palgrave Macmillan.

Hill, Fiona (2004) 'Caspian conundrum: pipelines and energy networks', 211–39, in Martin, Leonore G. and Keridis, Dimitris (eds) *The future of Turkish foreign policy*, Cambridge, Massachusetts: MIT Press.

Hirsch, Robert L. (2005) *Peaking of world oil production: impacts, mitigation, and risk management*, Washington, DC: Science Applications International Corporation/ Management Information Services, Inc., www.netl.doe.gov/publications/others/pdf/oil_peaking_netl.pdf.

Hudson, Alexandra (2008) 'Turkish Islamic preacher – threat or benefactor?', *Reuters UK*, http://uk.reuters.com, 14 May.

Hulsse, Rainer (2006) 'Cool Turkey: solving the image problem to secure EU membership', *Mediterranean Politics* 11(3): 309–27.

Human Rights Watch (2004) 'Claims in conflict: reversing ethnic cleansing in northern Iraq', www.hrw.org/en/reports/2004/08/02/claims-conflict, 2 August.

Hunt, Robert A. and Aslandogan, Yuksel A. (eds) (2006) *Muslim citizens of the globalized world: contributions of the Gulen movement*, Somerset, New Jersey: The Light, Inc. and IID Press.

Huntington, Samuel (1993), 'The clash of civilisations?', *Foreign Affairs* 72(3): 136–44.

—— (1996) *The clash of civilizations and the remaking of world order*, New York: Simon & Schuster.

Ibas, Selahattin (2007) 'Contributions of the Turkish armed forces to Middle East peace operations', *Policy Watch* 1199, Washington Institute for Near East Policy, www.washingtoninstitute.org/templateC05.php?CID=2568.

Ibrahim, Ferhad and Gurbey, Gulistan (2000) *The Kurdish conflict in Turkey: obstacles and chances for peace and democracy*, New York: St Martin's Press.

Icduygu, Ahmet (2004a) 'Demographic mobility over Turkey: migration experiences and government responses', *Mediterranean Quarterly* 15(4): 88–99.

—— (2004b) 'Transborder crime between Turkey and Greece; human struggling and its regional consequences', *Southeast European and Black Sea Studies* 4(2): 294–314.

—— (2006) 'International migrants remittances in Turkey', *Consortium for Applied Research on International Migration (CARIM)*, www.carim.org.

Icduygu, Ahmet and Toktas, Sule (2002) 'How do smuggling and trafficking operate via irregular border crossings in the Middle East?', *International Migration* 40(6): 25–52.

Idiz, Semih (2008) 'Ankara and northern Iraq break the ice', www.hurriyetdailynews.com, 9 May.

—— (2010) 'The Turkish–Armenian debacle', *Insight Turkey* 12(2): 11–19.

IMF (2008) 'Globalization: a brief overview', Washington, DC: International Monetary Fund, www.imf.org/external/np/exr/ib/2008/053008.htm.

Inbar, Efraim (2001) *The Israeli–Turkish entente*, London: King's College Mediterranean Studies.

International Crisis Group (2004a) *Iraq's Kurds: towards an historic compromise?* Middle East Report No. 26, www.crisisgroup.org/en/regions/middle-east-north-africa/iraq-syria-lebanon/iraq/026-iraqs-kurds-toward-an-historic-compromise.aspx.

—— (2004b) *The broader Middle East and North Africa initiative: imperilled at birth*, Middle East and North Africa Briefing 14, www.crisisgroup.org/en/regions/middle-east-north-africa/B014-the-broader-middle-east-and-north-africa-initiative-imperilled-at-birth.aspx.

—— (2005) *Iraq: allaying Turkish fears over Kurdish ambitions*, Middle East Report No. 35, www.crisisgroup.org/en/regions/middle-east-north-africa/iraq-syria-lebanon/iraq/035-iraq-allaying-turkeys-fears-over-kurdish-ambitions.aspx.

—— (2007a) *Islam and identity in Germany*, Europe Report 181, www.crisisgroup.org/en/regions/europe/181-islam-and-identity-in-germany.aspx?alt_lang=tr.

—— (2007b) *Iraq and the Kurds: resolving the Kirkuk crisis*, Middle East Report No. 64, www.crisisgroup.org/en/regions/middle-east-north-africa/iraq-syria-lebanon/iraq/064-iraq-and-the-kurds-resolving-the-kirkuk-crisis.aspx.

—— (2009) *Turkey and Armenia: opening minds, opening borders*, Europe Report 199, www.crisisgroup.org/en/regions/europe/caucasus/armenia/199-turkey-and-armenia-opening-minds-opening-borders.aspx.

—— (2010a) *Turkey and the Middle East: ambitions and constraints*, Europe Report No. 203, www.crisisgroup.org/en/regions/europe/turkey-cyprus/turkey/203-turkey-and-the-middle-east-ambitions-and-constraints.aspx.

—— (2010b) *Turkey's crises over Israel and Iran*, Europe Report No. 208, www.crisisgroup.org/en/regions/europe/turkey-cyprus/turkey/208-turkeys-crises-over-israel-and-iran.aspx.

IOM (2008) 'Migration in Turkey: a country profile', Geneva: International Organization for Migration, http://publications.iom.int/bookstore/free/Turkey_Profile2008.pdf.

Iraq Study Group (2007) 'The way forward – a new approach', Washington, DC: Iraq Study Group, http://media.usip.org/reports/iraq_study_group_report.pdf.

Irvine, Jill (2006) 'The Gulen movement and Turkish integration in Germany', 55–74, in Hunt, Robert A. and Aslandogan, Yuksel A. (eds) *Muslim citizens of the globalized world: contributions of the Gulen movement*, Somerset, New Jersey: The Light, Inc. and IID Press.

IWPR (2005) *Clampdown on Islamic teaching in Turkmenistan*, Reporting Central Asia 401, London: Institute for War and Peace Reporting.

Jacobs, Matthew F. (2006) 'The perils and promise of Islam: the United States and the Muslim Middle East in the early Cold War years', *Diplomatic History* 30(4): 705–39.

Jane's (2009) 'Gulen movement: Turkey's third power', *Jane's Islamic Affairs Analyst*, 29 January.

Jang, Ji-Hyang (2006) 'On the road to moderation: the role of Islamic business in transforming political Islamists in Turkey', *Journal of International and Area Studies* 13(2): 97–112.

Jellissen, Susan M. and Gottheil, Fred M. (2009) 'Marx and Engels: in praise of globalization', *Contributions to Political Economy* 28(1): 35–46.

Jenkins, Gareth (2001) *Context and Circumstance: the Turkish Military and Politics*, Adelphi Papers 337, London: International Institute for Strategic Studies.

—— (2007) 'Continuity and change: prospects for civil–military relations in Turkey', *International Relations* 8(2): 339–55.

—— (2008a) 'Explosion raises questions about the security of the BTC pipeline', *Eurasia Daily Monitor* 5(152), Jamestown Foundation, Washington, DC, www.jamestown.org.

—— (2008b) *Political Islam in Turkey: running west, heading east?* Basingstoke and New York: Palgrave Macmillan.

—— (2008c) 'A military analysis of Turkey's incursion into northern Iraq', *Terrorism Monitor* 6(5), Jamestown Foundation, Washington, DC, www.jamestown.org.

—— (2009) 'Between fact and fantasy: Turkey's Ergenekon investigation', Johns Hopkins University and Institute for Security and Development Policy, Central Asia-Caucasus Institute and Silk Road Studies Program, Silk Road Paper, Washington, DC and Stockholm. Available at www.silkroadstudies.org/new/docs/silkroadpapers/0908Ergenekon.pdf.

Jongerden, Joost (2001) 'Resettlement and reconstruction of identity: the case of the Kurds in Turkey', *Global Review of Ethnopolitics* 1(1): 81–86.

Jouejati, Murhof (1996) 'Water politics as high politics; the case of Turkey and Syria', 131–46, in Barkey, Henri J. (ed.) *Reluctant neighbour: Turkey's role in the Middle East*, Washington, DC: US Institute of Peace Press.

Jung, Dietrich (2005) 'Turkey and the Arab world: historical narratives and new political realities', *Mediterranean Politics* 10(1): 1–17.

Jung, Dietrich with Piccoli, Wolfgang (2001) *Turkey at the crossroads: Ottoman legacies and the greater Middle East*, London and New York: Zed Books.

Kaliber, Alper and Tocci, Nathalie (2010) 'Civil society and the transformation of Turkey's Kurdish question', *Security Dialogue* 41(2): 191–215.

Kalin, Ibrahim (2009) 'Debating Turkey in the Middle East: the dawn of a new geopolitical imagination?', *Insight Turkey* 11(1): 83–96.

Kapsis, James E. (2006) 'The failure of US–Turkish pre-Iraq War negotiations: an overconfident United States, political mismanagement, and a conflicted military', *Middle East Review of International Affairs* 10(3): 33–45.

Karaosmanoglu, Ali (1993) 'Officers, westernization and democracy', 19–34, in Heper, Metin, Oncu, Ayse and Kramer, Heinz (eds) *Turkey and the west: changing political and cultural identities*, London and New York: I.B. Tauris.

—— (2000) 'The evolution of the national security culture and the military in Turkey', *Columbia University Journal of International Affairs* 54(1): 199–216.

Karaveli, Halil M. (2010) 'An unfulfilled promise of enlightenment: Kemalism and its liberal critics', *Turkish Studies* 11(1): 85–102.

Kardas, Saban (2009a) 'Turkish government and opposition remain divided over foreign policy', *Eurasia Daily Monitor* 6(121), Jamestown Foundation, Washington, DC, www.jamestown.org.

—— (2009b) 'Ankara promotes stability in the Middle East', *Eurasia Daily Monitor* 6(148), Jamestown Foundation, Washington, DC, www.jamestown.org.

—— (2010a) 'Delays in Turkish-Azeri gas deal raises uncertainty over Nabucco', *Eurasia Daily Monitor* 7(39), Jamestown Foundation, Washington, DC, www.jamestown.org.

—— (2010b) 'Turkish–Iranian energy cooperation in the shadow of US sanctions on Iran', *Eurasia Daily Monitor* 7(144), Jamestown Foundation, Washington, DC, www.jamestown.org.

Karpat, Kemal H. (1975) 'Turkish and Arab–Israeli relations', 108–34, in Karput, Kemal H. (ed.) *Turkey's foreign policy in transition, 1950–1974*, Leiden, the Netherlands: E.J. Brill.

Kasapoglu, Cagil (2009) 'Turkish foreign policy and UNIFIL mission', http://cagilkasapoglu.wordpress.com/2009/06/29/turkish-foreign-policy-and-unifil-mission.

Kavakci, Merve (2009) 'Turkey's test with its deep state', *Mediterranean Quarterly* 20(4): 83–97.

Kaya, Ferzende (2001) 'Turks who fought in Afghanistan', www.hurriyetdailynews.com, 17 October.

Kaya, M. (2005) 'Cultural reification in Circassian diaspora: stereotypes, prejudices and ethnic relations', *Journal of Ethnic and Migration Studies*, 31(1): 129–49.

Kaya, M.K. (2008) 'Turkish political corruption: the AKP too?', *The Turkey Analyst* 1(14), www.silkroadstudies.org/new/inside/turkey/2008/080926A.html.

—— (2009) 'The "eastern dimension" in Turkish foreign policy grows', *The Turkey Analyst* 2(18), www.silkroadstudies.org/new/inside/turkey/2009/091012B.html.

Kaya, Serdar (2009) 'The rise and decline of the Turkish "deep state"; the Ergenekon case', *Insight Turkey* 11(4): 99–113.

Kazan, Isil (2005) 'Turkey: where geopolitics still matters', *Contemporary Security Policy* 26(3): 588–604.

Kazemi, Farhad and Ajdari, Zohreh (1998) 'Ethnicity, identity and politics: central Asia and Azerbaijan between Iran and Turkey', 52–70, in Menshari, David (ed.) *Central Asia meets the Middle East*, London: Frank Cass.

Kehl-Bodrogi, Krisztina (2003) 'Ataturk and the Alevis: a holy alliance?', 53–69, in White, Paul J. and Jongerden, Joost (eds) *Turkey's Alevi enigma: a comprehensive overview*, Leiden, the Netherlands: Brill.

Keohane, Robert O. and Nye, Joseph S. (1973), *Transnational relations and world politics*, Harvard, Connecticut; Harvard University Press.

Ker-Lindsay, James (2007) *Crisis and conciliation: a year of rapprochement between Greece and Turkey*, London: I.B. Tauris.

Keyman, E. Fuat (ed.) (2007) *Remaking Turkey: globalization, alternative modernities, and democracy*, Lanham, Maryland and Plymouth, UK: Lexington Books.

—— (2010) 'The CHP and the "democratic opening", reactions to the AK Party's electoral hegemony', *Insight Turkey* 12(2): 91–108.

Kilinc, Ramazan (2009) 'Turkey and the alliance of civilizations: norm adoption as a survival strategy', *Insight Turkey* 11(3): 55–75.

Kiniklioglu, Suat (2005) 'Turkey confronts history', www.hurriyetdailynews.com, 27 September.

Kinross, Lord (1977) *The Ottoman centuries: the rise and fall of the Turkish empire*, New York: Morrow Quill.

Kinross, Patrick (1995) *Ataturk: the rebirth of a nation*, London: Phoenix.

Kirisci, Kemal (2003) 'Turkey: a transformation from emigration to immigration', Washington, DC: Migration Information Service, www.migrationinformation.org/Feature/display.cfm?ID=176.

—— (2006) *Turkey's foreign policy in turbulent times*, Chaillot Paper 92, Paris: European Union Institute for Security Studies (EUISS), www.iss.europe.eu.

—— (2007) 'Turkey: a country of transition from emigration to immigration', *Mediterranean Politics* 12(1): 91–97.

—— (2009) 'The transformation of Turkish foreign policy: the rise of the trading state', *New Perspectives on Turkey* 40: 29–57.

Kirisci, Kemal and Winrow, Gareth M. (1997) *The Kurdish question and Turkey: an example of a trans-state ethnic conflict*, London and Portland, Oregon: Frank Cass.

Kirisci, Kemal, Tocci, Nathalie and Walker, Joshua (2010) *A neighbourhood rediscovered: Turkey's transatlantic value in the Middle East*, Brussels Forum Paper Series, The German Marshall Fund of the United States, www.gmfus.org/publications.

Klare, Michael T (2001) *Resource wars: the new landscape of global conflict*, New York: Metropolitan Books.

—— (2004) *Blood and oil*, London: Penguin Books.

—— (2008) *Rising powers, shrinking planet: the new geopolitics of energy*, New York: Metropolitan Books.

Koker, Levent (2010) 'A key to the "democratic opening", rethinking citizenship, ethnicity and the Turkish nation state', *Insight Turkey* 12(2): 49–69.

Kose, Talha (2009) 'The alliance of civilizations: possibilities of conflict resolution at the civilization level', *Insight Turkey* 11(3): 77–94.

—— (2010) 'The AKP and the "Alevi opening", understanding the dynamics of the rapprochement', *Insight Turkey* 12(2): 143–64.

Kosebalaban, Hasan (2003) 'The making of enemy and friend: Fethullah Gulen's national security identity', 170–83, in Yavuz, M. Hakan and Esposito, John L. (eds) *Turkish Islam and the secular state: the Gulen movement*, Syracuse, New York: Syracuse University Press.

—— (2008) 'Torn identities and foreign policy: the case of Turkey and Japan', *Insight Turkey* 10(1): 5–30.

—— (2009) 'Globalization and the crisis of authoritarian modernization in Turkey', *Insight Turkey* 11(4): 77–97.

Kramer, Heinz (1996) 'Turkey and the European Union: a multidimensional relationship with hazy perspectives', 203–32, in Mastny, Vojtech and Nation, R. Craig (eds) *Turkey between east and west: new challenges for a rising regional power*, Oxford and Boulder, Colorado: Westview Press.

—— (2000) *A changing Turkey: the challenge to Europe and the United States*, Washington, DC: Brookings Institution Press.

—— (2006) 'Turkey and the EU: the EU's perspective', *Insight Turkey* 8(4): 24–32.

Kubicek, Paul (2005) 'The European Union and grassroots democratization in Turkey', *Turkish Studies* 6(3): 361–77.

—— (2008) 'Turkey's inclusion in the Atlantic community', *Turkish Studies*, 9(1): 21–35.

—— (2009) 'The European Union and political cleavages in Turkish politics', *Insight Turkey* 11(3): 109–26.

Kucukkosum, Sevil (2010a) 'Turkey offers northern Iraq investment for peace', www. hurriyetdailynews.com, 3 June.

—— (2010b) 'Turkey tallies options in fight against PKK', www.hurriyetdailynews. com, 7 July.

Kuniholm, Bruce R. (1996) 'Turkey and the West since World War Two', 45–69, in Mastny, Vojtech and Nation, R. Craig (eds) *Turkey between east and west: new challenges for a rising regional power*, Boulder, Colorado and Oxford: Westview Press.

Kuru, Ahmet T. (2005) 'Globalization and diversification of Islamic movements: three Turkish cases', *Political Science Quarterly* 120(2): 253–74.

—— (2008) 'Secularism in Turkey; myths and realities', *Insight Turkey* 10(3): 101–10.

—— (2009) *Secularism and state policies towards religion: the US, France and Turkey*, Cambridge and New York: Cambridge University Press.

Kutschera, Chris (1995) 'Kurdistan Turkey: parliament in exile, a propaganda ploy?', *The Middle East Magazine*, www.chris-kutschera.com/A/parliament_exile.htm.

Laciner, Sedat (2009) 'Turkey's pipeline politics', Ankara: International Strategic Research Organization, www.usak.org.tr/EN/makale.asp?id=999.

Lapidot-Firilla, Anat (2004) 'Dancing with wolves: Turco–Iranian relations in perspective', 104–18, in Gammer, M. (ed.) *The Caspian region, Vol. I*, London: Routledge.

Larrabee, F. Stephen (2007) 'Turkey rediscovers the Middle East', *Foreign Affairs* 86(4): 103–14.

—— (2010) 'Turkey's new geopolitics', *Survival* 52(2): 157–80.

Larrabee, F. Stephen and Lesser, Ian O. (2003) *Turkish foreign policy in an age of uncertainty*, Washington, DC: RAND.

Lesser, Ian O. (1992) *Bridge or barrier? Turkey and the West after the Cold War*, Report R-4202-AF/A, Washington, DC: RAND.

—— (2000) 'Turkey in a changing security environment', *Journal of International Affairs* 54(1): 183–98.

—— (2006) 'Turkey, the United States and the delusion of geopolitics', *Survival* 48(3): 83–96.

LeVine, Mark (2003) '"Human nationalisms" versus "inhuman globalisms"; cultural economies of globalization and the reimagining of Muslim identities in Europe and the Middle East', 78–126, in Allievi, Stefano and Nielson, Jorgen (eds) *Muslim networks and transnational communities in and across Europe*, Leiden, the Netherlands and Boston: Brill.

Lewis, Bernard (2002) *The emergence of modern Turkey*, New York and Oxford: Oxford University Press, 3rd edn.

Lewis, Geoffrey (1999) *The Turkish language reform: a catastrophic success*, Oxford: Oxford University Press.

Lewy, Guenter (2005) *The Armenian massacres in Ottoman Turkey: a disputed genocide*, Salt Lake City: University of Utah Press.

Lochery, N. (1998) 'Israel and Turkey: deepening ties and strategic implications, 1995–98', *Israel Affairs* 5(1): 45–62.

Lundgren, Asa (2007) *The unwelcome neighbour: Turkey's Kurdish policy*, London: I.B. Tauris.

McCabe, Thomas R. (2007) 'The Muslim Middle East: is there a democratic option?', *Orbis* 51(3): 479–93.

McCurdy, Daphne (2008) 'Turkish–Iranian relations: when opposites attract', *Turkish Policy Quarterly* 7(2): 87–106.

McDowall, David (1996) *A modern history of the Kurds*, London and New York: I.B. Tauris.

McGrew, A.G. (1992) 'Conceptualizing global politics', 1–28, in McGrew, A.G. and Lewis P.G., *Global politics, globalization and the nation state*, Cambridge: Polity Press.

McKeeby, David (2000) '"Legislating history"? Congress and the US–Turkish strategic partnership', Washington, DC: Center for Strategic and International Studies, http://csis.org/publication/turkey-update-legislating-history-congress-and-us-turkish-strategic-partnership.

Maigre, Marie-Elisabeth (2006) 'Turkey; the emergence of Muslim ethics in the business world', *Islam in Business*, www.islaminbusiness.blogspot.com/2006/02/turkey-emergence-of-muslim-ethics-in.html, 17 February.

Makovsky, Alan (1996) 'Israel–Turkish relations: a Turkish "periphery strategy"?', 147–70, in Barkey, Henri J. (ed.) *Reluctant neighbour: Turkey's role in the Middle East*, Washington, DC: US Institute of Peace Press.

—— (1999) 'The new activism in Turkish foreign policy', *SAIS Review* 19(1): 92–113.

Mallinson, William (2005) *Cyprus; a modern history*, London: I.B. Tauris.

Mango, Andrew (1993) 'The Turkish model', *Middle Eastern Studies* 29(4): 726–57.

—— (1999) *Ataturk*, London: John Murray.

—— (2005) *Turkey and the war on terror*, London and New York: Routledge.

Mardin, Serif (1973) 'Centre-periphery relations: a key to Turkish politics?', *Daedalus* 102(1): 169–90.

—— (2005) 'Turkish Islamic exceptionalism yesterday and today: continuity, rupture and reconstruction in operational codes', *Turkish Studies* 6(2): 145–65.

Massicard, Elise (2003) 'Alevist movements at home and abroad: mobilization spaces and disjunction', *New Perspectives on Turkey* 28(9): 163–88.

Mastny, V. and Nation, R. Craig (eds) (1996) *Turkey between East and West: new challenges for a rising regional power*, Boulder, Colorado: Westview.

Mateescu, Dragos C. (2006) 'Kemalism in the era of totalitarianism: a conceptual analysis', *Turkish Studies* 7(2): 225–41.

Menon, Rajan and Wimbush, S. Enders (eds) (2007) *Is the United States losing Turkey?*, The Hudson Institute, www.hudson.org/files/pdf_upload/Turkey%20PDF.pdf.

Mercan, Murat (2009–10) 'Turkish foreign policy and Iran', *Turkish Policy Quarterly* 8(4): 13–19.

Michaud-Emin, Linda (2007) 'The restructuring of the military high command in the seventh harmonization package and its ramifications for civil–military relations in Turkey', *Turkish Studies* 8(1): 25–42.

Michel, Thomas (2003) 'Fethullah Gulen as educator', 69–84, in Yavuz, M. Hakan and Esposito, John L. (eds) *Turkish Islam and the secular state: the Gulen movement*, Syracuse, New York: Syracuse University Press.

—— (2005) 'Sufism and modernity in the thought of Fethullah Gulen', *The Muslim World* 95(3): 341–58.

Miller Jr, Kevin (2003) 'Islam in Kazakhstan and Kyrgyzstan: the Nurcu movement and Hizb ut Tahrir', *The Eurasian World*, www.amerasianworld.com/islam_in_kazakhstan.php, 23 December.

Mohapatra, Aswini K. (2008) 'Democratization in the Arab world: relevance of the Turkish model', *International Studies* 45(4): 271–94.

Morris, Chris (2005) *The new Turkey: the quiet revolution on the edge of Europe*, London: Granta Books.

Mufti, Malik (1998) 'Daring and caution in Turkish foreign policy', *Middle East Journal* 52(1): 32–50.

Muftuler-Bac, Meltem (1999) 'The never-ending story: Turkey and the European Union', 240–58, in Kedourie, S. (ed.) *Turkey before and after Ataturk: internal and external affairs*, London and Portland, Oregon: Frank Cass.

Murinson, Alexander (2006) 'The strategic depth doctrine of Turkish foreign policy', *Middle Eastern Studies* 42(6): 945–64.

Muslih, Muhammad (1996) 'Syria and Turkey: uneasy relations', 113–29, in Barkey, Henri J. (ed.) *Reluctant neighbour: Turkey's role in the Middle East*, Washington, DC: US Institute of Peace Press.

Muzalevsky, Roman (2009) 'Fethullah Gulen's movement in central Asia: a blessing or a curse?' *CACI Analyst*, www.cacianalyst.org/?q=node/5167.

Nafi, Basheer M. (2009) 'The Arabs and modern Turkey: a century of changing perceptions', *Insight Turkey* 11(1): 63–82.

Najibullah, Farangis (2009) 'Turkish schools coming under increasing scrutiny in central Asia', www.eurasianet.org/departments/insight/articles/pp042609.shtml, 25 April.

Narli, Nilufer (1999) 'The rise of the Islamist movement in Turkey', *Middle East Review of International Affairs* 3(3): 38–48.

—— (2000) 'Civil–military relations in Turkey', *Turkish Studies*, 1(1): 107–27.

Noureddine, Mohammed (2009) 'Arab–Turkish cooperation in the new era', *Insight Turkey* 11(1): 43–51.

Nugent, John T. Jr (2004) 'The defeat of Turkish Hizbollah as a model for counter-terrorism strategy', *Middle East Review of International Affairs* 8(1): 69–75.

Nuttall, Tom (2008) 'How Gulen triumphed', *Prospect* 148, 26 July.

Odmalm, Pontus (2009) 'Turkish organizations in Europe: how national contexts provide different arenas for participation', *Turkish Studies* 10(2): 149–63.

OECD (2010) *OECD factbook: economic, environmental and social statistics*, Paris: Organisation for Economic Co-operation and Development, www.oecd.org/site/0,3407,en_21571361_34374092_1_1_1_1_1,00.html.

Ogutcu, Mehmet (2010) 'Turkey and the changing dynamics of world energy: towards cleaner and smarter energy', *Insight Turkey* 12(3): 63–88.

Oguzlu, Tarik H. (2002) 'The "Turkomans" as a factor in Turkish foreign policy', *Turkish Studies* 3(2): 139–48.

—— (2008a) 'Middle easternization of Turkey's foreign policy: does Turkey dissociate from the West?', *Turkish Studies* 9(1): 3–20.

—— (2008b) 'Turkey's northern Iraq policy: competing perspectives', *Insight Turkey* 10(3): 5–22.

Oguzlu, Tarik H. and Gungor, Ugur (2006) 'Peace operations and the transformation of Turkey's security policy', *Contemporary Security Policy* 27(3): 472–88.

Oguzlu, Tarik and Kibaroglu, Mustafa (2009) 'Is the westernization process losing pace in Turkey? Who's to blame?', *Turkish Studies* 10(4): 577–93.

O'Leary, Brendan, McGarry, J. and Salih, Khalid (2005) *The future of Kurdistan in Iraq*, Philadelphia, Pennsylvania: University of Pennsylvania Press.

Olsen, Robert (1996) 'The Kurdish question and Turkey's foreign policy toward Syria, Iran, Russia and Iraq since the Gulf War', 84–113, in Olsen, Robert, (ed.) *The*

Kurdish nationalist movement in the 1990s: its impact on Turkey and the Middle East, Lexington, Kentucky: University Press of Kentucky.

Onis, Ziya (1999) 'Turkey, Europe and the paradoxes of identity', *Mediterranean Quarterly* 10(3): 107–36.

—— (2000) 'The Turkish economy at the turn of the new century', 95–115, in Abramowitz, Morton (ed.) *Turkey's transformation and American policy*, New York: Century Foundation Press.

—— (2001) 'An awkward partnership: Turkey's relations with the European Union in comparative-historical perspective', *Journal of European Integration History* 7(1): 105–19.

—— (2003) 'Domestic politics versus global dynamics: towards a political economy of the 2000 and 2001 financial crises in Turkey', *Turkish Politics* 4(2): 1–30.

—— (2007) 'Conservative globalists versus defensive nationalists: political parties and paradoxes of Europeanization in Turkey', *Journal of Southern Europe and the Balkans* 9(3): 247–61.

—— (2008a) 'Greek–Turkish rapprochement: rhetoric or reality?' *Political Science Quarterly* 123(1): 123–49.

—— (2008b) 'Turkey–EU relations: beyond the current stalemate', *Insight Turkey* 10(4): 35–50.

—— (2009) 'Beyond the 2001 financial crisis: the political economy of the new phase of neoliberal restructuring in Turkey', *Review of International Political Economy* 16(3): 409–32.

Onis, Ziya and Bakir, Caner (2007) 'Turkey's political economy in the age of financial globalization; the significance of the EU anchor', *South European Society and Politics* 12(2): 147–64.

Ostergaard-Nielson, Eva (2003) *Transnational politics: Turks and Kurds in Germany*, London and New York: Routledge.

O'Tuathail, Gearoid (2006) 'General introduction: thinking critically about geopolitics', 1–14, in O'Tuathail, Gearoid, Dalby, Simon and Routledge, Paul (eds) *The geopolitical reader*, London and New York: Routledge.

Ozbudun, Ergun (2000) *Contemporary Turkish politics: challenges to democratic consolidation*, Boulder, Colorado and London: Lynne Rienner.

—— (2007) 'Democratization reforms in Turkey, 1993–2004', *Turkish Studies* 8(2): 179–96.

Ozcan, Gencer (2001) 'The military and the making of foreign policy in Turkey', 13–30, in Rubin, Barry and Kirisci, Kemal (eds) *Turkey in world politics: an emerging multiregional power*, Boulder, Colorado and London: Lynne Rienner.

Ozcurumez, Saime (2009) 'Immigrant associations in Canada: included, accommodated, or excluded?', *Turkish Studies* 10(2): 195–215.

Ozdalga, Elizabeth (2003) 'Secularizing trends in Fethullah Gulen's movement: impasse or opportunity for further renewal?' *Critique: Critical Middle Eastern Studies* 12(1): 61–73.

—— (2005) 'Redeemer or outsider? The Gulen community in the civilizing process', *The Muslim World* 95(3): 429–46.

—— (2006) 'The hidden Arab: a critical reading of the notion of "Turkish Islam"', *Middle Eastern Studies* 42(4): 551–70.

Ozhan, Taha (2010) 'Turkey, Israel and the US in the wake of the Gaza flotilla crisis', *Insight Turkey* 12(3): 7–18.

Ozhan, Taha and Ete, Hatem (2009) 'A new agenda for the Kurdish question', *Insight Turkey* 11(1): 97–114.

Ozyurek, Esra (2009) '"The light of the Alevi fire was lit in Germany and then spread to Turkey": a transnational boundary debate on the boundaries of Islam', *Turkish Studies* 10(2): 233–53.

Page, Carter (2004) 'US involvement in the business and politics of the Caspian Sea region', 263–77, in Akiner, Shirin (ed.) *The Caspian: politics, energy and security*, London and New York: Routledge.

Pahlavan, Tschanguiz H. (1996) 'Turkish–Iranian relations: an Iranian view', 71–91, in Barkey, Henri J. (ed.) *Reluctant neighbour: Turkey's role in the Middle East*, Washington, DC: US Institute of Peace Press.

Park, Bill (2000) 'Turkey's European Union candidacy: from Luxembourg to Helsinki – to Ankara?', *Mediterranean Politics* 5(3): 31–53.

—— (2001) 'Turkey and the European Union: over the horizon?', *The World Today* 57(6): 25–27.

—— (2002) 'Turkey and Iraq: bridgehead or bridge?', *The World Today*, 58(10): 7–9.

—— (2003) 'Strategic location, political dislocation: Turkey, the United States, and northern Iraq', *Middle East Review of International Relations* 7(2): 11–23.

—— (2005) *Turkey's policy towards northern Iraq: problems and prospects*, Adelphi Papers 374, London: International Institute for Strategic Studies.

—— (2007) 'The Fethullah Gulen movement as a transnational phenomenon', 46–59, in Cantori, Louis J., Hermansen, Marcia K. and Capes, David B. (eds) *Muslim world in transition: contributions of the Gulen movement*, Leeds: Leeds Metropolitan University Press.

—— (2008a) 'The Fethullah Gulen movement', *Middle East Review of International Affairs* 12(3), www.gloria-center.org/meria/2008/12/park.asp.

—— (2008b) 'Turkey's deep state: Ergenekon and the threat to democratization in the republic', *The RUSI Journal* 153(5): 54–59.

Parris, Mark R. (2003) 'Starting over: US–Turkish relations in the post-Iraq era', *Turkish Policy Quarterly* 3(1), www.turkishpolicy.com.

Pascual, Carlos and Elkind, Jonathan (eds) (2010) *Energy security: economics, politics, strategies, and implications*, Washington, DC: Brookings Institution.

Patterson, Ruairi (2008) 'Rising nationalism and the EU accession process', *Turkish Policy Quarterly* 7(1): 131–38.

Petersen, Alexandros (2006) 'BTC security questions persist', www.eurasianet.org/departments/business/articles/eav071106.shtml.

Peterson, Laura (2002) 'The Pentagon talks Turkey', *The American Prospect* 13(16), 9 September.

Petkova, Lilia (2002) 'The ethnic Turks in Bulgaria: social integration and impact on Bulgarian–Turkish relations 1947–2000', *Global Review of Ethnopolitics* 1(4): 42–59.

Peuch, Jean-Christophe (2001a) 'Armenia: French parliament's recognition of 1915 genocide angers Turkey', www.rferl.org/content/article/1095555.html, 19 January.

—— (2001b) 'Turkey: uproar over genocide reflects need to reconcile with past', www.rferl.org/content/article/1095711.html, 9 February.

—— (2002) 'Turkey: court ruling shows authorities' refusal to see Alevism as a religious community', www.rferl.org/content/article/1098840.html, 18 February.

—— (2004a) 'Turkey: group seeks to create a new generation of Muslim believers', www.rferl.org/content/article/1053184.html, 7 June.

—— (2004b) 'Turkey: Fethullahci schools – a greenhouse for central Asian elites?' www.rferl.org/content/article/1053209.html, 8 June.

Phillips, David L. (2009) 'Turks, Iraqis becoming indispensable strategic partners', www.hurriyetdailynews.com, 18 June.

Pieterse, Jan Nederveen (1995) 'Globalization as hybridization', 99–105, in Featherstone, M. *et al.* (eds) *Global modernities*, London: Sage.

Pipes, Daniel (1995) 'Hot spot: Turkey, Iraq and Mosul', *Middle East Quarterly* II(3): 65–68, www.meforum.org/265/hot-spot-turkey-iraq-and-mosul.

—— (2009) 'Turkey: an ally no more', *FrontPage*, www.frontpagemag.com/2009/10/27/turkey-an-ally-no-more-by-daniel-pipes, 27 October.

Polat, Rabia Karakaya (2008) 'The Kurdish issue: can the AK Party escape securitization?', *Insight Turkey* 10(3): 75–86.

Pope, Nicole (2002) 'Cross border concerns', *Middle East International*, 683, 13 September.

—— (2003) 'Eyes on Turkey', *Middle East International*, 691, 10 January.

Poulton, Hugh (1997) *Top hat, grey wolf, and crescent: Turkish nationalism and the Turkish Republic*, London: Hurst.

Poyraz, Bedriye (2006) 'EU minority perspective and the case of Alevilik in Turkey', Robert Schuman Centre for Advanced Studies European University Institute Working, Paper no. 2006/24, Bada Fiesolana, Italy. Available at www.eui.eu/RSCAS/WP-Texts/06_24.pdf.

Rabasa, Angel and Larrabee, F. Stephen (2008) *The rise of political Islam in Turkey*, MG-726, Washington, DC: RAND Corporation.

Rabil, Robert (2002) 'The Iraqi opposition's evolution: from conflict to unity?', *Middle East Review of International Affairs* 6(4): 1–17.

Rafaat, Aram (2007) 'US–Kurdish relations in post-invasion Iraq', *Middle East Review of International Affairs* 11(4): 79–89.

Raphaeli, Nimrod (2008) 'The growing economic relations between Iran and Turkey', *The Middle East Media Research Institute (MEMRI) Economic Blog*, www.memrieconomicblog.org/bin/content.cgi?article=92, 1 April.

Republic of Turkey, Ministry of Energy and Natural Resources (undated) *Strategic Plan (2010–2014)*, www.enerji.gov.tr/yayinlar_raporlar_EN/ETKB_2010_2014_Stratejik_Plani_EN.pdf.

Republic of Turkey, Ministry of Foreign Affairs (2009) *Turkey's Energy Strategy*, Deputy Directorate General for Energy, Water and Environment, http://www.mfa.gov.tr/data/DISPOLITIKA/EnerjiPolitikasi/Turkey's%20Energy%20Strategy%20(Ocak%202009).pdf.

Republic of Turkey, Prime Ministry (2006) *Ninth Development Plan 2007–2013*, State Planning Organization, www.ekutup.dpt.gov.tr/plan/ix/9developmentplan.pdf.

Ripsman, Norrin M. and Paul, T.V. (2010) *Globalization and the national security state*, Oxford: Oxford University Press.

Risse, Thomas, Cowles, Maria Green and Caporaso, James (2001) *Transforming Europe: Europeanization and domestic change*, Ithaca, New York and London: Cornell University Press.

Roberts, John (2010) 'Turkey as a regional energy hub', *Insight Turkey* 12(3): 39–48.

Roberts, Paul (2005) *The end of oil: on the edge of a perilous new world*, New York: Mariner Books.

Robins, Philip (1993) 'Between sentiment and self-interest: Turkey's policy toward Azerbaijan and the central Asian states', *Middle East Journal*, 47(4): 593–610.

—— (1996) 'Avoiding the question', 179–203, in Barkey, Henri J. (ed.) *Reluctant neighbour: Turkey's role in the Middle East*, Washington, DC: US Institute of Peace Press.

—— (1997) 'Turkish foreign policy under Erbakan', *Survival* 39(2): 82–100.

—— (2003) *Suits and uniforms: Turkish foreign policy since the Cold War*, London: Hurst and Co.

—— (2007a) 'The Opium Crisis and the Iraq War: historical parallels in Turkey–US relations', *Mediterranean Politics* 12(1): 17–38.

—— (2007b) *Between the EU and the Middle East: Turkish foreign policy under the AKP government 2002–2007*, Working Paper 11, Milan: Turkish Programme, Italian Istituto per gli studi di politica international (ISPI).

Rogstad, Jon (2009) 'Towards a success story? Turkish immigrant organizations in Norway', *Turkish Studies* 10(2): 277–94.

Romano, David (2006) *The Kurdish nationalist movement; opportunity, mobilization and identity*, Cambridge: Cambridge University Press.

Rosenau, James, N. (1969) *Linkage politics: essays on the convergence of national and international systems*, New York: Free Press.

—— *Turbulence in world politics: a theory of change and continuity*, Princeton, New Jersey: Princeton University Press.

Rostow, W. W. (1960) *The stages of economic growth: a non communist manifesto*, Cambridge: Cambridge University Press.

Rouleau, Eric (2006) 'Turkey's dream of democracy', *Foreign Affairs* 79(6): 100–114.

Rubin, Barry and Kirisci, Kemal (eds) (2001) *Turkey in world politics: an emerging multiregional power*, Boulder, Colorado and London: Lynne Rienner.

Rubin, Michael (2005a) 'Green money, Islamist politics in Turkey', *Middle East Quarterly*, XII(1): 13–23, www.meforum.org/684/green-money-islamist-politics-in-turkey.

—— (2005b) 'A comedy of errors: American–Turkish diplomacy and the Iraq War', *Turkish Policy Quarterly* 4(1): 69–79.

—— (2008) 'Turkey's turning point: could there be an Islamic revolution in Turkey?', *National Review Online*, www.meforum.org/1882/turkeys-turning-point, 14 April.

Rumford, C. (2002) 'Failing the EU test? Turkey's national programme, EU candidature and the complexities of democratic reform', *Mediterranean Politics* 7(1): 51–68.

Saivetz, C.R. (2009) 'Tangled pipelines: Turkey's role in energy export plans', *Turkish Studies* 10(1): 95–108.

Saritoprak, Zeki (2003) 'Fethullah Gulen: a Sufi in his own way', 156–69, in Yavuz, M. Hakan and Esposito, John L. (eds) *Turkish Islam and the secular state: the Gulen movement*, Syracuse, New York: Syracuse University Press.

Saritoprak, Zeki and Griffith, Sidney (2005) 'Fethullah Gulen and the people of the book: a voice from Turkey for interfaith dialogue', *The Muslim World* 95(3): 329–340.

Sassen, Saskia (2000) 'Whose city is it? Globalization and the formation of new claims', 70–76, as reproduced in Lechner Frank J. and Boli, John (eds) *The Globalization reader*, Oxford: Blackwell, 1st edn.

Sayari, Sabri (1994) 'Turkey, the Caucasus and central Asia', 175–96, in Banuazizi, Ali and Weiner, Myron (eds) *The new geopolitics of central Asia and its borderlands*, London: I.B. Tauris.

—— (2000) 'Turkish foreign policy in the post Cold War era: the challenges of multi regionalism', *Journal of International Affairs* 54(1): 169–82.

Scholte, Jan Aart (2001) 'The globalization of world politics', 13–32, in Baylis, John and Smith, Steve (eds) *The globalization of world politics: an introduction to international relations*, Oxford: Oxford University Press, 2nd edn.

Schulte, Gregory L. (2009–10) 'Why Turkey cannot abstain on Iran's nuclear violations', *Turkish Policy Quarterly* 8(4): 21–26.

Schwartz, Stephen (2010) 'Islamist Gulen movement runs US charter schools', *American Thinker*, www.meforum.org, 29 March.

Seibert, Thomas (2009) 'Turkey confronts its past with review of 1930s operation against Kurds', *The National*, 10 December.

Sen, Mustafa (2010) 'Transformation of Turkish Islam and the rise of the Justice and Development Party', *Turkish Studies* 11(1): 59–84.

Seyrek, Demir Murat (2004) 'The role of Turkish NGOs in the integration of Turkey into the EU', *Turkish Political Quarterly* 3(3), www.turkishpolicy.com.

Sezgin, Yuksel (2002) 'The October 1998 crisis in Turkish–Syrian relations: a prospect theory approach', *Turkish Studies* 3(2): 44–68.

Shafak, Elif (2007) *The bastard of Istanbul*, London: Penguin.

Shankland, David (2003) *The Alevis in Turkey: the emergence of a secular Islamic tradition*, London: Routledge Curzon.

Sharon-Krespin, Rachel (2009) 'Fethullah Gulen's grand ambition: Turkey's Islamist danger', *Middle East Quarterly* XVI(1): 55–66.

Silova, Iveta, Johnson, Mark S. and Heyneman, Stephen P. (2007) 'Education and the crisis of social cohesion in Azerbaijan and central Asia', *Comparative Education Review* 51(2): 131–57.

Simsek, Sefa (2004) 'The transformation of civil society in Turkey: from quantity to quality', *Turkish Studies* 5(3): 46–74.

Smith, Michael Peter and Guarnizo, Luis Eduardo (eds) (1998) *Transnationalism from below*, New Brunswick: Transaction.

Socor, Vladimir (2009a) 'Gazprom, Turkey, revive and reconfigure Blue Stream Two', *Eurasia Daily Monitor* 6(154), Jamestown Foundation, Washington, DC, www.jamestown.org.

—— (2009b) 'Samsun–Ceyhan pipeline project designed to divert Kazakhstani oil', *Eurasia Daily Monitor* 6(195), Jamestown Foundation, Washington, DC, www.jamestown.org.

—— (2010) 'Nabucco pipeline, Azerbaijan's Shah Deniz field require synchronized development', *Eurasia Daily Monitor* 7(164), Jamestown Foundation, Washington, DC, www.jamestown.org.

Sohn, Janina and Ozcan, Veysal (2006) 'The educational attainment of Turkish migrants in Germany', *Turkish Studies* 7(1): 101–24.

Somer, Murat (2004) 'Turkey's Kurdish conflict: changing context, and domestic and regional implications', *Middle East Journal* 58(2): 235–53.

Sosay, Gul (2009) 'Delegation and accountability: independent regulatory agencies in Turkey', *Turkish Studies* 10(3): 341–63.

Soylemez, Yuksel (2005) 'Ottoman Armenians discussed', www.hurriyetdailynews.com, 23 October.

Stansfield, Gareth R.V. (2003) *Iraqi Kurdistan: political developments and emergent democracy*, London: Routledge Curzon.

Steinberg, Guido (2008a) 'A Turkish al Qaeda: the Islamic Jihad Union and the internationalization of Uzbek jihadism', *Strategic Insights* VII(3), Monterey, California: Naval Postgraduate School Center for Contemporary

Conflict, www.nps.edu/Academics/centers/ccc/publications/OnlineJournal/2008/Jul/steinbergJul08.html.

—— (2008b) 'The threat of jihadist terrorism in Germany', ARI 142, *Real Instituto Elcano*, www.realinstitutoelcano.org/wps/portal/rielcano_eng/Print?WCM_GLOBAL_CONTEXT=/wps/wcm/connect/elcano/Elcano_in/Zonas_in/ARI142-2008 6 November.

—— (2009) 'The evolving threat from jihadist terrorism in Turkey', *Real Instituto Elcano*, 16 February, www.realinstitutoelcano.org/wps/portal/rielcano_eng/Content?WCM_GLOBAL_CONTEXT=/elcano/elcano_in/zonas_in/international+terrorism/ari26-2009 16 February.

Subasi, Necdet (2010) 'The Alevi opening: concept, strategy and process', *Insight Turkey* 12(2): 165–78.

Swietochowski, Tadeusz (1994) 'Azerbaijan's triangular relationship: the land between Russia, Turkey and Iran'; 118–35, in Banuazizi, Ali and Weiner, Myron (eds) *The new geopolitics of central Asia and its borderlands*, London: I.B. Tauris.

Tait, Robert (2008) 'Islamic scholar voted world's no. 1 thinker', *The Guardian*, 23 June.

Taspinar, Omer (2003) *An uneven fit? The 'Turkish model' and the Arab world*, Brookings Institution Analysis Paper, www.brookings.edu/papers/2003/08islamicworld_taspinar.aspx.

—— (2007) 'The old Turks' revolt: when radical secularism endangers democracy', *Foreign Affairs* 86(6): 114–30.

—— (2008) 'The coming storm with Washington', www.todayszaman.com, 15 December.

Timmerman, Christiane (2006) 'Gender dynamics in the context of Turkish marriage migration: the case of Belgium', *Turkish Studies* 7(1): 125–43.

Tok, Evren (2008–09) 'Anatolian cities and the new spirit of Turkish capitalism', *Turkish Policy Quarterly* 7(4): 81–89.

Torbakov, Igor (2008) *The Georgia crisis and Russia–Turkey relations*, Washington, DC: The Jamestown Foundation, www.jamestown.org/uploads/media/GeorgiaCrisisTorbakov.pdf.

Torbakov, Igor and Ojanen, Hanna (2009) *Looking for a new strategic identity: is Turkey emerging as an independent regional power?*, Briefing Paper 30, Finnish Institute of International Affairs, www.fiia.fi/en/publication/74/looking_for_a_new_strategic_identity.

Travis, Hannibal (2006) '"Native Christians massacred", the Ottoman genocide of the Assyrians during World War I', *Genocide Studies and Prevention* 1(3): 327–71.

Tsereteli, Mamuka (2009) *The impact of the Russia-Georgia war on the South Caucasus transportation corridor*, Washington, DC: The Jamestown Foundation, www.jamestown.org/uploads/media/Full_Mamuka_RussiaGeorgia.pdf.

Turam, Bema (2003) 'National loyalties and international undertakings: the case of the Gülen community in Kazakhstan', 184–207, in Yavuz, M. Hakan and Esposito, John L. (eds) *Turkish Islam and the secular state: the Gulen movement*, Syracuse, New York: Syracuse University Press.

—— (2004) 'A bargain between the secular state and Turkish Islam: politics of ethnicity in central Asia', *Nations and Nationalism* 10(3): 353–74.

Turan, Ilter (1997) 'The military in Turkish politics', *Mediterranean Quarterly* 2(2): 123–35.

Ugur, Etga (2004) 'Intellectual roots of "Turkish Islam" and approaches to the "Turkish model"', *Journal of Minority Affairs* 24(2): 327–45.

Ulsever, Cuneyt (2010) 'National view vs Gulen movement', www.hurriyetdailynews. com, 14, 15, 16 August.

Ulusoy, Kivanc (2009) 'Europeanization and political change: the case of Cyprus', *Turkish Studies* 10(3): 393–408.

UNCTAD (2009) *World investment report*, Geneva: UN Conference on Trade and Development.

Unver, H. Akin (2009) *Turkey's 'deep state' and the Ergenekon conundrum*, Middle East Institute Policy Brief 23, Washington, DC. Available at www.mei.edu/Portals/0/ Publications/turkey-deep-state-ergenekonconundrum.pdf.

US Department of State (2008) '2008 human rights report: Turkey', Bureau of Democracy, Human Rights, and Labor, www.state.gov/g/drl/rls/hrrpt/2008/eur/ 119109.htm.

—— (2009) 'International religious freedom report', Bureau of Democracy, Human Rights, and Labor, www.state.gov/g/drl/rls/irf/2009/130299.htm.

—— (2010) 'Trafficking in persons report 2010', Office to Monitor and Combat Trafficking in Persons, www.state.gov/g/tip/rls/tiprpt/2010/142761.htm.

Uslu, Emrullah (2007) 'From local Hizbollah to global terror: militant Islam in Turkey', *Middle East Policy* 14(1): 124–41.

—— (2008a) 'Ulusalcilik: the neonationalist resurgence in Turkey', *Turkish Studies* 9(1): 73–97.

—— (2008b) 'The Kurdistan Workers' Party turns against the European Union', *Mediterranean Quarterly* 19(2): 99–121.

—— (2008c) 'AKP's dilemma: how to accommodate Alevi demands within the state structure', *Eurasia Daily Monitor* 5(234), Jamestown Foundation, Washington, DC, www.jamestown.org.

—— (2009a) 'Kurdish Hezbollah targets the Fethullah Gulen movement', *Eurasia Daily Monitor* 6(78), Jamestown Foundation, Washington, DC, www.jamestown.org.

—— (2009b) 'Turkish police target al Qaeda network in Turkey', *Eurasia Daily Monitor* 6(80), Jamestown Foundation, Washington, DC, www.jamestown.org.

—— (2009c) 'Turkish navy's fight against piracy in Gulf of Aden serves foreign policy goals', *Terrorism Monitor* 7(34), Jamestown Foundation, Washington, DC, www. jamestown.org.

Ustun, Kadir (2010) 'Turkey's Iran policy: between diplomacy and sanctions', *Insight Turkey* 12(3): 19–26.

Vaisse, Justin (2008) 'Slamming the sublime porte? Challenges in French–Turkish relations from Chirac to Sarkozy', www.brookings.edu/~/media/Files/rc/papers/2008/ 0128_turkey_vaisse/0128_turkey_vaisse.pdf, 28 January.

Vali, Ference A. (1971) *Bridge across the Bosporus: the foreign policy of Turkey*, Baltimore, Maryland and London: Johns Hopkins Press.

Vander Lippe, John M. (2000) 'Forgotten brigade of the forgotten war: Turkey's participation in the Korean War', *Middle Eastern Studies* 36(1): 92–102.

Vardan, Omer Cihad (2009) 'Turkey–EU relations and democracy in Turkey: problems and prospects', *Turkish Policy Quarterly* 8(1): 49–56.

Vertovec, Steven (2003) 'Diaspora transnationalism and Islam: sites of change and modes of research', 312–26, in Allievi, Stefano and Nielson, Jorgen (eds) *Muslim networks and transnational communities in and across Europe*, Leiden, the Netherlands and Boston: Brill.

Walker, Joshua (2006) 'Turkey and Israel's relationship in the Middle East', *Mediterranean Quarterly* 17(4): 60–90.

Walker, Joshua W. (2007) 'Learning strategic depth: implications of Turkey's new foreign policy doctrine', *Insight Turkey* 9(3): 32–47.

Weitz, Richard (2010) 'Turkey's efforts to support Afghanistan's reconstruction', *The Turkey Analyst* 3(3), www.silkroadstudies.org/new/inside/turkey/2010/100215B.html.

Weller, Paul (2006) 'Fethullah Gulen, religions, globalization and dialogue', 85–100, in Hunt, Robert A. and Aslandogan, Yuksel A. (eds) *Muslim citizens of the globalized world: contributions of the Gulen movement*, New Jersey: The Light, Inc. and IID Press.

West II, W. Jefferson (2006) 'Religion as dissident politics? Geopolitical discussions within the recent publications of Fethullah Gulen', *Geopolitics* 11(2): 280–99.

Wets, Johan (2006) 'The Turkish community in Austria and Belgium: the challenge of integration', *Turkish Studies* 7(1): 85–100.

White, Paul J. and Jongerden, Joost (eds) (2003) *Turkey's Alevi enigma: a comprehensive overview*, Leiden, the Netherlands: Brill.

Whittell, Giles (2010) 'Turkey recalls ambassador after US vote on Armenia "genocide"', *The Sunday Times*, 5 March.

William, Brian Glyn (2005a) 'Turkish volunteers in Chechnya', *Terrorism Monitor* 3(7), Jamestown Foundation, Washington, DC, www.jamestown.org.

—— (2005b) 'El Kaide Turke: tracing an al Qaeda splinter cell', *Terrorism Monitor* 2(22), Jamestown Foundation, Washington, DC, www.jamestown.org.

Williams, Paul A. and Tekin, Ali (2008) 'The Iraq War, Turkey, and renewed Caspian energy prospects', *Middle East Journal* 62(3): 383–97.

Wilson, Andrew (1979) *The Aegean dispute*, Adelphi Papers 155, London: International Institute for Strategic Studies.

Wilson, Ross (2010) 'Ross Wilson House Committee Testimony: 7/28/10 – Transcript: Turkey and the United States: how to go forward (and not back)', Statement for the Record, 28 July, House Committee on Foreign Affairs, Washington, DC: Atlantic Council, www.acus.org/highlight/ross-wilson-house-testimony-us-turkey-relations/transcript.

Winrow, Gareth (1995) *Turkey in post-Soviet central Asia*, London: Royal Institute of International Affairs.

—— (2009) *Turkey, Russia and the Caucasus: common and diverging interests*, Chatham House Briefing Paper REP/EP BP 2009/01, www.chathamhouse.org.

Winter, O. (2009) 'Recent attempts to form regional bloc: Syria, Turkey and Iran', *The Middle East Media Research Institute (MEMRI)*, http://memri.org, 6 January.

Wolfowitz, Paul (2002) Turgut Ozal Memorial Lecture, remarks by deputy secretary of defense Paul Wolfowitz, Washington Institute for Near East Policy, St Regis Hotel, Washington, DC, 13 March, www.defense.gov/speeches/speech.aspx?speechid=198.

World Bank (2009) Turkey Country Brief, www.worldbank.org.tr.

Yanasmayan, Zeynap (2010) 'Role of Turkish Islamic organizations in Belgium: the strategies of *Diyanet* and *Milli Gorus*', *Insight Turkey* 12(1): 139–61.

Yavuz, M. Hakan (1998) 'Turkish identity and foreign policy in flux: the rise of neo-Ottomanism', *Middle East Critique* 7(12): 19–42.

—— (2003a) *Islamic political identity in Turkey*, Oxford: Oxford University Press.

—— (2003b) 'The Gulen movement: the Turkish puritans', 19–47, in Yavuz, M. Hakan and Esposito, John L. (eds) *Turkish Islam and the secular state: the Gulen movement*, Syracuse, New York: Syracuse University Press.

—— (2004) 'Is there a Turkish Islam? The emergence of convergence and consensus', *Journal of Muslim Minority Affairs* 24(2): 213–32.

Yavuz, M. Hakan and Esposito, John L. (eds) (2003) *Turkish Islam and the secular state: the Gulen movement*, Syracuse, New York: Syracuse University Press.

Yavuz, M. Hakan and Ozcan, Nihat Ali (2006) 'The Kurdish question and Turkey's Justice and Development Party', *Middle East Policy* XIII(1): 102–19.

Yildiz, Ilhan (2007) 'Minority rights in Turkey', *Brigham Young University Law Review*, www.allbusiness.com/legal/constitutional-law-freedom-religion/8913213–1. html, 1 January.

Yildiz, Kerim (2005) *The Kurds in Turkey: EU accession and human rights*, London: Pluto Press.

—— (2007) *The Kurds in Iraq: past, present and future*, London: Pluto Press.

Yilmaz, Cevdet and Sahin, Mustafa (2006) 'Modernity and economic nationalism in the formation of Turkish nationalism', *Mediterranean Quarterly* 17(2): 53–71.

Yuce, Ayse (2003) 'Islamic financial houses in Turkey', *Journal of the Academy of Business and Economics* 1(1): 153–157.

Yurdakul, Gokce and Yukleyen, Ahmet (2009) 'Islam, conflict, and integration: Turkish religious associations in Turkey', *Turkish Studies* 10(2): 217–31.

Zebari, Abdul Hamid (2009) 'Turkish FM stresses importance of ties on Iraq visit', www.hurriyetdailynews.com, 1 November.

Zeidan, David (1999) 'The Alevi of Anatolia', *Middle East Review of International Affairs* 3(4), http://meria.idc.ac.il/journal/1999/issue4/jv3n4a5.html.

Zenginobuz, E. Unal (2008) 'On regulatory agencies in Turkey and their independence', *Turkish Studies* 9(3): 475–505.

Zurcher, Erik J. (2004) *Turkey: a modern history*, London and New York: I.B. Tauris, 3rd edn.

Index